Nick Holt has published a number of books on sport, music, film and other aspects of popular culture. He compiled the bestselling *Quizmaster*.

Also by Nick Holt

The Mammoth Quiz Book
The Mammoth Book of the World Cup
The Mammoth Football Quiz Book

The Mammoth
General Knowledge Quiz Book
Nick and Nicole Holt

ROBINSON

ROBINSON

First published in Great Britain in 2019 by Robinson

Copyright © Nick Holt, 2019

1 3 5 7 9 10 8 6 4 2

A CIP catalogue record for this book is available from the British Library

ISBN: 978-1-47214-115-6

Typeset in Whitman by Hewer Text UK Ltd, Edinburgh
Printed and bound in Great Britain by Clays Ltd, Elcograf S.p.A.

Papers used by Robinson are from well-managed
forests and other responsible sources

MIX
Paper from
responsible sources
FSC® C104740

Robinson
An imprint of
Little, Brown Book Group
Carmelite House
50 Victoria Embankment
London EC4Y 0DZ

An Hachette UK Company
www.hachette.co.uk

www.littlebrown.co.uk

Contents

Introduction

This is the umpteenth quiz book I've written and, I think, the best. I think it's the best because it's been tried and tested in front of a demanding audience.

For the last two years, my wife, Nicole, and I have been running a pub, The Stag Inn in Hastings. It's a small pub tucked away in a corner of Hastings Old Town, with very little passing trade, so we need ways of encouraging people to come through the door, even during quiet times. Hence, we started a Monday Quiz Night; it seemed a no-brainer, given I had previous as a quiz-book compiler. Before we took over, the pub wasn't even open on a Monday (a notoriously quiet night in the town, especially out of season). The pub seats forty-four. On a Monday, forty-four people is a quiet one – we often get upwards of fifty people crammed into the place.

Fifty customers make it an important night for the business, so we must get it right. Quizzes are social occasions and people want to feel part of the group. We hand out popcorn and liberal doses of banter, and we try to make sure everyone is comfortable, from the regulars to the odd random visitor who fancies having a go. We pitch the questions to our audience, who is mainly over thirty-five years old and pretty well educated. This doesn't make The Stag any different from most pubs that run a regular quiz; this is the general demographic both for pub quizzes and for quiz books. We do get some younger folk in – and we do mix it up occasionally to give them a better chance. The formula seems to work.

Hopefully this formula will translate into a fun book for the reader. Don't expect to breeze in and get ten out of ten every time, especially if you're just browsing through while you take a bath – some of the quizzes are far from easy. For a few of the quizzes, I've given a guide score that I think a team of four people should be able to get. Ten out of a ten means the quizmaster got the round wrong – a good score should be eight, not ten, and a low score should be four, not seven.

If you are using the book to host your own quiz (which is fine, by the way), remember to try to include a round that gives all the people attending a chance. If you think the quizzes are too tough, you can always make them multiple choice and give three alternative answers. There are some multi-choice questions included, but they tend to be a little off the wall.

One last thing: pub owners (Wetherspoons apart) aren't wealthy people; theirs is one of the toughest trades around. So when you go to a pub quiz, buy a couple of drinks, or you may find the pub isn't there the next time you visit.

Happy quizzing.

Nick & Nicole

QUIZ 1. HAPPY BIRTHDAY, ME

Let's start with an important date, shall we? August 13 is my birthday, on which occasion I presented the Quizzers with a series of questions about people who were born or died on the same date.

1. Annie Oakley, born 1860, was a female sharpshooter who was the subject of the 1946 musical *Annie Get Your Gun*. Who wrote the musical?

2. Which important Victorian reformer, who founded St Thomas' Nursing School, died on 13 August 1910, aged ninety?

3. Which film director, born in Leytonstone in 1899, has eight movies in the American National Film Registry as of 2018, including his personal favourite, *Shadow of a Doubt*?

4. Which comedian, born in Manchester in 1930, was the first compère of the TV show *Wheeltappers and Shunters Social Club*, launched on Granada TV in 1974?

5. John Slattery, American actor, born 1962, is best known for playing Roger Sterling in which hit TV series?

6. Which legendary American golfer, born in 1912 and winner of nine major tournaments, survived a head-on collision with a Greyhound bus in 1949, but recovered well enough to win further major events?

7. Which film director, born in 1955, won Academy Award nominations for *United 93* and *Captain Phillips*, as well as directing three of the Bourne movies?

8. Which famous inventor and engineer, who worked in Hastings while he developed his most famous piece of technology, died in Bexhill in 1946, aged fifty-seven?

9. *Match of the Day* pundit Alan Shearer remains the Premier League's top scorer with 260 goals in the competition: for which clubs did he score them?

10. Which major political figure of the twentieth century, born in 1926, died in Havana in 2016, aged ninety?

QUIZ 2. US PRESIDENTS

Questions about the occupants of the White House from the early days to Trump-time.

1. Who became America's youngest president at forty-two years of age when he succeeded to the post after the death of William McKinley?

2. What post did Ulysses S. Grant hold before becoming US president in 1869?

3. Who remains the only US president to serve a four-year term, lose the next election, and then regain office for a further four years?

4. Which two men served as president during the Second World War?

5. Who was the US president during the First World War, only bringing the US into the fray in 1917?

6. Who is the only man to have served in the House of Representatives, the Senate, as vice-president and as president?

7. Prior to running for office, Jimmy Carter was governor of which US state?

8. Which military man rose to the office of president on the back of his achievements in the Mexican–American War, but died in his second year in office, giving way to Millard Fillmore?

9. Who is the only man to have served as vice-president and president without being elected to either role?

10. Who lost the 1824 presidential election after intervention from the House of Representatives, but ran again for the newly formed Democratic Party in 1828 and served two full terms as the seventh president?

Answers to Quiz 1

1. Irving Berlin; it was released on Broadway in 1946 and a film followed four years later with Betty Hutton in the lead.

2. Florence Nightingale, the 'Lady with the Lamp'.

3. Alfred Hitchcock: the eight films on the National Registry are *Rebecca* (1940), *Shadow of a Doubt* (1943), *Notorious* (1946), *Rear Window* (1954), *Vertigo* (1958), *North by Northwest* (1959), *Psycho* (1960) and *The Birds* (1963). Others will surely follow – *Rope*, *Suspicion*, *Strangers on a Train* and *The 39 Steps* are all films of great quality.

4. Bernard Manning.

5. *Mad Men*.

6. Ben Hogan. Hogan won two PGA Championships and a US Open before the accident, but went on to win six further majors. He won the US Open again just sixteen months after suffering horrific injuries, and retained the title the following year, while adding his first Masters title. In 1953 he enjoyed a miraculous year, winning a fourth US Open, a second Masters, and his first Open Championship, at Carnoustie in Scotland, thus completing what was effectively a Grand Slam – the PGA clashed with the Open, so winning both was impossible. Hogan was a notable theorist and changed the way the golf swing was analysed and approached.

7. Paul Greengrass.

8. John Logie Baird – he was born in Dunbartonshire but moved to Hastings in 1923 due to ill health.

9. Blackburn Rovers and Newcastle United – two points for these, deduct one if your answer includes Southampton. Shearer scored twenty-three top-flight goals for Southampton but that was before the Premier League began. The England man scored 112 goals in 138 games for Blackburn, winning the Premier League in the process, and added 148 in 303 games for Newcastle.

10. Fidel Castro, Marxist revolutionary and President of Cuba.

QUIZ 3. IN THE NEWS

This is a quiz about people or incidents that hit the headlines in January 2019, which is when the book was completed. A test for the memory – although hopefully nothing too ephemeral here, so a bit of general knowledge comes into play.

1. Nicolás Maduro, currently resisting pressure to hold fresh elections, replaced Hugo Chavez as president of which country in 2013?

2. Emiliano Sala's aeroplane went missing en route to him taking up employment with which organisation in January 2019?

3. Which Democrat leader of the US House of Representatives became a thorn in the side of President Trump when her party regained a house majority in January 2019?

4. Which politician, arrested in January 2019, was the MP for Banff and Buchan from 1987 to 2010?

5. Who was the subject of the documentary *Leaving Neverland*, shown for the first time at the 2019 Sundance Film Festival?

6. Which overseas organisation bought the Chiswick-based brewer, Fullers, in January 2019?

7. What was the majority by which Teresa May's first draft Brexit deal was rejected in Parliament in January 2019; was it 46, 98, 145 or 230?

8. Paweł Adamowicz was murdered in Poland on Sunday 13 January 2019. What position did he hold?

9. Swedish activist Greta Thunberg organised marches in Brussels and Berlin to protest about climate change in January 2019. What was unusual about them?

10. In early 2019 the Weddell Sea Expedition set off for the Antarctic to look for which lost vessel?

Answers to Quiz 2

1. Theodore Roosevelt.

2. Commanding General of the US army (or anything that indicates head of the armed forces).

3. Grover Cleveland (Democrat, 1885–9 and 1893–97).

4. Franklin D. Roosevelt and Harry S. Truman.

5. Woodrow Wilson.

6. Lyndon B. Johnson.

7. Georgia.

8. Zachary Taylor.

9. Gerald Ford – he became vice-president on the resignation of Spiro Agnew and succeeded Nixon as president.

10. Andrew Jackson.

Donald Trump is the forty-fifth President of the United States: here's a full list of the other forty-four:

1 George Washington 1789–97

2 John Adams 1797–1801

3 Thomas Jefferson 1801–9

4 James Madison 1809–17

5 James Monroe 1817–25

6 John Quincy Adams 1825–9

7 Andrew Jackson 1829–37

8 Martin van Buren 1837–41

9 William H. Harrison 1841

10 John Tyler 1841–5

11 James Polk 1845–9

12 Zachary Taylor 1849–50

13 Millard Fillmore 1850–3

14 Franklin Pierce 1853–7

15 James Buchanan 1857–61

16 Abraham Lincoln 1861–5

17 Andrew Johnson 1865–9

18 Ulysses S. Grant 1869–77

19 Rutherford B. Hayes 1877–81

20 James A. Garfield 1881

21 Chester Alan Arthur 1881–5

22 Grover Cleveland 1885–9

23 Benjamin Harrison 1889–93

24 Grover Cleveland 1893–7

25 William McKinley 1897–1901

26 Theodore Roosevelt 1901–9

27 William Howard Taft 1909–13

28 Woodrow Wilson 1913–21

29 Warren G. Harding 1921–3

30 Calvin Coolidge 1923–9

31 Herbert Hoover 1929–33

32 Franklin D. Roosevelt 1933–45

33 Harry S. Truman 1945–53

34 Dwight Eisenhower 1953–61

35 John F. Kennedy 1961–3

36 Lyndon B. Johnson 1963–9

37 Richard Nixon 1969–74

38 Gerald Ford 1974–7

39 Jimmy Carter 1977–81

40 Ronald Reagan 1981–9

41 George H.W. Bush 1989–93

42 Bill Clinton 1993–2001

43 George W. Bush 2001–9

44 Barack Obama 2009–17

QUIZ 4. PEOPLE AND PLACES

Geography in twenty-first-century schools is a very different beast to the subject we studied as children, but it still seems to attract the same loathing from those who don't feel drawn to it. My gorgeous other half simply switches off if someone uses the word 'map' . . .

1. Iona, Mull, Skye, Stronsay: which of these islands is not part of the Inner Hebrides group?

2. Which peak, the highest in the Alps, was first climbed by Jacques Balmat in 1786?

3. Which state capital is the southernmost of the major Australian cities on the mainland of the country?

4. The Barents Sea takes its name from an explorer from which country?

5. Bremen, Dortmund, Hannover, Leipzig: which of these was in East Germany during the Soviet bloc's domination of Eastern Europe after the Second World War?

6. Santander, Madrid, Sevilla, Valencia: which of these Spanish cities is furthest to the south?

7. The island of Götland, a Swedish territory, is located in which body of water?

8. Kibo peak in Tanzania is the highest summit in Africa: by what name is it more commonly known in the West?

9. Which mountain range provides the source for the River Rhine?

10. What is the name of the Russian province and city wedged between Poland and Lithuania on the Baltic coast and separated from the rest of Russia?

Answers to Quiz 3

1. Venezuela. Maduro is engaged in a running dispute with the President of the National Assembly, Juan Guaidó, a dispute that may well teeter into civil war.

2. Cardiff City FC. Sala was the Argentinian striker Cardiff bought from Nantes in France: he and pilot David Ibbotson went down over the Channel and Sala's body was later found in the wreckage.

3. Nancy Pelosi. The Representative from California's 12th District replaced Paul Ryan as Speaker of the House when the Democrats took control in the 2018 November mid-term elections. She is the first woman to be Speaker and the highest-ranked female official in US history to date.

4. Alex Salmond. The former SNP leader was arrested and charged on 24 January, but no trial has yet determined his guilt or innocence.

5. Michael Jackson. The film follows the testimony of two men who claim to have been abused by Jackson when they were young boys. No judgement has ever been made against Jackson on this issue, although rumours and allegations persist.

6. Asahi, Japan's biggest brewer. The expanding company purchased Peroni, Grolsch and Meantime as part of the purchase of SABMiller in 2016, and added Fuller's in 2019.

7. 230. The Brexit debate rumbles interminably on – it may still not be resolved by the time you read these answers!

8. Mayor of Gdansk. Adamowicz, a liberal, was stabbed at a charity event.

9. The marchers were all schoolchildren – which is a nice thing to reflect on considering how negative most of the news items were that played out around the time.

10. Shackleton's *Endurance*. Launched in 1912, the ship was lost in the Weddell Sea in the Antarctic in 1915.

QUIZ 5. MIXED BAG

A general knowledge quiz. A good pub quiz should have a couple of rounds out of six that are just basic general knowledge, unless the entire quiz has a pre-advertised theme.

1. The 'color line', the rule that barred black players from competing in Major League Baseball, was finally broken when which player signed for the Brooklyn Dodgers in 1946?

2. What term did Thomas Macaulay first apply to the press in a report on activity in the House of Commons in 1828?

3. Magnus Carlsen has spent (to January 2019) 103 weeks as the world's top-rated what? And who is the only player to have eclipsed that 103-week statistic?

4. In which country did the Knesset first meet on St Valentine's Day, 1949?

5. The Night Riviera sleeper train runs between London and which destination?

6. Which former West Indian fast bowler stood at six foot eight inches tall and was known as Big Bird?

7. If an epidemic is a widespread infection over a large area, what is a worldwide infection?

8. Which private bank has its headquarters at 440, The Strand, London?

9. DCLXIV. What is this in Arabic numbers?

10. Who was the Commander-in-Chief of the British forces in France from 1915 until the end of the First World War?

Answers to Quiz 4

1. Stronsay is in the Orkney Islands. Skye is comfortably the largest and most populous of the Inner Hebrides, home to over ten thousand of the population of just under nineteen thousand. Mull, along with Islay, also has over a thousand inhabitants. Iona is a tiny island best known for an abandoned abbey.

2. Mont Blanc, the highest peak in the Alpine massif and the highest in Europe west of the Russian Caucasus peaks. Mont Blanc lies in an area that forms the border between France and Italy, and climbers and visitors are served principally by the town of Chamonix, home to the inaugural Winter Olympics in 1924.

3. Melbourne.

4. The Netherlands; it was first seen by Willem Barentsz.

5. Leipzig.

6. Sevilla.

7. The Baltic Sea – Götland lies on the east coast of Sweden almost halfway to the Lithuanian coast.

8. Kilimanjaro. Kibo is the highest of the three peaks (cones, technically; the others are Mawenzi and Shira) that make up this dormant volcano.

9. The Alps.

10. Kaliningrad. The area, and the major city of Kaliningrad, give Russia a vital port on the Baltic Sea, meaning its shipping no longer has to travel to the strait between Finland and Estonia.

QUIZ 6. SPORT – MIXED

A nice, doable starter for the first all-sports quiz in the book. I would always advise caution when using sports questions in a pub quiz; they can be divisive and put off large sections of your potential quizzers. Better to mix them in with themed rounds rather than have an entire sports one.

1. How many of Serena Williams' fourteen major doubles titles have been won with her sister Venus as her partner?

2. Ray Harroun won the first running of which historic motor race on 30 May 1911?

3. Which sport has more players on the playing surface at any one time: basketball, netball, ice hockey or volleyball?

4. Why would it have been impossible for the great racehorse Sea the Stars to compete in the Epsom Oaks?

5. Fencing, rowing, shooting, swimming. Which of these is not a constituent event of the Olympic Modern Pentathlon?

6. Who were the first team to beat England as World Cup holders, winning a famous match 3–2 at Wembley in 1967?

7. David Hemery won Britain's only gold medal on the track at the 1968 Olympics; what was his discipline?

8. Which famous cricket commentator was the captain of the Australian team during the 1961 and the 1962–3 Ashes series?

9. Which two-time World Champion snooker player was known as the Hurricane?

10. What name have American sports journalists given to their country's 1980 Winter Olympics ice hockey victory over the heavily fancied Soviet Union?

Answers to Quiz 5

1. Jackie Robinson.

2. The fourth estate.

3. Chess. Carlsen, a Norwegian, was a child prodigy known for his devastating attacking play. He has matured into a complete player and, still only twenty-eight, is talked about as one of the game's greatest exponents. Garry Kasparov, the Azerbaijani-born Soviet player, now a citizen of Croatia and a fierce opponent of Vladimir Putin, is the only player currently to have eclipsed him.

4. Israel. The State of Israel was declared in 1948 and its Parliament, the Knesset, met early the following year.

5. Penzance, Cornwall – it is the only night train in Britain apart from the Caledonian sleeper between London and Edinburgh.

6. Joel Garner. Garner was a key part of the fearsome West Indies fast-bowling attack that dominated cricket from the mid-1970s until the early 1990s. First came Andy Roberts and Michael Holding, then Garner and Malcolm Marshall, and later Courtney Walsh and Curtly Ambrose. Garner was the least quick of these six great bowlers, but with his height and reach he was able to make the ball bounce more steeply. Contemporaries write that the white sight-screens behind the bowler at every ground rarely extended high enough for the batsman to see the top of Garner's arm when he was bowling!

7. A pandemic; they are rare, the last being a 2009 flu outbreak. The most talked-about pandemic in modern times was the HIV outbreak.

8. Coutts, formed in 1692 by a Scottish goldsmith. Coutts was bought by NatWest in 1969, which in turn was purchased by the Royal Bank of Scotland Group in 2000.

9. 664. Roman numbering is based around seven symbols. I = 1, V = 5, X = 10, L = 50, C = 100, D = 500, M = 1,000. Any Arabic number can be converted by using these symbols and stacking them as appropriate. For example, 277 is 2 × C (200) + 1 × L (50) + 2 × X (20) + 1 × V (5) + 2 × I (2): CCLXXVII. Simple. If you like that sort of thing.

10. Douglas Haig.

QUIZ 7. HERE COMES THE SUMMER

Summer is the theme, but don't expect too many questions on sunshine or beachwear . . .

1. Which band, still gigging today, were at No. 1 for six weeks in 1970 with 'In the Summertime'?

2. Shakespeare; Sonnet 18: 'Shall I compare thee to a summer's day? / Thou art more lovely and more temperate / Rough winds do shake . . .' What do they shake?

3. To Germans it is *altweibersomer* (old ladies' summer), to East Europeans a gypsy summer, and we used to call it St Martin's summer? What do we call it now?

4. What was the name of Buffy Summers' mum in *Buffy the Vampire Slayer*?

5. Jacqueline Gold is the businesswoman behind the success of which high-street chain?

6. Comic-book character Scott Summers is better known as what?

7. According to Aristotle, what doesn't make a summer?

8. Musician Andy Summers is best known for being the guitarist in which band.

9. In the Bryan Adams' song 'Summer of 1969', where does the singer buy his 'first real six-string'?

10. The tune 'Summertime' was written by George Gershwin for which 1935 opera?

Answers to Quiz 6

1. All of them; the sisters have won every major doubles final they have contested, four at the Australian Open, two French Opens, six Wimbledon titles and two US Open Championships.

2. Indianapolis 500; the winners of the Indy 500 were all American for many years, but this hegemony has been broken in the last thirty years as manufacturers have looked abroad for talented drivers and a number of drivers from other disciplines have tried their luck at Indianapolis.

3. Netball (seven) – volleyball and hockey have six, basketball five.

4. Sea the Stars raced as a colt (a boy), and the Oaks is exclusively for the girls (or fillies, as they are properly termed). Sea the Stars was a brilliant Irish-bred horse that won a rare treble of the 2,000 Guineas, the Derby and the Eclipse Stakes at Sandown. He then made the season a uniquely successful one by winning the Prix de l'Arc de Triomphe at Longchamp in the autumn.

5. Rowing – the other two are equestrian and running, although the equestrian event is under review as it is too easily affected by different standards of horses.

6. Scotland. A maverick Rangers' star called Jim Baxter ran the show for Scotland, who could have won by more. They were a really strong team at the time, featuring, as well as Baxter, four of the Celtic team that had just won the European Cup, including Denis Law and Billy Bremner.

7. The 400-metre hurdles. He was the last, and only the second, British athlete to win a gold medal over hurdles – the first was Lord Burghley, played by Nigel Havers in the film *Chariots of Fire*.

8. Richie Benaud. Benaud was a leg-spin bowler and effective lower-order batsman, and as a captain was as astute as one would expect, having heard him in the commentary box.

9. Alex Higgins.

10. The Miracle on Ice. The Soviets were a fully professional team and had won the previous six Olympic tournaments. In a fiercely contested match, the US prevailed 4–3, having trailed for much of the game.

QUIZ 8. OSCAR TIME

Here we need you to match the actor in the first list to the film that won them an Academy Award as Best Actor or Actress.

1. Audrey Hepburn.

2. Gary Cooper.

3. Ingrid Bergman.

4. Robert Duvall.

5. Jane Fonda.

6. Susan Sarandon.

7. Lee Marvin.

8. Sean Penn.

9. Kate Winslet.

10. Robert Donat.

A. *Goodbye Mr Chips*

B. *The Reader*

C. *Cat Ballou*

D. *Roman Holiday*

E. *Mystic River*

F. *Sergeant York*

G. *Dead Man Walking*

H. *Klute*

I. *Tender Mercies*

J. *Gaslight*

Answers to Quiz 7

1. Mungo Jerry. The follow-up, 'Baby Jump', also went to No. 1, and they had two more Top 10 hits before their star declined.

2. *The Darling Buds of May*; H.E. Bates used these lines for the title of his 1958 novel, which became a hit TV series with David Jason, Pam Ferris and Catherine Zeta-Jones in the early 1990s.

3. Indian summer.

4. Joyce; Buffy's mum is killed off in a devastating episode in Series 5 of the show.

5. Anne Summers, the retailer of sexy lingerie and toys.

6. Cyclops in *X-Men*; he has been played by James Marsden, Tim Pocock and Tye Sheridan in the Marvel Cinematic Universe.

7. One swallow – the suggestion being that one fine day doesn't mean that no more cold weather will come. It's similar to the old wives' saying, 'ne'er cast a clout 'til May is out' – meaning don't start shedding layers of clothing until May is finished. Clearly a saying used before global warming.

8. The Police, along with Sting (bass and vocals) and Stewart Copeland.

9. The next line goes: 'bought it in a five and dime' – a five and dime being a budget store in the US until the mid-twentieth century.

10. *Porgy and Bess*. The song has become a jazz standard, with perhaps Billie Holiday's being the most famous rendition.

QUIZ 9. MONEY-GO-ROUND

Money makes the world go round, as Joel Grey sang in *Cabaret*. It is, alas, true, so here's one for the capitalists. Match the countries in the first list to the domestic currency they use from the second list.

1. Brazil.

2. Poland.

3. Iran.

4. Japan.

5. Finland.

6. Norway.

7. Taiwan.

8. Thailand.

9. Philippines.

10. Malaysia.

A. Rial

B. Euro

C. Ringgit

D. Baht

E. Real

F. Peso

G. Dollar

H. Zloty

I. Yen

J. Krone

Answers to Quiz 8

1. Audrey was in *Roman Holiday* (D, 1953) with Gregory Peck.

2. Gary Cooper won his award for *Sergeant York* (F, 1946), Howard Hawks' biopic of the decorated US soldier.

3. Ingrid Bergman plays Paula in *Gaslight* (J, 1944), manipulated by her husband (Charles Boyer) into believing herself insane. Also nominated was eighteen-year-old Angela Lansbury for her work in a supporting role.

4. In *Tender Mercies* (I, 1983) Robert Duvall plays a recovering alcoholic country singer.

5. Jane Fonda deserved her gong (they don't always) for her work in *Klute* (H, 1971) as a prostitute helping a private detective (Donald Sutherland) solve a missing-person crime.

6. Susan Sarandon won for *Dead Man Walking* (G, 1995), a study of the relationship between a nun and a death-row prisoner.

7. Lee Marvin starred in two roles in *Cat Ballou* (C, 1965), a rare beast in being a successful comedy western.

8. Sean Penn was nominated for an Academy Award for *Dead Man Walking* (see 6 above) but won for his part in Clint Eastwood's *Mystic River* (2003, E) alongside Tim Robbins and Kevin Bacon.

9. Kate Winslet starred in the 2008 drama *The Reader* (B) with Ralph Fiennes.

10. Robert Donat was a between-the-wars matinee idol who won his Oscar for his part as the schoolteacher in *Goodbye Mr Chips* (A, 1939) opposite Greer Garson.

QUIZ 10. MILITARY MIGHT

Ten questions about battles and campaigns across the ages. The world seems a bleak place at the moment.

1. Which battle during the War of Spanish Succession, won by the allies under John Churchill, Duke of Marlborough, gives its name to the Churchills' huge country house in Oxfordshire?

2. Who led the Prussian forces that joined with the British to defeat Napoleon at Waterloo?

3. Edward III inflicted a crushing defeat on the French at the Battle of Crécy in 1346. Ten years later, his son, the Black Prince, inflicted another defeat on the same opposition near which French town?

4. At which Virginia town was General Cornwallis forced to surrender, ending the American Revolutionary War?

5. The Gallipoli Campaign in the First World War took place in which modern country? Which Imperial power controlled that country at the time?

6. United States; United Kingdom; South Korea; Australia; Philippines; New Zealand; Japan: which two of these were not belligerents alongside the South Vietnamese during the Vietnam War?

7. From 1899 to 1901, Western powers and the Japanese allied to quash which major anti-colonial uprising?

8. The Battle of Lepanto (1571) was a naval battle and was the last major engagement to feature which particular type of vessel?

9. The tribes that fought a nine-year civil war against the Soviets were known as the Mujahideen and they later formed the basis of the Taliban's fighting force: who were the primary sponsors of the Mujahideen in their struggle against the Soviets?

10. Control of the city of Sebastopol was a principal reason for which war of the mid-nineteenth century?

Answers to Quiz 9

1. Brazil – Real (E).

2. Poland – Zloty (H).

3. Iran – Rial (A).

4. Japan – Yen (I).

5. Finland – Euro (B).

6. Norway – Krone (J).

7. Taiwan – Dollar (G).

8. Thailand – Baht (D).

9. Philippines – Peso (F).

10. Malaysia – Ringgit (C).

Trivia spot:
According to September 2018 statistics, the ten
most-traded currencies in the world are:
US Dollar (USD)
Euro (EUR)
Japanese Yen (JNY)
Pound Sterling (GBP)
Australian Dollar (AUD)
Canadian Dollar (CAD)
Swiss Franc (CHF)
Chinese Renminbi (CNH)
Swedish Krone (SEK)
New Zealand Dollar (NZD)

QUIZ 11. THIS OR THAT

This or That is a popular occasional round at The Stag. It's a good, quirky filler and runs really quickly, so it's a useful device to have on stand-by when you have a deadline or need an early finish.

Here's how it works: I give you twelve names, all of whom are either a vice-president, a character in *The Wire* or a famous baseball hitter. If you happen to be American, you'll do pretty well . . .

1. Tommy Carcetti.

2. Adlai Stevenson.

3. Cedric Daniels.

4. Jackie Robinson.

5. Andrew Johnson.

6. Willie Mays.

7. Spiro Agnew.

8. Joe DiMaggio.

9. Alex Rodriguez.

10. Stringer Bell.

11. Avon Barksdale.

12. Hannibal Hamlin.

Answers to Quiz 10

1. Blenheim; the War of Spanish Succession was a dispute as to who would inherit the Spanish throne, the French candidate (Philip) or the Habsburg candidate (Charles). Protestant Britain supported the Habsburg claim and were (sort of) victorious, ensuring there was no line of succession that would combine Spain and France into a Catholic super-power.

2. Von Blücher. Gebhard Leberecht von Blücher led the Prussian armies in the alliance that defeated Napoleon at Leipzig in 1813, and he arrived, albeit a trifle late, to turn Waterloo decisively in the allies' favour and end Napoleon's military effectiveness.

3. Poitiers; these two victories, along with Agincourt in 1415, suggested that the English Plantagenet kings might prove victorious in their long dynastic struggle for control of France, but later victories for the French, inspired by Jeanne d'Arc at Orléans, proved more decisive and the English ended their ambitions in France in 1453. The Hundred Years War is a misnomer – the conflict ran from 1337 to 1453.

4. Yorktown. Cornwallis was a competent commander and went on to serve in India and Ireland after the loss of the American colonies.

5. Turkey; the Ottoman Empire that, along with Austria-Hungary, were the main allies of Germany in the First World War.

6. UK and Japan. Laos, Cambodia and Thailand also piled in on the side of the South Vietnamese. Against them were North Vietnam, China and all the Chinese-sponsored communist rebels in the other Southeast Asian countries.

7. The anti-Western and anti-Imperial Boxer Rebellion in China.

8. Lepanto was the last battle to feature galleys, or rowed vessels; it resulted in a victory for the Venetian Republic, assisted by Spain, against the Ottoman Empire.

9. United States. Obvs.

10. Crimean War. Sebastopol remains a crucial Black Sea port. Russia annexed the Crimea in 2014 just to get access to the Black Sea. The West still views the Crimea and Sebastopol as part of the Ukraine.

QUIZ 12. MUSIC

Everyone loves a music quiz. Usually we do an audio round for the music element of the quiz, but three or four times a year we have just a music quiz – the pub is invariably rammed.

1. In 1983–4 Lionel Richie had a No. 1 hit on both sides of the Atlantic with an album and a huge-selling single taken from the album: can you name both?

2. Who topped the UK album chart with the prog-rock epic *Journey to the Centre of the Earth* in 1974?

3. Richard Thompson is a veteran of the folk scene and one of the world's premier guitar players: with which band did he make his name in the late 1960s?

4. Tina Turner includes the song 'Addicted to Love' in her live shows: who wrote and had the original hit with the song in 1986, from his album, *Riptide*?

5. Born Chaim Witz, who co-founded the glam-metal band Kiss with Paul Stanley?

6. What was Gloria Gaynor's massive 1978 hit, a No. 1 on both sides of the Atlantic? And what was her earlier 1974 hit, which reached the Top 10 in both the US and the UK?

7. Barry Gibb formed the Bee Gees with his two younger twin brothers, both now deceased: what were their names?

8. Frank Beard was the drummer in which trio, in which, humorously, he was the only one not sporting a long beard?

9. Apart from a song recorded with Manchester United, Status Quo had only one UK No. 1 hit. Was it 'Caroline', 'Down Down', 'Rockin' All Over the World' or 'In the Army Now'?

10. Which rock star won a Tony Award for his sold-out residency of anecdotes and songs at the Walter Kerr Theatre on Broadway?

11. In the context of 2019, when this book was completed and published, what connects these artists?

Answers to Quiz 11

1. Tommy Carcetti (played by Irish actor Aiden Gillen) is a devious wannabe mayor (and later actual mayor) of Baltimore in *The Wire*.

2. Adlai Stevenson was a Democrat vice-president to Grover Cleveland from 1893 to 1897. His grandson was Adlai Stevenson III (in true American fashion), who stood unsuccessfully as a Democratic presidential candidate in 1952 and 1956.

3. Cedric Daniels (Lance Reddick) is one of the few honest policemen in *The Wire*.

4. Jackie Robinson was the first African-American player to appear in Major League Baseball.

5. Andrew Johnson was a Democrat who served as vice-president under Republican president Abraham Lincoln in 1865 and assumed the presidency when Lincoln was assassinated.

6. Willie Mays was a centre fielder who played eighteen consecutive seasons for the San Francisco Giants.

7. Spiro Agnew was Richard Nixon's vice-president until he was forced to resign as he was facing corruption charges.

8. Joe DiMaggio was a hitter who played for the New York Yankees for thirteen years either side of the Second World War. He is also remembered as Marilyn Monroe's second husband.

9. Alex 'A-Rod' Rodriguez is a former short-stop and hitter with the Seattle Mariners, Texas Rangers and New York Yankees, and currently a broadcaster. Rodriguez has been romantically linked with both Madonna and Jennifer Lopez.

10. Stringer Bell (Idris Elba) is a drug-dealer in *The Wire*, and a wannabe intellectual and businessman; he is killed by a rival in Season 3.

11. Avon Barksdale (Wood Harris) is Stringer's boss, a kingpin of the Baltimore drug scene.

12. Hannibal Hamlin sounds like a character from *The Wire* but in fact was Abraham Lincoln's first vice-president – he was a Democrat turned Republican and was picked to help Lincoln get some of the anti-slavery Democrats on board with his agenda.

QUIZ 13. NAME THE YEAR

We give you four events from a particular year, you give us the year. Two points for spot on, one point if you are within the leeway given. These are surprisingly difficult, even the recent ones. You'll probably find those you get right are because one of the events given as a clue resonates somehow with an incident or memory from your life.

1. Playstation 2 is released; Ridley Scott's *Gladiator* is released; the computer virus ILOVEYOU causes havoc for Windows users; Steve Redgrave wins a fifth Olympic gold medal (two years).

2. Bertrand Russell launches CND; Brazil beat Sweden 5–2 in the World Cup Final; the hula hoop is launched; transatlantic air travel exceeds sea travel for the first time (two years).

3. Australia cuts its last political ties to Britain with the Australia Act; Ferdinand Marcos is removed from office in the Philippines; the Hand of God; Glasnost and Perestroika are introduced into the global lexicon (one year).

4. Jimmy Carter is sworn in and immediately pardons all Vietnam draft-dodgers; The Clash, The Jam and The Sex Pistols all release their debut albums; Marc Bolan is killed in a car crash; Egyptian president Anwar Sadat visits Israel (one year).

5. Mickey Mouse makes his first appearance in a comic strip; Mahatma Gandhi initiates the Salt March protest; Haile Selassie is crowned Emperor of Ethiopia; Arsenal win the first of their thirteen FA Cups (three years).

6. Anthony Blunt admits to spying for the Russians; Burton and Taylor marry for the first time; President Lyndon B. Johnson declares a war on poverty; Radio Caroline is launched (one year).

7. Juan Péron is elected President of Argentina; the first Formula One race takes place in Turin, Italy; Dean Martin and Jerry Lewis make their debut as a comedy duo; Dolly Parton, David Lynch, George Best and George W. Bush are all born (three years).

8. A general strike is declared in the UK; Rudolph Valentino dies aged only thirty-one; Route 66 is given its iconic name, along with a multitude of other American highways; Huddersfield Town win a third successive League title, the first club to do so (three years).

9. The first American cinema opens in Los Angeles; Edward VII is crowned King of England; the first borstal in the UK opens in Kent; Gilbert Jessop scores a sensational century as England pull off a famous Ashes victory (three years).

10. The US Government sets up a 700-billion-dollar fund to purchase failing bank assets; the large Hadron Collider is officially commissioned; Mark Ronson, Kate Nash and the Arctic Monkeys win the three main awards at the Brit Awards; the Champions League Final is contested by two English teams for the first and only time (one year).

Answers to Quiz 12

1. *Can't Slow Down* was the album, 'Hello', complete with extraordinarily tacky video, was the single. Proof, if ever it were needed, that the general public and good taste are entire strangers.

2. Rick Wakeman. The classically trained pianist and former Yes keyboard player had three successful concept albums, of which this was the second. *The Six Wives of Henry VIII* and *King Arthur and the Knights of the Round Table* were the other two. They were the essence of prog rock – elaborate neo-classical compositions with the occasional catchy riff to keep the rock audience engaged.

3. Fairport Convention; Thompson is still going strong at seventy.

4. Robert Palmer.

5. Gene Simmonds.

6. 'I Will Survive', a staple of school discos and 1980s' nightclubs; her 1974 hit was 'Never Can Say Goodbye'.

7. Robin and Maurice; Barry, the eldest, has outlived both the twins and his youngest brother, Andy.

8. ZZ Top: main songwriter and guitarist Billy Gibbons and bass player and singer Dusty Hill both sport long beards, Frank is clean-shaven. Billy, for trivia lovers, plays a scary father in the TV comedy crime drama *Bones*.

9. 'Down Down'; I would have gone for 'Rockin' All Over the World' every time.

10. Bruce Springsteen; watch the video, it's mesmerising stuff.

11. All turn seventy in 2019 (Francis Rossi of Status Quo is the connection in Q9).

QUIZ 14. SFTV

Some of the most innovative TV programmes screened have been science-fiction programmes. Just as poetry can sometimes eclipse prose in its power to evoke feeling, taking away the constraints of the real world can similarly allow heightened moments of pleasure in a TV show.

1. Which UK sci-fi series starred a pre-*Poldark* Aidan Turner as a vampire called John Mitchell?

2. Which series, with Charlie Cox in the lead, was the first of Netflix's forays into the Marvel Universe in 2015?

3. Which US sci-fi franchise is based on a 1994 film starring James Spader and Kurt Russell as the leads in a team exploring wormholes in space?

4. What is the name of Charlie Brooker's sci-fi series, inspired by *The Twilight Zone*, launched on Channel 4 in 2011 and later purchased and re-energised by Netflix?

5. Phil Coulson leads which team of good guys in their struggles against Hydra, the Kree and various rogue Inhumans?

6. Eliza Taylor as Clarke Griffin is the lead role in which sci-fi drama, developed and launched by Jason Rothenberg in 2014?

7. The Daleks were created and cleverly copyrighted by Terry Nation, who also devised which cult British sci-fi show, which ran for four series from 1978 to 1981?

8. What was Russell T. Davies' *Dr Who* spin-off, using the character Captain Jack Harkness played by John Barrowman?

9. Which TV sci-fi series explores the relationships and ethics between humans and sentient androids known as 'hosts'?

10. What was the name of the 1998 sci-fi series starring Jack Davenport, Susannah Harker and a young Idris Elba about a secret government body hunting Code Nines (or vampires)?

Answers to Quiz 13

1. 2000 – Redgrave would be a give-away for any sports fan.

2. 1958 – the 1958 World Cup saw the emergence of the game's greatest player, Pelé. After a drab 0–0 draw with an ordinary England team, coach Feola threw the teenager into the team. In the knockout stage he scored the only goal against Wales, a stunning hat-trick against France and two more in the Final against Sweden.

3. 1986.

4. 1977.

5. 1930.

6. 1964: Burton and Taylor married in 1964, were divorced a decade later, remarried the following year, and divorced again less than a year after that. Burton was married to Suzy Miller before 1976 was done.

7. 1946: Péron was a former general and minister who came to power in 1946, remaining as president until 1955, three years after the death of his wife, Eva (as in *Evita*, the musical). Peronism remains a strong thread in Argentinian politics, a platform of social justice woven into a capitalist structure with a dash of nationalism.

8. 1926: Huddersfield's first two titles were under the management of Herbert Chapman, English football's greatest pre-war manager. Chapman went on to win two further titles with Arsenal before his premature death in 1934.

9. 1902: Edward, Queen Victoria's eldest surviving son, was already sixty-one when he took the throne. Elizabeth II's great-grandfather, he died in 1910.

10. 2008.

QUIZ 15. FREDERICK

Themed rounds always prove popular. There will invariably be some teams who baulk at an entire sports round or who don't do well on movies or history, or whatever their *bête noire* happens to be. If you mix a couple of sports questions into a themed round – the theme in this case being the name Fred – then they notice (and protest) less. You can't please all of the people all of the time, but you can stop them moaning . . . Identify the following:

1. Actor best known for being in the *Scooby-Doo* movies and marrying Sarah Michelle Gellar, whom he met on the set of *I Know What You Did Last Summer*.

2. The former CEO of the Royal Bank of Scotland. He presided over a near-decade of boom and bust at the bank, the bust part forcing the UK government into taking RBS into public ownership. He was knighted in 2004 but this honour was annulled in 2012, a rare move.

3. The birth names of movie dance couple Fred Astaire and Ginger Rogers.

4. Nickname of former England Test cricketer Andrew Flintoff.

5. The villainous killer in the *Nightmare on Elm Street* franchise, he of the flayed face and scalpel finger.

6. The guitarist with the MC5s and, later, Patti Smith's band. He and Patti were married in 1980 and remained a couple until Smith's premature death in 1994, aged forty-six.

7. German film-maker who moved to Hollywood in the 1930s, best known for the early sci-fi masterpiece *Metropolis*. In Hollywood he made a series of excellent films noir, including *Big Heat*, with Glenn Ford and Gloria Grahame, one of the best of the genre.

8. Of Manchester United and Brazil; United paid Shakhtar Donetsk around £50m for him in the summer of 2018 – at the time of writing it seems that the Ukrainian side got the better of that deal.

9. A Louisiana band who had a one-off hit in 1968 with 'Judy in Disguise (with Glasses)'.

10. A basset hound in a classic *Daily Mail* comic strip first launched in 1963.

Answers to Quiz 14

1. *Being Human*: the show co-starred Russell Tovey and Lenora Crichlow as a werewolf and a ghost respectively, and a deliciously malevolent Jason Watkins as chief adversary Herrick.

2. *Daredevil*: Netflix went über dark with their Marvel series. Fisks in *Daredevil* and Kilgrave in *Jessica Jones* are two of the bleakest villains imaginable.

3. *Stargate*: Richard Dean Anderson and Michael Shanks took Russell and Spader's roles and the show ran for ten seasons and two spin-offs, *Stargate Atlantis* (five seasons) and *Stargate Universe* (two seasons).

4. *Black Mirror*: initially a cult watch, this series has won awards aplenty and enormous critical approval. A fifth season is due in 2019.

5. *Agents of S.H.I.E.L.D.*: the show has been renewed for a sixth season, even though Coulson has retired from duty.

6. *The 100*: based on Kass Morgan's books, this show is part coming-of-age drama, part sci-fi adventure, and a sixth season will air in 2019.

7. *Blake's Seven*: cardboard sets apart, there was something dark about Avon (Paul Darrow) and something compelling about Servalan (Jacqueline Pearce), a pioneer of the sci-fi lady bad-ass.

8. *Torchwood*: *Dr Who* with more overtly adult content, *Torchwood* was interesting and successful but flawed.

9. *Westworld*: Closer to the Michael Crichton novel than the original movie with Yul Brynner.

10. *Ultraviolet*: No spoilers, just watch it. Cult viewing.

QUIZ 16. VOCAB TEST

I like to slip in the odd Words Round; people usually score quite well in these, and such rounds don't demand any specialist knowledge. The questions here are more like those in a crossword than a straight quiz, but they work nicely as a bit of a change. The number in brackets is the number of letters in the answer – it eliminates most of the potential ambiguities. All these words begin with the same letter (R).

1. From the French, mildly suggestive or naughty (6).

2. To restore or restock to a former or agreed level (9).

3. In heraldry, to describe an animal standing on one hind foot with both forefeet in the air (7).

4. The entourage of a VIP or royal personage (7).

5. Policy or diplomacy based on pragmatism rather than ideology or ethics (11).

6. Small ceramic serving dish, usually with round edges (7).

7. A slender blade used in the sixteenth and seventeenth centuries and in some forms of sports fencing (6).

8. The restoration of a lost item, or the payment of compensation for losses caused (11).

9. An even-toed ungulate cud-chewing mammal (8).

10. Difficult to control or handle, turbulent and noisy, wildly boisterous, especially of social behaviour or children (12).

Answers to Quiz 15

1. Freddie Prinze Jr.

2. Fred Goodwin.

3. Frederick Austerlitz and Virginia McKath.

4. Freddie Flintoff.

5. Freddy Krueger.

6. Fred 'Sonic' Smith.

7. Fritz Lang (Fritz is short for Friedrich)

8. Frederico Rodrigues de Paula Santos.

9. John Fred and His Playboy Band.

10. Fred Basset.

QUIZ 17. FOOD AND DRINK

We all eat. We all drink. But how much do you know about what you consume?

1. Which famous food emporium is found at 181 Piccadilly, London?

2. Who baked the cake featured on the front cover of The Rolling Stones' album, *Let It Bleed*?

3. What is the clarified butter used as a base oil in Indian cooking?

4. Who opened a small chocolate shop in Bull Street, Birmingham, in 1824?

5. What became known as 'Wilson's gravy' in the 1960s, due to then-Prime Minister Harold Wilson's supposed enthusiasm for the product?

6. Which of these peppers is graded as the hottest: jalapeno, tabasco or Scotch bonnet?

7. If you are served slices of edible raw fish in Japan, what are you eating?

8. Grüner Veltliner is a trendy white wine grape first sold to the UK by winemakers from which country?

9. Which vitamin's primary function is to promote the hormone that aids bone growth and formation?

10. The mango is a member of which fruiting plant family, the name of which is most commonly applied to a type of nut?

Answers to Quiz 16

1. Risqué.

2. Replenish.

3. Rampant.

4. Retinue.

5. Realpolitik.

6. Ramekin.

7. Rapier.

8. Restitution.

9. Ruminant.

10. Rambunctious.

The first 'word-cross' puzzle appeared in the *New York World* in 1913 and was devised by Arthur Wynne. Prior to that, various diagrammatic puzzles had appeared in a number of Victorian publications, but without any consistency. The *New York World* began to feature such puzzles on a regular basis, and the *Boston Globe* and other American publications followed.

The UK picked up the bug in the early 1920s, when crosswords in the US were becoming an all-consuming fad, in the same way that Sudoku would sweep across the West from Japan in the early 2000s. The *Sunday Express* was the first newspaper to publish a crossword, with most of the dailies following soon after. Cryptic crosswords are a variation peculiar to the UK, with most broadsheet newspapers running a cryptic and a plain crossword in every edition since the Second World War. The crossword setters each developed independent quirks and signatures, and became minor celebrities among a rather clannish circle of aficionados.

QUIZ 18. CANADA

Here's a tip. If you meet a North American and you can't place their accent, guess Canadian. If you guess American and they are Canadian, they will hate you, whereas the reverse is less likely. Canadians view Americans with the same contempt that many Scots hold for the English.

So here's a quiz for you, our Canadian friends.

1. Which is the only Canadian city to host the Summer Olympics?

2. In which decade did the colonies of Canada, New Brunswick and Nova Scotia amalgamate to form the beginnings of modern Canada?

3. Who won a gold medal for Canada in the men's super-heavyweight boxing division at the 1988 Olympic Games in Seoul?

4. Toronto is Canada's largest city: which are the next two largest? And what is the country's administrative capital?

5. Which Canadian territory comprising the north-east of the country was separated formally from the Northern Territories as a separate entity in 1999? It has a population of around 36,000 spread over a space the size of Mexico.

6. Which book by Michael Ondaatje, made into an Academy Award-winning film by Anthony Minghella a few years later, made the author the first Canadian winner of the Booker Prize?

7. What is Canada's only Major League baseball team?

8. *The Edible Woman* (1969) was the first full-length novel by which Canadian writer?

9. Which Western Canadian settlement, originally named Gastown, shares a connection with Hastings, having been built to service the Hastings Mill logging business?

10. Who are the only father and son to have served as prime minister of Canada?

Answers to Quiz 17

1. Fortnum & Mason.

2. Delia Smith. Delia was a then unknown cookery writer who was employed by sleeve designer Robert Brownjohn to provide an elaborate cake-style topping to a sculpted stack of items. Brownjohn was the graphic designer who created the iconic titles for two early Bond movies, *From Russia with Love* and *Goldfinger*.

3. Ghee.

4. John Cadbury. Cadbury developed the business with his brother, Benjamin. It was his sons, Richard and George, who moved the business in 1879 to the famous Bournville village, a commune based around the Cadbury factory that reflected the family's Quaker values. Cadbury's other significant act was to form the Animal Friends Society, a forerunner of the RSPCA.

5. HP brown sauce. Wilson's wife once let slip that Harold drowned most of his meals in the sauce and the company leapt on the marketing opportunity. The move did Wilson no harm; it was seen as a sign that he was one of the people.

6. Scotch bonnet. Peppers are measured for the intensity of heat on a scale developed by Wilbur Scoville. Down at the bottom are bell peppers and pimentos at less than a hundred units – Scotch bonnets are over one hundred thousand, with jalapenos and tabasco somewhere in between.

7. Sashimi; sushi is just the specially prepared rice, often with a piece of sashimi on top.

8. Austria: the wines are not dissimilar to a dry Riesling.

9. Vitamin D. Vitamin D is not commonly found in most foods (although fatty fish are a good natural source); much of what we take in is added to foodstuffs such as milk or bread or breakfast cereal. The body needs sunshine to synthesise the chemicals, and sunshine deficiency in Victorian times was a common cause of bone diseases such as rickets.

10. Cashews. You may well not have got this, but I threw it in as a cracking piece of triv. A mango is a cashew. Who knew that?

QUIZ 19. MIXED BAG

A good, old-fashioned general knowledge round, which may well come as a blessed relief after all that complicated themed stuff.

1. Constantinople is an old Western name for which modern city? What name did the Romans give this city?

2. Which card game has a gin version to it?

3. Which Latin phrase is used to describe one's old school or college?

4. Which award-winning Polish-French film director is unable to visit the United States because of unresolved charges dating back to the early 1970s of sexual relations with a minor?

5. What is the other alcoholic element alongside vodka in a Cosmopolitan?

6. Which American author left ten years between writing *The Secret History*, her debut novel, and *The Little Friend*, then a further eleven years until she wrote the Pulitzer Prize-winning *Goldfinch*?

7. Tariff, almanac and hazard are all words that came into the English language via which other tongue? Is it Arabic, Greek, Indian or Serbo-Croat?

8. Spanish giant Santander gained a significant foothold in the UK banking market with their purchase of which company in 2004?

9. Which artist is at the heart of the novel and film *Girl with a Pearl Earring*?

10. The US-backed dictator General Batista was overthrown and deposed in 1959 in which country?

Answers to Quiz 18

1. Montreal. Calgary (1988) and Vancouver (2010) have both hosted the Winter Olympics, but Montreal in 1976 was the only time Canada has hosted the Summer games.

2. 1860s (1867). The new Confederation comprised Ontario, Quebec (the two halves of old Canada), New Brunswick and Nova Scotia. The Northwest territories came under Confederation control almost immediately and Manitoba (1870) and British Columbia, including Vancouver Island (1871), joined soon after.

3. Lennox Lewis, that well-known British heavyweight . . .

4. Montreal and Vancouver come next. Sixth in that list would be Ottawa, the official capital.

5. Nunavut. The population density, or lack of it, is mostly explained by the fact that much of the province lies within the Arctic Circle.

6. *The English Patient*. I found the film a bit tortuous if I'm honest, but mine was a rare dissenting voice; it won nine Academy Awards.

7. Toronto Blue Jays. The Blue Jays play in the American League (East) division, alongside the New York Yankees, the Boston Red Sox, the Tampa Bay Rays and the Baltimore Orioles.

8. Margaret Atwood.

9. Vancouver. Vancouver lies on the western coast of Canada, not far north of the border with the United States. Further to the west is Vancouver Island, with the state capital of British Columbia, Victoria, at the southern tip. Victoria is equidistant by ferry from Vancouver City and Seattle in the state of Washington in the US.

10. Pierre and Justin Trudeau.

Canada comprises ten provinces:

Quebec (capital Quebec City); Ontario (Toronto); Nova Scotia (Halifax); New Brunswick (Fredericton); Manitoba (Winnipeg); British Columbia (Victoria); Prince Edward Island (Charlottetown); Saskatchewan (Regina); Alberta (Edmonton); Newfoundland and Labrador (St John's).

In addition, there are three territories – Northwest Territories (Yellowknife); Yukon (Whitehorse); Nunavut (Iqaluit). The difference is constitutional, the territories being absolutely controlled by the federal government, while the provinces wield more constitutional power and have more autonomy.

QUIZ 20. MOVIE MIXED BAG

A broad-based selection of movie questions. Movies are tricky because, unless they are outstanding, they are easily forgotten and not re-watched in the way we listen to music over and over again. We've tried to mix it up, with a nod to genre and indie movies as well as including mainstream and award-winning stuff.

1. Which 1994 film involved the hiring of a detective to find a mascot lost by the Miami Dolphins football team?

2. Which Taiwanese film director became part of the Hollywood mainstream after winning the Best Foreign Film Academy Award for *Crouching Tiger, Hidden Dragon*?

3. Who appeared in the third *Die Hard* film (*Die Hard with a Vengeance*) as Simon Gruber, brother of Hans, the main antagonist played by Alan Rickman in the first movie in the series?

4. Robert Altman assembled an impressive array of talent for his 2001 portmanteau country-house film *Gosford Park*: which of them played singer/composer Ivor Novello? Was it Charles Dance, Tom Hollander, Jeremy Northam or Clive Owen?

5. What type of creature is Sid (voiced by John Leguizamo) in *Ice Age* and its sequels?

6. Who wrote the eerie music to John Carpenter's siege thriller *Assault on Precinct 13* (1974)?

7. *Crazy Heart* saw which respected Hollywood star play a declining country star called Bad Blake?

8. Who directed the hit 1994 comedy *Four Weddings and a Funeral*? Was it Richard Curtis, Sam Mendes, Mike Newell or Christopher Nolan?

9. Marion Cotillard won an Academy Award for her role in *La Vie en Rose*: who was she playing in this 2007 biopic?

10. In the 1970 film *A Man Called Horse*, starring Richard Harris as an English aristocrat, what other language is spoken apart from English?

Answers to Quiz 19

1. Istanbul; Byzantium – hence the use of the term Byzantine Empire for what is more formally known as the Eastern Roman Empire.

2. Rummy – there are any number of variants. The game bears similarities to the popular, but much more complex, Chinese tile game, Mah Jong.

3. Alma mater; and former pupils are known as alumni.

4. Roman Polanski: the case is immensely complex, so I shall refrain from any further observations.

5. Triple sec: add two parts of vodka to one part of triple sec, one part of cranberry juice and a squeeze of lime juice, shake with ice and strain into a cocktail glass. Garnish with a wedge of lime or a slice of burnt orange.

6. Donna Tartt.

7. Arabic: alcohol, caravan, muslin and zenith are others.

8. Abbey National – Santander also added Bradford and Bingley to their portfolio in 2010.

9. Vermeer. Colin Firth plays the artist while Scarlett Johansson plays Griet, the maid in Vermeer's household who was the subject for the painting and the main protagonist in Tracy Chevalier's 1999 novel.

10. Cuba. Fidel Castro seized power with the support of the Russians, who wanted a base of operations in the Caribbean. Despite the best efforts of the CIA, Cuba has remained outside US control since.

QUIZ 21. KINGS

A themed quiz on Kings. We're not necessarily talking about the sceptred kind of king; you know, the ones with the big jewelled hats and ermine-trimmed robes.

1. Which King died on 4 April 1968?

2. Ben E. King, who had a huge hit with 'Stand by Me', also had a hit as the lead singer in which American soul vocal group?

3. Which King won an Academy Award for his performance in the musical film of *My Fair Lady*?

4. 'Your Love is King' was the debut single and a Top 10 hit off *Diamond Life*, the debut album of which soul band?

5. Billie Jean King won twelve major singles titles in her tennis career and also a ton of doubles titles, both ladies and mixed. Which younger player, a protégée of King, was her partner for her final three major wins?

6. England footballer Ledley King was forced to retire early after a series of chronic knee problems dogged his career. Which was his only club?

7. *The Gunslinger* (1982) was the first in which series of novels by Stephen King?

8. Don King is best known as an entrepreneur in which sport?

9. Who starred as psychotic Frank White in Abel Ferrara's 1990 crime thriller *The King of New York*?

10. Mark King was the distinctive bass guitar player and singer in which band, formed in the 1980s?

Answers to Quiz 20

1. *Ace Ventura: Pet Detective*: Jim Carrey plays Ace in this and a limp follow-up.

2. Ang Lee: *Crouching Tiger, Hidden Dragon* was also nominated for the 'big one' (Best Picture), which Lee later won with *Brokeback Mountain* and *The Life of Pi*.

3. Jeremy Irons, who had the sense (and talent) to recycle Rickman's classy English malevolence.

4. Jeremy Northam played Novello, and his brother played the piano when Novello was portrayed as doing so.

5. Sid is a sloth; his friends are Manny, a mammoth; Diego, a smilodon or prehistoric big cat; and Scrat, a sabre-toothed squirrel.

6. John Carpenter – he composed the music for most of his films.

7. Jeff Bridges. The film also starred Colin Farrell as an up-and-comer and Robert Duvall (who had previously starred as a country singer in *Tender Mercies*) as an old stager; Maggie Gyllenhaal provides the love interest as a young journalist.

8. Mike Newell, from a script by Curtis.

9. Edith Piaf, the legendary French singer known as 'little bird'.

10. Sioux: Harris's character joins the Native American tribe.

QUIZ 22. KINGS AND QUEENS

Now you can put your history hats on and remember those family trees and chronologies. This one is about crowned heads and dynastic deeds.

1. Gustavus Adolphus, killed at the Battle of Lützen in 1632, was a great military commander who briefly turned which European nation into a major power?

2. Umberto II had a brief reign as the last king of which country before a referendum voted in a Republic in 1946?

3. What connects Jack Daniels and the French throne for two hundred years? (1589–1792)

4. Which battle in Ireland in 1690 cemented William of Orange's place on the English throne and effectively ended Roman Catholic influence on the royal family?

5. Who was the first woman to reign as undisputed sole monarch of England after the Norman conquest?

6. Harold Harefoot, King of England from 1035 to 1040, was the son of which powerful Danish-born king?

7. Who, in 1743, at the Battle of Dettingen, was the last English king to be present on an active battlefield?

8. Edward VII, who acceded to the British throne on the death of Queen Victoria, was the first monarch of which Royal House, which later changed its name to the rather less Germanic Windsor?

9. Henri II of France had four sons. All died without issue, leaving Henri III, King of Navarre, as the clear rightful heir to the throne. Why was his claim disputed?

10. Who was sitting on the throne of England and Scotland when the Act of Union formally joined the states of England and Scotland in 1707, forming, along with Wales, the new state of Great Britain?

Answers to Quiz 21

1. Martin Luther King, assassinated by James Earl Ray.

2. The Drifters – he sang on the masterpiece that is 'Save the Last Dance for Me'. King died in 2015.

3. Rex Harrison (Rex is king in Latin). Here's a thing about *My Fair Lady*. Harrison and Julie Andrews starred in the theatrical hit production, but Andrews was overlooked for the film role, which went to Audrey Hepburn. *My Fair Lady* cleaned up at the Academy Awards, winning Best Director and Best Picture, and Best Actor for Harrison. Hepburn was controversially ignored, it is believed because of revelations that Marni Nixon overdubbed her singing parts. The winner of the Best Actress Award? Julie Andrews for *Mary Poppins*.

4. Sade, the band name used by Helen Folasade Adu.

5. Martina Navratilova. King won twelve singles titles, eighteen doubles and eleven mixed doubles. Navratilova eclipsed her mentor, winning eighteen singles titles, an incredible thirty-one doubles titles and ten mixed doubles titles.

6. Tottenham Hotspur. King fought a constant battle with injuries, and was playing some of his best football at thirty years old when a final injury before the 2010 World Cup curtailed his international career.

7. *The Dark Tower*. The series in full: (1) 'The Gunslinger'; (2) 'The Drawing of the Three'; (3) 'The Waste Lands'; (4) 'Wizard and Glass'; (4.5) 'The Wind Through the Keyhole'; (5) 'Wolves of the Calla'; (6) 'Song of Susannah'; (7) 'The Dark Tower'.

8. Boxing. Remember him, the guy with the vertical hair who looked as if he had just stuck his finger in an electric socket?

9. Christopher Walken. Walken was so good he typecast himself as a psycho for a while.

10. Level 42. They had a string of successful albums in the 1980s and 90s until they split in 1994, before re-forming in 2001. The band still tour and King is still the front man.

QUIZ 23. QUEENS

As per Quiz 21, not crowned heads, but Queen as a name, a place name, a fictional name, all that kind of stuff.

1. Who rode a motorbike into a barbed-wire fence after a memorable chase scene in *The Great Escape*?

2. In which Queen song did she keep her 'Moet and Chandon in a pretty cabinet'?

3. What is the name of the stadium in the borough of Queens in New York that plays host to the US Open Tennis Tournament?

4. Which fictional mystery writer and amateur sleuth was created in book form and for TV by Frederic Dannay and Manfred Bennington Lee, writing jointly under the same name as their fictional character?

5. Who was nominated for a Best Supporting Actress award for her performance in the 2002 musical film, *Chicago*?

6. In which book did Lewis Carroll create a character called The Red Queen?

7. Which movie directed by Steve McQueen won an Academy Award for Best Film, although McQueen failed to win the Best Director award?

8. Under what guise does Oliver Queen conduct his superhero activities on TV?

9. *The White Queen*, *The Red Queen* and *The Kingmaker's Daughter* make up The Cousins' War trilogy, a series of historical novels set in Tudor England by which author?

10. Marc Bolan nicked the riff for his hit 'Get It On' from 'Little Queenie', a rock-and-roll song covered by both The Beatles and The Rolling Stones. Who wrote the song and recorded the original version?

Answers to Quiz 22

1. Sweden. Gustavus Adolphus was a brilliant and innovative general, and one of the principal leaders of the North European alliance in the Thirty Years War against the Habsburg Empire. He was killed halfway through the war in 1632 at the Battle of Lützen, still aged only thirty-seven.

2. Italy. Ousted by Mussolini, Umberto II enjoyed a brief stint back on the throne after the Second World War before the Italians decided they had had enough of monarchs.

3. France was ruled by the House of Bourbon during that period – Jack Daniels is a Bourbon whiskey.

4. The Battle of the Boyne, when William's army crushed an ill-prepared army raised to further the claim of the deposed King James II. The Orange Order (Protestants in mainly Northern Ireland) still celebrate the victory with a march.

5. Mary Tudor, who was immediately followed by the second, Queen Elizabeth I.

6. Æthelred the Unready, who was a bit rubbish, was removed as king by Sweyn Forkbeard, but later restored by the Saxons. Canute or Cnut (the correct answer here . . . just watch that spelling), Sweyn's son, invaded again and wrestled most of the country from Æthelred's son, Edmund. On Edmund's death, Cnut became undisputed king, and his younger son Harold Harefoot and older son Harthacnut briefly ruled after him. Both died young, Harthacnut in 1042, and there was a brief Saxon revival before the Norman invasion of 1066.

7. George II. The game old boy was sixty years old and was in genuine danger of capture had not a precipitate attack by the French cavalry given the allies an opportunity for counter-attack to strengthen their position. In truth, George was fighting more in defence of his other principal territory of Hannover than of Britain.

8. Saxe-Coburg and Gotha. The name change came during the First World War, when it was pointed out that the British Royal Family sporting a German name was a bit rum, what!

9. He was a Protestant. Henri agreed to convert to Catholicism but he introduced an era of greater tolerance towards French Protestants.

10. Queen Anne. The succession towards the end of the House of Stuart was complicated. Charles II, restored to the throne after the Civil War and interregnum, was succeeded by his Catholic brother, James II, who was deposed when it became clear he was planning to revert England to Catholicism. His successors were Mary, his daughter, and William, the Dutch Prince of Orange, who she had married. They both died childless, so Anne, Mary's sister, took the throne. She also died childless, hence the Hanoverian accession with George I.

QUIZ 24. WORLD CUP RECORDS

Move on quickly if you aren't a footie buff. If you're unsure, give it a try; these aren't too horrendous. We love the World Cup; it is much bigger than just football. Some younger commentators argue that the Champions League is a bigger test, but that's nonsense. The Champions League is determined by money – the World Cup, for all FIFA's nauseous marketing, is determined by talent.

1. Which team was allowed to keep the original Jules Rimet Trophy when they won the World Cup for a third time in 1970?

2. Which is the only country to have competed in three World Cup Finals and lost all of them (to 2018)?

3. Canada, Kuwait, Israel, Venezuela: which of these nations has never appeared in a World Cup Finals tournament?

4. Which two sides have won the World Cup on just one occasion (to 2018)?

5. And which two have ended up as the losers on their only appearance in the final?

6. Belgium, Netherlands, Russia (incl. USSR), Switzerland: which of these has played in the most Finals tournaments?

7. Which country has played in the most tournaments (eight) without ever making it past the first round/group stage?

8. Which team, never to have won the World Cup, has lost the most matches (twenty-seven) in World Cup Finals' tournaments?

9. Which two participants at the 2018 World Cup were competing in a Finals tournament for the first time?

10. England declined to send a team to the World Cup in the years before the Second World War. Since their first appearance in 1950, on how many occasions have they failed to qualify for the Finals?

Answers to Quiz 23

1. Steve McQueen as Hilts, the Cooler King. Amid a stellar cast, McQueen and James Garner, the two American attractions, were given top billing alongside Richard Attenborough.

2. 'Killer Queen': '"Let them eat cake," she said, just like Marie Antoinette' goes the next line.

3. Flushing Meadows or, more formally, Flushing Meadows Corona Park. Citi Fields, home of the New York Mets baseball team, is also found in the same park.

4. Ellery Queen.

5. Queen Latifah. Bit of a tricksy question (although the theme should have given you the correct answer). Catherine Zeta-Jones actually won the Academy Award for Best Supporting Actress for her performance as Velma Kelly, while Latifah and Renée Zellweger were nominated but failed to pick up the prize.

6. *Through the Looking-Glass* (*Alice's Adventures in Wonderland* is not just mildly inaccurate, it is wrong).

7. *12 Years a Slave*. Alfonso Cuarón won Best Director for *Gravity*.

8. Arrow or Green Arrow.

9. Philippa Gregory. The books are set during the Wars of the Roses, and, in turn, view the conflict from the eyes of Elizabeth Woodville, wife of Edward IV, Margaret Beaufort, mother of the later Tudor King, Henry VII, and Anne Neville, wife of Richard III.

10. Chuck Berry.

QUIZ 25. LORDS AND LADIES

Not quite the crowned heads of the last couple of rounds, but folk of title, whether inherited, earned or assumed.

1. Which political party was founded by Screaming Lord Sutch in 1983?

2. By what name is the long-haired Countess of Mercia, who died in 1067, better known?

3. By what name was comic character Lord Marmaduke of Bunkerton better known?

4. Who directed the 1938 mystery thriller *The Lady Vanishes*, starring Margaret Lockwood and Michael Redgrave?

5. Ralph, Jack and Piggy are the main protagonists in which dystopian novel, a standard school text since its publication in 1954?

6. The musical film *My Fair Lady* is based on the play *Pygmalion*, written by which Irish dramatist?

7. What did Thomas Lord establish in north-west London in 1814?

8. 'Children at your feet; wonder how you manage to make ends meet?' Who are we singing about?

9. The Chancellor of the Duchy of Lancaster is a sinecure, or honorary title, that is usually paired with which Cabinet post?

10. Which novel, published by Penguin in 1928, was the subject of a ground-breaking obscenity trial in 1960, won by the publisher against Her Majesty's Crown Prosecution Service?

Answers to Quiz 24

1. Brazil. They beat Sweden in 1958, Czechoslovakia in 1962 and Italy in 1970. The 1970 side played what is regarded as some of the finest football ever seen. Masterminded by the incomparable Pelé and with top-quality players in almost every position (except the goalkeeper, who was terrible but scarcely needed), they were simply unstoppable.

2. The Netherlands. They lost to West Germany in 1964, despite the presence of the great Johan Cruyff in the team; four years later they were beaten finalists again, this time losing to Argentina; in 2010 they put in a dismal, bad-tempered display and were deservedly beaten by Spain.

3. Venezuela. They have the misfortune to always compete in the tough South American round-robin qualifying tournament. Israel made the 1970 Finals, and performed respectably, drawing with Sweden and eventual finalists, Italy. Kuwait made the Finals in 1982 and played in England's group, drawing with Czechoslovakia and avoiding humiliation. Canada played in 1986 and lost all three games without scoring, but without getting slaughtered.

4. England and Spain. England won their solitary final, against West Germany, in 1966; Spain won against the Netherlands in 2010.

5. Sweden and Croatia. Sweden lost to Brazil in 1958 (and were beaten by Brazil again when they made the semi-finals in 1994); Croatia lost to France in 2018.

6. Belgium, with thirteen, followed by USSR/Russia, with eleven; Switzerland (who in recent years always seem to plod into the second phase and lose a drab game on penalties), also with eleven; and ten by The Netherlands (who seem to either do well or screw up completely and fail to qualify).

7. Scotland. Hard to believe if you've only followed football in the twenty-first century, but Scotland were once a significant force. They went to the 1978 and 1982 Finals as genuine dark horses, but managed to make a Horlicks of both tournaments. In fairness, they have encountered Brazil in their group in four of the last six tournaments in which they appeared, which effectively reduces any chance of progressing to one in three rather than two in four.

8. Mexico. They always make the Finals, because they play in a weak qualifying region (CONCACAF, the North and Central American region), but they never threaten the business end of the show.

9. Iceland and Panama. Neither did terribly well – Iceland's time came at the 2016 European Championships when they eliminated England.

10. Three (1974, 1978 and 1994). The first of these, 1974, cost Alf Ramsey his job; 1978 was just after Ron Greenwood took over, so he was given a little longer; and 1994 was the reign of Graham 'Do I Not Like That' Taylor, a low ebb for the national team.

QUIZ 26. IDENTIFY AND EXPLAIN

This is a music round. We've given you ten names and phrases – you have to tell us something about them. Two points per question; the more detail you give, the better. For example, if I'd written *Quadrophenia*, a good answer would be '1973 album by The Who made into a 1979 film directed by Franc Roddam'. Mention of only the album or only the film would get you just one point.

1. Trout Mask Replica.

2. Héloise Létissier.

3. Dan Auerbach and Patrick Carney.

4. Andrew Loog Oldham.

5. Earl Sweatshirt.

6. Aston 'Family Man' Barrett.

7. Anohni.

8. One Little Indian.

9. Vince Clarke.

10. Greil Marcus.

Answers to Quiz 25

1. The Monster Raving Loony Party.

2. Lady Godiva: as legend has it, she rode naked through the streets of Coventry with only her long hair to cover her modesty, all in protest at taxes imposed by her own husband.

3. Lord Snooty (*Beano* character). Snooty was first introduced as the leader of the Ash Can Alley gang in 1938. He acquired a new set of friends in 1950, but one constant was his long-suffering and tolerant maiden aunt Matilda.

4. Alfred Hitchcock – not to be confused with a sub-par 1979 American remake.

5. *Lord of the Flies* – it still gives me the heebie-jeebies.

6. George Bernard Shaw. He wrote *Pygmalion* in 1912, and it features an even more acerbic version of Henry Higgins than Rex Harrison gives us in the film. Pygmalion was a character in Greek mythology who fell in love with a statue, which then comes to life.

7. Lord's cricket ground. It has always been the home of Marylebone Cricket Club – the first site was on what is now Dorset Square, next to the station – which for years was the arbiter of cricket's rules and regulations. It remains England's premier Test match ground and the home of Middlesex County Cricket Club.

8. 'Lady Madonna', a non-album single from 1968 by The Beatles.

9. Leader of the House of Lords; other titles include the Lord Privy Seal and the Lord President of the Council – all are notional titles.

10. *Lady Chatterley's Lover*. Penguin published this in 1960 and won a landmark court case against the CPS in 1960, thirty-two years after the book was first privately published. It changed publishing for ever.

QUIZ 27. A POT POURRI OF POINTLESS TRIVIA

Or, in other words, a general knowledge round.

1. In a book called *The Encyclopedia of Animal Rights and Animal Welfare*, which other Victorian book is described by the editor as 'the most influential anti-cruelty novel of all time'?

2. What is the name of the political party that champions Welsh nationalism?

3. Which European capital city's name means White City?

4. Which French city houses a museum devoted entirely to the works of the Russian-born artist Marc Chagall? Is it Marseille, Nice, Cannes or Monte Carlo?

5. What is the width of the English Channel between Dover and Calais? Is it 15 miles/24 km, 21 miles/34 km, 25 miles/40 km or 35 miles/56 km?

6. Which director made the startling TV film *Cathy Come Home* and the award-winning social drama *Kes* in the 1960s?

7. *Tomorrow Never Dies* starred which actor as 007 James Bond?

8. What was cloned by the Roslin Institute in 1997?

9. Which cartoon villain had a dog called Muttley?

10. Which fashion designer set up his (mainly) menswear company in the mid-1970s and burst into the limelight with his costumes for Richard Gere in *American Gigolo* (1980)?

Answers to Quiz 26

1. A 1969 Captain Beefheart album; it was Beefheart's third album and the first to bring him significant commercial success.

2. Lead singer and songwriter of Christine and the Queens.

3. The Black Keys, garage blues-rock duo from Akron, Ohio.

4. Legendary music entrepreneur, he managed The Rolling Stones in their early days. Loog Oldham was a good promoter who helped promote The Beatles before working for The Rolling Stones from 1963. While with the Stones he launched the career of Marianne Faithfull with 'As Tears Go By'.

5. Chicago-born Thebe Kgositsile is a rapper and producer.

6. Bass player and part of the rhythm section (along with his brother, Carlton) of The Wailers. Family Man is still part of The Wailers at seventy-two years old; his brother Carlton, like fellow Wailer Peter Tosh, was murdered in Jamaica.

7. She is a singer, formerly Antony of Antony and the Johnsons.

8. UK indie rock label that has furthered the careers of Bjork, Chumbawamba and Skunk Anansie, among others.

9. Songwriter and synth player with Erasure, formerly a founder member of Depeche Mode and the other half of Yazoo alongside Alison Moyet.

10. Rock journalist with *Rolling Stone* and other publications. His 1989 book, *Lipstick Traces*, was one of rock journalism's more intelligent attempts to put popular music in a proper social context and discuss its generational influence.

QUIZ 28. THE APPLIANCE OF SCIENCE

No, not a round on Zanussi, but a general science-based quiz. I often get complaints from people who have studied sciences that quiz books or TV programmes like *University Challenge* are biased towards the arts. It's true, but there are perfectly good reasons for this. Well-read science students are much more common than scientifically knowledgeable arts students, and people of all persuasions enjoy film, music and sports, hence the dominance of these topics in pub quizzes and books.

1. Which comet was last seen in 1986 and appears in the Bayeux Tapestry?

2. We've most of us sent or received an image as a JPEG, but for what does this acronym stand?

3. Which element, listed as atomic number 12 and found in the periodic table with the alkaline earth metals, exists only in compound state and burns when exposed to heat with a fierce white light?

4. When did the ounce cease to be a measurement in the UK for legal purposes? Was it 1972, 1990, 2000 or 2012?

5. Jane Goodall is best remembered for her work and research with which species?

6. Which scientist, inventor of the zinc-carbon battery and flash photography, gives his name to an essential piece of equipment in any laboratory?

7. American mathematician Grace Hopper was the pioneer and primary mover behind which computer system, the most widely used in the last century?

8. Sir Joseph Banks was a botanist and traveller who served as King George III's adviser on which major botanical project?

9. Why is the jackrabbit misnamed?

10. Bariatric surgery is an interventionist medical procedure for what condition?

Answers to Quiz 27

1. *Black Beauty* by Anna Sewell. The book was published in 1877, and Sewell died shortly afterwards. She would be pleased to know that the book has sold over 50 million copies and had a pervasive positive influence on animal welfare.

2. Plaid Cymru. Their stance post-Brexit vote is to advocate Welsh independence within the EU; the party is left of centre and had four MPs elected to the Westminster Parliament at the 2017 General Election.

3. Belgrade, the capital of Serbia.

4. Nice; both Chagall and Matisse worked extensively on the French coast and have museums of their works in the region.

5. The distance is 21 miles, or 34 km.

6. Ken Loach. Loach turns eighty-three this year (2019) but *I, Daniel Blake* (2016) showed that he still has plenty to say and can say it with great potency.

7. *Tomorrow Never Dies* (1997) was the second Bond film to star Pierce Brosnan as the super-agent; the first was *Goldeneye* in 1995.

8. Dolly the sheep.

9. Dick Dastardly. Dastardly's sidekick first appeared in *Wacky Races* aboard the Mean Machine. He joined Dick in trying to catch the ever-evasive pigeon in the spin-off *Dastardly and Muttley in Their Flying Machines*. I do a particularly good impression of Muttley's laugh . . .

10. Giorgio Armani. Armani has always been clever at hooking in to popular culture – in recent years he has formed a successful partnership with Lady Gaga.

QUIZ 29. MIXED BAG – WITH A CONNECTION

A general knowledge round with a connection at the end. A good way to approach a round like this, especially if you have all the questions laid out in front of you, is to pick the ones you know the answers to, and see if they give you the connection. This can sometimes help with the trickier components of the round.

1. Who won the seat of Uxbridge and South Ruislip for the Conservatives in the 2015 General Election?

2. Who plays Sherlock Holmes in the New York-based updated version of the stories, *Elementary*?

3. Who went from playing Gary in *Miranda* to the devil on Amazon Prime?

4. What is the real name of Baby Spice?

5. Which pop star made a successful foray into film as the lead character Jim Maclaine in *That'll Be the Day* and *Stardust* in 1973 and 1974?

6. Who made her first film appearance aged seventeen in *The Belles of St Trinian's* in 1954?

7. What was the character played by Hugh Bonneville in *Downton Abbey*?

8. Which pair of brothers played the Kray Twins in the 1990 biopic of their life?

9. Who, with Matt Lucas, was the main star of *Little Britain*?

10. What's the connection?

Answers to Quiz 28

1. Halley's Comet, named after British astronomer Edmond Halley, who established the comet's regularity in 1705. It is due again in 2061, so if I live to be a hundred . . .

2. Joint Photographic Experts Group.

3. Magnesium; the other alkaline earth metals are beryllium, calcium, strontium, barium and radium.

4. The year 2000. From this date shops were obliged to sell only in grams; an ounce is 28.3 g.

5. Chimpanzees. Goodall is a conservationist and anthropologist specialising in primates and especially chimps.

6. (Robert) Bunsen, a German scientist who lived from 1811 to 1899. He also gave his name to Bunsen Honeydew, who runs the laboratory in *The Muppet Show*. Just thought we'd share that . . .

7. COBOL, or common business-oriented language.

8. The Royal Botanic Gardens at Kew. He also travelled extensively, often with James Cook, and was a prime mover in the establishment of Botany Bay as a British penal colony in Australia.

9. It is a species of hare, and hares belong to the genus Lepus, which makes up the other half of the family Leporidae, alongside the rabbits.

10. Obesity – it involves the insertion of a gastric band or removal of part of the stomach or similar.

QUIZ 30. ARTS AND LIT – MIXED BAG

One for the culture vultures: some questions on the highbrow arts.

1. The celebrated Japanese artist Hokusai painted a set of thirty-six views of which major feature of his country's landscape?

2. Where in England does theatrical company the RSC have its home?

3. Which English romantic poet's illustrations to Dante's *Divine Comedy* are on show at the Tate in London?

4. Pop artist Peter Blake is best known for which famous piece of album cover art? Was it *Tubular Bells*, *Dark Side of the Moon*, *Sgt Pepper's Lonely Hearts Club Band* or *Nevermind*?

5. *Early Sunday Morning* was a 1930 work by which famous New York painter, a specialist in urban character scenes?

6. Which English portrait artist was also the first President of the Royal Society, of which he was also the co-founder?

7. Whose portrait of Winston Churchill was destroyed by his wife, who loathed it? Was it (a) Lucian Freud; (b) David Hockney; (c) Stanley Spencer; or (d) Graham Sutherland?

8. Vanessa Bell and Roger Fry were both part of which London-based artistic group active in the years between the two world wars?

9. Which of these was not a founder member of the Pre-Raphaelite brotherhood: William Holman Hunt; Frederick, Lord Leighton; John Everett Millais; Dante Gabriel Rossetti?

10. In 1984 Malcolm Morley became the first recipient of which British art prize?

Answers to Quiz 29

1. Boris Johnson. His old seat of Westminster was vacated when he became Mayor of London so the party needed a safe seat to return Johnson to Parliament.

2. Jonny Lee Miller, alongside Lucy Liu as Dr Watson; the show is a novel take on the stories, with Holmes in rehab for his addiction and living in a New York brownstone.

3. Tom Ellis, the star of Amazon's original show, *Lucifer*.

4. Emma Bunton.

5. David Essex; the first film, with Ringo Starr in support as a cynical teddy boy, was terrific, the second an indulgence, despite a bigger budget and impressive cast.

6. Barbara Windsor, before she hooked up with the Carry On team.

7. Robert Crawley, Earl of Grantham; the show ran for six seasons up to 2015 and was a ratings smash, especially in the US where it conformed to Americans' notions of the upper-class British.

8. Martin and Gary Kemp; the former guitarist and bassist with Spandau Ballet were oddly compelling as the gangsters; in a 2015 version, *Legend*, Tom Hardy played both brothers with typical vigour and menace.

9. David Walliams, who has enjoyed even more success as a writer of children's books than he did as an actor and comedian.

10. They have all appeared in *Eastenders*: Boris Johnson made a cameo appearance in 2009; Jonny Lee Miller played Jonathan Hewitt in 1993; Tom Ellis played Dr Oliver Cousins in 2006; Emma Bunton made a cameo in 1992; David Essex joined the cast as Alfie Moon's uncle, Eddie, in 2011; Barbara Windsor played Peggy Mitchell for years; Hugh Bonneville appeared as a headmaster in an episode in 1995; Martin Kemp played Steve Owen, a key antagonist to the Mitchell Brothers, for four years from 1998; David Walliams played a fake registrar at Alfie and Kat's wedding in 2003.

QUIZ 31. MOMMIE DEAREST

Questions all about mummy, (as opposed to *The Mummy*). A general knowledge round about mothers and their sons and daughters.

1. Who was the subject, played by Faye Dunaway, of the 1981 melodrama *Mommie Dearest*?

2. Who was the mother of the late model and IT girl, Peaches Geldof?

3. According to the majority of sources, who was the human mother of Helen of Troy, daughter of the Greek god, Zeus?

4. Rufus and Martha Wainwright are the singer children of Loudon Wainwright III. Who is their mother, one of a pair of singing Canadian folk singers?

5. Whose maternal grandmother was Cecilia Bowes-Lyon, Countess of Strathmore?

6. What is the name of Harry Potter's mum?

7. If Katherine of Aragon was the mother of Mary Tudor, and Anne Boleyn was the mother of Queen Elizabeth I, who was the mother of their brother and the primary heir to Henry VIII, Edward VI?

8. What was Lionel Shriver's best-selling 2003 novel, written from the perspective of the mother of the perpetrator of a school killing?

9. Who wrote about her relationship with her mother, actress Debbie Reynolds, in the book and self-scripted film, *Postcards from the Edge*?

10. Who is the mother of Brooklyn, Romeo, Cruz and Harper?

Answers to Quiz 30

1. Mount Fuji.

2. Stratford-upon-Avon – the RSC is the Royal Shakespeare Company, who are based in the Bard's home town. The theatre was extensively remodelled and reopened in 2010 in its current guise.

3. William Blake. Blake also created artwork to match some of his own poetry – his drawings are at once innocent and disturbing, perhaps unsurprising for a poet whose best work, according to many, was an anthology called *Songs of Innocence and Experience*.

4. Peter Blake did the multi-charactered montage for The Beatles' *Sgt Pepper's Lonely Hearts Club Band* album.

5. Edward Hopper.

6. (Sir) Joshua Reynolds; he was a significant mover and shaker in the art world as well as a painter of portraits.

7. Graham Sutherland; portraiture was a new venture for Sutherland, whose reputation was built on bleak industrial scenes.

8. The Bloomsbury Group. The group also included the novelist Virginia Woolf, the economist John Maynard Keynes and the novelist and critic E.M. Forster.

9. Lord Leighton: although he was a direct contemporary of Millais and the others, and painted in a not dissimilar milieu and style, he wasn't strictly a member of the brotherhood.

10. The Turner Prize – after tricky early years it would become the most publicised and best-known art prize in Britain.

QUIZ 32. SITCOMS

Sitcoms are a bit like marmite: one tends to either love them or hate them. I can't watch *Last of the Summer Wine*, but they made 295 episodes, so a lot of people clearly did watch it. My lovely hated *The League of Gentlemen*, which was generally hailed as mad genius.

1. Steve and Becky live in Walthamstow, London, and do very little. What's the sitcom and who plays Steve?

2. Which sitcom launched the careers of Richard Ayoade and Catherine Parkinson? Which writer, creator of *Father Ted* and *Black Books*, also created this show?

3. Penelope Keith became a major name after her work in *The Good Life* as which character? Who played her husband in the series, and what was her next big TV comedy role?

4. Which major US sitcom is set in the fictional town of Pawnee, Indiana? Who first appeared in the second season as a state auditor who ends up working in the town?

5. Who writes, directs and appears in the award-winning *Detectorists*? Which earlier sitcom made his name?

6. Who plays an exaggerated comedy version of himself in the media comedy *Episodes*? And which anarchic British comedy also starred the show's other leading actors?

7. In *Bojack Horseman*, who plays the Persian cat, Princess Carolyn? And what is the name of the Labrador Retriever played by Paul F. Tompkins?

8. Which city provided the setting for *Cheers*, and who played the barman, Sam Malone, for the entire run?

9. Who created the British sitcom, *The Thick of It*, and what was the American comedy he created as a follow-up?

10. Which TV sitcom follows the lives of Jay Pritchett and his family in Los Angeles, and who plays Jay's second wife, Gloria?

Answers to Quiz 31

1. Joan Crawford.

2. Paula Yates, who was married to, and had three children (Fifi, Peaches and Pixie), with Bob Geldof. Yates left Geldof and started a relationship with Michael Hutchence, the lead singer of INXS. Peaches died from a heroin overdose in 2013.

3. Leda, with whom the chief of the gods, Zeus, mated in the form of a swan.

4. Kate McGarrigle, who sang alongside her sister, Anna, until her death in 2010.

5. Queen Elizabeth II. Cecilia was the mother of Elizabeth, wife of King George VI.

6. Lily (Evans).

7. Jane Seymour, Henry's third wife – Edward was a delicate child who died aged fifteen, leaving the throne open for Catholic Mary and, subsequently, Elizabeth.

8. *We Need to Talk about Kevin* – Eva, the mother, is played by Tilda Swinton in the film version.

9. Carrie Fisher; the book was a fictionalised version of the relationship between the two.

10. Victoria Beckham.

QUIZ 33. RATTLE BAG

Another mixed round. A Rattle Bag is a bag of pebbles or pellets used to attract deer while hunting, but now the term has a less macabre meaning, generally referring to a miscellany or ragtag collection. A female a cappella singing group in Hastings uses the name, and on their monthly sing-a-round they pass the Rattle Bag and the recipient is invited to contribute a song.

1. Jamie Lee Curtis made her screen debut as a teenager in which 1978 horror movie?

2. Which botanical provides the pre-eminent flavouring in traditional gin distillation?

3. If you had a Katzenjammer in Germany, would you have (a) a pain-killer; (b) a hangover; (c) a child born outside marriage; or (d) gender reassignment?

4. Who composed the ballet and orchestral work *The Rite of Spring*?

5. The snaky head of Medusa is the symbol of which famous Italian fashion house?

6. The Charles Dickens Museum in London is at Doughty Street, Holborn, where he wrote his first three novels. Where is the Charles Dickens Birthplace Museum?

7. The word columbine is associated with which species of bird? Is it a dove, an eagle, a gull or a wren?

8. Which famous financial institution was formed in West Yorkshire in 1853?

9. What is the name of the Milan Opera House, opened in 1778 after a fire destroyed the theatre previously occupying the site?

10. 'Speakeasies' flourished in the 1920s in the US. What was/is a 'speakeasy'?

Answers to Quiz 32

1. *Him and Her*: Russell Tovey plays Steve, with Sarah Solemani as Becky.

2. *The IT Crowd*, which also launched the career of Chris O'Dowd; Graham Linehan.

3. Margot Leadbetter: Paul Eddington plays Jerry and they are the snobbish neighbours of the central couple, Tom and Barbara Good, played by Richard Briers and Felicity Kendal. Penelope Keith went on to play Audrey fforbes-Hamilton opposite Peter Bowles in *To the Manor Born*.

4. *Parks and Recreation*; Rob Lowe.

5. MacKenzie Crook; Crook played Gareth in the Ricky Gervais-led sitcom, *The Office*.

6. Matt LeBlanc; the main stars are played by Tamsin Greig and Stephen Mangan, who also appeared together in *Green Wing*.

7. Amy Sedaris voices the cat, and the Labrador retriever is called Mr Peanutbutter (voiced by Paul F. Tompkins).

8. Boston; Ted Danson.

9. Armando Iannucci; *Veep*, with Julia Louis-Dreyfus as the vice-president of the United States.

10. *Modern Family*; Sofia Vergara.

QUIZ 34. EXPLODING DRUMMERS

This is a film round, just in case you didn't twig! We need you to explain the names given. As with the previous quiz of this nature, the more detail, the better. For example, if I gave you 'William "Bill the Butcher" Cutting', and you wrote 'character in Gangs of New York', you would get one point, but if you added 'played by Daniel Day-Lewis' you would get both.

1. Deadly Viper Assassination Squad.

2. Fay Wray.

3. Xander Cage.

4. Maria Schneider.

5. Alex Winter.

6. Sugar Kane Kowalczyk.

7. Lois Lane.

8. Travis Bickle.

9. Derek Smalls.

10. Optimus Prime.

Answers to Quiz 33

1. *Halloween*; Curtis played the central character Laurie Strode in John Carpenter's original movie, and reprised the role both in *Halloween II* and the 2018 fortieth-anniversary version, which is set up as a direct sequel to the original forty years on and ignores the other nine films made in the interval – rightly so, most of them were rubbish.

2. Juniper is usually the principal botanical. It is the floral juniper combined with the bitterness of the tonic that makes the classic gin-and-tonic combination.

3. You might take a painkiller, but you would have a hangover – the expression means 'cat's wailing', which sounds about right.

4. Igor Stravinsky; he wrote it for the Ballets Russes in 1913.

5. Versace: Medusa was the mythological beast whose hair was living snakes and whose gaze turned a person to stone. She was slain by Perseus with the help of the gods.

6. Portsmouth. Dickens was born in Portsmouth and went to work in a factory as a child to ease his father's debts, hence his distaste for Victorian work practices. He was almost entirely self-taught and published his first novel in serial form when he was twenty-four.

7. Dove – doves and pigeons form the family Columbidae.

8. Halifax Building Society. The other option, the Bradford & Bingley, was only formed in 1960 as a merger between two older mutual societies.

9. La Scala. Teatro alla Scala, to give its proper name, was opened in 1778 with an opera from Salieri, he of *Amadeus* notoriety.

10. A speakeasy was an illegal drinking establishment during the US prohibition years, when the sale of any alcoholic drink was illegal.

QUIZ 35. THIS OR THAT

You'll get the hang of these. Twelve names: you have to guess which of them is a college at Cambridge University, which a House at Harrow School and which just the name of a UK public school. There are four of each.

1. Fitzwilliam.

2. Moretons.

3. Radley.

4. Darwin.

5. Newnham.

6. Rendalls.

7. Hurstpierpoint.

8. Elmfield.

9. Peterhouse.

10. Alleyn's.

11. The Knoll.

12. Stonyhurst.

Answers to Quiz 34

1. They are a group of assassins in Tarantino's *Kill Bill*. One of the group, Beatrix Kiddo (Black Mamba), has left the group and sworn to kill the others, and their leader, Bill (the snake charmer).

2. Fay Wray played Anne Darrow in the original 1933 *King Kong* film; the part has also been played by Jessica Lange (1976, her film debut) and Naomi Watts (2005). Fay Wray is referenced in *The Rocky Horror Picture Show* ('whatever happened to Fay Wray, that delicate satin-draped frame . . .').

3. Vin Diesel's character in the *xXx* films, a Hollywood attempt to out-Bond the Bond movies.

4. Maria Schneider is the actress who starred alongside Brando in *Last Tango in Paris*, but she has been little used outside her native France since.

5. The American actor who played Bill opposite Keanu Reeves' portrayal of Ted in *Bill and Ted's Excellent Adventure*; Winter also appeared in the sequel and in the earlier (1987) cult vampire film, *Lost Boys*, but has worked more as a director this century.

6. Marilyn Monroe's character in *Some Like It Hot*.

7. Lois Lane was the journalist who became the love interest of Clark Kent (Superman). The best-known movie incarnations are Margot Kidder opposite Christopher Reeve in the 1980s and Amy Adams opposite Henry Cavill in the recent reboot.

8. Robert De Niro's character in Scorsese's *Taxi Driver*. Scary.

9. The drummer (played by Harry Shearer) in the fictional heavy metal band Spinal Tap at the time of the movie; the band had various other fictional drummers, most of whom exploded, hence the title of this round.

10. Leader of the Autobot faction (the goodies) in *Transformers*.

QUIZ 36. ASIA

A general socio-political-geographical round about Southeast Asia. There's a few of these, selecting random countries or regions. Just another themed quiz, really.

1. In which country did the Khmer Rouge take control and wreak havoc from 1975 to 1979?

2. What is the principal religion of Mongolia?

3. Which Asian country's flag is a white band to the left of a larger green block containing a white crescent moon and star?

4. Indonesia and Malaysia share the bulk of the island of Borneo: which third small state lies to the north end of the island?

5. Vientiane is the capital of which Southeast Asian country?

6. Which revolutionary leader declared North Vietnam independent from France in 1945?

7. Manila (Philippines), Colombo (Sri Lanka) and Kuala Lumpur (Malaysia): which lies furthest south?

8. Which state was created as a result of a civil war in Pakistan in 1971?

9. Which J-League (Japanese pro soccer league) was managed by Arsène Wenger and had Gary Lineker in the line-up when they won the league title in 1995?

10. What is the Japanese word for 'harbour wave'?

Answers to Quiz 35

1. Cambridge college.

2. House at Harrow.

3. Public school.

4. Cambridge college.

5. Cambridge college.

6. House at Harrow.

7. Public school.

8. House at Harrow.

9. Cambridge college.

10. Public school.

11. House at Harrow.

12. Public school.

Here are the thirty-one colleges of Cambridge University, listed in order of their achieving collegiate status rather than their establishment. The less familiar names are likely to be postgraduate colleges or research colleges.

Cambridge University has sixteen old colleges, founded between 1284 and 1596: Peterhouse (1284), Clare, Pembroke, Gonville and Caius, Trinity Hall, Corpus Christi, Magdalene, King's, Queen's, St Catherine's, Jesus, Christ's, St John's, Trinity College, Emmanuel, Sidney Sussex (1596).

The fifteen new colleges were added from 1800, starting with Downing, then followed by Girton, Newnham, Selwyn, St Edmund's, Hughes Hall, Murray Edwards, Churchill, Darwin, Lucy Cavendish, Wolfson, Clare Hall, Fitzwilliam, Homerton, Robinson.

In the interests of even-handedness, here are the thirty-eight constituent colleges of Oxford University. There was no long hiatus in according status, so the thirty-eight are simply listed in the order of their acceptance as a college: St Edmund Hall (1226), University, Balliol, Merton, Exeter, Oriel, The Queen's College, New College, Lincoln, All Souls, Magdalen, Brasenose, Corpus Christi, Christ Church, St John's, Trinity, Jesus, Wadham, Pembroke, Worcester, Hertford, Keble, Lady Margaret Hall,

Somerville, St Hugh's, St Hilda's, Nuffield, St Andrew's, St Anne's, St Peter's, Linacre, St Antony's, St Catherine's, St Cross, Wolfson, Kellogg, Mansfield, Harris Manchester, Green Templeton (2008, the most recent).

Oxford also has six single-denomination Permanent Private Halls, but these are governed by single-faith charities.

QUIZ 37. MIXING BOWL

Another general knowledge round, with a mix of subjects. Just so you know, these rounds are set so that a decent team of four can get seven or eight out of ten. The winning team in a quiz should average about eight out of ten per round – forty-eight points in a six-round quiz. The losers should still get about half marks. It doesn't always work – the demographic at our place is thirty to sixty-five, so teams comprised solely of younger members struggle, unless I know they are coming, in which case I throw in a round on recent pop culture.

1. Which Irish poet, born in Northern Ireland but resident in Dublin for the second half of his life, won the 1995 Nobel Prize of Literature?

2. Which other capital city lies across the Gulf of Finland from Helsinki?

3. Which figure, as recognisable as the president for a few years, was US Senator for Wisconsin from 1947 until 1957?

4. Who confessed to the killing of Cock Robin?

5. Which 1993 film won Steven Spielberg his first Academy Award for Best Director?

6. Which famous dandy was Master of Ceremonies of the spa town of Bath from 1704 until his death in 1761 at the impressive age of ninety-six?

7. Which satirical TV programme gave the phrase 'omnishambles' to the language?

8. Which great Victorian novelist, born in 1840, regarded himself as primarily a poet and confined his writing to that discipline in the twentieth century until his death in 1928?

9. What office did Michelle Robinson hold between January 2009 and January 2017?

10. Linus Pauling is one of two people to have won a Nobel Prize in two different fields (Chemistry and Peace): who was the earlier winner of a joint award for Physics in 1903 and a sole award in Chemistry in 1911?

Answers to Quiz 36

1. Cambodia. Pol Pot assumed leadership of Cambodia after the Khmer Rouge proved victorious in the Civil War – subsequently, between 20 and 25 per cent of Cambodia's population were exterminated by one of history's most savage genocidal regimes.

2. Buddhism. Just over half of Mongolians identify as Buddhist, while around a third identify as secular.

3. Pakistan.

4. Brunei. The islands of New Guinea and Timor are also shared by Indonesia, with Papua New Guinea and East Timor respectively.

5. Laos, the only land-locked country on the Southeast Asian peninsula, wedged between Vietnam and Thailand with small northern borders to Burma and China.

6. Ho Chi Minh. A slow nine-year war with French-backed forces ended in 1954 when Ho Chi Minh's forces won a decisive victory at the Battle of Dien Bien Phu. Ho Chi Minh died in 1969, but his name lives on as the country's capital city, replacing Hanoi.

7. Kuala Lumpur.

8. Bangladesh. Formerly Pakistan consisted of two territories separated by northern India, East and West Pakistan – East Pakistan became the state of Bangladesh.

9. Nagoya Grampus 8; this was the heyday of the J-League, formed in 1993. Nagoya Grampus have remained an ever-present in the J-League top tier since, but have never won the title again.

10. A tsunami.

QUIZ 38. MUSIC MIX-TAPE

Lots of music questions, about all sorts of styles and eras. Music is a tricky one; people have such different tastes. If you set a quiz for musos and include artists like Nick Cave and St Vincent, you alienate the folk who only listen to commercial radio, and if you just set questions on pop, the musos aren't interested. We try and get a balance, and reserve the tough stuff for our 'music only' quizzes.

1. Which band was fronted by the outspoken Chrissie Hynde, a pioneer female guitar-wielding band leader?

2. Which band recorded the song for the 2012 Olympic Games in London? What was the title of their 2008 Mercury Prize-winning album?

3. *Surrealistic Pillow* (1967) was a psychedelic classic from which band? What was the hallucinogenic hit single, loosely based on 'Alice in Wonderland'?

4. Who was the subject of the eight-and-a-half-minute song 'Hurricane', from Bob Dylan's 1976 album, *Desire*?

5. If two of the original members were Rick Buckler and Bruce Foxton, who was the third? What was the band he formed next, with keyboard player Mick Talbot?

6. Actress Riley Keough (*Magic Mike*, *Mad Max: Fury Road*, *The Girlfriend Experience*) is the granddaughter of which recording star?

7. Who performed to 125,000 people at Knebworth in 1996, at the time the largest outdoor concert ever played?

8. Brooks and Dunn, Ian Jackson, Toby Keith and Ronnie Milsap have all topped which chart on more than twenty occasions?

9. Which song was released just before Elvis's death, hitting the top of the UK chart immediately afterwards?

10. What was the 2009 debut album of Florence + the Machine? Apart from Florence Welch, who is the other mainstay of the band, co-writing some songs, playing keyboards and sharing production credits?

Answers to Quiz 37

1. Seamus Heaney.

2. Tallinn, Estonia.

3. Joseph McCarthy, who led the witch-hunt against so-called communist agitators in the US, especially Hollywood.

4. 'I, said the Sparrow, with my bow and arrow, I killed Cock Robin.' A full and frank confession.

5. *Schindler's List*, based on *Schindler's Ark* by Thomas Keneally, a Booker Prize winner from 1982. In all, to 2019, Spielberg has been nominated seven times for Best Director, winning twice, for *Schindler's List* and for *Saving Private Ryan*.

6. Beau Nash; Beau Brummel was a London-based contemporary.

7. *The Thick of It*; omnishambles was one of many fabulous phrases uttered by Peter Capaldi as spin doctor Malcolm Tucker – most of them could not be printed here.

8. Thomas Hardy; Hardy's final novel (*Jude the Obscure*) was published in 1895, thirty-three years before the author's death.

9. First Lady of the United States – Robinson is the maiden name of Michelle Obama.

10. Marie Curie.

QUIZ 39. ODD ONES OUT

It's strange, but when a straight question is asked, it engenders less debate than a multiple-choice or odd-one-out question. Maybe something about putting the potential answer in front of someone encourages all the members of the team to *think* they know the answer, whereas a straight question will only elicit a response from the one or two team members who *do* know the answer. As a quizmaster it is quite entertaining listening to the debates around these questions.

1. 'She Loves You'; 'Please Please Me'; 'A Hard Day's Night'; 'Paperback Writer': which of these Beatles songs did not reach No. 1 in the UK?

2. Staphylococcus; campylobacter; bacillus cereus; streptococcus: which of these is not a pathogen commonly transmitted through poor food safety?

3. Donetsk; Kazan; Murmansk; Novosibirsk: which of these is not a city in Russia?

4. Portugal; the Republic of Ireland; Serbia; Sweden: which of these countries is not an EU member state?

5. Pink Floyd; the Moody Blues; Led Zeppelin; The Rolling Stones: which of these never had a UK No. 1 hit single?

6. Alan Minter; Nigel Benn; Amir Khan; Anthony Joshua: which of these British boxers never won an Olympic medal?

7. *The Bourne Identity*; *The Martian*; *Spotlight*; *The Talented Mr Ripley*; which of these does not star Matt Damon?

8. Gary Lineker; Alan Shearer; Nat Lofthouse; Jimmy Greaves: which of these England goal-scorers won the league title in England at least once?

9. Celery; rice; sesame; soya: which of these is not one of the fourteen listed allergens on the FSA list?

10. Bavaria; Bremen; Munich Stadt; Rhineland-Palatinate: which of these is not one of the sixteen German states?

Answers to Quiz 38

1. The Pretenders. Chrissie is still going strong at sixty-seven, despite most of her band having died in tragic circumstances.

2. The song, 'First Steps', was by Elbow, who were at the height of their popularity at the time; The *Seldom Seen Kid* contained 'One Day Like This', Elbow's 'big anthem'. The singer and front man, Guy Garvey, is now a popular presenter on BBC 6 Music.

3. Jefferson Airplane; 'White Rabbit': 'One pill makes you larger, and one pill makes you small, and the one that mother gives you doesn't do anything at all.' The powers that be at the Beeb didn't click that the song was about drugs.

4. Rubin 'Hurricane' Carter; 'Hurricane' was the opening song on the album and railed against the injustice of Carter's conviction for a triple murder; the boxer was released in 1985, nine years after Dylan's song.

5. Paul Weller; they were the three members of The Jam. The Style Council was Weller's other 'band' project, before he started his long and successful solo career.

6. Elvis. She is Lisa Marie Presley's daughter by Danny Keough, her first husband. Presley has subsequently been married to Michael Jackson, Nicolas Cage and record producer Michael Lockwood.

7. Oasis; the support acts included The Charlatans, Kula Shaker, Manic Street Preachers, Ocean Colour Scene, Chemical Brothers and the Prodigy.

8. The US country chart.

9. 'Way Down'.

10. *Lungs*; Isabella Summers.

QUIZ 40. ART FOR ART'S SAKE

1. By what more common name is the painting La Gioconda usually known?

2. Which US architect invented the Geodesic Dome? Was it Richard Buckminster Fuller, Charles Rennie Mackintosh, Louis Sullivan or Frank Lloyd Wright.

3. Who placed a telephone box with a pickaxe buried in it in Soho, London, in protest at BT's removal of most of the iconic red boxes from London's streets?

4. Canaletto is best remembered for his portraits of Venice and which other European city?

5. Who famously painted a ceiling for Pope Julius II between 1508 and 1512?

6. Forensic scientist and crime novelist Patricia Cornwell has obsessively tried to prove that which late nineteenth-century artist was the man behind the Jack the Ripper killings?

7. Which mythological creature is the subject of Harrison Birtwistle's popular 2008 opera?

8. With which art movement, in some ways a forerunner of Surrealism, was the Romanian-born poet Tristan Tzara an important figure?

9. Who lays claim to the largest Renaissance oil painting, a thirty-by-seventy-four-foot masterpiece, *Paradiso*, on show at the Doge's Palace?

10. Whose painting of a naked Venus admiring herself in a mirror held by Cupid (known as the *Rokeby Venus*) was damaged by suffragette Mary Richardson in 1914?

Answers to Quiz 39

1. 'Please Please Me' only hit No. 2 (see list below).

2. Streptococcus more commonly leads to a sore throat, not a dodgy gut. Staphylococcal poisoning is most likely to be contracted via poor handling of foods like cooked meats, cheeses or other foods that aren't cooked before being served. Bacillus cereus is typically contracted in takeaways where fried rice has sat for too long. Campylobacter causes what we think of as serious food poisoning, with diarrhoea, vomiting and sweats.

3. Donetsk is in the Ukraine.

4. Serbia has still not been invited, after the civil wars of the 1990s.

5. The Rolling Stones had eight No. 1s, the last being 'Honky Tonk Women' in 1969. The Moody Blues went to No. 1 in 1964 with 'Go Now', and reached No. 2 with 'Question' – 'Nights in White Satin' made only No. 19 on original release, and No. 9 when it was reissued in 1972. Neither Led Zeppelin nor Pink Floyd were really singles bands, but Floyd bucked the trend with 'Another Brick in the Wall, Pt. 2', which topped the chart in 1979. The answer, therefore, is Led Zeppelin.

6. Nigel Benn; Minter won light-middleweight gold in 1972, Khan won lightweight silver in 2004 and Joshua won super-heavyweight gold in London in 2012.

7. *Spotlight*.

8. Shearer won with Blackburn Rovers.

9. More trivia from The Stag kitchen: rice is not an allergen although it can cause problems if not reheated correctly.

10. Munich Stadt: Munich is the capital of the state of Bavaria.

UK No. 1 singles for The Beatles: 1963 – 'From Me to You', 'She Loves You', 'I Want to Hold Your Hand'; 1964 – 'Can't Buy Me Love', 'A Hard Day's Night', 'I Feel Fine'; 1965 – 'Ticket to Ride', 'Help!', 'We Can Work It Out'/'Day Tripper'; 1966 – 'Paperback Writer', 'Yellow Submarine'/'Eleanor Rigby'; 1967 – 'All You Need is Love', 'Hello Goodbye'/'I Am the Walrus'; 1968 – 'Lady Madonna', 'Hey Jude'; 1969 – 'Get Back', 'The Ballad of John and Yoko'.

QUIZ 41. IT'S ALL JUST GREEK TO ME

We love myths, wherever they are from, and we throw in more mythology rounds than we probably ought. No apologies, they are fun and available to be read by all, so are not a specialist subject. This quiz is limited exclusively to the Greek myths – they remain the most popular source in the West.

1. Who led the Greek expedition to besiege Troy after the Trojan Prince Paris stole Helen?

2. Who rescued Andromeda from the Sea Monster?

3. Who should never have looked back?

4. Who was condemned to kill his own father and sleep with his mother?

5. Who is the sorceress encountered by Odysseus on his long voyage home after the Trojan wars?

6. What was the name of the boat in which Jason sailed off to find the fabled Golden Fleece, accompanied by the cream of Greece's warriors?

7. After killing his children in a drug-induced frenzy, Heracles was condemned to perform a number of labours for the cowardly King Eurystheus: how many?

8. Who was the only Amazon to marry and who was the lucky husband?

9. Who escaped the sack of Troy and went on to become a major figure in the creation of Rome as a key ancestor of Romulus and Remus?

10. Scylla and Charybdis were twin hazards on a sea voyage. Charybdis was a pair of clashing rocks; what was Scylla?

Answers to Quiz 40

1. *The Mona Lisa.*

2. Buckminster Fuller; here's three top bits of trivia about Buckminster Fuller, who was an architect and theorist about the future. He was expelled from Harvard University, and was also president of Mensa. Fuller and his wife died within thirty-six hours of each other – he suffered a stroke while sitting by her side when she was dying of cancer.

3. Banksy, or Geoff, as his friends call him. (I made that up, I have no idea who Banksy is.)

4. London: Canaletto was born in Venice in 1697. He worked in England between 1746 and 1756 – his style was popular there and King George III purchased a number of Canaletto's works.

5. Michelangelo – the ceiling was in the Sistine Chapel.

6. Walter Sickert; it is not a theory without supporters, but after all this time no one will ever 100 per cent verify who the criminal was, without DNA evidence.

7. Minotaur, the half-man, half-bull who stalks the Labyrinth on Crete.

8. Dada(ism).

9. Tintoretto – it was painted in the late 1980s.

10. Velázquez. Painted around 1750, and sold to England in the early nine-teenth century, the *Rokeby Venus* was bought for the National Gallery in 1906 where, after restoration, it is still exhibited.

QUIZ 42. TERMS SCIENTIFIC

More science. I set this one and the scores varied between zero and nine, so who knows where you fit into this scheme? Trying to be realistic, I think I would have got five without research, so see if you can beat the quizmaster.

1. The trachea is the medical term for what?

2. The American Space programme is run by NASA: for what does NASA stand?

3. Which group of chemical elements takes its name from the first in the series, element no. 57, which takes its place in the main periodic table while the rest of the group are set in a separate pink block beneath the table?

4. Which scientist, born in 1546 in what was then a Danish-held part of modern Sweden, paved the way for Keppler and Newton by measuring the orbit of Mars with a reasonable degree of accuracy?

5. Hippocrates is the most significant classical scholar in which field of science?

6. Which scientist (1791–1867) was, among many fine achievements, the first to liquefy a gas at low temperature and discover the cooling properties of such liquefied elements?

7. Which Persian poet and polymath first accurately calculated the length of a year? His calculations are still valid today.

8. What is the highest level of the earth's atmosphere that can be used by jet-powered aircraft?

9. What threatened species of big cat native to Central and South Asia is sometimes known as an Ounce?

10. Major Mitchell's, galah and gang-gang are all types of which showy bird, mainly native to the Australasian region?

Answers to Quiz 41

1. Agamemnon, King of Mycenae – Helen was his sister-in-law, married to Menelaus, King of Sparta.

2. Perseus. Andromeda was the daughter of Cepheus and Cassiopeia, rulers of Aethiopia, and she was offered as a sacrifice to the monster to assuage the wrath of Poseidon, whom Cassiopeia had offended.

3. Orpheus: when he escorted Eurydice from the Underworld he was told that, if he looked back, he would lose her, but he couldn't help himself.

4. Oedipus – hence the Oedipus complex.

5. Circe; the enchantress turned Odysseus's men into pigs, but the trickster god Hermes advised him on how to guard against her wiles and he ended up spending a year frolicking on her island.

6. Argo, hence the story of Jason and the Argonauts.

7. Ten (he ended up performing ten because Eurystheus claimed he cheated in two of them).

8. In many versions of the Greek tales, Theseus and Herakles abduct Hippolyta and Theseus claims her as his bride as spoils of war – in others, she comes willingly.

9. Aeneas, as recounted in Virgil's *Aeneid*.

10. A whirlpool. Jason encounters them, as does Odysseus on his return from Troy.

QUIZ 43. HORSE AND CARRIAGE

A quiz on married couples. We don't do a lot of celebrity rounds, nor ones about reality TV, tabloid gossip-column stuff or YouTuber stars – that stuff doesn't live long in the memory. Most of these ladies and gents have a less ephemeral claim to fame.

1. Who is married to the Earl of Wessex?

2. Martha Dandridge was the first wife to hold which position?

3. Whose parents were Jim and Mary, third wife Nancy and second child Stella?

4. Which American model and actress was married to Trevor Engelson from 2011 to 2013?

5. If Conrad Hilton Jr was the first, Mike Todd the third and Richard Burton the fifth and sixth, who were the fourth and eighth?

6. Which celebrity couple had a son, Saint, in December 2015?

7. Which twenty-one-year-old actress did Humphrey Bogart marry in 1945, when he was forty-five?

8. Who left her husband, cartoonist Spencer McCallum, after falling in love with Matthew Macfadyen on the set of TV spy drama *Spooks*?

9. Mary; Audrey; _____; Norma; Cherie; Sarah; _____; Philip: fill in the two _____ gaps.

10. Which former sports star is married to the sixteenth in line to the British throne?

Answers to Quiz 42

1. The windpipe.

2. National Aeronautics and Space Administration, established during the Eisenhower administration in 1958.

3. Lanthanides.

4. Tycho Brahe: Tycho picked up the work of Copernicus and took it to the next level; others followed and arrived at a more scientific definition of planet Earth and its place in the universe.

5. Medicine: from him comes the notion of the Hippocratic Oath, whereby doctors make a commitment to heal without malpractice or divulging confidentiality.

6. Michael Faraday.

7. Omar Khayyam, he of the *Rubayait* (an Arabic word for a four-line stanza, or quatrain).

8. The stratosphere.

9. The snow leopard; it is listed as vulnerable on the Red List, as there are believed to be fewer than ten thousand living adults.

10. Cockatoos.

QUIZ 44. HISTORY MASH

A selection of history questions, from all ages of mankind, concerning war and peace and all that stuff. Our pub dates from the sixteenth century, so it is, of itself, a piece of history; it's appropriate, therefore, that we ask a lot of history questions.

1. On whose instruction were Sharon Tate and four others murdered at 10050 Cielo Drive in Hollywood in 1969?

2. Which wars were fought between the British and militia formed by colonial Dutch farmers?

3. Which major battle in Pennsylvania ended Confederate General Lee's march north during the American Civil War?

4. Who was married to Emma Wedgwood, granddaughter of the founder of the famous pottery factory? Was it (a) Charles Dickens; (b) Benjamin Disraeli; (c) Charles Darwin; or (d) Alfred, Lord Tennyson?

5. Which ocean liner was sunk by a German submarine in 1915 with the loss of 1,198 lives?

6. Which significant piece of modern architecture opened in San Francisco on 27 May 1937?

7. Which was the only country in Southeast Asia to remain self-governing during the colonial peak of the seventeenth and eighteenth centuries?

8. Which political event interrupted the 1913 Epsom Derby?

9. The Roman province of Lusitania roughly equates to which modern country? Is it Morocco, Portugal, Switzerland or Tunisia?

10. Who surrendered to Eisenhower in September 1943 and changed sides during the Second World War a month later?

Answers to Quiz 43

1. Sophie Rhys-Jones; the Earl is Prince Edward.

2. First Lady of the US, she was the wife of George Washington.

3. Paul McCartney; his first wife was Linda Eastman, and Stella is their daughter. After Linda's premature death from cancer McCartney married Heather Mills – that didn't work out well and he married for a third time, to Nancy Shevell, in 2011.

4. Meghan Markle – he was her first husband before Prince Harry.

5. Eddie Fisher and Larry Fortensky; they were husbands of Elizabeth Taylor.

6. Kanye West and Kim Kardashian.

7. Lauren Bacall; they remained married until Bogart's death in 1957, and Bacall later married another actor, Jason Robards.

8. Keeley Hawes.

9. They are the first names of spouses of the sitting prime ministers from Harold Wilson to Theresa May, so the missing ones are Denis Thatcher and Samantha Cameron.

10. Mike Tindall.

Succession to the British throne as of January 2019: (1) Charles, Prince of Wales; (2) William, Duke of Cambridge, his son; (3, 4, 5) George, Charlotte and Louis, William and Kate's children; (6) Harry, Duke of Sussex, Charles's second son; (7) Andrew, Duke of York, Charles's brother; (8, 9) the Princesses Eugenie and Beatrice, his children; (10) Edward, Duke of Wessex, Charles's brother; (11, 12) James and Louise, his children; (13) Anne, Princess Royal, Charles' sister; (14) Peter Phillips, her son; (15, 16) Savannah and Isla, Peter's children; (17) Zara Tindall, Anne's daughter; (18, 19) Mia and Lena, Zara's daughters.

This is all the immediate family stemming from Queen Elizabeth II.

QUIZ 45. STUFF

Numbers. These are good quizzes, but hard to set and research. Question 1 has one answer, question 2 has two answers and so on . . . it means fifty-five points if you go up to ten, so we tend to make this style of quizzes the equivalent of at least two, sometimes three rounds.

1. From 2005 to the end of 2018, who is the only non-European man to win one of tennis's Grand Slam tournaments?

2. The two actors who played Philip Marlowe in different versions of *The Big Sleep* (1946 and 1978).

3. What three bones make up the human inner ear?

4. Which four players have scored more than two hundred career goals for Manchester United (up to the 2018–19 season, although no one threatens to join that group)?

5. Which five non-American actresses scooped the Best Actress award at the Academy Awards between 2000 and 2017?

6. Who are the six players to have scored over eight thousand Test match runs for England? (Joe Root, barring calamity, will join this list while the book remains in circulation.)

7. Name the seven London boroughs beginning with the letter H.

8. London lies second (behind Bangkok) in the Mastercard list of cities visited by the most international visitors: what are the other eight European cities in the Top 20?

9. Bremen, with just over half a million inhabitants, is officially the tenth most populous German city: which nine have more inhabitants?

10. Which ten countries have been beaten in a World Cup Final? (In one instance, the country has changed its name, but it still counts as one team.)

Answers to Quiz 44

1. Charles Manson, the leader of the Manson family. It was a particularly ghoulish series of murders.

2. The Boer Wars in South Africa.

3. Gettysburg, where Lincoln made his famous address. The battle cost around fifty thousand lives and proved a turning point in the war.

4. Darwin.

5. RMS *Lusitania* – the number included over a hundred Americans and the event turned public opinion against Germany in the US.

6. The Golden Gate Bridge.

7. Thailand, which was then the Kingdom of Siam, and remained cleverly neutral (or picked the right side) in the various colonial conflicts.

8. The suffragette Emily Davison threw herself in front of a horse and was killed.

9. Portugal – it formed part of the Iberian Peninsula with Hispania, although the two Roman regions never exactly matched modern Portugal and Spain.

10. Italy.

QUIZ 46. OLYMPIANS

The Olympic Games. Along with the FIFA World Cup, it is the greatest global sporting event. You could fill a book with questions on the record holders and medal winners, and stories of triumph and anguish across all the sports over the 120-plus years of the modern games. But we don't have a whole book, so here's ten questions.

1. Who became the first man to win gold in five separate games in Sydney in 2000?

2. Who won four gold medals at the 1936 Berlin Games, much to Hitler's chagrin?

3. Who defeated World Champion and favourite Mike Powell to win a third long-jump gold at the Barcelona Olympics in 1992?

4. In what discipline is Sarah Storey a multiple Olympic gold medallist?

5. Who was the seventeen-year-old Belarus-born gymnast who became the darling of the 1972 Olympics?

6. Four-hundred-metre hurdler Ed Moses won 122 consecutive races between 1977 and 1987. Given he was injury-free, why was the 1980 Olympic Final not one of these races?

7. Whose legendarily inept performances at the 1988 Winter Olympics in Calgary forced the authorities to toughen up qualification rules for most events?

8. Yusra Mardini was one of the great stories of the 2016 Olympic Games. Explain.

9. Which city will host the 2020 Olympic Games?

10. Johnny Weissmuller won Olympic swimming gold in 1924 and 1928, as well as a water polo medal. For what else is he known?

Answers to Quiz 45

1. Juan Martín del Potro won the US Open in 2009.

2. Humphrey Bogart and Robert Mitchum.

3. Malleus, incus and stapes – also accept hammer, anvil and stirrup.

4. Wayne Rooney, Bobby Charlton, Denis Law, Jack Rowley.

5. Nicole Kidman (Australia, 2002, *The Hours*); Charlize Theron (South Africa, 2003, *Monster*); Helen Mirren (Britain, 2006, *The Queen*); Marion Cotillard (France, 2007, *La Vie en Rose*); Cate Blanchett (Australia, 2013, *Blue Jasmine*).

6. Alastair Cook, Graham Gooch, Alec Stewart, David Gower, Kevin Pietersen, Geoff Boycott.

7. Hackney, Hammersmith and Fulham, Haringey, Harrow, Havering, Hillingdon and Hounslow.

8. Paris (No. 3), Istanbul (8), Barcelona (12), Amsterdam (13), Milan (14), Rome (16), Vienna (18), Prague (20).

9. Berlin, Hamburg, Munich, Cologne, Frankfurt, Essen, Dortmund, Stuttgart, Dusseldorf.

10. Germany (including West Germany) × 4; Argentina and Holland × 3; Brazil, Czechoslovakia, Hungary, Italy × 2; France, Sweden, Croatia × 1.

QUIZ 47. ALL SORTS

Another mixed bag of questions to keep you on your toes.

1. Which shipping area, named after a famous battle, is the southernmost of the areas covered by the BBC Shipping Forecast?

2. What is the unlucky number in Japan and Mandarin, the equivalent of thirteen in our culture?

3. On which London street can the headquarters of BAFTA be found?

4. How many faces does a dodecahedron possess?

5. Which Hollywood actress was denounced by the US senate in the 1940s for her affair with Italian film director Roberto Rossellini?

6. What connects author Margaret Atwood, singer Shania Twain, actor Ryan Gosling and celebrity Justin Bieber?

7. Who would attend to your coiffure?

8. Adjani or Huppert?

9. Who rode a winner in all seven races on the card at Ascot in September 1996?

10. Which work, based on thirteenth-century Latin secular poems, was set to music in 1937 by Carl Orff?

Answers to Quiz 46

1. Steve Redgrave.

2. Jesse Owens; he won the 100m, the 200m, the long jump and the 100m relay. The story goes that Owens was given advice on technique by Luz Long, his German rival, before his winning jump in the long-jump competition – a sporting gesture Herr Hitler would never emulate.

3. Carl Lewis. Lewis was a latter-day Owens, winning the same four events in Los Angeles in 1984. He retained his 100m title and won a second long-jump gold in Seoul, followed by a third long-jump plus a relay gold in Barcelona. Impressively, he won a fourth long-jump title at the age of thirty-five in Atlanta in 1996.

4. This is something of a trick question. Storey is a remarkable athlete. She won five gold medals as a teenage swimmer, but was less successful from 1992 to 2000, picking up a series of medals in the pool, but no more golds. So she switched disciplines and was in the saddle for Beijing, adding nine further cycling gold medals at the next three games, including three in Rio at the age of thirty-nine.

5. Olga Korbut. Korbut won three gold medals at Munich and a further team medal in Montreal in 1976.

6. The US boycotted the Moscow games; in retaliation the Soviet athletes were a no-show at the Los Angeles games four years later.

7. Michael 'Eddie the Eagle' Edwards – his ability as a self-publicist far outstripped his ability on the ski-jump run.

8. She was the swimmer with the Refugee Olympic Team at Rio: on her way from Syria to Europe, she and two others pulled a boatload of desperate people to safety when their boat threatened to capsize.

9. Tokyo; in 2024 it will be back to Europe for the second Paris games, and in 2028 another city, Los Angeles, gets a second go.

10. Weissmuller played Tarzan in twelve movies between 1932 and 1948, and in another thirteen as Jungle Jim.

QUIZ 48. FILM NIGHT

A mixed bag of film questions. Nothing too tricky here; we've found that the film rounds score very divisively. You get the odd film buff who gets the lot, and entire teams who appear to have never seen the inside of a cinema. Or maybe they just watch Adam Sandler films, which don't feature heavily in this book.

1. In Spike Jonze's 2002 film *Adaptation*, written by Charlie Kaufman, a character called Charlie Kaufman (any similarities purely intentional) is played by Nicolas Cage. Who plays Charlie's brother, Donald?

2. Who won an Academy Award for his work in the title role of the 2005 film *Capote*, directed by Bennett Miller?

3. Who played the title character in Richard Fleischer's 1967 adaptation of Hugh Lofting's books for children, *Dr Dolittle*?

4. Richard Attenborough, James Coburn, James Garner, Alec Guinness: which of these was NOT in John Sturges's *The Great Escape* (1963)?

5. Who made an Indecent Proposal to Demi Moore in 1993?

6. What is the name of the Blade Runner played by Harrison Ford in Ridley Scott's film of that name from 1982, and what is the name given to the AI characters he is hunting?

7. If Richard Bohringer is The Cook, Michael Gambon is The Thief and Alan Howard is Her Lover, who is His Wife?

8. Terry Zwigoff's cult coming-of-age drama *Ghost World* (2001) starred Thora Birch and which other young actress as the two central teenage characters? Was it Emily Blunt, Bryce Dallas Howard, Scarlett Johansson or Emily Mortimer?

9. *The Left-Handed Gun*, a 1958 western starring Paul Newman, told the story of which legendary Wild West outlaw?

10. There have been two versions of *The Manchurian Candidate*. In the 2004 version the action is set during the Gulf War. What military action provides the backdrop for the original 1962 film? Who plays the lead role in both versions of the story?

Answers to Quiz 47

1. Trafalgar.

2. Four.

3. Piccadilly: BAFTA was founded in 1947 by a group of film luminaries – David Lean was the first president. The first BAFTA awards were presented in 1949.

4. Twelve.

5. Ingrid Bergman; she left her Swedish husband, Petter Kindström, for Rossellini, and they had a daughter, Isabella, also an actress.

6. All are Canadian.

7. Your hairdresser.

8. Isabelle; Huppert, born 1953, has the most nominations for César Awards (sixteen), winning twice. Adjani, born two years later in 1955, has the most César wins, with five.

9. Frankie Dettori; this was a feature racing day, not some wet Wednesday at a minor all-weather course. The seven horses were: Wall Street (2–1); Diffident (12–1); Mark of Esteem (100–30); Decorated Hero (7–1); Fatefully (7–4); Lochangel (5–4); Fujiyama Crest (2–1). For those who don't follow horse racing, this is an unprecedented sequence of wins for one jockey – one punter won £500,000 for a very modest outlay.

10. *Carmina Burana*. Orff's work, with its famous opening piece, 'O Fortuna!', uses only 24 of the original 254 poems.

QUIZ 49. THE BOOK OF DAVID

David, in all its incarnations. A general quiz about all aspects of Dave, be they sporting, filmic, political or from any other walk of life. It always amazes me in these quizzes that a team of intelligent people, when asked 'Which Manchester United footballer . . .?' in a quiz with Dave as a theme, will then answer 'Paul Scholes'. Use the theme, folks, it's a big clue.

1. *A Book of Mediterranean Food*, *French Country Food* and *French Provincial Cooking* are among the works of which influential post-war British food writer?

2. Which former sports presenter and author of over twenty books, expounds a theory that a reptilian race known as the Archons have control of the planet?

3. Bruce Forsyth; Larry Grayson; Bruce Forsyth; MISSING; Graham Norton. What is the list and who is missing?

4. How did David Peacock achieve fame, alongside his partner Charles Hodges?

5. Which former Lancashire and England cricketer, later an umpire and after-dinner speaker, now a Sky Sports commentator, goes by the nickname Bumble?

6. Apart from Manchester United, which was the only other English club for whom David Beckham played, making five league appearances on loan in 1994–5?

7. In 2009 the TV channel Dave launched its first original scripted shows. The three-episode mini-series *Back to Earth* was a revival of which sci-fi comedy show?

8. Dave Vanian is the singer in which long-running punk band?

9. Who made an Important Astrology Experiment and had a Googlewhack Adventure before asserting that Modern Life is Goodish?

10. *Mr Stink*, *Ratburger* and *Demon Dentist* are among the children's books written by which author?

Answers to Quiz 48

1. Nicolas Cage – Donald is a twin.

2. Philip Seymour Hoffman; it was his only Best Actor nomination and a rare lead part for a brilliant character actor.

3. Rex Harrison; the film took an age to shoot, as live animals were used for all the sequences with animals, in what were pre-CGI days.

4. Alec Guinness didn't appear in the film (pretty much everyone else was in it).

5. Robert Redford; the film was panned and both Redford and Moore were nominated for Razzies (Golden Raspberry Awards for the worst film of the year).

6. Deckard; the Blade Runners are responsible for bringing in rogue replicants.

7. Helen Mirren (in Peter Greenaway's *The Cook, The Thief, His Wife & Her Lover*).

8. Scarlett Johansson, a mere niblet of sixteen at the time.

9. Billy the Kid. It's a bleak, revisionist version of the tale, showing a Billy Boney who hates the glamorisation of his adventures.

10. The aftermath of the Korean War: Frank Sinatra and Denzel Washington.

QUIZ 50. AND THE . . .

There are an awful lot of bands over the years who have been So-and-So and the Such-and-Suches, usually reflecting that the band leader is the main mover and shaker and the backing band are also-rans. Some of the backing bands have been just that, session musicians sitting behind a 'star', while others form an integral part of the group's sound. Where would Gladys Knight have been without her loyal Pips?

1. The Jordanaires were a studio band famous for backing which star?

2. Who started out with the Attractions and later adopted the Imposters?

3. If Will Sergeant and Les Pattinson are playing guitar and bass, who is singing and what is the band?

4. Mike Campbell, Howie Epstein, Stan Lynch and Benmont Tench comprise whose famous backing band?

5. *Burnt Weeny Sandwich* and *Weasels Ripped My Flesh* were two 1970 albums released at the height of the output of which innovative band?

6. Which band was formed in Bromley, London, by Susan Ballion and Steve Severin in 1976?

7. What was the name of the fictional band Elton John sang about on his 1974 album, *Goodbye Yellow Brick Road*?

8. Which band all played together with Delaney and Bonnie and Friends before striking up their own partnership? Who was their main guitarist, what was their biggest hit and who played a famous slide guitar part on that song?

9. Which early rappers delivered 'The Message' in 1982?

10. 'Tears of a Clown' was the only UK No. 1 single for which Motown act? And which more disco-oriented song returned them to the top of the US charts (UK No. 3) with Billy Griffin on lead vocals?

Answers to Quiz 49

1. Elizabeth David. David was an upper-class wild child who spent much of her formative years gallivanting across Europe and North Africa. She can claim considerable credit for bringing better standards of cooking and eating to Britain after the war.

2. David Icke.

3. Jim Davidson – they are the presenters of the *Generation Game*. The show was revived in 2018 with Mel and Sue as the new presenters.

4. They were Chas and Dave, until Chas Hodges died in 2018. The duo produced a boogie woogie/skiffle/music hall hybrid music that they called Rockney, and had a string of hits from 1979, including 'Gertcha', 'Rabbit', 'Ain't No Pleasing You' and 'Snooker Loopy'.

5. David Lloyd. The former Lancashire batsman played nine Test matches for England, but was unlucky enough to be on the 1974–5 tour to Australia when Dennis Lillee and Jeff Thomson destroyed a number of international careers and reputations.

6. Preston North End; he played five games on loan for them in 1994–5.

7. *Red Dwarf*; the show launched in 1988 and has had various revivals.

8. The Damned.

9. They are all TV shows by Dave Gorman.

10. David Walliams.

Walliams' books, in order – all of them best-sellers – are: *The Boy in the Dress*; *Mr Stink*; *Billionaire Boy*; *Gangsta Granny*; *Ratburger*; *Demon Dentist*; *Awful Auntie*; *Grandpa's Great Escape*; *The Midnight Gang*; *Bad Dad*; *The Ice Monster*; *Fing*.

QUIZ 51. MORE STUFF

I have little more to say about the general knowledge rounds. Aim for 7/10 on this one.

1. In business terms, what is the ERM?

2. Which famous footballer's name means a dwelling place by a brook?

3. If you are British and a member of the NFU, what is your occupation?

4. In 1984 Dr Kathryn Sullivan became the first woman to (a) serve as Mayor of New York (b) walk in space (c) perform open heart surgery, or (d) play a round of golf at St Andrews golf course?

5. England and Scotland compete for the Calcutta Cup at which sport?

6. Who was the first female Chancellor of Germany?

7. Which company was the first to produce instant coffee in 1937?

8. What is the difference between a troglodyte and a speleologist?

9. Karen Carpenter of The Carpenters died aged thirty-two from complications caused by which medical and psychological affliction?

10. Which head of Dior fashion house was suspended in 2011 after he was overheard making anti-Semitic remarks in a Paris bar?

Answers to Quiz 50

1. Elvis Presley.

2. Elvis Costello; the Attractions were a tight band, with Steve Nieve's distinctive organ playing gelling with Costello's taut guitar. Bruce Thomas (bass) and Pete Thomas (no relation, drums) provided the beats.

3. Ian McCulloch; Echo and the Bunnymen.

4. They are the Heartbreakers, as in Tom Petty and the Heartbreakers; the band formed in 1976 and had few line-up changes in the forty years to Petty's demise in 2017 – guitarist Mike Campbell and keyboard player Benmont Tench were ever-presents in this time.

5. Frank Zappa and the Mothers of Invention.

6. Susan Ballion is Siouxsie Sioux, so the band is Siouxsie and the Banshees; the classic line-up was the early 1980s quartet of Siouxsie, Severin (bass), John McGeoch (formerly of Magazine, on guitar) and Budgie on drums.

7. Bennie and the Jets; the song wasn't a huge success as a single when it came out in the UK in 1976, but it has long been a staple of Elton John's live sets.

8. Derek and the Dominos; Eric Clapton; Layla; Duane Allman.

9. Grandmaster Flash and the Furious Five.

10. Smokey Robinson and the Miracles; 'Love Machine'.

QUIZ 52. ANIMAL INSTINCTS

Questions about animals. Or are they? Some of these questions are straight natural history, but to keep you on your toes, others look at the use of animal symbolism in different disciplines. It's never straightforward, is it?

1. If the Bulls played the Rhinos at Rugby League, which two Yorkshire towns or cities are represented?

2. Zeus mated with Europa and Leda in the guise of animals: which specific forms did he take?

3. What type of creatures are Firenze and Mrs Norris in the Harry Potter novels?

4. Along with anteaters, which creatures make up the order of mammals Pilosa? To which part of the world are they exclusively native?

5. Black Lace Weaver, Bush Widow, Common Crab, Green Huntsman, Marbled Orb-Weaver, Reed Runner, Spotted Wolf: which two of these are not types of spider native to the UK?

6. A griffin or gryphon is a mythological creature and is a composite of which two animals?

7. Under what name do Sussex CCC play T20 cricket? And which team represents Warwickshire CCC?

8. What comes between Species and Family in the modern taxonomic system, and who was the Scandinavian scientist who developed the system in the first half of the eighteenth century?

9. What is the name of the main equine character in Michael Morpurgo's classic *War Horse*? Which playwright adapted the book for the hugely successful National Theatre stage production?

10. In the horse-breeding world, how would a male horse under four years old with a pale or white coat be described?

Answers to Quiz 51

1. The Exchange Rate Mechanism for currency exchange; the mechanism is a complex method of ensuring currency stability within the European Union.

2. David Beckham.

3. The NFU is the National Farmers' Union of England and Wales (Scotland has a separate body). The body was formed in 1908 and current membership (2019) stands at around 55,000 active farming members with over 30,000 supporting Countryside members.

4. She was the first woman to walk in space.

5. Rugby Union; not including 2019's Six Nations, England currently have seventy victories to Scotland's forty.

6. Angela Merkel; the powerful centre-right politician assumed office in 2005 and will stand down in 2021.

7. Nestlé.

8. A troglodyte lives in a cave (or underground), while a speleologist studies caves.

9. Anorexia nervosa.

10. John Galliano. Galliano's career never recovered and his French Légion d'Honneur award from 2009 was officially withdrawn in 2012 by President Hollande.

QUIZ 53. LIFE STORIES

A poll of the most popular biographies on a US website threw up these titles in the Top 50. Match the book to its originator. We enjoy pulling questions from random internet lists. Accepted, the lists are arbitrary, but they tend to be populist, so the quizmaster has a ready-made list of stuff that will probably be familiar to most of the audience. A popular vote of 'Which are the best ten?' of anything will probably produce ten answers of which a quiz team would be able to guess more than half.

1. *Long Walk to Freedom.*
2. *A Child Called It.*
3. *Girl, Interrupted.*
4. *Lucky Man.*
5. *Bossypants.*
6. *The Diving Bell and the Butterfly.*
7. *Bad Blood.*
8. *Wishful Drinking.*
9. *Notes of a Native Son.*
10. *Dreams from My Father.*

A. Dave Pelzer.
B. Nelson Mandela.
C. Lorna Sage.
D. Jean-Dominique Bauby.
E. James Baldwin.
F. Barack Obama.
G. Susannah Kayser.
H. Tina Fey.
I. Carrie Fisher
J. Michael J. Fox.

Answers to Quiz 52

1. Bradford vs Leeds; the match-up doesn't happen at the moment, as three-time league champions, the Bulls, are fighting their way back to the top after a few years of financial difficulty. The Rhinos have been ever present since the Super League was formed and have won a record eight championships.

2. He mated with Europa in the form of a bull, and Leda in the form of a swan.

3. Firenze is a centaur, while Mrs Norris is Filch's cat who roams the corridors of Hogwart's.

4. Sloths, which are native to the Central and South American jungle.

5. Bush Widow, Reed Runner.

6. A gryphon has the back legs and tail of a lion, and the head and talons of an eagle.

7. Sussex Sharks and Birmingham Bears.

8. Genus, and Carl Linnaeus was the scientist whose charts are still the basis of the system nearly two hundred years later.

9. Joey; Nick Stafford wrote the play, and in 2011 Lee Hall and Richard Curtis developed the book for Steven Spielberg's movie version.

10. Grey colt.

Here are the twelve teams making up Rugby League's Super League in 2019, with a new format introduced: Castleford Tigers, Catalans Dragons (the only non-English team, based in Perpignan, France), Huddersfield Giants, Hull FC, Hull Kingston Rovers, Leeds Rhinos, London Broncos, Salford Red Devils, St Helens, Wakefield Trinity, Warrington Wolves, Wigan Warriors.

QUIZ 54. RIVER RUNS

Here are ten rivers – you need to match them to the body of water into which they pour. It is unlikely you will simply know the answers here, so a certain amount of patience and logic is required and a process of elimination will take place. A great quiz should always demand some reasoning as well as regurgitation of facts. We lost an experienced quiz team after a few months because we 'don't deal in facts'. We do, but we sometimes make you work for them. What they really meant was, 'We don't win every week, like we used to . . .'

1. Colorado (the longer one).
2. Great Ouse.
3. Brahmaputra.
4. Potomac.
5. Loire.
6. Dnieper.
7. Nile.
8. Orinoco.
9. Liffey.
10. Mississippi.

A. Bay of Bengal.
B. Eastern Mediterranean.
C. Black Sea.
D. Gulf of Mexico.
E. North Sea.
F. Bay of Biscay.
G. Irish Sea.
H. Atlantic (south).
I. Chesapeake Bay.
J. Gulf of California.

Answers to Quiz 53

1. B: *Long Walk to Freedom* was Nelson Mandela's 1994 autobiography, made into a very worthy and well-acted but rather dull film starring Idris Elba.

2. A: Dave Pelzer's *A Child Called It* was a searing 1995 account of an abusive childhood.

3. G: Susannah Kayser's account of time spent in a psychiatric hospital was *Girl, Interrupted*, a best-seller in 1993.

4. J: *Lucky Man* is Michael J. Fox's upbeat account of his struggle with Parkinson's disease, he having been diagnosed at the age of twenty-nine.

5. H: Comedian Tina Fey's comic autobiography topped the best-seller lists in 2011.

6. D: This account of locked-in syndrome by former editor of *Elle* magazine, Bauby, recounted to a helper via a series of eye movements, is a staggering work from 1997, made into a surprisingly hilarious and moving film starring Mathieu Amalric in 2007.

7. C: Lorna Sage, a writer and teacher, lived just long enough to see her autobiography win the Whitbread Biography award in 2001.

8. I: Carrie Fisher's *Wishful Drinking* (2008) was adapted from her stage show, and is a comic account of her struggles with addiction.

9. E: *Notes of a Native Son* is African-American writer James Baldwin's autobiography, told in the form of ten previous essays re-edited to produce a coherent narrative of his life and philosophy.

10. F: *Dreams from My Father* is Barack Obama's account of his early years in Hawaii and Chicago.

QUIZ 55. WHAT DO YOU KNOW?

More stuff. This is a little easier than one or two of the general rounds – aim for 8/10 if you have a team of four.

1. Baku in Azerbaijan, at 28 metres below sea level, is the lowest-lying capital city in the world, and is known as the Windy City due to the winds blowing in off which body of water?

2. When I was sixteen I lived up on the moors above Bolton, a notoriously breezy spot. On a clear day I could see a man-made landmark a full fifty miles to the west. What was it?

3. Which production team had their first UK No. 1 hit with Dead or Alive's 1985 song 'You Spin Me Round (Like a Record)'?

4. Who owns the Asda chain of superstores?

5. Which game is played between players acting as Planeswalkers? Which colour in the game represents fire, lightning, chaos and passion, among other things?

6. Denali, or Mount McKinley, is the highest peak in the United States: in which state can it be found?

7. Rubella is the proper name – what is the old-fashioned common name for the rubella virus?

8. Bronze is usually comprised of copper mixed with around 12 per cent of which other metal (along with various traces)?

9. What should one not get wet or feed after midnight?

10. Whose *Common Sense Book of Baby and Child Care* was first published in 1946?

Answers to Quiz 54

1. J: Colorado – Gulf of California.

2. E: Great Ouse – North Sea.

3. A: Brahmaputra – Bay of Bengal.

4. I: Potomac – Chesapeake Bay.

5. F: Loire – Bay of Biscay.

6. C: Dnieper – Black Sea.

7. B: Nile – Eastern Mediterranean.

8. H: Orinoco – Atlantic (south).

9. G: Liffey – Irish Sea.

10. D: Mississippi – Gulf of Mexico.

Here are the world's ten longest rivers. Rivers are complex; they often comprise two or three named watercourses that are, technically, one river.

- Nile – runs through much of North and East Africa into the Mediterranean.
- Amazon – passes through seven South American countries into the Atlantic.
- Chang Jiang (Yangtze) – cuts across a huge swathe of China.
- Mississippi/Missouri – empties into the Gulf of Mexico.
- Yensisei – comes up as the Ider in Mongolia, then flows through Russia and empties into the Kara Sea on the Siberia coast.
- Huang He (Yellow River) – proceeds through China and into the Yellow Sea, which divides north-east China from Korea.
- Ob-Irtysh – flows through Mongolia, China and Russia on its way to the Arctic.
- Rio de la Plata/Rio Grande – runs through South America and into the Atlantic, where it forms part of the border between Argentina and Uruguay.
- Congo – flows through Africa into the Atlantic to the west of the continent – the Congo is the world's deepest river.
- Amur-Kherlen – forms part of the Russo-Chinese border and empties into the Sea of Okhotsk.

QUIZ 56. AMERICAN ARTS

American art is distinct from English. The new world is a very different experience from Europe, and while the language may be common to Britain, the view of the world is very different. Here are some questions on uniquely American artists whose work extends beyond their country while wholeheartedly reflecting it.

1. Which revered American poet had her first volume of work published in 1890, four years after her death?

2. Captain Ahab, the captain of the whaling ship *Pequod*, was in obsessive pursuit of what?

3. Bruce Springsteen's album *The Ghost of Tom Joad* takes its title from which great American novel?

4. Which of these is NOT a novel by F. Scott Fitzgerald: *The Great Gatsby*; *Tender is the Night*; *This Side of Paradise*; *The Torrents of Spring*?

5. Who earned fame/notoriety for his 1952 work 4'33" in which the musicians sit and do nothing for that length of time, and the sounds of the auditorium and humanity become the composition?

6. Which modern American artist (1912–56) was nicknamed Jack the Dripper after his unique style of painting?

7. Which American artist, known especially for large detailed paintings of flowers, died in Santa Fe in 1986 aged ninety-eight?

8. Which American poet and protester howled his way to fame (or notoriety if you are a reactionary bigot) in 1956?

9. Hemingway's 1940 work *For Whom the Bell Tolls* was based on his experiences during which war?

10. Who gave up the law to write full time after his first book *A Time to Kill* (1989) became a best-seller?

Answers to Quiz 55

1. The Caspian Sea, which is technically the world's largest lake.

2. Blackpool Tower; the moors around the reservoirs at Anglezarke are part of the West Pennine Moors and have a beauty at odds with the image of the industrial Northwest.

3. Stock, Aitken, Waterman.

4. Walmart.

5. Magic: The Gathering; Red.

6. Alaska.

7. German measles.

8. Tin.

9. A Gremlin, according to the 1984 movie.

10. Dr Benjamin Spock.

Stock Aitken Waterman had over a hundred Top 40 hits, including the following number ones. Impressive stats, even if the music left much to be desired.

1985: Dead or Alive – 'You Spin Me Round (Like a Record)'.

1987: Mel and Kim – 'Respectable'.

1987: Ferry Aid, in aid of the Zeebrugge disaster – 'Let It Be'.

1987: Rick Astley – 'Never Gonna Give You Up'.

1987: Kylie Minogue – 'I Should Be So Lucky'.

1988: Kylie and Jason – 'Especially for You'.

1989: Jason Donovan – 'Too Many Broken Hearts'.

1989: Kylie Minogue – 'Hand on Your Heart'.

1989: Aid for victims of the Hillsborough Disaster – 'Ferry Cross the Mersey'.

1989: Jason Donovan – 'Sealed with a Kiss'.

1989: Sonia – 'You'll Never Stop Me Loving You'.

1989: Band Aid II – 'Do They Know It's Christmas'.

1990: Kylie Minogue – 'Tears on My Pillow'.

QUIZ 57. BY GEORGE!

Another themed round, revolving around the name George. Odd how names go in and out of fashion. There was a George in my year at school and it seemed such a quaint, old-fashioned name, redolent of wartime kings. Now those names, George, Ben, Thomas etc., are cool and back in fashion.

1. Which country has exactly 365 churches dedicated to St George?

2. Who takes the role of Parisian Inspector Maigret in the recent TV adaptations of the classic Georges Simenon novels?

3. By what name is the singer George O'Dowd better known?

4. The flamboyant Bobby George was one of the first superstars of which sport?

5. Ricky George, playing for non-league Hereford United, scored a famous winning goal to knock out which first-division team in the FA Cup in 1972?

6. Who plays Inspector George Gently in the TV series of that name?

7. Lowell George was the singer and main songwriter in which country rock band?

8. Who was vice-president under the first president of the United States, George Washington?

9. Which writer was born in Dublin in 1856 and died in Hertfordshire in 1950?

10. How old is Prince William and Catherine's eldest child, George?

Answers to Quiz 56

1. Emily Dickinson; she died, aged fifty-five, in Amherst, Massachussetts, where she had always lived. It was 1955 before a properly original volume of her work was published.

2. Moby Dick, the whale, in Herman Melville's epic novel.

3. *The Grapes of Wrath*, an account of the difficulties of living in the Midwest during the Great Depression and the hope (and subsequent crushing of that hope) offered by new opportunities in California.

4. *The Torrents of Spring* is by Hemingway; Fitzgerald's other two full-length novels are *The Beautiful and Damned* and the unfinished book, *The Last Tycoon*. He left these and a host of short stories as a robust legacy of Jazz Age America.

5. John Cage – the idea still divides critics. If the duty of art is to stimulate and challenge, then Cage certainly did that; if entertainment is a prerequisite, then less so.

6. Jackson Pollock.

7. Georgia O'Keeffe; the Wisconsin-born artist worked in New York before she began visiting New Mexico. She died in Santa Fe, now home to the Georgia O'Keeffe Museum.

8. Allen Ginsberg, a key figure in American 1950s and 60s counter-culture.

9. The Spanish Civil War – Hemingway worked as a journalist in Spain during the conflict.

10. John Grisham. The year 2019 will see the publication of Grisham's thirty-ninth full-length novel, including the five Theodore Boone novels for older kids.

QUIZ 58. THE NOBLE GAME

A quiz about the pugilistic art of boxing, though why two guys or girls pummelling each other's face for a living is called the Noble Game is beyond me. You can understand why they do it if they have the talent – the purses for the big fights are eye-watering. And even though it's not my sport, I do like the fact that, in the Olympic Games, it is strictly amateur.

1. Muhammad Ali lost three of his last four fights, when he was clearly past his prime: which two boxers beat him in his pomp?

2. Brian London was one of three British fighters to go up against Ali: who were the other two, both beaten twice?

3. What is the name of Ali's daughter, who had a 24–0 unbeaten record in her eight-year career?

4. During the 1980s four boxers named the 'Fabulous Four' kept public interest alive in pro boxing. Americans Thomas Hearns and Marvin Hagler were two: who was their Panamanian rival, and who was the other American boxer who beat all the other three?

5. Who was the 'Celtic Warrior' who won the WBO middleweight and super-middleweight titles, making him unquestionably Ireland's most successful professional boxer?

6. Which two British boxers have won the Olympic super-heavyweight boxing title since 2000?

7. Which British boxer, who enjoyed a long rivalry with Chris Eubank, was known as the Dark Destroyer?

8. Which flyweight British boxer became the first woman to win an Olympic boxing gold medal, and at which games did women first box for medals?

9. Which US boxer won titles at five professional weights, from super-flyweight to light middleweight, before retiring in 2017 with a 50–0 unbeaten record?

10. Which Senator of the Philippines was also the only boxer to win eight world titles in different weight divisions across the various awarding bodies?

Answers to Quiz 57

1. Georgia; the clue is in the name.

2. Rowan Atkinson.

3. Boy George, singer with Culture Club and then a solo artist. George was at the forefront of the New Romantic movement in the 1980s, and 'Do You Really Want To Hurt Me?' and 'Karma Chameleon' were massive global hits.

4. Darts.

5. Newcastle United; the game was the *Match of the Day* debut for a new commentator, John Motson – the upset did him a great service.

6. Martin Shaw, with Lee Ingleby as his flaky deputy, John Bacchus.

7. Little Feat.

8. John Adams.

9. George Bernard Shaw. Shaw moved to London when he was twenty years old and was awarded the Nobel Prize for Literature in 1925.

10. Depends on when you do the quiz – he was born on 22 April 2013.

QUIZ 59. OH, THOSE RUSSIANS

As Boney M said at the end of their disco hit, 'Rasputin'. A quiz on Russia, with a few about the former Soviet Union. And I didn't even mention Salisbury . . .

1. Where might one find the Krasnaya Ploshchad, one of the most significant landmarks in Russia?

2. The Sea of Okhotsk forms a maritime border between Russia and which other major nation?

3. Which famous museum was established in St Petersburg in Russia in 1754?

4. Larisa Latynina and Nikolai Andrianov won thirty-three medals between them in which Olympic sport?

5. How many separate states made up the Soviet Union?

6. And which of them lies to the west of Russia between Ukraine and the Baltic states?

7. Rasputin came to wield power in Russia around 1915 through his influence on Alexandra, the wife of which ruler?

8. Which ethnic group formed the majority of the anti-Bolshevik White Army immediately after the Russian revolution, and were exiled and persecuted as a consequence?

9. Where did Matthias Rust land a Cessna 142 light aircraft in 1987?

10. Up until the end of the 2018 season, which club has won the Russian Premier League on the most (ten) occasions?

Answers to Quiz 58

1. Ali lost his thirty-second professional fight to Joe Frazier in 1971 in Madison Square Garden, and his forty-third to Ken Norton in San Diego in 1973. He beat Norton later the same year and took revenge on Frazier the following January. He then beat George Foreman (The Rumble in the Jungle) to regain all his titles, and beat Frazier again in 1975 (The Thriller in Manila). In 1978 Ali lost to Leon Spinks, then beat him and retired. Two attempted comebacks resulted in easy victories for Larry Holmes and Trevor Berbick, and there were signs of the Parkinson's disease that would eventually end Ali's life.

2. Henry Cooper and Joe Bugner.

3. Laila.

4. Roberto Dúran and Sugar Ray Leonard.

5. Steve Collins.

6. Audley Harrison and Anthony Joshua; Harrison was quickly found out, while the jury remains undecided on Joshua as a true great.

7. Nigel Benn; they fought twice, Eubank winning the first, a classic, and the second ending in a draw. Both were beaten not long after by Steve Collins.

8. Nicola Adams, London 2012; Adams retained her title in Rio in impressive style.

9. Floyd Mayweather Jr – he features in most boxing pundits' Top 10 Fighters list.

10. Manny Pacquaio. Ditto.

QUIZ 60. HISTORY MIX

Another pot pourri of historical titbits.

1. The Duke of Monmouth, beheaded aged thirty-six for leading a rebellion against his uncle, was the illegitimate son of which English king and his mistress, Lucy Walter?

2. Who was the German propaganda minister, appointed Chancellor as successor to Adolf Hitler in Hitler's will, but only holding office for one day before committing suicide?

3. Who invented the labour-saving device the Spinning Jenny in Lancashire in 1746?

4. What are the first three words of the US constitution?

5. In which year was the *Jazz Singer*, the first 'talkie' or movie with sound, released?

6. Which Disney movie was the first full-length animated feature film when it was released in 1939?

7. Who became Prime Minister of India when the country achieved independence in 1947, retaining his position until his death in 1964?

8. Who committed suicide rather than surrender to the Romans in 182 BCE?

9. On which island off the coast of modern Namibia did Napoleon Bonaparte die in exile in 1821?

10. Where in the Crimea in February 1945 did Churchill, Roosevelt and Stalin meet to discuss the future of Europe as the Second World War drew to a close?

Answers to Quiz 59

1. Moscow, it is Russian for Red Square.

2. Japan.

3. Hermitage; it was founded by Catherine the Great to house her own expanding collection, and opened to the public in 1852.

4. Gymnastics; Latynina (who was born in the Ukraine) won eighteen medals between 1956 and 1964, nine of them individual gold, while Andrianov won fifteen, with seven gold, between 1972 and 1980.

5. Fifteen.

6. Belarus.

7. Tsar Nicholas II, the last tsar.

8. Cossacks.

9. Red Square; it was a hugely embarrassing incident for the Soviets and Rust served fourteen months of a four-year jail sentence.

10. Spartak Moscow.

The former Soviet States are: Armenia, Azerbaijan, Belarus, Estonia, Georgia, Kazakhstan, Kyrgyzstan, Latvia, Lithuania, Moldova, Russia, Ukraine, Tajikistan, Turkmenistan, Uzbekistan.

QUIZ 61. MAY 21

We set this quiz – unsurprisingly – on 21 May. It's just another way of doing a mixed round – ask questions about stuff that happened on a certain day/week; there's usually enough, especially if you throw in folk who were born on that day.

1. In 1349 Dusan the Mighty established the constitution of which modern country? Was it (a) Serbia; (b) Italy; (c) Turkey; (d) Albania?

2. In 1703 which author was imprisoned for seditious libel? Was it (a) Alexander Pope; (b) Jane Austen; (c) Daniel Defoe; (d) Oscar Wilde?

3. In 1864 the Ionian Islands became once again part of Greece. Who ruled the islands for around four hundred years before Napoleon took control in 1797? Was it (a) The Ottoman Empire; (b) Great Britain; (c) Venice; (d) Spain?

4. Which engineering feat, designed by Edward Leader Williams, was opened by Queen Victoria in 1894? Was it (a) Clifton Suspension Bridge; (b) the Manchester Ship Canal; (c) Waterloo Bridge; (d) Battersea Power Station?

5. What was founded in Paris in 1904? Was it (a) the French Foreign Legion; (b) Air France; (c) FIFA; (d) The International Red Cross?

6. Who landed in Paris in 1927 after crossing the Atlantic? Was it (a) The Montgolfier Brothers; (b) Charles Lindbergh; (c) Amelia Earhart; (d) Howard Hughes?

7. In 1936 Sada Abe was arrested in Tokyo. What did she have in her handbag? Was it (a) a pipe bomb destined for the government offices; (b) the severed head of her baby daughter; (c) her husband's mutilated genitals; (d) a packet of cigarettes and a lipstick?

8. In which city did the White Nights riots take place in 1979 after the lenient sentencing of the murderer of liberal Mayor George Moscone and Councillor Harvey Milk? Was it (a) New York; (b) San Francisco; (c) Toronto; (d) Sydney?

9. In 1991 who was assassinated by a female suicide bomber near Madras, India? Was it (a) Rajiv Gandhi; (b) Indira Gandhi; (c) General Bhutto; (d) Saeed Jaffrey?

10. In 2008 Chelsea and Manchester United contested the only all-English Champions League Final. In the penalty shoot-out, which Chelsea legend slipped as he took a crucial spot-kick and missed the chance to win the cup? Was it (a) Peter Osgood; (b) Didier Drogba; (c) Gianfranco Zola; (d) John Terry?

Answers to Quiz 60

1. Charles II; Monmouth laid claim to the throne as a Protestant alternative to King James II; had he waited a while, Parliament might have endorsed his claim.

2. Joseph Goebbels.

3. James Hargreaves; Richard Arkwright's water spinner soon followed, and ten years after that, Crompton's spinning jenny arrived. Between them they ushered in the Industrial Revolution.

4. 'We the People . . .' – an unequivocal affirmation that the state exists to serve the people.

5. It was 1927; the film still used black-screen dialogue but interjected a few words. The move to fully synchronised sound was swift.

6. *Snow White and the Seven Dwarves.*

7. Jawaharlal Nehru.

8. Hannibal; he was a general of the Carthaginian Empire and handed out a couple of drubbings to the Romans before he fell.

9. St Helena; he was first exiled to Elba, but returned to rekindle the wars, so he was sent a lot further away the second time.

10. Yalta – how complicit were the Western leaders in the formation of the Iron Curtain they came to fear?

QUIZ 62. MOVIES

I was in a bit of a hurry one week, and I did a movie round off the top of my head. So it does reflect my personal taste a bit. If you get 10/10 on this round, we would probably get on. And you would probably do well at the Stag quiz.

1. Which daughter of a famous father starred alongside Leslie Nielsen in *The Naked Gun* movies?

2. What is the subject matter of the 1996 film *Tin Cup*, starring Kevin Costner and Rene Russo?

3. Gene Kelly in 1948; Michael York in 1973; Chris O'Donnell in 1993; Logan Lerman in 2011. Which character?

4. How did Catherine Tramell uncrossing her legs cause a stir in 1992?

5. Apart from relationships, what is the main subject matter of the surprise 2004 hit drama *Sideways*?

6. Who provides the voice of Princess Fiona in the *Shrek* movies?

7. What part was played by chameleon actor Michael Sheen in the 2006 biopic *The Queen*, starring Helen Mirren?

8. Who stars as a gay private eye alongside Robert Downey Jr in the 2005 noir comedy *Kiss Kiss Bang Bang*?

9. Which big Hollywood star made his debut in the 1958 B-movie *The Blob*?

10. Who are the Turnbull ACs, the Orphans, the Baseball Furies, the Lizzies and the Punks?

Answers to Quiz 61

1. Dusan set up the original constitution of Serbia. It pretty much went 'do as I tell you'.

2. Daniel Defoe was a pamphleteer and dissenter who was an obvious target during a clampdown by Queen Anne's government.

3. Geographically, the Ionian Islands should have fallen to the Ottoman Empire, but they were under the protection of the Venetian Republic until they rejoined Greece.

4. The Manchester Ship Canal – Leader Williams was later knighted for his efforts.

5. Commercial air traffic hadn't begun, and the Foreign Legion and Red Cross were both founded in the previous century – the answer is FIFA.

6. It was Lindbergh. Impressive feat, but he was still a fascist.

7. Yep, it was her old man's goolies.

8. San Francisco.

9. Rajiv Gandhi – his mother, Indira, had been assassinated by her own Sikh bodyguards seven years earlier.

10. John Terry. Terry's missed penalty meant the shoot-out continued and French striker Nicolas Anelka also missed his kick to leave United the winners.

QUIZ 63. BROWN-ENVELOPE QUIZ

We set this quiz as a giggle. One week, the crowd challenged us to do a quiz about sex, so we did, and we handed it out in brown envelopes. The next time we advertised a brown-envelope quiz, this was the first round – it's about brown envelopes. (I was told it was the most boring round I'd ever set – I'm inclined to agree . . .)

1. What kind of durable stationery takes its name from a hemp made from banana plants grown in the Philippines?

2. In the US, A4 paper is more commonly replaced with what size (6mm wider and 18mm shorter)?

3. Which ubiquitous office item (100 billion units and counting) was first introduced to the market in 1950 by a French company that later enjoyed similar success with the first mass-produced disposable lighter?

4. Which stationery item has a crown, two legs and teeth?

5. Which Edinburgh-based stationer and newsagent, founded in 1833, sold its retail business to W.H. Smith in 1998?

6. A DL envelope is specifically designed to take what kind of paper and how?

7. What does DL stand for?

8. Which then-unique adhesive product was designed by a Henkel researcher and first released in 1969?

9. Which American stationery company opened its first branch in Massachusetts in 1986, but sold its British enterprise in 2016 for a nominal sum after failure to achieve market penetration?

10. Which manufacturer of writing instruments, founded in 1888, closed its only UK plant in Newhaven, East Sussex, in 2011, moving it to Nantes, in France?

Answers to Quiz 62

1. Priscilla Presley, Elvis's daughter.

2. Golf; unusually for a sports movie, it's not awful, and Costner actually looks as though he can play golf.

3. D'Artagnan in various versions of *The Three Musketeers*; the Kelly version also had Vincent Price as a scenery-chewing Richelieu, while Oliver Reed made Athos into a cynical alcoholic in the 1970s films.

4. Tramell is Sharon Stone's character in *Basic Instinct* – the stir was down to the fact that Stone wasn't wearing any underwear . . .

5. Wine, the characters are on a vineyard tour.

6. Cameron Diaz, to Mike Myers' Shrek, Eddie Murphy's Donkey and – in the later films – Antonio Banderas' Puss in Boots.

7. UK prime minister Tony Blair.

8. Val Kilmer; glorious piece of neo-noir kitsch, with both actors in splendid form. The title is from the famous critic Pauline Kael, who saw it on a movie poster in Europe and thought it the perfect expression of the excitement of the movies.

9. Steve McQueen.

10. Gangs in *The Warriors*, the 1979 cult film directed by Walter Hill and based on a 1965 novel by Sol Yurick.

QUIZ 64. SCIENCE

Another mixed round of science questions. Again, you can use me as a yardstick – I knew six of these without looking them up.

1. Which oil, produced from flax seed, was traditionally used for oiling cricket bats?

2. Which planet lies about 250 million kilometres from the sun?

3. What name is given to a chemical substance made of more than one element bonded together?

4. Subrahmanyan Chandrasekhar discovered which now commonly accepted astronomical phenomenon during his distinguished career?

5. Frances Kelsey earned the thanks of the US government in the early 1960s for her work in blocking the use and exposing the risk of which controversial drug?

6. What was the major scientific invention of Stephanie Kwolek, a unique substance used in military armour, car manufacturing and sports equipment?

7. James Chadwick led the British scientific contribution to which wartime scientific collaboration?

8. Cirrostratus and altocumulus are both types of what naturally occurring phenomenon?

9. The nocturnal aardvark is unique to the southern half of which continent?

10. Jackdaws, ravens, rooks and magpies are all part of which bird family?

Answers to Quiz 63

1. Manila envelope.

2. Letter size – it appears as the default option on most Microsoft software.

3. Bic biro.

4. Staple.

5. John Menzies. They were my first full-time employer; I joined as a graduate trainee in 1984. I never got into stationery, but I enjoyed the book side and soon migrated into that industry.

6. A4 folded into thirds.

7. Dimension lengthwise.

8. Pritt stick – most people guessed Blu Tack.

9. Staples; the big office sheds never took off here like they did in the US – maybe due to the ubiquitous nature of W.H. Smith.

10. Parker pens. It was a controversial decision by the Wisconsin-based firm. Special relationship, right?

QUIZ 65. GENERAL KNOWLEDGE

Another mix of subjects. Nothing too tricky here; you should aim for 8/10.

1. *The Remains of the Day* (1993), an understated love story starring Anthony Hopkins and Emma Thompson, was based on a novel by which Anglo-Japanese writer?

2. In which city in Virginia can the headquarters of the CIA be found?

3. Why would DOA not be a good thing to have on your hospital admission form?

4. What brand of soup can did Andy Warhol famously paint?

5. Who is the actress wife of film director Joel Coen?

6. Which tune from *Mary Poppins* won an Academy Award for Best Song?

7. *Amadeus* (1984) was an Academy Award-winning film about the life of which great classical composer?

8. Who was Nick Grimshaw's predecessor as the host of the *Radio 1 Breakfast Show*?

9. Oxford and Cambridge are Britain's oldest universities; which is the third oldest, founded in 1413?

10. A calotte is (a) a wide-bottomed trouser; (b) a gendarme's cap; (c) a type of hair pin; or (d) a skullcap worn by Catholic clergy?

Answers to Quiz 64

1. Linseed oil; it's an intoxicating smell, with memories of summer afternoons (and hay fever).

2. Mars.

3. A compound.

4. Black holes. It's probably unscientific to say he discovered them; I should probably say 'first postulated the theory' or some such. But I'm not a scientist, so I allow myself linguistic vagaries.

5. Thalidomide; the US was largely free of the spate of malformed limbs on birth that accompanied the release of the drug into the market. Around ten thousand children were affected worldwide, with about 50 per cent not surviving.

6. Kevlar, most commonly seen (via TV and the movies) in bulletproof vests.

7. The Manhattan Project, the allied project to develop a nuclear arsenal.

8. Clouds; they come in five forms: stratiform, cirriform, strato cumuliform, cumuliform, cumulonimbiform. Fog is surface-level stratiform cloud.

9. Africa.

10. Corvidae (accept crows), which also includes jays, choughs and nutcrackers.

QUIZ 66. NAME THE ALBUM

We give you three tracks from an album, and the year it was released (because we're generous). You give us the album title and the artists responsible. That seems to me a perfectly fair exchange. Our teams did poorly, but if you're up on your music you should do better.

1. 'Daddy Lessons'; 'Formation'; 'Hold Up' (2016).

2. 'Victims'; 'Church of the Poisoned Mind'; 'Karma Chameleon' (1983).

3. 'One'; 'Who's Gonna Ride Your Wild Horses'; 'The Fly' (1991).

4. 'Pachucho Cadaver'; 'Ant Man Bee'; 'The Dust Blows Forward 'n the Dust Blows Back' (1969).

5. 'Song Cry'; 'Takeover'; 'Girls, Girls, Girls' (2001).

6. 'Subterranean Homesick Blues'; 'Maggie's Farm'; 'It's Alright Ma (I'm Only Bleeding)' (1965).

7. 'Freddie Freeloader'; 'Flamenco Sketches'; 'Blue in Green' (1959).

8. 'Redondo Beach'; 'Free Money'; 'Land pts I, II and III' (1976).

9. 'Glam Slam'; 'When 2 R in Love'; 'Alphabet St.' (1988).

10. 'Sour Times'; 'Numb'; 'Glory Box' (1994).

Answers to Quiz 65

1. Kazuo Ishiguro; he's had a pretty good couple of years, winning the Nobel Prize for Literature in 2017 and getting a knighthood the following year.

2. Langley.

3. It means Dead on Arrival.

4. Campbell's; the New Jersey-based company are still going.

5. Frances McDormand. She made her film debut in the Coen Brothers' *Blood Simple*, and also had main parts in *Raising Arizona*, *Fargo* (for which she won an Academy Award as Best Actress), *The Man Who Wasn't There*, *Burn After Reading* and *Hail, Caesar!*

6. The Sherman brothers won the award for Chim Chim Cher-ee.

7. Mozart – his full name was Wolfgang Amadeus Mozart. Mozart was played in the film by Tom Hulce, but it was F. Murray Abraham as the jealous court composer Salieri who stole the show, winning an Academy Award as Best Actor – both he and Hulce were nominated for the award, the most recent example of both leads earning nominations.

8. Chris Moyles. Big ego, big ratings.

9. St Andrew's on the east coast of Scotland.

10. It is the skullcap worn by Roman Catholic clergy.

QUIZ 67. WORDS OF LOVE

The essence of love. Mainly literary, but a few from more recent popular culture. We did a few quote books years back and they were popular; they make good by-the-loo books. Like quiz books.

1. 'If music be the food of love, play on, / Give me excess of it . . .' Which Shakespeare play begins with this line?

2. 'Who, being loved, is poor?' Which Victorian writer and wit?

3. 'In vain I have struggled. It will not do. My feelings will not be repressed. You must allow me to tell you how ardently I admire and love you.' Which Jane Austen character finally lets his feelings out?

4. 'How do I love thee? Let me count the ways. I love thee to the depth and breadth and height. My soul can reach . . .' Which Victorian female poet?

5. 'He was my North, my South, my East and West, my working week and my Sunday rest.' Which film massively increased the profile and popularity of the W.H. Auden poem from which these lines are taken?

6. 'GIRL: I fear I'll never see you again. BOY: Of course you will. GIRL: But what if something happens to you? BOY: Hear this now: I will come for you. GIRL: But how can you be sure? BOY: This is true love. You think this happens every day?' From which cult movie do these lines come? Who wrote the brilliant script?

7. 'You should be kissed, and often, by someone who knows how.' From which novel of 1936, made into a movie three years later?

8. 'Whatever our souls are made of, his and mine and are the same.' About whom is Cathy Earnshaw talking?

9. 'The amusement park rises bold and stark, / Kids are huddled on the beach in a mist, / I want to die with you Wendy, on the streets tonight, / In an everlasting kiss.' Which New Jersey singer?

10. 'To love, or have loved. Ask nothing further. There is no other pearl to be found in the dark folds of life.' Which novel, now more famous as a musical?

Answers to Quiz 66

1. Beyoncé: *Lemonade*; Beyoncé's sixth album drew massive critical acclaim, but weaker sales than most of its predecessors.

2. Culture Club: *Colour by Numbers*.

3. U2: *Achtung Baby*.

4. Captain Beefheart and his Magic Band: *Trout Mask Replica*.

5. Jay-Z: *The Blueprint*.

6. Bob Dylan: *Bringing It All Back Home*.

7. Miles Davis: *Kind of Blue*; add the opening track 'So What' and the eleven-and-a-half-minute 'All Blues' and you have the entire album, just five tracks.

8. Patti Smith: *Horses*; the album was a key release in the punk movement, influencing a host of New York bands as well as many British admirers like Johnny Marr and P.J. Harvey.

9. Prince: *Lovesexy*.

10. Portishead: *Dummy*. The Bristol band, named after a nearby coastal town, were part of a burgeoning West Country trip-hop scene with Massive Attack at its heart. The electronic tracks were bleak and the sound hinged on the tortured, haunting vocals of Beth Gibbons.

QUIZ 68. PEOPLE AND PLACES

Another general set of questions on the Big Out There.

1. Four islands make up the Greater Antilles – which of Antigua, Cuba, Jamaica and Puerto Rico is not one of them?

2. What is the name of the nineteen-mile-mile strait that makes up part of the link (with the Dardanelles) between the Asian and European parts of Turkey?

3. The Bass Strait separates Australia from which island territory to the south?

4. Which other European capital city lies nearest geographically to Vilnius, the capital of Lithuania? Is it Minsk, Riga, Tallinn or Warsaw?

5. Allemagne is the name given to which country by the French?

6. Most of us are familiar with cayenne pepper, but where exactly is Cayenne? Is it a city in French Guiana, Haiti, Senegal or the US?

7. The French territory of St Pierre and Miquelon lies off the south coast of which Canadian province?

8. Lake Seneca is the largest of the Finger Lakes and can be found in which US state?

9. Which river passes through Washington DC before emptying into Chesapeake Bay?

10. What is the southernmost region of Spain, containing the cities of Sevilla, Malaga and Granada?

Answers to Quiz 67

1. *Twelfth Night.* These are the opening words of the play, spoken by the lovesick Duke Orsino.

2. Oscar Wilde in uncharacteristically maudlin mood.

3. Mr Darcy in *Pride and Prejudice.*

4. Elizabeth Barrett Browning. Achingly beautiful.

5. *Four Weddings and a Funeral*, when John Hannah as Matthew recites Auden's 'Funeral Blues' at the funeral of his lover, Gareth (Simon Callow).

6. *The Princess Bride.* Best. Film. Ever.

7. Rhett Butler speaks these words to Scarlett O'Hara in *Gone with the Wind.*

8. Heathcliff (from *Wuthering Heights*).

9. Bruce Springsteen; the lines are from 'Born to Run'.

10. *Les Misérables*, by Victor Hugo.

QUIZ 69. THIS OR THAT

Hopefully you've got the hang of these. Twelve expressions: you have to decide whether each one is an album by Thin Lizzy, the Anglo-Irish-American hard-rock band, a horse that won the Grand National, or a horse that appears in the works of J.R.R. Tolkien.

1. Bad Reputation.

2. Aurora's Encore.

3. Fatty Lumpkin.

4. Snowmane.

5. L'Escargot.

6. Black Rose.

7. Silver Birch.

8. Renegade.

9. Little Polveir.

10. Shadowfax.

11. Bill.

12. Johnny the Fox.

Answers to Quiz 68

1. Antigua (and Barbuda) is part of the Leeward Islands – the island missing from the Greater Antilles is Hispaniola.

2. The Bosporus.

3. Tasmania. Australia has six states and two territories – Tasmania is the only non-mainland state.

4. Minsk, the capital of Belarus – Vilnius is in the south-east corner of Lithuania, close to Belarus.

5. Germany.

6. Cayenne is the capital of French Guiana, on the South Atlantic coast of South America.

7. Newfoundland and Labrador (accept just Newfoundland).

8. New York State. The Finger Lakes lie to the south of Lake Ontario to the south-west of the city of Syracuse.

9. Potomac.

10. Andalusia. As Andalusia stretches down to the Strait of Gibraltar, which cuts off the Mediterranean from the Atlantic, this makes it the only European province with a coastline on the Med and the Atlantic.

QUIZ 70. MATCH THE PAINTER

A simple mix-and-match round. Ten painters and ten paintings. Match the painter to his work. Shame we're not doing this book in colour; the picture rounds are among the most popular.

1. Edouard Manet.

2. Thomas Gainsborough.

3. Edward Degas.

4. Pablo Picasso.

5. Michelangelo.

6. David Hockney.

7. Botticelli.

8. Salvador Dalí.

9. Paul Gauguin.

10. Vincent van Gogh.

A. *My Parents.*

B. *La Primavera.*

C. *Dancers.*

D. *Van Gogh's Chair.*

E. *Guernica.*

F. *A Bar at the Folies-Bergère.*

G. *Street in Tahiti.*

H. *The Last Judgment.*

I. *Persistence of Memory.*

J. *The Blue Boy.*

Answers to Quiz 69

1. Thin Lizzy, 1997; it included the hit single 'Dancing in the Moonlight'.

2. Grand National winner, 2013. Aurora's Encore won at 66–1 from Cappa Bleu and Teaforthree.

3. Tolkien; Fatty Lumpkin is Tom Bombadil's horse in that somewhat surreal chapter in *Lord of the Rings*.

4. Tolkien; Snowmane is the horse of Theoden, King of Rohan.

5. Grand National winner, 1975. Having finished third and second behind the great Red Rum in the two previous years, L'Escargot finally got the better of his rival in 1975, winning at 7–2. Red Rum was second again in 1976 behind Rag Trade, but finally got his hat-trick in 1977.

6. Thin Lizzy, 1979 – the seven-minute title track is a four-part mini opera and fabulous.

7. Grand National winner, 2007. Silver Birch won at 33–1 ahead of McKelvey and Slim Pickings.

8. Thin Lizzy, 1981 – the band were past their best by this stage.

9. Grand National winner, 1989. Little Polveir won as a 28–1 shot ahead of West Tip and The Thinker.

10. Tolkien; Shadowfax is the swiftest horse in Rohan, gifted to Gandalf.

11. Tolkien; Bill is the pack-pony that carries the Fellowship's gear from Bree to the Gates of Moria via Rivendell – Sam is delighted when he discovers on the return journey that Bill survived and made his way back to Bree.

12. Thin Lizzy, 1976 – Lizzy were in their pomp and 1976 was an *annus mirabilis* that saw them release two albums, *Jailbreak* and *Johnny the Fox*, which were both outstanding.

QUIZ 71. HAPPY BIRTHDAY

The phrase 'Happy Birthday' appears here in twelve different languages. You have to tell us which language they are. To make it (a lot) easier, we've listed the twelve languages below. Some are approximations of the native language where a different alphabet or writing system is used.

1. *La multi ani.*

2. *Fijne verjaardag.*

3. *Penblwydd hapus.*

4. *Tillykke med fodselsdagen.*

5. *Doğum günün kutlu olsun.*

6. *Feliz cumpleaños.*

7. *Hau'oli lā hānau.*

8. *Boldog születésnapot.*

9. *Selamat ulang tahun.*

10. *Ra whanau koa.*

11. *Bon anniversaire.*

12. *Felican naskigtagon.*

The languages featured are: Danish, Dutch, Esperanto, French, Hawaiian, Hungarian, Indonesian, Maori, Romanian, Spanish, Turkish, Welsh.

Answers to Quiz 70

1. Manet – *A Bar at the Folies-Bergère*.

2. Gainsborough – *The Blue Boy*.

3. Degas – *Dancers*.

4. Picasso – *Guernica*.

5. Michelangelo – *The Last Judgment*.

6. Hockney – *My Parents*.

7. Botticelli – *La Primavera*.

8. Dalí – *Persistence of Memory*.

9. Gauguin – *Street in Tahiti*.

10. Van Gogh – *Van Gogh's Chair* (it wasn't a trick question).

QUIZ 72. RELIGIOUS HISTORY

A history quiz, but focusing on major religious figures or events. We haven't included much on religions, comparative or otherwise, as we don't really feel qualified. We're not religious ourselves, but would hate to offend people of faith by asking crass or incorrectly worded questions.

1. Who was French King Louis XIII's chief minister from 1624 to his death in 1642, a period that included the events fictionalised in Alexandre Dumas' *The Three Musketeers*?

2. What nationality is the current Pontiff, Pope Francis?

3. Who presided over the wedding of Charles and Diana in 1981?

4. In what way are we coming to the end of the year 1438?

5. What did Libby Lane first achieve in January 2015?

6. What name is given to the Vedic teachers and priests in Hinduism?

7. Where is the headquarters of the Church of Jesus Christ of Latter-Day Saints?

8. What is the largest country in the world with a Muslim majority?

9. When Protestantism was established in the early sixteenth century, two main strands developed: one followed the teachings of Martin Luther; whose teachings did the other main faction follow?

10. Which evangelist and preacher developed a long-standing relationship with Queen Elizabeth II after he met her on a visit to London in 1955?

Answers to Quiz 71

1. *La multi ani* – Romanian.

2. *Fijne verjaardag* – Dutch.

3. *Penblwydd hapus* – Welsh.

4. *Tillykke med fodselsdagen* – Danish.

5. *Doğum günün kutlu olsun* – Turkish.

6. *Feliz cumpleaños* – Spanish.

7. *Hau'oli lā hānau* – Hawaiian.

8. *Boldog születésnapot* – Hungarian.

9. *Selamat ulang tahun* – Indonesian.

10. *Ra whanau koa* – Maori.

11. *Bon anniversaire* – French.

12. *Felican naskigtagon* – Esperanto.

QUIZ 73. MIXED BAG

A very eclectic mix of questions here; we're pleased with this set.

1. Which Ford motor car, made between 1950 and 1972, was named after the god of the west wind?

2. Which spin bowler is the all-time leading wicket-taker in Test cricket?

3. Which Australian spin doctor managed the Conservative election victory in 2015, but failed spectacularly to repeat the dose in 2017?

4. Vladimir Kramnik of Russia unified the two conflicting world titles in which game in 2006? Who was the last American to hold the title of World Champion, between 1972 and 1975?

5. Of the countries making up the peninsula of Southeast Asia to the south of China, which is the only one that is entirely land-locked?

6. Which city in Uruguay became important in the 1860s when the 'Liebig's Extract of Meat Company' was based there?

7. Which element, atomic number 6, is the second most abundant in the human body after oxygen?

8. For what condition would you most likely take an ACE inhibitor?

9. What does the IUCN Red List monitor?

10. The comic strip *Peanuts* launched in 1950: who was the author?

Answers to Quiz 72

1. Cardinal Richelieu. Dumas' historical aspect was heavily skewed; while Richelieu, historically, was an arch manipulator and political schemer, there seems little historical evidence that he worked against the crown as persistently as the novel suggests.

2. Argentinian.

3. Robert Runcie, Archbishop of Canterbury; Runcie was Archbishop from 1980 to 1991, when George Carey succeeded him. Rowan Williams took over in 2002 and served until 2013, when the current incumbent, Justin Welby, took office.

4. It is 1438 on the Islamic calendar, which began, in Western terms, in 622 CE.

5. The first woman bishop in the UK, Lane was consecrated in York Minster as the Bishop of Stockport – in 2019 she moved to take over as head of the diocese of Derby.

6. Brahmins.

7. Salt Lake City, Utah. Church of Jesus Christ of Latter-Day Saints is the formal name for what is often referred to as the Mormon Church, begun by John Smith in New York in the late 1820s and relocated later in the century to Utah.

8. Indonesia.

9. John (Jean) Calvin, a French writer and dissident operating out of Geneva in Switzerland.

10. Billy Graham, the North Carolina minister who died in 2018.

QUIZ 74. WHERE IN THE WORLD?

Where indeed? An assortment of questions on places near and far.

1. The Royal Naval College, the Woolwich Artillery and the O2 Arena all lie within which London borough?

2. The Cook Strait divides the two sections of which country in the southern hemisphere?

3. Which European state lies closer to the coast of Syria and Lebanon than to any of its European allies?

4. Which other European capital city lies nearest geographically to Vienna? Is it Berne, Bratislava, Budapest or Prague?

5. Which country is bordered by France, Belgium and Germany and no others?

6. Upolu is the most populated island of which Pacific nation group?

7. The Caribbean island of Hispaniola comprises the Dominican Republic and which other country?

8. Aconcagua is the highest peak in which mountain range, the world's longest?

9. The city of Melbourne was built on the lower side of which river, with its source on Mount Matlock?

10. Which mountain, with strong biblical connections, is the highest point in Turkey?

Answers to Quiz 73

1. Ford Zephyr: In Greek mythology Aeolus was the chief god of the winds, with Boreas looking after the north, or winter wind, Notus the south wind, Eurus the east wind and Zephyrus the west wind.

2. Muttiah Muralitharan, who took an astonishing 800 Test wickets in 133 matches. He also holds the record for wickets in one-day-international matches, with 534.

3. Lynton Crosby.

4. Chess. Bobby Fischer, whose matches against Boris Spassky became synonymous with Russo–American Cold War rivalry.

5. Laos; I've a horrible feeling I may have given the answer to this one away in an earlier quiz. But you probably forgot. One week, at the pub, I asked a question I'd asked two weeks earlier by mistake – half the teams still got it wrong.

6. Fray Bentos; tough question, but what a great bit of triv. Those of us of a certain age were brought up on Fray Bentos without having the foggiest idea where the name came from.

7. Carbon.

8. High blood pressure; ACE stands for angiotensin-converting enzyme, which, if allowed to run riot, can raise the blood pressure; hence the inhibitor.

9. The conservation status of species.

10. Charles M. Schulz.

IUCN (International Union for Conservation of Nature) Red List status
There are seven levels to the IUCN Red List as per current categorisation:

- Extinct – we have failed these species.
- Extinct in the wild – a handful of species exist only in breeding programmes: occasionally these end well and the species is released back into the wild.
- Critically endangered – close to extinction, with breeding programmes under way where possible.

- Endangered – likely to become extinct without necessary action.
- Vulnerable – at risk of extinction without action.
- Near threatened – not currently high risk but may become so without due watchfulness.
- Conservation dependent – species where current rates of predation will lend to risk.

All the above levels would be included on a list of species that it is proscribed to hunt/pick/destroy. Any other species would be listed as 'Least concern' – this includes *homo sapiens*, which is ironic, given that, as a species, we are of greatest concern to the well-being of the planet we share.

QUIZ 75. STUFF (AGAIN)

Random questions on random subjects – random answers not recommended.

1. A law enforcement officer who is in the RCMP would colloquially be known as what?

2. Lundy Island is a popular spot off the coast of Britain for bird-watchers: after what type of bird is Lundy named?

3. Nicholas Hawksmoor was (a) an adventurer in a series of novels by John Buchan; (b) the founder of the East India Company; (c) an architect who designed several notable London churches; or (d) an English nobleman who became a lover of Russian ruler Catherine the Great.

4. Which series of topographical landmarks are named after Sir Hugh Munro (1856–1919)?

5. Genesis and Exodus are the first two books of the Old Testament: what is the third?

6. What was the setting for the novel by Nevil Shute and subsequent film *A Town Like Alice* (1956)?

7. What is the main constituent of falafel?

8. Which paprika-flavoured stew is the most familiar dish in Hungarian cuisine?

9. Which comedian fell off his roof and died while trying to fix his TV aerial in 1999?

10. Piccadilly Weepers are (a) long sideburns with no beard; (b) red and white brogues; (c) Victorian street cleaners; (d) a destructive ivy common to city centres?

Answers to Quiz 74

1. Greenwich. We used to live there; it's a very special place. Standing in the grounds of the Naval College at twilight looking across the river at the twinkly lights of Canary Wharf – great memories.

2. New Zealand; named after James Cook, the explorer, the first European to navigate the strait – the Maori call the strait Raukawa.

3. Cyprus.

4. Bratislava; the cities are only an hour's drive apart, as Bratislava is to the south-west of Slovakia, and Vienna to the north-east of Austria.

5. Luxembourg; the population of the country is only 600,000 people, with 100,000 living in the capital, Luxembourg City. Luxembourg City is one of the EU's bases, with the Court of European Justice sitting there.

6. The Independent State of Samoa (formerly Western Samoa).

7. Haiti; the two countries have similar populations, of around 10.8 million, but Haiti occupies only the smaller western third of the island.

8. The Andes; they run the length of South America for around seven thousand kilometres.

9. Yarra.

10. Mount Ararat: it is accepted among Christians that Ararat was the resting place of Noah's Ark. Scholars deem this unlikely, but then science and faith have never been easy companions, have they?

QUIZ 76. AMERICAN SPORT

A quiz about uniquely American sports. I've always been curious as to how the US managed to cultivate a set of sports entirely different from the rest of the planet. It's another aspect of their insularity, which is at odds with the size and scale of the country. Maybe because it's so big they can develop things purely for their market and not give a monkeys about the rest of us. Although I've always suspected there is an element of fear of exposure and failure involved. Having said that, I do love a baseball match.

1. Which two players, both retired in the last few years, are the joint top-scorers for the US men's football team?

2. Which National League side won the 2001 World Series Baseball against the Yankees, only four years after competing in the league for the first time? Which Florida-based side joined the American League at the same time, making them the joint-newest sides in the competition?

3. After the Montreal Canadiens and the Toronto Maple Leafs, which US team have won ice hockey's premier event, the Stanley Cup, the most times (eleven)?

4. Half of these cities have teams in the America Football League, half do not. Identify the cities that do NOT have a franchise in the league: Austin, Des Moines, Detroit, Indianapolis, Miami, New Orleans, Orlando, San Diego.

5. Ferdinand Alcindor Jr played his best basketball after he changed his name in 1971 to what?

6. Who won their sixth Superbowl in 2009 and became the first team to score six wins in the competition, and who matched them in 2019 when they beat the Los Angeles Rams in the final?

7. And who are the only team to have won consecutive Superbowls twice?

8. Which quarterback, mainly with the Green Bay Packers, won the NFL most valuable player award in 1995, 1996 and 1997, the only player to win three consecutive awards?

9. Which player, nicknamed the Georgia Peach, holds the record for the highest batting average at .366, after a twenty-five-year career at the beginning of the last century?

10. Which Philadelphia Warriors superstar of the 1960s enjoyed a run of 126 basketball matches scoring twenty-plus points in every one?

Answers to Quiz 75

1. A Mountie – the RCMP is the Royal Canadian Mounted Police.

2. Lundy is another word for a puffin.

3. Hawksmoor (1661–1736) designed several churches, including Spitalfields and St Alfege in Greenwich. He worked with Christopher Wren as a young man, and later for John Vanbrugh, and recently his reputation has risen to sit alongside those luminaries.

4. Scottish peaks or hills over a certain height (3,000 feet), as catalogued by the Scottish Mountaineering Club.

5. Leviticus.

6. A Japanese POW camp for women.

7. Chickpea; it can be mixed with various other ingredients (we use broad bean and red pepper at the pub) and is then shallow- or deep-fried.

8. Goulash; it became a popular thrifty dish across Europe after the war, as the strong paprika flavouring could mask cheap cuts of meat.

9. Rod Hull.

10. Long sideburns on a beardless face. Tried it; looked awful on me.

QUIZ 77. AMERICAN ENGLISH

Ten American words we'd like you to translate. No match-up list here; just give us the equivalent in Queen's English.

1. Realtor.
2. Garbanzo bean.
3. Chips.
4. Eggplant.
5. Sedan.
6. Peeler.
7. Faucet.
8. Billfold.
9. Thumb tack.
10. Vest.

Answers to Quiz 76

1. Clint Dempsey and Landon Donovan; Dempsey managed his goals in sixteen fewer games and was pretty good for Fulham for five years.

2. Arizona Diamondbacks; that victory made them the fastest new admission to the WSB to win the pennant. They have won their mini-league, the National League West Division, on five occasions. Tampa Bay (Devil) Rays compete in the American League; they won the American League in 2008 but lost the WSB to the Philadelphia Phillies. They have won their own mini-league only twice, but they compete against two wealthy clubs in the Yankees and the Red Sox.

3. Detroit Red Wings.

4. Austin, Des Moines, Orlando, San Diego. From 1961 to 2016 the San Diego Chargers were in the old AFO and later the AFC, but the franchise moved back to its original home in LA for the 2017 season.

5. Kareem Abdul-Jabbar; not being a huge basketball fan, I remember him more for playing the co-pilot in *Airplane!* . . .

6. Pittsburgh Steelers; New England Patriots.

7. Also the Pittsburgh Steelers, in 1974 and 1975, then again in 1978 and 1979.

8. Brett Favre.

9. Ty Cobb.

10. Wilt Chamberlain.

QUIZ 78. WORLD OF FILM

A slightly trickier set of movie questions – 6/10 would be a perfectly respectable score.

1. What are the names of the father and mother of the Addams Family, played by Raul Julia and Anjelica Huston in two films (1991 and 1993) directed by Barry Sonnenfeld?

2. *Raindrops Keep Falling on My Head* won an Academy Award as best movie song: in which 1969 box-office smash was the song used?

3. Where does most of the action take place in Nicolas Roeg's creepy 1973 thriller, *Don't Look Now*, starring Donald Sutherland and Julie Christie?

4. What part was played by Max Von Sydow in the 1965 Hollywood epic *The Greatest Story Ever Told*?

5. In which 1999 film do Al Pacino and Russell Crowe star as a journalist and a whistle-blower trying to expose secrets of the tobacco industry?

6. *Billy Elliot*, the hit 2000 film starring Jamie Bell as an aspiring ballet dancer, featured which enduring British actress as his tutor, Mrs Wilkinson?

7. Who played Ruth Ellis, the last woman to be hanged in Britain, in Mike Newell's 1985 account of her crime and trial, *Dance with a Stranger*?

8. Who endowed the removal of a single glove with a world of understated eroticism in the title role of Gilda in Charles Vidor's 1946 movie of that name?

9. What was the title of Bernardo Bertolucci's controversial erotic drama starring Marlon Brando, which caused something of a furore on its release in 1972?

10. What does the 1975 film *The Man Who Would Be King*, starring Sean Connery and Michael Caine, have in common with Disney's *The Jungle Book*?

Answers to Quiz 77

1. Estate agent.

2. Chickpea; a garbanozo is actually just one type of chickpea, but in the US it's a generic term for all types.

3. Crisps; not to confused with chips, which are fries in the US.

4. Aubergine; it is usually called brinjal in most Asian cookbooks. Bracketed as a vegetable, aubergine is technically a berry.

5. Saloon car.

6. Stripper; in English the term Peeler is an old term for a Police Constable, from Prime Minister Robert Peel, who initiated the force.

7. Tap.

8. Wallet.

9. Drawing pin; tack is still used for a short nail employed in certain construction projects, for example attaching a waterproof layer to a shed roof.

10. Waistcoat, whereas in the UK a vest is a sleeveless undergarment.

QUIZ 79. NAMESAKES

Each question has two answers, which feature the same surname. So 'American actor who is only ever six steps away, and brilliant polymath born in 1561 – scientist, legal adviser, politician, writer' – would yield an answer of Kevin and Francis Bacon. Or it should do.

1. A prolific England goal-scorer and the film *The Red Shoes*.

2. A World Cup Winner with England in 1966 and Ali G.

3. A great British Olympian and a great British acting dynasty.

4. Actress turned MP turned actress and a civil rights activist and former Democratic presidential nominee.

5. An Australian film actress and a Rolling Stones drummer.

6. An American golfer and Kurt Cobain's missus.

7. England's most-capped full back and *Minder*'s boss.

8. *Twilight* meets *Star Trek: The Next Generation*.

9. The main character in *Cabaret* and a gentleman *To the Manor Born*.

10. Racing-car father and son and sexy Victorian ingénue.

Answers to Quiz 78

1. Gomez and Morticia; one of cinema's great loving couples.

2. *Butch Cassidy and the Sundance Kid*; B.J. Thomas sang the song (written by Burt Bacharach and Hal David) while Butch (Paul Newman) bicycles round the house of Etta (Katharine Ross), the girlfriend of Kid (Robert Redford).

3. Venice; the foggy city provides a perfect backdrop for the film's wintry tones.

4. Jesus; it was a narrative of the life of Christ.

5. *The Insider*; it was Mann's follow-up to *Heat*, also starring Pacino, alongside Robert De Niro.

6. Julie Walters.

7. Miranda Richardson, with Rupert Everett as her obnoxious lover, David Blakely.

8. Rita Hayworth.

9. *Last Tango in Paris*.

10. Both were based on works by Rudyard Kipling.

QUIZ 80. BASTILLE DAY WEEK

A set of general questions on the days around 14 July – this quiz actually took place on Monday 16 July 2018.

1. In which year did the citizens of Paris storm the Bastille prison on 14 July?

2. Which businessman and later recluse set a new world record for flying around the world (ninety-one hours), completing the flight on 14 July, 1938?

3. Which enduring rock-and-roll band performed their first concert at the Marquee in London on 12 July 1962?

4. On 13 July 1878, Serbia, Montenegro and Romania became independent of which fading super-power?

5. Which debilitating disease was first given a name by Emil Kraepelin in his 1910 book, *Clinical Psychiatry*, released on 15 July?

6. Which piece of music was premiered on 17 July 1717 when it was played by fifty musicians for King George I aboard a barge on the Thames?

7. What was changed from eighteen to twenty-one by American Federal Law on 17 July 1984?

8. In 1903, on 18 July, Maurice Garin won the first running of which sporting event, still going annually?

9. On 11 July 1924, Eric Liddell won GB a gold medal in the 400 metres at the Olympic Games: which famous film portrayed the story of Liddell and other British athletes?

10. Who took office as the first President of the Russian Federation on 10 July 1991?

Answers to Quiz 79

1. Alan Shearer, Southampton, Blackburn, Newcastle, England and subsequently a pundit with the BBC; Moira Shearer's career-defining performance came aged twenty-two in the Powell and Pressburger drama – she got the role as much for her ballet training as for her acting.

2. George and Sasha Baron Cohen.

3. Steve, the rower; and the Redgraves. Michael, his children Vanessa, Corin and Lynn, Vanessa's children, Natasha and Joely, and Corin's daughter, Jemma.

4. Glenda Jackson, Academy Award winner and former MP for Hampstead and Highgate; and Jesse Jackson.

5. Naomi Watts (*Mulholland Dr*, *The Impossible*); and Charlie Watts.

6. Davis Love III, 1997 PGA winner and Ryder Cup player; and Courtney Love, frontwoman of American grunge band, Hole.

7. Ashley Cole, Arsenal, Chelsea and England; and George Cole, the actor who played wheeler and dealer Arthur Daley, looked after by his minder, Terry McCann (Dennis Waterman).

8. Kristen Stewart (Bella in the *Twilight* movies); and Patrick Stewart (Captain Jean-Luc Picard in *Star Trek: The Next Generation*).

9. Sally Bowles (played by Liza Minnelli in the film); and Peter Bowles (who played Richard DeVere in the TV sitcom).

10. Graham Hill (twice World Championship winner, in 1962 and 1968), and his son Damon, (who won in 1996); and Fanny Hill, subject of a Victorian erotic novel.

QUIZ 81. BARBED TONGUES

Some wonderful quotes here; some catty, some snide, some clever and some downright rude.

1. 'It is no use telling me there are bad aunts and good aunts. At the core, they are all alike. Sooner or later, out pops the cloven hoof.' Which comic literary figure?

2. 'Christian Dior's New Look consists of clothes by a man who doesn't know women, never had one, and dreams of being one.' Which earlier fashion designer wasn't onside with the latest wave.

3. Which opposition politician did Winston Churchill describe as a 'modest man with much to be modest about'.

4. 'One has no great hopes for Birmingham. I always say there is something direful in the sound.' Which author, in a book of 1816?

5. 'He can lie out of both sides of his mouth at the same time, and if he ever caught himself telling the truth, he'd lie just to keep his hand in.' Harry S. Truman on which other American politician?

6. 'I fart in your general direction! Your mother was a hamster and your father smells of elderberries.' Which film?

7. Which New Labour politician could 'skulk in broad daylight' according to columnist Simon Hoggart?

8. 'He wears a No. 10 jersey. I thought it was his position but it turns out to be his IQ.' George Best on which famous footballer?

9. 'He has a face like a warthog that has been stung by a wasp . . .' Which fellow professional golfer was Ryder-Cup-player-turned-commentator David Feherty describing?

10. 'I am as shallow as a puddle.' Which modern writer created a diarist who could easily have uttered these words herself?

Answers to Quiz 80

1. 1789.

2. Howard Hughes.

3. The Rolling Stones.

4. Ottoman Empire.

5. Alzheimer's.

6. Handel's *Water Music*; born in Germany in 1685, Georg Friedrich Handel moved to England in his twenties and became a nationalised British citizen in 1727. The success of his choral work *Messiah* (1742) cemented his reputation and he was buried with full state honours in 1759.

7. The legal age for purchasing alcohol – states vary greatly in how they deal with actual consumption.

8. The Tour de France.

9. *Chariots of Fire*, which highlighted the competitive rivalry between Liddell, a devout Christian who refused to compete on a Sunday, and the Jewish sprinter Harold Abraham.

10. Boris Yeltsin. He probably had a drink to celebrate.

QUIZ 82. MUSIC

A mix of music questions. Not the easiest; be happy with 5 or 6/10.

1. 'What's that coming over the hill, is it a monster?' *Monster* was a 2006 hit for which Welsh pop-rock band?

2. Who was the bass player and lyricist of the Manic Street Preachers who went missing in 2005 and was declared dead in absentia in 2008?

3. What was the third, final and most successful album by the Jimi Hendrix Experience? Why was it mildly controversial? Which Bob Dylan song did Hendrix famously cover on the record?

4. What was Holland-Dozier-Holland's primary contribution to popular music?

5. What was the first UK single (and No. 1) for the twenty-one-year-old Buddy Holly, released under his band name, The Crickets?

6. What personal aspect of his life drove the work on Bob Dylan's 1979 *Slow Train Coming*? Who provided the album's distinctive guitar playing?

7. What was the name of the band with which Beyoncé first enjoyed chart success? Which other member of the band had a No. 1 hit with 'Dilemma'?

8. Which media franchise, back then principally a magazine, published the first US popular music chart in 1940?

9. What was Mariah Carey's third and best-selling album from 1993, her first to top the charts on both sides of the Atlantic? What was Carey's first UK No. 1 hit single, a cover of a Badfinger song taken from this album?

10. Strathclyde Park, Balado airfield and Strathallan Castle all played host to which festival, which ran from 1994 to 2016?

Answers to Quiz 81

1. Bertie Wooster.

2. Coco Chanel.

3. Clement Attlee.

4. Jane Austen (from *Emma*).

5. Richard Nixon.

6. *Monty Python and the Holy Grail*.

7. Peter Mandelson.

8. Paul Gascoigne.

9. Colin Montgomerie.

10. Helen Fielding, creator of *Bridget Jones*.

QUIZ 83. THIS OR THAT

These twelve folk are either an Australian fast bowler, a character from *Grand Theft Auto V*, or an MP sitting in the UK Parliament in December 2018.

1. Terry Alderman.

2. Stephen Lloyd.

3. Michael De Santa.

4. Garth McKenzie.

5. Thangam Debbonaire.

6. Keith Miller.

7. Trevor Philips.

8. Devon Weston.

9. Brett Lee.

10. Graham Brady.

11. Greg Hands.

12. Lester Crest.

Answers to Quiz 82

1. The Automatic.

2. Richey Edwards (accept Richey James – James was his middle name and he went by this moniker at times).

3. *Electric Ladyland*; it had naked women on the cover, in a very sixties summer-of-love kind of way; 'All Along the Watchtower'.

4. They were the Tamla Motown house song-writing team. The trio wrote ten of the Supremes' twelve Billboard No. 1 singles, most of the Four Tops' big hits, plus songs for Marvin Gaye and Martha Reeves, as well as the classic 'Band of Gold' for Freda Payne.

5. 'That'll be the Day'; it was Holly's only UK No. 1 in his lifetime, his next chart topper being the posthumously released 'It Doesn't Matter Anymore'.

6. It was his first album after embracing Christianity; Mark Knopfler, the main man in Dire Straits.

7. Destiny's Child and Kelly Rowland.

8. Billboard.

9. *Music Box*; the single was 'Without You', written by Pete Ham and Tom Evans – it had already been a massive hit for Harry Nilsson.

10. T in the Park.

QUIZ 84. TV CRIME

Everyone loves a crime drama on TV, otherwise they wouldn't make so many of them. From the early days of *Dixon of Dock Green* and American shows like *Perry Mason*, good cop shows have always been ratings winners. Some are formulaic and get a bit tiresome, others challenge and provoke as effectively as any contemporary non-genre drama.

1. Suranne Jones and Lesley Sharp – what's the crime drama?

2. Who took the title role in the 1960s-set crime drama *Inspector George Gently*?

3. Which anthology crime series is loosely based (or inspired) by a 1996 Coen Brothers film?

4. Who co-stars alongside Idris Elba as the barking mad Alice Morgan in detective series *Luther*?

5. If Krister Henriksson played the title role in the Swedish adaptation of Henning Mankell's stories, who played the English version?

6. The year 2018 saw the twenty-first series of which long-running crime series, which many predicted would fade when its lead actress left after series eight?

7. In the US comedy crime drama *Castle*, Nathan Fillion plays a civilian helping an LAPD police unit solve crimes: what is his civilian occupation?

8. Who led the cold case unit in the BBC's crime series *Waking the Dead*?

9. Steven Bochco, who died last year, devised a number of crime procedurals, including one that lasted twelve years and depicted the struggles of the 15th squad in Manhattan: what was that series?

10. If Woody Harrelson and Matthew McConaughey were Season 1, and Colin Farrell and Rachel McAdams were Season 2, who is Season 3 and what is the programme?

Answers to Quiz 83

1. Terry Alderman took 170 Test wickets for Australia between 1981 and 1991. He had a particularly fine record against England, but is less kindly remembered for missing a year through injury after trying to rugby tackle a pitch invader in Perth, and for missing three years after joining an unsanctioned tour of Apartheid South Africa.

2. Stephen Lloyd is the MP for Eastbourne. He won back his seat as a Lib Dem in 2017 (having briefly lost it in 2015) but has since resigned his party whip over their opposition to Brexit.

3. Michael De Santa is one of three playable characters in *GTAV*.

4. Garth McKenzie took 246 Test wickets for Australia and was the spear-head of their attack during the 1960s.

5. Thangam Debbonaire is the Labour MP for Bristol West.

6. Keith Miller enjoyed a fruitful fast-bowling partnership with Ray Lindwall, and took 170 Test wickets, as well as scoring 2,958 Test runs. Arguably Australia's greatest all-rounder, Miller was a handsome Golden Boy who had served in the Royal Australian Air Force in the Second World War.

7. Trevor Philips is another playable character in *GTAV*, a comrade and sometimes rival to De Santa.

8. Devin Weston is a corrupt businessman and antagonistic NPC (non-playable character) in *GTAV*.

9. Brett Lee, along with Glenn McGrath and Jason Gillespie, made up the triumvirate of Australian fast bowlers who helped their team dominate Test cricket in the late 1990s to early 2000s. Lee finished with 310 Test wickets and was a competent attacking lower-order batsman.

10. Graham Brady has been MP for the north-west constituency of Altrincham and Sale West since 1997, and is the Chairman of the influential 1922 Committee within the Conservative Party.

11. Greg Hands is the Conservative MP for Chelsea and Fulham.

12. Lester Crest is an NPC in *GTAV*, a hacker and business associate of the protagonists.

QUIZ 85. MIXED BAG

Another assortment of neat nuggets.

1. What was George Orwell's last book, published in 1949, the year before his death?

2. Members of which famous Italian family were the basis for the Magi in Botticelli's *Adoration of the Magi*?

3. Queen Elizabeth II signs herself ER. For what does the R stand?

4. Which planet in our solar system has moons named after characters in plays by William Shakespeare?

5. *Hue and Cry* (1946), starring Alistair Sim and Jack Warner, was the first in a string of successful comedy films to come out of which British studio?

6. Which comedy team gave rock band Queen a couple of album titles?

7. If he was played by James Garner in the TV series that started in 1958, who played him in the 1994 movie?

8. What is the name given to a poker hand containing two black Aces and two black Eights?

9. Who did John Hinckley try to assassinate in 1981?

10. Who launched a New Look in 1947 that took the fashion world by storm?

Answers to Quiz 84

1. *Scott & Bailey*. Lesley Sharp plays DC Janet Scott and Suranne Jones plays DC (later DS) Rachel Bailey; the show ran for five series, ending in 2011.

2. Martin Shaw, with Lee Ingleby as DS John Bacchus. The final series of this bleak view of the north-east in the 1960s aired in 2017.

3. *Fargo*; the show has run for three well-received seasons to date, with each season set in the same location but at a different point in time.

4. Ruth Wilson; Alice is a psychopath and murderer who evades conviction and becomes an unlikely ally for Luther.

5. Kenneth Branagh played Wallander in the UK TV versions of the stories.

6. *Silent Witness*, which seemed to have run its course when Amanda Burton left.

7. Crime-fiction writer; he is writing a series of books using the LAPD officer he shadows as a role model for his protagonist, Nikki Heat – surprise, surprise, they fall in love . . .

8. Peter Boyd (Trevor Eve).

9. *NYPD Blue*; Bochco also created *Hill Street Blues* and *L.A. Law*.

10. Mahershala Ali. The show is *True Detective*: like *Fargo*, it is what is termed an 'anthology series', where each series has separate characters and incidents, but each is also loosely connected.

QUIZ 86. HOW'S YOUR LATIN?

It's impossible to overstate how key Latin is to most Western languages – hence the continuation of its teaching long after it seemed irrelevant to the modern day. Communication has become frighteningly dumbed down in the twenty-first century, and etymology seems to hold little fascination for anyone other than pedants like me. So here's a round for you fellow pedants.

1. Which word to describe an extra reward is taken from the Latin adjective for good?

2. What Latin phrase is often used when something is done for the public good rather than personal gain, especially in legal circumstances?

3. The Latin phrase 'ad hoc' is used to describe what circumstance?

4. In which film does the phrase *Romani ite domum* appear a hundred times?

5. *Malleus Scotorum* was a nickname given to King Edward I of England. What does it mean?

6. 'E.g.' is a Latin abbreviation meaning 'for example'. What does it stand for? (The correct spelling is needed for a full point.)

7. Which Latin term means pretty much the same as 'you scratch my back and I'll scratch yours'?

8. What is the subject matter of the book, *Malleus Malificarum*, published by the Catholic cleric, Heinrich Kramer in 1487?

9. Which philosopher first expounded the Latin proposition, *cogito, ergo sum* – 'I think, therefore I am'?

10. Which rock band take their name from the Latin for the current state of affairs?

Answers to Quiz 85

1. *Nineteen Eighty-four*. He wrote it in 1948 and just transposed the last two digits to give him the futuristic setting.

2. The Medici family; it was common among Renaissance painters to paint their patrons or sponsors in a heroic or saintly light.

3. *Regina*, the Latin word for queen.

4. Uranus. The five major moons are Ariel, Miranda, Umbriel, Titania and Oberon: while Ariel is a character in *The Tempest*, and a number of the irregular moons are named from that play, Ariel and Umbriel in this instance are spirits in Alexander Pope's epic satirical poem, *The Rape of the Lock*.

5. Ealing studios – the list of hits includes *The Ladykillers*, *Kind Hearts and Coronets* and *The Lavender Hill Mob*. It was the heyday of British movie making. The studios are still working today.

6. *A Night at the Opera* (1975) and *A Day at the Races* (1976) were Queen albums with titles from Marx Brothers films released in 1935 and 1937 respectively.

7. Mel Gibson – the character is Brett Maverick (Garner played his father in the film).

8. A dead man's hand – this was, according to legend, the last hand dealt to Wild Bill Hickok before he was killed.

9. Ronald Reagan – Hinckley missed the president but Reagan was hit and wounded by a ricochet.

10. Christian Dior.

QUIZ 87. WHAT'S MY LINE?

Four people, all sharing a common thread. All you need to do is tell us what *they* do.

1. Simon Starling, Wolfgang Tillmans, Keith Tyson, Richard Wright.

2. Mitch McConnell, Bernie Sanders, Marco Rubio, Dick Durbin.

3. Mr Mistoffelees, Thomas O'Malley, Crookshanks, Jones.

4. Cash Asmussen, Andrea Atzeni, Javier Castellano, Christophe Soumillon.

5. John Bodkin Adams, Charles Peace, David Berkovitz, Harold Shipman.

6. Amy Zoller, Elsa Schiaparelli, Tom Ford, Dirk Bikkembergs.

7. Katie Bell, Padma Patil, Alicia Spinnet, Susan Bones.

8. Bobbie Wickham, Aline Hemingway, Gertrude Winkworth, Madeline Bassett.

9. Joseph Paxton, Norman Foster, Jørn Utzon, Renzo Piano.

10. Karol Wojtyla, Giovanni Montini, Roderic de Borja, Nicholas Breakspear.

Answers to Quiz 86

1. Bonus.

2. *Pro bono.*

3. Often mistakenly used to mean random, whereas it means almost the opposite: specifically tailored to a situation; for example, in the event of a flood, an ad hoc solution might be to use sandbags to shore up the affected area, rather than the more obvious long-term solution of improving the drainage.

4. *Monty Python's Life of Brian*; when John Cleese's centurion catches Brian scrawling on the city wall, he corrects his grammar and makes him write 'Romans go home' on the wall a hundred times.

5. Hammer of the Scots; Edward I took advantage of the lack of an obvious successor to the Scottish throne to try and rule the country for some time – his main opponent was William Wallace, whom he eventually captured and executed.

6. *Exempli gratia.*

7. *Quid pro quo*; the exchange of one favour for another – just watch the Hitchcock movie *Strangers on a Train*.

8. Witchcraft; some of the author's suggestions of how to combat witchcraft make the blood run cold, particularly when you realise that the Church used these methods as an excuse to weed out undesirables rather than criminals.

9. René Descartes; the phrase appears in its Latin form in the key 1644 work *Principles of Philosophy*, but had earlier appeared in French ('*Je pense, suis je donc*') in the earlier pamphlet, *Discourse on the Method of Rightly Conducting One's Reason and of Seeking Truth in the Sciences*.

10. Status Quo, playing under that name since 1967.

QUIZ 88. THE STATES

A round on places in the United States – picked at random, this could make a book all by itself.

1. San Juan, with a population of around 400,000, is the capital of which US territory?

2. Manhattan, Brooklyn, Staten Island: these are three of the five New York boroughs. What are the other two?

3. The city of St Louis lies on which river?

4. Which state lies between New York and Rhode Island on the Eastern Seaboard of the US?

5. What is the only US state beginning with a D?

6. Mount Whitney in the Sierra Nevada is the highest peak in which US state?

7. Milwaukee and Green Bay, Wisconsin, are ports on which body of water?

8. Which two US states have a largest city called Portland?

9. What was the US's first National Park, established in 1872 across the states of Wyoming, Montana and Idaho?

10. In which US state is the Wild West town of Tombstone; is it Idaho, California, Arkansas or Arizona?

Answers to Quiz 87

1. Turner Prize winners from the 2000s (2005, 2000, 2002, 2009 respectively).

2. US Senators: McConnell is a Republican from Kentucky and leads his party in the Senate; Sanders is a left-leaning Independent who stood for the Democratic nomination against Hillary Clinton in 2016; Rubio (Republican, Florida) also stood in 2016, pulling out of the race when Trump beat him in his home state; Durbin is the Democratic whip and a Senator for Illinois.

3. Fictional cats; Mr Mistoffelees is from T.S. Eliot's *Old Possum's Book of Practical Cats*, O'Malley is the alley cat in Disney's *The Aristocats*, Crookshanks is Hermione's cat in the Harry Potter books and Jones was the cat aboard the spaceship in *Alien*.

4. Jockeys.

5. Serial killers.

6. Fashion designers.

7. Harry Potter characters.

8. Characters from P.G. Wodehouse's Jeeves and Wooster series.

9. Architects.

10. Popes – Breakspear is notable as the only British-born pope, serving from 1154 until 1159.

QUIZ 89. AGGREGATOR

Question 1 has one answer, question two has two, and so forth. Lots of points up for grabs. If you go the whole hog and count this as fifty-five, I tend to think that thirty-five is a good score. For questions six to ten, it's always hard to remember ALL the answers.

1. Name the only team (to the end of the 2018–19 season) to have finished a Premier League season unbeaten.

2. Name two countries on mainland Europe (exclude city states) that share a land border with only one other.

3. Name the three movies that make Daniel Day-Lewis the only actor to date to win three Best Actor Academy Awards.

4. You board the Jubilee Line at West Hampstead to get to Canary Wharf. Fill in the gaps in your stopping points: Finchley Road, Swiss Cottage, _____, Baker Street, Bond Street, _____, Westminster, Waterloo, _____, London Bridge, Bermondsey, _____, Canary Wharf.

5. Adam West was the first big screen Batman in the 1960s. Name the five actors to have played the role in an official movie since Tim Burton revived the character in 1989.

6. Name the six monarchs who ruled England for over forty years.

7. Name the seven children of Arthur and Molly Weasley in the Harry Potter world.

8. Name the first eight films directed by Quentin Tarantino (to 2019; films in two parts count as one entry).

9. Name the nine male players who have won over a hundred England caps at football. (Given that none of the current squad have hit fifty at the time of writing, there will be no change for a few years.)

10. Starting with the current No. 2 to Donald Trump (as of January 2019), name the last ten US vice-presidents.

Answers to Quiz 88

1. Puerto Rico.

2. Queens and the Bronx.

3. Mississippi. The giant river flows through or borders ten states on its journey of over 2,300 miles, watering the cities of Minnesota, St Louis, Memphis and Baton Rouge (among others), before emptying into the Gulf of Mexico at New Orleans.

4. Connecticut. Only Rhode Island and Delaware are smaller by area, but Connecticut is populous and wealthy, boasting the highest income per head of population in the US.

5. Delaware.

6. California. The range spreads into Nevada and is home to Lake Tahoe and Yosemite National Park among its many features.

7. Lake Michigan, which also has Chicago at its south-western corner.

8. Oregon and Maine. Although Salem and Augusta are the capital cities of these states, both have a Portland. Oddly, neither Salem nor Augusta is the one most people have heard of – the witch town Salem is in Massachusetts and the golf course Augusta is in Georgia.

9. Yellowstone.

10. Arizona: the town's population of around 1,300 is boosted by nearly half a million tourists – more than 340 per person!

QUIZ 90. MOVIES

How are we on pugilism in the movies? Identify the actor (from the list) who played the boxer in these movies (no name given for the boxer means that the movie title is also the name of the boxer).

1. *Kid Galahad* (1962).

2. *Ali* (2001).

3. Micky Ward in *The Fighter* (2010).

4. Rocky Graziano in *Somebody Up There Likes Me* (1956).

5. Rubin Carter in *The Hurricane* (1999).

6. Maggie Fitzgerald in *Million Dollar Baby* (2004).

7. Apollo Creed in *Rocky I, II* and *III* (1976, 1979, 1982).

8. Adonis Johnson Creed in *Creed* (2015).

9. Jake La Motta in *Raging Bull* (1980).

10. James J. Braddock in *Cinderella Man* (2005).

A. Russell Crowe.

B. Robert De Niro.

C. Michael B. Jordan.

D. Paul Newman.

E. Elvis Presley.

F. Will Smith.

G. Hilary Swank.

H. Carl Weathers.

I. Mark Wahlberg.

J. Denzel Washington.

Answers to Quiz 89

1. Arsenal in 2003–4.

2. Denmark (borders only Germany) and Portugal (borders only Spain).

3. *My Left Foot*, *There Will Be Blood* and *Lincoln*.

4. St John's Wood; Green Park; Southwark; Canada Water.

5. Michael Keaton (two films); Val Kilmer (one); George Clooney (one); Christian Bale (three) and Ben Affleck (one and one upcoming).

6. Elizabeth II, Victoria, George III, Henry III, Edward III, Elizabeth I.

7. Bill, Charlie, Percy, Fred and George (twins), Ron, Ginny.

8. *Reservoir Dogs*, *Pulp Fiction*, *Jackie Brown*, *Kill Bill*, *Death Proof*, *Inglourious Basterds*, *Django Unchained*, *Hateful Eight*.

9. Peter Shilton, Wayne Rooney, David Beckham, Steven Gerrard, Bobby Moore, Ashley Cole, Bobby Charlton, Frank Lampard, Billy Wright.

10. Running backwards: Mike Pence (Trump); Joe Biden (Obama); Dick Cheney (Bush Jr); Al Gore (Clinton); Dan Quayle (Bush Snr); George H.W. Bush (Reagan); Walter Mondale (Carter); Nelson Rockefeller (Ford); Gerald Ford (Nixon; Ford was promoted to president on Nixon's resignation); Spiro Agnew (Nixon; resigned, and replaced by Gerald Ford).

QUIZ 91. ITALY

1. If you ate polpette in Italy, what would you be eating?

2. Which Italian city was once the centre of a republic that survived from the seventh century until 1797? What nickname was applied to the republic (and later the city itself as part of Italy)?

3. If the region of Calabria makes up the toe of the boot-shape of Italy, which region makes up the heel; is it Abruzzo, Campania, Puglia or Sardinia?

4. Maranello, a town in northern Italy, is the home of which iconic Italian manufacturer?

5. Which Italian port is Italy's busiest and also the biggest in the Mediterranean?

6. Who did Italy beat in their first Six Nations match in February 2000?

7. An assault on the site of which sixth-century abbey saw the Allied forces in Italy suffer heavy losses en route to Rome?

8. Umberto Eco, who died in 2016, is best remembered for which 1980 medieval mystery, which combined thriller elements with theological and philosophical literary musings?

9. How did no club manage to win the Serie A title in 2004–5?

10. Which family held control of the powerful republic based around the city of Firenze (Florence) for the bulk of the fifteenth century, when the republic was at its zenith?

Answers to Quiz 90

1. E: Elvis Presley.

2. F: Will Smith. The film was generally well received, especially Smith's performance, but it lost a ton of money.

3. I: Mark Wahlberg. It was Christian Bale who picked up an Academy Award as Ward's half-brother, Dicky.

4. D: Paul Newman. Graziano was a rags-to-riches middleweight boxer, not to be confused with the undefeated heavyweight champion Rocky Marciano.

5. J: Denzel Washington. Carter was the boxer framed and jailed for murder, immortalised in this movie and in the Bob Dylan song 'Hurricane', which was part of a campaign to have him released from prison.

6. G: Hilary Swank.

7. H: Carl Weathers played the original rival to Rocky Balboa.

8. C: Michael B. Jordan played Balboa's son in the recent reboot of the series, with Stallone still there as an ageing Balboa mentoring the young fighter.

9. B: Robert De Niro, who played the boxer with famous intensity, and was coached by La Motta himself to fight in a similar style – De Niro became mightily proficient and won a couple of amateur fights that he undertook to enhance authenticity.

10. A: Russell Crowe.

QUIZ 92. HISTORY MIXED BAG

Some history questions from across the ages.

1. If you fought in the ANZAC division in the Second World War, where would you most likely be from?

2. Which of the Seven Wonders of the Ancient World was located at the palace of Nebuchadnezzar south of modern-day Baghdad?

3. Which Polish politician was voted in as President of the European Council in 2014 and again in 2017?

4. Which British statesman and figure of Empire featured on Alfred Leete's iconic 1914 recruiting poster for the British army?

5. The Roman Emperor Augustus died in 44 CE: what was the name of his nominated successor, who cemented his position by murdering Augustus' son, Agrippa Postumus?

6. Which historical figure is sometimes known as the Maid of Orléans?

7. What year is MCCLXIV?

8. Bulgaria, Czechoslovakia, Romania, Yugoslavia: which of these countries was not a signatory to the 1955 Warsaw Pact?

9. Anton Cermak, Mayor of Chicago, was shot and killed in 1933 by an assassin. Who was believed to be the intended target, with whom Cermak was shaking hands at the time?

10. Who shot Billy the Kid in 1881?

Answers to Quiz 91

1. Meatballs; we serve some mightily tasty ones in the dining room at the pub . . .

2. Venice; La Serenissima (it translates as 'most serene').

3. Puglia; Basilicata fills in the space between (the arch of the foot), while Campania, including the city of Naples, is the shin. The principal city of Puglia is the coastal city of Bari.

4. Ferrari; the company was founded by Enzo Ferrari in 1939 and started manufacturing commercially in 1947.

5. Genoa, in Liguria, the coastal province in the north-west spur of Italy.

6. Scotland. Times have got a lot tougher; the Azzurri have won only twelve matches in twenty seasons at the top table, and have still never beaten England.

7. Monte Cassino; the retreating German army fought for every inch of ground as the Allies pushed north, despite having lost their Italian allies.

8. *The Name of the Rose*; later made into a film (which wisely used only the narrative elements) starring Sean Connery and Christian Slater as his young apprentice.

9. A major match-fixing scandal was exposed and Juventus were stripped of the title (and runners-up Milan were also implicated). Serie A and scandals have been familiar partners over the years.

10. The Medici family – they produced four popes from within the family, which helped them cement their power base.

QUIZ 93. RADIO DAYS

Quiz books tend to have lots of questions on TV and few on radio. This one is no exception, so here is a quiz for those of you who like your fix of the wireless, as it once was known. And is again, in these days of Bluetooth and connectivity.

1. Who presented the first *Radio 1 Breakfast Show* at 7.00 a.m. on 30 September 1967?

2. The first song heard on Radio 1, apart from intros and jingles, was 'Flowers in the Rain'. Which 1960s pop-rock band released this song?

3. Who has hosted the Live Lounge since 2015, where artists perform either a cover version or one of their own songs live on air?

4. The Radio 1 Roadshow has been rebadged as what for the modern era?

5. Which Manchester band played the most sessions (thirty-two) for John Peel?

6. Which singer did Andy Peebles interview two days before his (the singer's) death in December 1980?

7. Which broadcasting legend made his radio debut in 1967 on Radio 2's *Late Night Extra* show?

8. Who opened his first *Radio 1 Breakfast Show* with the quip 'From now until they fire his ass, the saviour of Radio 1 is here'?

9. Who was the first female presenter of the *Radio 1 Breakfast Show*?

10. Whose 2015 single 'Living for Love', caused a controversy when it was omitted from Radio 1 playlists, with suggestions of ageism ensuing?

Answers to Quiz 92

1. Australia or New Zealand (the Australia and New Zealand Army Corps).

2. The Hanging Gardens of Babylon.

3. Donald Tusk.

4. Lord Kitchener. The former military commander was Secretary of State for War at the beginning of the First World War until 2016, when the ship on which he was sailing to Russia hit a mine and sank.

5. Tiberius.

6. Joan of Arc: the French resistance fighter was a key figure in the turning of the tide against the English forces in France during the Hundred Years War. Burned at the stake, her inspirational qualities only increased when Pope Callixtus III declared her trial invalid and St Joan a martyr.

7. 1264.

8. Yugoslavia.

9. Franklin D. Roosevelt, the president.

10. Pat Garrett.

The Seven Wonders of the World

The Seven Wonders of the World generally refers to the wonders of the early and classical civilisations. They are as follows:

The Great Pyramid at Giza (the only surviving ancient wonder).

The Hanging Gardens of Babylon (destroyed).

The Temple of Artemis at Ephesus (destroyed).

The Statue of Zeus at Olympia (destroyed).

The Tomb of Mausolus at Halicarnassus (destroyed by earthquakes in the Western medieval era; the tomb gives its name to the word mausoleum).

The Colossus of Rhodes (a gigantic statue of the sun god, Helios, destroyed by an earthquake in 226 BC).

The Lighthouse (or Pharos) of Alexandria (destroyed in the fifteenth century).

QUIZ 94. SPORTS MATCH

Match the sportsperson from List 1 to another from List 2 and explain your reason for matching them. Be careful – some may match up in one way, but you need the BEST match. For example, Roger Federer would match to Andy Murray as both are winners of major tennis tournaments, but he would match better to Stan Wawrinka, because both are also Swiss.

1. Raymond Barneveld.
2. Kenenisa Bekele.
3. Gail Devers.
4. Roberto De Vicenzo.
5. Katherine Grainger.
6. Meg Lanning.
7. Anna Meares.
8. Phil Mickelson.
9. Makhaya Ntini.
10. Alan Rough.
11. Jason Robinson.
12. Lindsey Vonn.

A. Donovan Bailey.
B. Angel Cabrera.
C. Bob Charles.
D. Craig Gordon.
E. Iestyn Harris.
F. Jean-Claude Killy.
G. Elisabeta Lipă.
H. Morné Morkel.
I. Anya Shrubsole.
J. Phil Taylor.
K. Laura Trott-Kenny.
L. Lasse Virén.

Answers to Quiz 93

1. Tony Blackburn.

2. The first song played was 'Flowers in the Rain' by The Move (The Move included Roy Wood, later of Wizzard, and Jeff Lynne, later of ELO and the Travelling Wilburys). Less well known is that the second song was 'Massachusetts' by the Bee Gees.

3. Clara Amfo. The slot was first introduced during Jo Whiley's time on the morning show, and continued by Fearne Cotton when she took over.

4. The Big Weekend.

5. The Fall.

6. John Lennon.

7. Terry Wogan.

8. Chris Moyles. He actually held on to the *Breakfast Show* longer than any other presenter, despite a few *contretemps* along the way.

9. Zoe Ball.

10. Madonna.

Here are all the *Radio 1 Breakfast Show* presenters:

Tony Blackburn   30 September 1967–1 June 1973

Noel Edmonds   4 June 1973–28 April 1978

Dave Lee Travis   2 May 1978–2 January 1981

Mike Read   5 January 1981–11 April 1986

Mike Smith   5 May 1986–17 May 1988

Simon Mayo   23 May 1988–3 September 1993

Mark Goodier   6 September 1993–24 December 1993

Steve Wright   10 January 1994–21 April 1995

Chris Evans   24 April 1995–17 January 1997

Mark and Lard   17 February 1997–10 October 1997

Kevin Greening and Zoe Ball   13 October 1997–25 September 1998

Zoe Ball   28 September 1998–10 March 2000

Sara Cox   3 April 2000–19 December 2003

Chris Moyles   5 January 2004–14 September 2012

Nick Grimshaw   24 September 2012–9 August 2018

Greg James   20 August 2018–present

QUIZ 95. MIXED BAG

Another set of questions pulled from across the knowledge spectrum.

1. The tortured Mr Rochester is the central male character in which Victorian novel?

2. Iraq's invasion of which gulf state precipitated the first Gulf War?

3. Bicycle Motocross is a long-hand way of describing which sporting endeavour?

4. American artist Mark Rothko was born in which state, at the time a part of the Soviet Union. Was it Estonia, Georgia, Kazakhstan or Latvia?

5. Which song from *8 Mile* won Eminem an Academy Award?

6. British actor Paul Bethany married which American actress in 2003?

7. Who turned H.G. Wells' *War of the Worlds* into a star-studded musical extravaganza narrated by Richard Burton?

8. George Mallory died in 1924: where was his body found seventy-five years later?

9. The Peninsular and Oriental company are mainly concerned with which business?

10. Which fashion house started in Basingstoke in 1856 making rainwear?

Answers to Quiz 94

1. J: Dutchman Barneveld and Englishman Phil 'the Power' Taylor were superstar darts players.

2. L: Bekele of Ethiopia and the Finn, Virén, have won Olympic medals at 5,000m and 10,000m.

3. A: Devers (American) and Bailey (Canadian) have both have won Olympic 100m medals.

4. B: De Vicenzo and Cabrera are both Argentinian winners of major golf tournaments.

5. G: Both Grainger and the German Lipă are Olympic gold-medal-winning rowers.

6. I: Meg Lanning of Australia and England's Anya Shrubsole are both international women's cricketers.

7. K: Both are Olympic gold-medal-winning cyclists, Meares for Australia and Trott-Kenny for Team GB.

8. C: Phil Mickelson and Bob Charles are left-handed golfers who won at least one major tournament. Charles won the first (the Open in 1963), Mickelson has five majors, while the other two, Canadian Mike Weir and Bubba Watson, have both won the US Masters, Watson twice.

9. H: Ntini and Morkel are both South African fast bowlers. Ntini did more than anyone to bury the myth of tokenism concerning inclusion of black players in the post-Apartheid South African cricket team.

10. D: Rough and Gordon are Scottish goalkeepers.

11. E: Both are dual-code rugby internationals, having represented England (Robinson) and Wales (Harris) at both Rugby League and Rugby Union.

12. F: American Vonn and Frenchman Killy are Olympic gold-medal-winning skiers – some would say Vonn is *the* Olympic skier.

QUIZ 96. MUSIC

We give you the members of the band, you name the band. It's that simple. Provided you happen to be over forty. (There's one for the toddlers later.)

1. Eric Clapton, Ginger Baker, Jack Bruce.

2. Roger Daltrey, John Entwistle, Keith Moon, Pete Townshend.

3. Pete Shelley, Steve Diggle, John Maher, Steve Garvey.

4. Diana Ross, Florence Ballard, Mary Wilson.

5. David Byrne, Chris Frantz, Jerry Harrison, Tina Weymouth.

6. Stuart Adamson, Mark Brzezicki, Tony Butler, Bruce Watson.

7. Gene Clark, Michael Clarke, David Crosby, Chris Hillman, Roger McGuinn.

8. Brian Bennett, Hank Marvin, John Rostill, Bruce Welch.

9. David Illsley, David Knopfler, Mark Knopfler, Pick Withers.

10. Ernie, Marvin, O'Kelly, Ronald, Rudolph, Chris Jasper.

Answers to Quiz 95

1. *Jane Eyre*. Don't worry, she gets her man . . . sorry, SPOILER ALERT.

2. Kuwait. This was a much less drawn-out affair than the Second Gulf War post 9/11. The Iraqis invaded Kuwait over an oil dispute and the international community agreed on retaliatory action to throw them out – this consensus was the BIG difference between the two engagements.

3. BMX.

4. Latvia.

5. 'Lose Yourself'. The film was pretty good, and seemed to open up new opportunities for the rapper, which he has declined to exploit.

6. Jennifer Connelly. They married in 2003 and are still together.

7. Jeff Wayne. The rather OTT prog-rock musical extravaganza also included the vocal talents of Julie Covington, Phil Lynott and Justin Hayward.

8. On the slopes of Mount Everest. Mallory led a number of expeditions in the Himalayas and died trying to conquer Everest nearly thirty years before Hillary did so.

9. Ferries and cruises – they are P&O.

10. Burberry.

QUIZ 97. BANKS

A quiz on banks; you know, places where you leave your money and they misuse it. Although it isn't that simple (is it ever?) – some of the questions are just about people called Banks . . .

1. Tony Banks was a popular East End Labour MP: which ministerial post did he hold from 1997 to 1999?

2. With which band was another Tony Banks the keyboard player from 1967 to 1998 and again more recently?

3. Which bank was brought down by rogue trader Nick Leeson in 1995?

4. What was the title of Banksy's 2010 film? Was it (a) *We're Bored of Fish*; (b) *Ozone's Angel*; (c) *Exit Through the Gift Shop*; or (d) *The Son of a Migrant from Syria*?

5. Whose ghost reappears to haunt Macbeth in Shakespeare's tragedy?

6. Which European corporation have gobbled up Abbey National, Alliance & Leicester and Bradford & Bingley in recent years?

7. ITV cancelled its arts programme *The South Bank Show* in 2010, because of the retirement of which presenter, who had written and hosted the show since it started in 1978?

8. Which famous children's books and family musical concerns the antics of the Banks' family nanny?

9. Which fashion designer launched a range of clothes and a perfume called Rive Gauche in 1966?

10. Who took the lead role in the 2008 heist movie, *The Bank Job*?

Answers to Quiz 96

1. Cream. The trio squeezed four albums of improv-style jam blues into their three-and-a-half-year career.

2. The Who: the classic line-up remained the same until Moon's death in 1978, when he was replaced by Kenny Jones of the Small Faces.

3. The Buzzcocks, who kept on playing through to Shelley's death in 2018.

4. The Supremes. Originally a four-piece, this became the classic early line-up until head of Tamla Motown Berry Gordy renamed the band Diana Ross and the Supremes, and Ballard was replaced by Cindy Birdsong.

5. Talking Heads. Probably the band I most regret not seeing (excluding those I could never have realistically seen play).

6. Big Country, formed by Adamson when the Skids broke up – the band was based around the bagpipe-like guitar of Adamson and Brzezicki's crisp drumming.

7. The Byrds.

8. The Shadows.

9. Dire Straits. Mark Knopfler, the songwriter and brilliant guitarist, was the mainstay of this four-piece who were, for a spell in the 1980s, the world's biggest band, leaving six multi-platinum albums. *Brothers in Arms* achieved staggering sales for what was not obviously commercial music.

10. The Isley Brothers – the band were actually brothers, with their cousin Chris Jasper on keyboards. Originally a vocal group comprising O'Kelly, Ronald and Rudolph, their addition of the massively talented Ernie and bassist Marvin increased their scope and ambition.

QUIZ 98. SCIENCE STUFF

More stuff to torment you with memories of being bullied by the physics teacher at school (No? Just me?)

1. What is deoxyribose nucleic acid?

2. The nucleus of an atom contains protons and which other sub-atomic particles?

3. What factor in physics is measured in ohms?

4. In the Periodic Table, each element shows two numbers. The bottom left number is the atomic number: what is the number at the top left?

5. Exothermic reactions like burning give out energy: what name is given to reactions that take in energy?

6. Plants use chlorophyll from light sources to synthesise water and which other compound into glucose?

7. If a lot of amino acids join up, what do they form?

8. What name is given to a base with a pH greater than 7 when dissolved in water?

9. When the body uses glucose and oxygen during exercise, what two waste products ensue?

10. What is measured by multiplying force applied (in newtons) by the distance moved (in metres)?

Answers to Quiz 97

1. Sports Minister. Banks was MP for Newham and later West Ham from 1993 until 1995 when he entered the House of Lords as Baron Stratford, but he died less than a year later in 2006.

2. Genesis. Banks made up the classic early line-up, with Peter Gabriel singing, Steve Hackett on guitar, Mike Rutherford on bass and Phil Collins on drums.

3. Barings Bank.

4. *Exit Through the Gift Shop*.

5. Banquo.

6. Santander, the Spanish bank.

7. Melvyn Bragg, now Lord Bragg, Carlisle's finest.

8. *Mary Poppins*. The first of P.L. Travers' eight books was published in 1934.

9. Yves St Laurent (Rive Gauche means Left Bank, a reference to the trendy artistic quarter of Paris).

10. Jason Statham – the film was written by Dick Clement and Ian La Frenais (writers of *The Likely Lads*, *Porridge* and *Auf Wiedersehen, Pet*), and the story was based on a real bank job in Baker Street in 1971.

QUIZ 99. HOLIDAYS

A general knowledge round, with a fair bit of pop culture, riffing on the idea of holidays or vacations.

1. Who had a UK No. 1 hit in 2009 with 'Holiday'?

2. What name is given to a vacation during which one engages in activity that is similar to one's usual work.

3. What kind of holiday did Gregory Peck and Audrey Hepburn take in 1953?

4. By what name was the May Bank Holiday known when it first became an official public holiday in 1871?

5. Michael O'Leary is the outspoken CEO of which budget holiday-related business?

6. Who starred in the 1963 movie *Summer Holiday*, and had a hit with the theme tune?

7. Who had a 1978 Number 1 with the song 'Dreadlock Holiday'?

8. Who, in the movies, had a 1983 *Vacation*, a 1985 *European Vacation* and a 1989 *Christmas Vacation*?

9. What is the minimum age you have to be to take a Saga holiday?

10. Who were the two female stars (opposite Jack Black and Jude Law) in the 2006 romantic comedy, *The Holiday*?

Answers to Quiz 98

1. DNA.

2. Neutrons.

3. Resistance.

4. Mass.

5. Endothermic.

6. Carbon dioxide.

7. Enzymes / proteins.

8. Alkaline.

9. Water and carbon dioxide.

10. Work, in joules.

Base SI units

These are the base units on which, for consistency, all scientific measurements are based, SI denoting Systéme Internationale, or International System of Units. Would it surprise you to know that the United States is one of three countries that does not accept this standardisation? The others are Myanmar and Liberia.

Length is measured by the metre (m).
Weight is measured by the kilogram (kg).
Time is measured by the second (s).
Electric current is measured by the ampere (A).
Thermodynamic temperature is measured in kelvin (K).
Mass, or amount, is measured by the mole (mol).
Luminous intensity is measured in candela (cd).
There are many derived units, like the hertz (frequency), joule (work) and tesla (magnetic flux), but the list above covers the key units.

QUIZ 100. THE BARD

A quiz all about Shakespeare. If you know nowt about Shakespeare, consider yourself to have missed out. I don't mean sitting in class reading through the text and deciphering what it all means; that has killed Shakespeare for entire generations. Just go and watch it in a real live theatre.

1. Who had three daughters called Goneril, Regan and Cordelia?

2. Which Shakespeare play is set on the island state of Illyria?

3. Who played Romeo in *Romeo + Juliet*, Baz Luhrmann's modern take on *Romeo and Juliet*?

4. Which Shakespeare tragedy is reputed to bring bad luck to any actor who utters its title aloud while not actually performing the play on stage?

5. Which is the first (chronologically) of Shakespeare's history plays, which cover the Wars of the Roses?

6. What series title did the BBC give to their transmission of the history plays between 2012 and 2016?

7. In which Shakespeare play did David Tennant and Catherine Tate play together on the London stage after their successful collaboration on *Dr Who*?

8. Indicated in the play's subtitle, Othello was a general in the employment of which city state?

9. In a 1990 film version of *Hamlet*, with Glenn Close and Helena Bonham Carter as Gertrude and Ophelia, who played the title role?

10. Which Shakespeare play is set during the siege of Troy by the Greek armies?

Answers to Quiz 99

1. Calvin Harris – not Madonna, that was much earlier (1983).

2. Busman's holiday.

3. *Roman Holiday*. The film is a romantic comedy and concerns the adventures of a princess in Rome who slips her chaperones and larks around with a journalist as her companion. It won Hepburn an Academy Award.

4. Whit Monday.

5. Ryanair. Here's a tip: if you haven't seen it, check out Fascinating Aida's 'Cheap Flights' song online – a clever dig at budget airlines clearly aimed at Ryanair. It's funny without being offensive.

6. Cliff Richard.

7. 10cc: 'I don't like cricket, I love it' was heard around many a school playground. Well, middle-class grammar-school playgrounds, at least.

8. National Lampoon. The films were derived from a popular satirical magazine, *National Lampoon* – their first one was the 1978 cult comedy *Animal House*.

9. Fifty-five. Two years in and I haven't been tempted yet . . .

10. Cameron Diaz and Kate Winslet.

QUIZ 101. FOOD AND DRINK

1. Is a radish a form of carrot, a member of the cabbage family or a small onion?

2. In 2013, GlaxoSmithKline sold Lucozade and which other traditional soft drink brand to Japanese company Suntory for £1.35 billion? Was it Kia-Ora, Ribena, Vimto or Irn-Bru?

3. What is riboflavin?

4. Which important foodstuff is the seed of the Oryza grasses?

5. What is added to sparkling wines to make a Kir Royale?

6. What 'R' is a root vegetable created by crossing a cabbage and turnip?

7. Which edible plant is synonymous with non-specific chatter?

8. Which confectionery company first manufactured Rolo in 1937?

9. Which grape varietal, developed in the Rhine Valley, is the flagship grape of the German wine industry?

10. Currant; prune; raisin; sultana. Which of these is not a dried grape?

Answers to Quiz 100

1. *King Lear*.

2. *Twelfth Night*. The main character, Viola, is washed up on the shore of Illyria and disguises herself as a young man in service to the local bigwig – cue much gender-based hilarity and musings about love.

3. Leonardo DiCaprio, opposite Clare Danes, and a fine and feisty adaptation it is.

4. *Macbeth*. Watch the fabulous *Blackadder* episode 'Sense and Senility' for a spoof on this old superstition.

5. *Richard II*.

6. *The Hollow Crown*.

7. *Much Ado About Nothing*.

8. (The Moor of) Venice.

9. Mel Gibson.

10. *Troilus and Cressida*.

Shakespeare's plays

The categories into which I have put the plays, below, are moveable and various criteria exist:

The history plays (11): *King John*; *Richard II*; *Henry V*; *Henry IV* (*Part 1* and *2*); *Henry VI* (*Part 1*, *2* and *3*); *Richard III*; *Henry VIII*; *Edward III* (possibly).

The Roman tragedies (6): *Coriolanus*; *Julius Caesar*; *Antony and Cleopatra*; *Titus Andronicus*; *Troilus and Cressida*; *Timon of Athens*.

The great tragedies (4 + 1): *Hamlet*; *Macbeth*; *King Lear*; *Othello*; with *Romeo and Juliet* as an early prototype.

Early comedies (4): *Two Gentlemen of Verona*; *The Comedy of Errors*; *The Merry Wives of Windsor*; *The Taming of the Shrew*.

Mature comedies (5): *As You Like It*; *Love's Labour's Lost*; *Much Ado About Nothing*; *A Midsummer Night's Dream*; *Twelfth Night*.

Late romances / problem plays (8): *All's Well that Ends Well*; *Measure for Measure*; *Cymbeline*; *The Tempest*; *Pericles, Prince of Tyre*; *The Merchant of Venice*; *A Winter's Tale*; *Two Noble Kinsmen* (*Troilus and Cressida* is sometimes categorised with these plays).

QUIZ 102. GROWN-UP TELLY

A quiz about TV, but the serious kind – documentaries and factual programming.

1. Peter Dimmock was the first presenter of *Grandstand*, briefly, in 1958, and Steve Rider saw the programme through from 1993 to its end in 2007: who were the three presenters in between?

2. In May 1997, which *Newsnight* presenter asked the question 'Did you threaten to overrule him?' of then Home Secretary, Michael Howard, twelve consecutive times?

3. On the death of its originator Robert McKenzie, who took over the results analysis using the famous Swingometer during the BBC's *Election Night* coverage?

4. What was David Attenborough's first major attempt on the BBC to catalogue the planet, broadcast in 1979 after three years in the making?

5. Alan Shearer has served as the principal analyst on BBC's *Match of the Day* since 2018, when he replaced which long-serving pundit?

6. Who presents a cornerstone BBC programme from Longmeadow in Herefordshire?

7. Philip Avery, Louise Lear, Helen Willetts and Tomasz Schafernaker all help present what on the BBC?

8. What is the world's longest-running current affairs programme, having first been aired in 1953?

9. Biddy Baxter led the team behind which children's programme between 1958 and 1988?

10. Which event boasts the most viewers in TV history in the UK, pushing Diana's funeral into second place?

Answers to Quiz 101

1. It is a brassica root, so technically a cabbage.

2. Ribena.

3. Vitamin B2 – it is obtainable through dairy products or fat heavy fruits such as avocado and banana.

4. Rice.

5. Crème de cassis, which is a dark red blackcurrant liqueur made in Burgundy. It can be drunk with white wine to make a simple Kir – the fizz adds the Royale.

6. Rutabaga.

7. Rhubarb.

8. Mackintosh's. The Halifax-based company started in 1890, and developed brands such as Quality Street, Rolo and Toffee Crisp. In 1969 they merged with Rowntree's of York, who already had Kit Kat, Smarties and Fruit Pastilles. The merged company was bought, in turn, by Nestlé in 1988 – the business still operates from the Rowntree headquarters in York.

9. Riesling.

10. Prune (it's a dried plum).

QUIZ 103. PIRATES

Forgive the indulgence here – Hastings is a Pirate Town (see question 1) so it was inevitable I included a pirate round. We have a Pirate Day every July in the town, when thousands of people dressed in piratical garb descend on the Old Town for a party. Pewter tankards and rum cocktails are the order of the day.

1. The South Coast town of Hastings holds the record for the most people dressed up as pirates in one place at one time in Britain. How many people were counted? Was it around six thousand, ten thousand, fourteen thousand or twenty-two thousand?

2. The Pirates represent which American city at baseball? Is it Philadelphia, Pittsburgh, Seattle or Tampa Bay?

3. What was the 1960 hit that made the careers of Johnny Kidd and his backing band, the Pirates?

4. By what name was the pirate captain Edward Teach colloquially known?

5. What surname connects the notorious Caribbean pirate Calico Jack and the Victorian children's book illustrator named Arthur?

6. And who was the female pirate who became Calico Jack's consort and partner, and fought alongside him when he was captured and later hanged?

7. Which story begins in the Admiral Benbow Inn and continues aboard the schooner, *Hispaniola*?

8. Which successful theatrical actor stars as Captain Flint in the pirate TV drama *Black Sails*?

9. Poole Pirates are a hugely successful team in which sport?

10. With whom, in the light opera *The Pirates of Penzance*, is Mabel, the daughter of Major-General Stanley, besotted?

Answers to Quiz 102

1. David Coleman (1958–68), Frank Bough (1968–82) and Desmond Lynam (1982–91).

2. Jeremy Paxman. The incident was typical both of the evasiveness of politicians in general, and of the cult-of-personality news-presentation style of Paxman, gleaned from Robin Day.

3. Peter Snow. His buccaneering hands-on graphics have been replaced by sophisticated algorithm-based predictive charts.

4. *Life on Earth*.

5. Alan Hansen.

6. Monty Don. The programme is *Gardeners' World*, and Monty is currently in his second stint as the main presenter, following in the footsteps of enduring favourites, Percy Thrower, Geoff Hamilton and Alan Titchmarsh.

7. Weather.

8. *Panorama*.

9. *Blue Peter*. While Biddy may have retired, *Blue Peter* soldiers on and is now the world's longest-running children's programme.

10. The 1966 World Cup Final.

QUIZ 104. FILM STUFF

A mix of film questions, exclusively on movies from the last century. We're not going to argue that films are better or worse in the modern era, but we will argue that massive advances in technical resources, including CGI, have been a mixed blessing.

1. The 1976 Alan J. Pakula film *All the President's Men* told the story of two reporters uncovering the Watergate scandal: which two Hollywood big names played the reporters, Bob Woodward and Carl Bernstein?

2. If the scary killer in the 1962 original was Robert Mitchum, who was it in Martin Scorsese's 1992 remake?

3. What was the 1976 film starring Michael Caine and Donald Sutherland concerning a plot to kill Churchill during the Second World War?

4. Who played Doc Halliday to Burt Lancaster's Wyatt Earp in *Gunfight at the O.K. Corral* (1957)?

5. What is the name of Indiana Jones' young sidekick, played by Jonathan Ke Quan?

6. Alan Cummings voiced which character as the narrator of the 1994 film of the classic novel *Black Beauty*?

7. Who plays PI Rigby Reardon in Carl Reiner's 1982 homage to film noir, *Dead Men Don't Wear Plaid*?

8. After box-office success with *The Deer Hunter*, Michael Cimino's next project was a commercial disaster, listed as one of cinema's most expensive flops. What was this 1980 film, its budget $44 million, but its box-office take less than $4 million?

9. Mel Gibson appeared in four *Lethal Weapon* films as Martin Riggs: who played his buddy, Roger Murtaugh?

10. Which film won Julie Andrews an Academy Award as Best Actress?

Answers to Quiz 103

1. Fourteen thousand. Penzance briefly took the record, but sanity has been restored.

2. Pittsburgh.

3. 'Shakin' All Over'. Johnny Kidd died young in 1966, but the band carried on playing into the 2000s, until the death of guitarist Mick Green in 2010 took the flag down.

4. Blackbeard. Teach was less murderous than many of his ilk, relying on his fearsome appearance and reputation rather than outright violence.

5. The surname Rackham.

6. Mary Read, one of many female pirates of the age.

7. *Treasure Island*, by Robert Louis Stevenson, published in book form in 1883.

8. Toby Stephens. The successful Starz show ran for four seasons from 2013 to 2017: the setting is a prequel to *Treasure Island*, explaining the nature of the treasure that the party in Stevenson's book are seeking.

9. Speedway – the Pirates are still a major force and the current national champions.

10. Frederick, the pirate, who is indentured to the Pirate King.

QUIZ 105. WHO IS BEING DESCRIBED?

We give you a clue to someone's identity and you have to give us a name –
no explanation needed, although the answers provide some.

1. The original Wonder Woman.

2. Tennis player who won loads of major titles, married for a while to a
   British player who won none.

3. Antigua sportsman, born with the given name Isaac, who was a key
   member of the all-conquering West Indies team of the 1980s.

4. Film director who made his name with *She's Gotta Have It* and *Do the
   Right Thing*.

5. Welsh rugby full back who was known by his initials.

6. Former MP for Hartlepool who is credited as the architect of New
   Labour.

7. White soul singer who started with the Q-Tips and had a string of hits
   in the 1980s, reaching No. 1 with a splendid Marvin Gaye cover.

8. She went Moonlighting with Bruce Willis.

9. The man who 'invented' the internet.

10. Half a bottom, celebrity husband and chef.

Answers to Quiz 104

1. Robert Redford and Dustin Hoffman play the two journalists, whose work brought down President Nixon.

2. Robert De Niro, who plays Max Cady in Scorsese's version of *Cape Fear*.

3. *The Eagle Has Landed*. Sutherland plays an IRA agent working for the Germans – Caine apparently declined that part and asked to play the U-Boat Commander.

4. Kirk Douglas.

5. Short Round.

6. The horse itself, Blackie or Black Beauty.

7. Steve Martin.

8. *Heaven's Gate*.

9. Danny Glover.

10. *Mary Poppins*. Most of the Academy Awards that year went to *My Fair Lady*, except Best Actress, where Andrews pipped Audrey Hepburn in an ironic twist: Andrews had been overlooked for the part of Eliza Doolittle, despite having been a success in the stage musical.

QUIZ 106. WELCOME TO THE NORTH

It's not all mill towns, black brick, flat caps and whippets. Mostly, but not all. Here are ten questions about the north. If you live north of Watford, aim for seven or eight points; if you've never left the south, you'll get about three.

1. Which city, other than Manchester, can be found within the confines of Greater Manchester?

2. Croxteth, Fazakerley, Riverside and Waverley are all council wards in which city?

3. Blackpool, Hull, Sheffield, York: which lies furthest north?

4. The Lancashire town of Preston lies on which river?

5. Apart from Headingley in Leeds and Old Trafford in Manchester, which other northern cricket ground has hosted Test Matches in recent years?

6. The city of Chester is the county town of Cheshire. But which town on the border with Lancashire is the county's biggest?

7. Barnsley, Doncaster, Mansfield, Rotherham: which of these is NOT in Yorkshire?

8. Scafell Pike is England's highest mountain: is it in the Lake District, the Peak District or the Pennines?

9. In which North Yorkshire coastal town did Count Dracula first appear in England in Bram Stoker's novel?

10. Newcastle is at the mouth of the River Tyne: which city is situated at the mouth of the River Wear to the south?

Answers to Quiz 105

1. Lynda Carter, who played Diana Prince/Wonder Woman in the original TV series from 1975 to 1979. Gal Gadot plays the more recent incarnation of the character.

2. Chris Evert-Lloyd, who won eighteen Grand Slam singles titles. We are being a little unfair on John Lloyd, who was good enough to reach the Australian Open Final in 1977 and won three Grand Slam Mixed Doubles titles with Australian Wendy Turnbull.

3. Isaac Vivian Alexander Richards.

4. Spike Lee, who produced his best work since with 2018's *BlacKkKlansman*.

5. JPR Williams, part of the fantastic Wales and British Lions team of the 1970s.

6. Peter Mandelson.

7. Paul Young – the Marvin Gaye cover was 'Wherever I Lay My Hat'.

8. Cybill Shepherd played Maddie Hayes and Willis co-stars as David Addison, her partner in a detective agency.

9. Tim Berners-Lee.

10. Ade Edmondson, who made *Bottom*, the TV sitcom, with Rik Mayall, is married to Jennifer Saunders and won *Celebrity MasterChef*.

QUIZ 107. THIS OR THAT

Your task here is to decide whether each of these twelve names represents a member of Bruce Springsteen's band, the E Street Band, a character from *Breaking Bad*, or a Premier League manager at the start of the 2018–19 season.

1. Max Weinberg.
2. Gustavo Fring.
3. David Warner.
4. Steve Van Zandt.
5. Hank Schrader.
6. Eddie Howe.
7. Claude Puel.
8. Danny Federici.
9. Hector Salamanca.
10. Clarence Clemons.
11. Saul Goodman.
12. Javi García.

Answers to Quiz 106

1. Salford is a city in its own right as well as part of Greater Manchester.

2. Liverpool.

3. York.

4. The Ribble. It starts in North Yorkshire and flows across Lancashire through Preston before emptying in a ten-mile-wide estuary near Lytham.

5. The Riverside Stadium in Durham.

6. Warrington, with a population of around 210,000 to Chester's 120,000.

7. Mansfield is in Nottinghamshire.

8. The Lake District.

9. Whitby; the count's ship is seen foundering off the coast and soon afterwards he begins appearing at Holmwood's ancestral home to prey on Lucy.

10. Sunderland – while Middlesbrough is at the mouth of the River Tees a little further south.

QUIZ 108. LYRICS

Song lyrics. I find these difficult – it's tricky looking at the words or hearing them read without the tune and trying to place them. Aim for six out of a ten; that would be a decent score, we think.

1. 'By the look in your eye, I can tell you're gonna cry – is it over me?'

2. 'Every time you kiss me, I'm still not certain that you love me.'

3. 'Up in the club, just broke up, I'm doing my own little thing / You decided to dip and now you wanna trip / Cos another brother noticed me.'

4. 'Well I heard there was a secret chord, that David played and it pleased the Lord.'

5. 'Once upon a time you dressed so fine, threw the bums a dime in your prime . . .'

6. 'I'd sit alone and watch your light, my only friend through teenage nights.'

7. 'I used to rule the world, seas would rise when I gave the word / Now in the morning I sleep alone, sweep the streets I used to own.'

8. 'I live in an apartment on the 99th floor of my block / And I sit at home looking out the window / Imagining the world has stopped.'

9. 'Yellow diamonds in the light, and we're standing side by side / As your shadow crosses mine, what it takes to come alive.'

10. 'It was a slow day, and the sun was beating on the soldiers by the side of the road.'

THE MAMMOTH GENERAL KNOWLEDGE QUIZ BOOK | 223

Answers to Quiz 107

1. E Street Band; Max has been Springsteen's drummer since 1974.

2. Giancarlo Esposito plays Gus Fring, a meth distributor and owner of Los Pollos Hermanos in *Breaking Bad*.

3. David Warner lost his job at Huddersfield Town in mid-season with the team struggling.

4. Steve Van Zandt is a guitarist in the E Street Band – he did have a recurring role in *The Sopranos*, so it wouldn't have been a major surprise had he turned up in *Breaking Bad*.

5. Hank (Dean Norris) is an agent in *Breaking Bad*, tracking down the meth manufacturer, unaware it is his brother-in-law.

6. Eddie Howe has overseen another season of keeping Bournemouth in the Premier League.

7. Claude Puel was another Premier League managerial casualty during the season, giving way to Brendan Rodgers at Leicester City.

8. Danny Federici is the organ player in the E Street Band, and was an original 1972 member.

9. Hector is an elderly wheelchair-bound Don in *Breaking Bad*.

10. Clarence Clemons was an original member of the E Street Band. The giant sax player was Springsteen's right-hand man until his death in 2011 – he was replaced by his nephew, Jake.

11. Saul Goodman is one of the names used by Bob Odenkirk's character in *Breaking Bad* – he is a lawyer and conman.

12. Javi García has overseen another good season for Watford in the Premier League.

QUIZ 109. STUFF, STUFF AND MORE STUFF

Again, a mixed bag of questions – bit of this, bit of that.

1. No. 5 is a distinctive and enduring scent from which fashion house?

2. The video-sharing forum YouTube is now owned by which media giant?

3. Sentimental things are often referred to as schmaltzy. From what language does the word derive?

4. The Cthulhu Mythos is a fictional world used as the base for a number of works: on whose work is the world based?

5. Which English fast bowler was the first to take 300 wickets in Test matches?

6. Who is Robert Galbraith?

7. If bovine refers to cows, cattle or oxen, what word similarly describes sheep?

8. Which new bank in a new style was set up by Midland Bank in 1989?

9. Kemal Atatürk was the founder and first president of which modern country in 1923?

10. How is a reindeer known in most of North America?

Answers to Quiz 108

1. 'Wherever I Lay My Hat (That's My Home)' (written by Marvin Gaye with the song-writing team of Norman Whitfield and Barrett Strong, the song was a B-side, and later a UK No. 1 hit for Paul Young).

2. 'Suspicion' was a Doc Pomus and Mort Shuman song written and released in 1962.

3. 'Single Ladies (Put a Ring On It)', with its catchy chorus, was a 2008 hit single for Beyoncé.

4. 'Hallelujah': written by Leonard Cohen and recorded by John Cale, Jeff Buckley, k.d. lang, Rufus Wainwright and a hit for *X Factor* winner Alexandra Burke in 2008.

5. 'Like a Rolling Stone' – one of modern music's iconic songs, written by Bob Dylan in 1965 for his *Highway 61 Revisited* album.

6. 'Radio Ga Ga' – a 1984 Queen song (from *The Works*) written by drummer Roger Taylor.

7. 'Viva la Vida' – the title song from a 2008 Coldplay album.

8. 'Get Off of My Cloud' is a chart-topping (US and UK) single written by Keith Richards and Mick Jagger of The Rolling Stones.

9. 'We Found Love' (Rihanna), written for the singer's 2011 *Talk That Talk* album.

10.' Boy in the Bubble' (Paul Simon), one of the lead tracks on his 1986 multi-platinum album *Graceland*.

QUIZ 110. OPERA

A round for the culture vultures. We have included lots of pop culture – a cornerstone of quizzes – but we do like to throw in an occasional round on slightly more highbrow artistic endeavour. People rarely score well.

1. In 1934 the Christie family first hosted an opera festival at which country estate near Lewes?

2. Who wrote the opera *Lucia di Lammermoor*, and on which British writer's work is it loosely based?

3. What word is used to describe the playful elaborations of a soprano singer, as heard in, for example, the part of the Queen of the Night in Mozart's *Magic Flute*?

4. In 1732, theatrical entrepreneur John Rich put on the first show at the new Theatre Royal, Covent Garden, a production of Congreve's *Way of the World*. By what name is this theatre now more commonly known?

5. Which controversial film director shot the 1975 film version of Pete Townshend's 1969 concept album, or rock opera, *Tommy*?

6. Which male voice comes between a tenor and a bass?

7. Which British composer enjoyed a long-standing personal and professional relationship with the tenor Peter Pears?

8. Which one-act opera by Pietro Mascagni is often performed on a double bill with *Pagliacci* by Ruggero Leoncavallo?

9. Which famous Verdi opera is based on *La Dame aux Camélias* by Alexandre Dumas *fils*?

10. Which opera tells of the love between Rodolfo, a poet, and Mimi, a seamstress?

Answers to Quiz 109

1. Chanel.

2. Google. YouTube was created in 2005 and bought by Google the following year.

3. Yiddish.

4. H.P. Lovecraft – a virtual unknown in his lifetime (he died from cancer in 1937, aged only forty-six), Lovecraft has acquired cult status as an influential horror writer.

5. Fred Trueman. Trueman finished his career with 307 wickets and an outstanding average and strike rate. His wicket total has since been superseded by Bob Willis, then Ian Botham, Jimmy Anderson and Stuart Broad.

6. J.K. Rowling – Galbraith is the pseudonym she uses when she writes the Cormoran Strike crime books.

7. Ovine.

8. First Direct, the first mainstream commercial bank without a retail customer interface.

9. Turkey. Atatürk was a Turkish general during the First World War and was instrumental in clearing out the last remnants of the Ottoman Empire after the conflict.

10. Caribou.

QUIZ 111. FOR PETE'S SAKE

Pete, Peter, Petey, Peterson, Petra – a round on Peter and all its derivatives. These rounds can be a little easier than the pure general knowledge rounds, as the theme gives a bit of a clue.

1. St Petersburg in Russia was known by what name in the Soviet era?

2. World Cup winner Martin Peters was involved in Britain's first £200,000 transfer when he moved from West Ham United to which club in 1970?

3. St Peter is recognised by the Eastern Christian Church as their first spiritual leader: by what title is he referred to in this context? Is it (a) the Bishop of Constantinople; (b) the Patriarch of Antioch; (c) the Cardinal of Byzantium; or (d) the Bishop of Jerusalem?

4. Mary Peters from Northern Ireland won a gold medal for Great Britain and Northern Ireland at the 1972 Olympic Games in which athletic discipline?

5. Actor William Petersen is best known for his portrayal of Gil Grissom for thirteen years in which US TV series?

6. The Peterloo Massacre of 1819, when armed cavalry charged a crowd of protesters, killing fifteen, took place in St Peter's Field in which English city?

7. The American city of St Petersburg is home to which baseball team?

8. J.M. Barrie's Peter Pan (as we know the character) was first seen as a stage play in which decade of the twentieth century?

9. The city of Petra, founded close to 300 BCE by the Nabateans, an early Arabic nomadic culture, is the most visited tourist attraction in which modern country?

10. Norwegian Suzann Pettersen, born 1981, is a leading exponent of which sport?

Answers to Quiz 110

1. Glyndebourne. Apart from five years during the war, the festival has taken place every year since, latterly in a specially commissioned opera house in the grounds.

2. Donizetti; Sir Walter Scott.

3. Coloratura – purists regard it as showing off!

4. The Royal Opera House, the home of The Royal Opera and The Royal Ballet.

5. Ken Russell. It is a terrible mess but with fleeting moments of high entertainment.

6. Baritone.

7. Benjamin Britten.

8. *Cavalieri Rusticana*.

9. *La Traviata*.

10. *La Bohème*.

Classification of singing voices

Soprano – the highest range for female singers.

Mezzo-soprano – slightly lower.

Contralto – the lowest female voice, occasionally dipping towards the male range.

Tenor – the highest male range, usually the lead singer in an opera.

Baritone – a more stately male voice.

Bass – a deep, rumbling male voice, often used in choral works as a counterpoint to the higher voices.

A man singing within the female range is usually labelled '**countertenor**' and will either sing falsetto (a technique) or be able to reach higher notes due to some genetic quirk.

QUIZ 112. SCIENCE – BIRDLIFE

One for the twitchers among you. We were surprised by how badly this round scored – the best score was six, and, despite us not being birdwatching types, we didn't think it was that tricky.

1. Which species of bird has the largest population in the UK?

2. Puffin Books, established in 1940, is one of Britain's longest-standing children's book imprints. Which was the parent company that launched it as an adjunct to their adult imprint?

3. At twelve feet, which bird has the largest known wingspan?

4. Which mythological god was often accompanied by his two ravens, Huginn and Muninn?

5. What was Richard Bach's multi-million-selling novella, published in 1970, about a bird learning to fly and survive?

6. The PDSA Dickin Medal for animal courage and sacrifice in the war was awarded fifty-four times between 1943 and 1949: to eighteen dogs, three horses, one ship's cat and thirty-two what?

7. What kind of bird is Zazu in *The Lion King* and who provided his voice in the 1994 Disney film?

8. What is the name we give to the fused collarbone of a bird?

9. Where might we read about Gwaihir, the Windlord, a great eagle?

10. Egrets and bitterns are part of the avian family Ardeidae, which is comprised mainly of which type of bird?

Answers to Quiz 111

1. Leningrad, between 1924 and 1991.

2. Tottenham Hotspur.

3. The Patriarch of Antioch, which always sounds to me like a character from a fantasy novel.

4. Pentathlon (now the heptathlon). The seven events in the heptathlon are 100m hurdles, high jump, shot putt, 200m sprint, long jump, javelin, and 800m race. The men's decathlon replaces the 100m hurdles with 110m hurdles, and the sprint is 100m, not 200m, while the middle-distance run is 1,500m. The three extra disciplines are a 400m race, discus, and pole vault.

5. *CSI: Crime Scene Investigation* (the original series, set in Las Vegas). Grissom retired after nine seasons and was replaced as the lead character by Dr Ray Langston (Laurence Fishburne), and later D.B. Russell (Ted Danson).

6. Manchester.

7. Tampa Bay Rays; originally called the Devil Rays, the franchise dropped the Devil in 2007 at the insistence of owner Stuart Sternberg, with immediate benefit as the Rays reached the World Series for the first time in 2008.

8. The year was 1904 (so 1900s): a character called Peter Pan appeared in a novel, *The Little White Bird* (also by Barrie), in 1902.

9. Jordan – the city is ancient, having been established as a trading post, and is on many lists of extant wonders of the world.

10. Golf. Pettersen is a two-time Major winner and former world number two.

QUIZ 113. ODDLES

Simple set-up; just pick the odd one out based on the criteria we give you. This is another round that scored surprisingly badly – apparently giving people the answer within the question isn't always a big help!

1. Which of these is NOT a play by William Shakespeare: *All's Well that Ends Well*; *Measure for Measure*; *Never for Ever*; *Twelfth Night*?

2. Which of these was NOT President of the United States: Grover Cleveland: Calvin Coolidge; Charles P. Durning; Martin Van Buren?

3. Which of these is not a car currently manufactured by Volkswagen: Jetta; Nomad; Polo; Sharan?

4. Which of these NEVER played guitar with Thin Lizzy: Rory Gallagher; Scott Gorham; Gary Moore; Midge Ure?

5. Which of these was NOT an album by The Stranglers: *Aural Sculpture*; *Baroque Bordello*; *No More Heroes*; *The Raven*?

6. Which of these is NOT an element in the Periodic Table: palladium; tellurium; vestigium; zirconium?

7. Which of these is NOT one of Marvel's Avengers: Hawkeye; Iron Man; Thor; Wonder Woman?

8. Which of these was NEVER an Austrian international footballer: Marko Arnautović; Hans Krankl; Herbert Prohaska; Robert Prosinečki?

9. Which of these was NEVER a member of Boyzone: Keith Duffy; Niall Horan; Ronan Keating; Shane Lynch?

10. Which of these individuals was NOT born in India: former Lib Dem leader Paddy Ashdown; former England cricket captain Ted Dexter; actress Vivien Leigh; comedian and writer Spike Milligan?

Answers to Quiz 112

1. Wren. I was surprised, but then I know nothing about wildlife, to my shame.

2. Penguin Books.

3. The wandering albatross (accept albatross).

4. Odin. He's a bit of an animal lover, having two wolf companions (Geri, Freki) and he rides an eight-legged horse called Sleipnir.

5. Jonathan Livingston Seagull.

6. Pigeons.

7. Hornbill. Rowan Atkinson provided the voice; the character is the main source of humour in the film.

8. Furcular, or wishbone.

9. In the works of J.R.R. Tolkien. He uses Gwaihir as something of a device, as the eagles intervene in a number of key scenes in Tolkien's work, including the rescue of Frodo and Sam after they have completed their quest.

10. Herons.

QUIZ 114. SOVIET BLOCK (SIC)

Lots of new modern states were created by the break-up of the Soviet Union and Yugoslavia in the 1990s and after. Match the new state to its new capital city.

1. Bosnia and Herzegovina.

2. Chechnya.

3. Azerbaijan.

4. Georgia.

5. Croatia.

6. Slovenia.

7. Latvia.

8. Kazakhstan.

9. Kosovo.

10. Moldova.

A. Riga.

B. Chişinău.

C. Zagreb.

D. Pristina.

E. Grozny (aka Dohar).

F. Tbilisi.

G. Ljubljana.

H. Baku.

I. Astana.

J. Sarajevo.

Answers to Quiz 113

1. *Never for Ever* (alternate title for *Twelfth Night*; also a Kate Bush album).

2. Charles P. Durning. We made him up, although there was an American actor called Charles (Edward) Durning.

3. Nomad, although one type of VW Touareg is sub-named the Nomad.

4. Rory Gallagher; although Gallagher would have fitted the bill, he was Irish and a direct contemporary.

5. 'Baroque Bordello' is the title of a track on *The Raven*, their fifth album.

6. Vestigium; the others are all metallic elements – zirconium in a compound, as zirconium dioxide, is used to manufacture gemstones and makes a convincing diamond substitute.

7. Wonder Woman is a DC Comics character and thus not part of the Marvel Universe – she interacts with Batman and Superman in the recent reboots of those characters.

8. Robert Prosinečki (Croatia): Prosinečki first played for Yugoslavia, and later Croatia, and is currently the manager of the Bosnia and Herzegovina national team.

9. Niall Horan is a member of One Direction – the other two Boyzone members were Mikey Horan and the late Stephen Gately.

10. Ted Dexter was born in Italy. Very much an establishment figure, Dexter is remembered as much for his bumbling performances as manager of the England team as for his brilliant and powerful attacking batsmanship.

QUIZ 115. KEEP UP WITH THE JONESES

There have many Joneses over the years, some Welsh, some not – it remains the UK's second most common surname (after Smith) and the fourth most common in the US (after Smith, Johnson and Williams).

1. Revered singer-songwriter David Jones died on 10 January 2016: under what pseudonym did most of us know him?

2. Harrison Ford played Indiana Jones Jr in the popular film franchise: who played Indiana Jones Snr in the third film?

3. Who is the superhero love interest of superhero Jessica Jones?

4. Jack Jones was a major influence in British domestic politics in the 1970s: in what capacity?

5. Phil Jones is the only Jones to play football for England in the twenty-first century. With which club did he make his Premier League debut in 2009?

6. Which song from the animated Christmas film *The Snowman* took teenager Aled Jones into the UK Top 10 in 1985?

7. Which famous sci-fi film features a ship's cat called Jones?

8. Davy Jones, who died in 2012, is best remembered as the lead singer of pop group The Monkees. In which Lionel Bart musical did he first achieve fame as a teenager in the show's initial London and Broadway runs in 1960?

9. Which sitcom character was always trying to bed Miss Jones, one of his tenants, played by Frances de la Tour?

10. Australian Alan Jones won the F1 World Drivers' Championship in 1980. He was the first to win driving for which motor racing team?

Answers to Quiz 114

1. Bosnia and Herzegovina: J. Sarajevo. The country and the city suffered greatly during a civil war in the 1990s when the Bosnian Serbs wanted to remain within Yugoslavia, while the Bosniaks and Croats wanted independence.

2. Chechnya: E. Grozny was the unofficial capital of the Chechen Republic, which fought a bitter campaign to wrest independence from Russia (they ultimately failed).

3. Azerbaijan: H. Baku, a large and crucial port on the Caspian Sea.

4. Georgia: F. Tbilisi.

5. Croatia: C. Zagreb.

6. Slovenia: G. Ljubljana, an increasingly popular tourist city.

7. Latvia: A. Riga. Latvia is the middle of the three post-Soviet Baltic states, wedged between Estonia and Lithuania. It is a Baltic port in a large natural bay (Gulf of Riga), and the largest city within the three states.

8. Kazakhstan: I. Astana.

9. Kosovo: D. Pristina. Kosovo unilaterally declared independence from Serbia in 2008, and most of the international community has since recognised that independence (but not Serbia).

10. Moldova: B. Chişinău.

QUIZ 116. MIXED SPORT

A selection of questions across various sporting disciplines.

1. Teófilo Stevenson and Félix Savón both won three consecutive gold medals at the Summer Olympics: for which country and in which discipline?

2. Who was the only British golfer to win a Major Championship in the 1960s?

3. Who won the ice dance gold medal, scoring a perfect set of marks for artistic expression, at the 1984 Winter Olympics in Sarajevo?

4. Who was the last American male to win one of tennis's four major tournaments? (to the end of 2019).

5. If you were visiting Wincanton, Lingfield or Naas, what sport would you most likely be following?

6. Which three Australian cricketers received lengthy bans for their part in the ball-tampering scandal during the series against South Africa in 2018?

7. Who scored five points from five matches in the 2018 Ryder Cup as the European team reclaimed the trophy?

8. David Beckham and Simon Fuller's MLS team will begin competition in 2020: under what name will they play? Is it Inter Miami, Tampa Bay Mutiny, The Everglades, or Red Star Florida?

9. Dylan Hartley, at the start of the 2019 Six Nations, sits at ninety-seven test caps for England: who is the only man with more (119)?

10. Look at any list of National Hockey League player records, or any list of all-time great players – which name stands out?

Answers to Quiz 115

1. David Bowie.

2. Sean Connery.

3. Luke Cage (played on Netflix by Mike Colter). He appears in Jessica Jones' (Krysten Ritter) TV series and then had a spin-off series of his own – both characters appeared in *The Defenders*, alongside Dardevil and Iron Fist.

4. General Secretary of the Transport and General Workers' Union, at a time when trade union power was at its apex.

5. Manchester United. Great things were expected, but Jones has been hampered by persistent injury problems.

6. *Walking in the Air*. Jones has continued to have a career as an adult singer, but will always be remembered for this song.

7. *Alien*.

8. *Oliver!* – he was the original Artful Dodger.

9. Rigsby, played by Leonard Rossiter, in *Rising Damp* (written by Eric Chappell).

10. Williams – the team won the Constructors' Championship nine times (second to Ferrari), all in the 1980s and 1990s.

QUIZ 117. GAMES

Not sport, this time, but indoor games. Board games have had a massive revival in recent years, with clubs devoted to the pastime in every town. We have an open evening for gamers every Wednesday at the pub and always have a selection of board games available, both traditional and modern.

1. How many pieces does each player begin with in a game of backgammon? Which famous publisher on games published the first set of written rules for backgammon in 1753?

2. In a traditional game of Bingo, what is the highest number? And how many numbers need to be crossed off to call Full House?

3. In which country was *Trivial Pursuit* first released in 1981? Was it the UK, US, Canada or Australia? What is the designated colour for history questions?

4. Which popular tile-laying game takes its name from a city in the Languedoc region of France, and where was it developed?

5. In which decade was *Dungeons and Dragons* first published? And which company (now a subsidiary of Hasbro) has been distributing the game in recent years?

6. Which game is named from the Swahili word 'to build'? In which decade was it launched?

7. How many points does SEXY ELF score in Scrabble with the F on a double-letter score?

8. What lies between Trafalgar Square and Leicester Square on a standard London *Monopoly* board? Which property sits directly opposite?

9. Which version of Poker starts with two face-down hole cards in front of each player and five face-up community cards on the table? What colloquial name is given to the final card drawn in this version, sometimes known as Fifth Street?

10. In a game of cribbage, you have a 4H, 5C, 6C and JD in your hand, with a 5D at the top of the pile: how many points would you score this round?

Answers to Quiz 116

1. Cuba, boxing (heavyweight division). Stevenson won in 1972, 1976 and 1980, Savón in 1992, 1996 and 2000.

2. Tony Jacklin.

3. Jayne Torvill and Christopher Dean.

4. Andy Roddick, who won the 2003 US Open – earlier the same year Andre Agassi won his eighth and final major at the Australian Open.

5. Horse racing.

6. Steve Smith, David Warner and Cameron Bancroft.

7. Francesco Molinari, topping off a fabulous year in which he had already won his first major at the Open Championship.

8. Inter Miami.

9. Jason Leonard.

10. Wayne Gretzky. This seems a vague question but I can't think of any other sport, notwithstanding Ali in boxing, where there is such a strong consensus about who is the game's dominant player.

British winners of major golf titles since Tony Jacklin.

Jacklin broke a long wait, winning the Open eighteen years after Max Faulkner won the Open Championship in 1951 – against less stiff opposition then, as American golfers mainly stayed away from British links courses in the years after the war.

Tony Jacklin (Open Championship 1969, US Open 1970).
Sandy Lyle (Open 1985, Masters 1988).
Nick Faldo (Open 1987, 1990, 1992, Masters 1989, 1990, 1996).
Ian Woosnam (Masters 1991).
Paul Lawrie (Open 1999).
Graeme McDowell (US Open 2010).
Rory McIlroy (US Open 2011, PGA 2012, 2014, Open 2014).
Darren Clarke (Open 2011).

Justin Rose (US Open 2013).
Danny Willett (Masters 2016).

In addition to these, eight other European players have won major titles in the same period:

Seve Ballesteros (Masters × 2, Open × 3).
Bernhard Langer (Masters × 2).
José-María Olazábal (Masters × 2).
Padraig Harrington (Open × 1, PGA × 2).
Martin Kaymer (US Open × 1, PGA × 1).
Henrik Stenson (Open).
Sergio García (Masters).
Francesco Molinari (Open).

QUIZ 118. DOGS ON FILM

You may notice we have quite a few doggie questions. We hold a charity quiz for rescue dogs every year in honour of Martha, our gorgeous pub dog, who herself was rescued from a Romanian pound with only a few weeks left to live – which is absurd for a perfectly healthy, beautiful dog.

1. 'Toto,' says Dorothy to her dog in *The Wizard of Oz*. 'I've a feeling we're not in . . . anymore.' Where weren't they?

2. In which film does Frank, an alien disguised as a pug, first feature?

3. *Reservoir Dogs* was Quentin Tarantino's debut feature film: in which year was it released?

4. In the *Back to the Future* films, after which scientist does Doc Brown name his dog?

5. How did Rudd Weatherwax make a lot of money out of his rough collie, Pal?

6. Who played a starring role in the 1975 crime movie with a twist, *Dog Day Afternoon*?

7. In which film, starring Reese Witherspoon, does the main character own a chihuahua called Bruiser?

8. What are the names of the two parent dogs in the original animated Disney version of *One Hundred and One Dalmatians*?

9. Asta, a wire fox terrier, helps Nick and Nora Charles solve crimes in which series of 1930s/1940s movies?

10. Neil Fanning provided the voice for which cartoon movie dog in 2002 and 2004 movies?

Answers to Quiz 117

1. Fifteen; Edmund Hoyle. *Hoyle's Games* remains a go-to publication on the rules of traditional games and card games.

2. Ninety; fifteen. A classic bingo card has twenty-seven squares, in three rows of nine. Five squares per row contain fifteen numbers between 1 and 90. The caller gives out numbers and the player must concentrate and cross off the numbers on their card. If their card is full before anyone else's, they call 'House' and they have won.

3. Canada; history is yellow. The other categories are geography (blue), entertainment (pink), arts and literature (brown or purple), science and nature (green), and sports and leisure (orange).

4. Carcassonne, Germany.

5. The 1970s; Wizards of the Coast.

6. Jenga; the 1980s.

7. Twenty-four. S, E, E and L score one point each = four. Y gets four, X gets eight, making sixteen. F gets four, so doubled that makes eight, giving a total of twenty-four. And yes, we do know sexy elf is two words – it was a running gag at Christmas.

8. Fenchurch Street Station; The Angel, Islington.

9. Texas Hold'em; The River.

10. Fourteen; fifteen if playing one for his nob. There are four ways of making fifteen (two points each) and two alternative runs of three, making a further six points – total, fourteen points.

QUIZ 119. ALL SORTS

Not the liquorice kind, sadly, but another mash-up of general knowledge questions. This isn't the toughest – a team of four should definitely get seven points, even eight or nine.

1. What did newspaper editor Larry Lamb introduce into popular culture in 1970, before it was abandoned in 2015 in the face of vigorous opposition?

2. Who took over as the presenter of Radio 4's *Desert Island Discs* in 2006?

3. Autobots and Decepticons are types of what?

4. Which fêted Irish poet was among the founders of the Abbey Theatre in Dublin?

5. Which European ruler was the subject of lurid tales, probably apocryphal, of sex with the horses in her stables?

6. Baby Shark. Explain.

7. A madeleine is (a) a device for curing meat; (b) a small sponge cake; (c) a small soft-shelled Mediterranean crab; or (d) a Swiss liqueur chocolate?

8. Which model and celebrity dancer is married to footballer Peter Crouch?

9. What word for a large lorry comes from a statue of Krishna that is dragged through the streets of Puri during an annual festival?

10. Who entered Parliament as MP for Doncaster North in May 2005 and has held the seat since?

Answers to Quiz 118

1. Kansas, and they were in colour.

2. *Men in Black*.

3. 1992.

4. Einstein.

5. Pal played Lassie. The first Lassie film, *Lassie Come Home*, was released in 1943 and was a huge success. Pal played the part in a further six films and his descendants have been selected to play the role in more recent incarnations on film and on TV.

6. Al Pacino.

7. *Legally Blonde*.

8. Pongo and Perdita. The film is based on a 1956 novel by Dodie Smith – in the book, Missis is the wife of Pongo, and it is they who have the adventure, while Perdita, a stray, stays with the Dearlys.

9. The *Thin Man* series, based on a novel by Dashiell Hammett. The six films are: *The Thin Man* (1934), *After the Thin Man* (1936), *Another Thin Man* (1939), *Shadow of the Thin Man* (1941), *The Thin Man Goes Home* (1945), *Song of the Thin Man* (1947).

10. Scooby-Doo. Don Messick was the main voice of Scooby-Doo on TV, fulfilling the role from 1969 to 1996.

QUIZ 120. NAME THE ALBUM

Relatively straightforward. We give you three tracks from a successful album, you give us the name of the album and the band that made it. A variety of eras, though nothing too old and nothing too recent in there.

1. 'British Legion'; 'Me Plus One'; 'Shoot the Runner' (2006).

2. 'What'll I Do'; 'Again'; 'That's the Way Love Goes' (1993).

3. 'Tears Are Not Enough'; 'All of My Heart'; 'Poison Arrow' (1982).

4. 'Hard Times'; 'Love Goes Down'; 'Prayin'' (2010).

5. 'Money Can't Buy It'; 'Why'; 'Walking on Broken Glass' (1992).

6. 'Lenny', 'Mansize Rooster'; 'Caught by the Fuzz' (1995).

7. 'Nightblindness'; 'Sail Away'; 'Babylon' (1998).

8. 'Walking Away'; 'Rendezvous'; 'Fill Me In' (2000).

9. 'Tears and Rain'; 'No Bravery'; 'Wisemen' (2004).

10. 'Mindfields'; 'Breathe'; 'Firestarter' (1997).

Answers to Quiz 119

1. The Page Three Girl in the *Sun* newspaper.

2. Kirsty Young. The show's creator, Roy Plomley, was presenter from 1942 to 1985, when Michael Parkinson started a three-year stint. In 1988, Sue Lawley took over, and eighteen years later she handed over the reins to Kirsty Young. Some concepts are so simple and adaptable they become timeless.

3. Transformers.

4. W.B. Yeats (1865–1939). The Abbey Theatre opened in 1904 and in 1925 became the first state-funded theatre in the world.

5. Catherine the Great.

6. A kids' song that became a viral phenomenon in 2018, with over three billion views across all media platforms.

7. It is a small sponge cake.

8. Abigail Clancy Crouch. The presenter of *Britain's Next Top Model* was the 2011 winner of *Strictly Come Dancing*.

9. A juggernaut.

10. Ed Miliband.

QUIZ 121. ONLY CONNECT

This is basically a general knowledge round. But we can give you a clue – the answers are connected in that all the countries played a part in the 2018 World Cup Finals tournament in Russia.

1. The Walloon region is an important French-speaking area of which country?

2. Which country seceded from the Republic of Gran Colombia in 1903 and promptly allowed American engineers to start construction on a vital piece of twentieth-century transport infrastructure?

3. In which modern country was the Inca Empire the dominant political entity on its continent from the late thirteenth to the fifteenth century?

4. Incursion into South America by which European country put a violent end to that dominance?

5. Which Asian country is the biggest military spender after the United States and China, according to 2018 stats?

6. Which is the most populous country in the Arabic world?

7. After negotiating a deal to end a long-standing military conflict with the FARC rebels, which country's president, Juan Manuel Santos, was awarded the 2016 Nobel Peace Prize?

8. What name is given to the twenty-six administrative regions of Switzerland?

9. Which country has topped the last three Happy Planet lists of the most environmentally and sociologically well balanced?

10. The island groups the Azores and Madeira both come under the sovereignty of which European country?

Answers to Quiz 120

1. *Empire*, Kasabian's second album.

2. *Janet* (written as *janet.*) was the 1993 fifth album from Janet Jackson; it went to No. 1 on both sides of the Atlantic, her first UK No. 1 album.

3. ABC, *The Lexicon of Love*. The classic eighties beat-pop album was much hyped and went straight to No. 1 in the UK.

4. Plan B, *The Defamation of Strickland Banks*.

5. Annie Lennox, *Diva*. This was Lennox's first solo album after the break-up of The Eurythmics, one of the most successful British bands of the 1980s.

6. Supergrass, *I Should Coco*. Supergrass were one of the key Britpop bands and this was their debut album.

7. David Gray, *White Ladder*. It took a year or so for Gray's fourth album to hit its peak, but it became one of those ubiquitous albums that seem to insinuate their way into every household.

8. Craig David, *Born to Do It*.

9. James Blunt, *Back to Bedlam*.

10. Prodigy, *The Fat of the Land*.

QUIZ 122. GENERAL SCIENCE

Groans are heard around the pub when I announce a science round – but the scoring is generally okay; most teams have at least one member with inclinations towards the empirical, or who can at least remember what they studied for their GCSEs.

1. For what might one use an analgesic?

2. In astronomy, how did nine become eight in 2006?

3. What name is given to the different forms taken by some elements? For example, diamond and graphite are both forms of pure carbon.

4. *The Revolutions of the Celestial Spheres*, a massively influential treatise that put the sun, not the earth, at the centre of the solar system, was written in the 1530s and published in 1543 just before its author's death. Who was he?

5. The theory of animal magnetism was developed by which theoretical experimentalist, whose name is now given to this area of mind control and suggestion?

6. What discovery, by eighteen-year-old William Perkin in 1856, changed the face of the textile industry and also had a significant impact on food and medicine?

7. Which American Founding Father coined the terms positive and negative to describe different aspects of electricity?

8. What is the specialist branch of taxonomy known as Alpha Taxonomy?

9. The class of creatures grouped as Gastropoda comprise mainly which two types of common creature?

10. Which type of bird accounts for over half the avian species in the world?

Answers to Quiz 121

1. Belgium. The country comprises three regions. One is the capital, Brussels; another is the Flemish region, comprising the northern half of Belgium; while the south is the region of Wallonia, and is mainly French-speaking.

2. Panama.

3. Peru.

4. Spain. The Conquistadores beat down the Aztec civilisation in Mexico under Cortès, and later did the same to the Peruvian Inca Empire under Pizarro and others.

5. Saudi Arabia.

6. Iran, which ranks eighteenth in the world, three places ahead of the UK.

7. Colombia.

8. Cantons.

9. Costa Rica.

10. Portugal.

The Top 10 military spenders in 2018 were:

United States.

China.

Saudi Arabia (forget the human rights, think of the cash . . .).

Russia.

India.

United Kingdom.

France.

Japan.

Germany.

South Korea.

QUIZ 123. TOMFOOLERY

Tom, Thomas, Thomson – Tommies in all their glory. Alas, no Thomasinas.

1. Which Tom contested a number of major tournaments with Jack Nicklaus in Nicklaus's heyday, winning eight in the 1970s and 1980s?

2. Which Midlands cabinet maker started a railway company in 1841 to transport protesting temperance groups?

3. Which Sicilian-born friar, philosopher and theologian was canonised in 1323, nearly fifty years after his death?

4. Which singer did English actor Tom Hiddleston portray in the 2015 biopic *I Saw the Light*?

5. Who married Dustin Lance Black in May 2017?

6. Which songwriter and performer set a list of chemical elements to the tune of the 'Major-General's Song' from *The Pirates of Penzance*?

7. Tom Brady is the only player to win six Superbowl championships – with which north-east-based American Football franchise has he achieved this?

8. 'It's Not Unusual' (1965) was the debut single and first No. 1 for Welsh singer Tom Jones: what was his only other solo UK No. 1?

9. A member of Springsteen's E Street Band in recent years, Tom Morello was previously best known as the guitarist and songwriter in which political rock band, who enjoyed a surprise UK No. 1 in 2009?

10. Who wrote about the mystery-solving duo Tommy and Tuppence?

Answers to Quiz 122

1. Pain relief.

2. Pluto was relegated in status to a dwarf planet, leaving only eight true planets in our solar system: the decision was made by the International Astronomical Union.

3. Allotropes.

4. Nicolaus Copernicus.

5. (Franz) Mesmer.

6. Purple dye – purple had hitherto been prohibitively expensive, but Perkin's work opened up a host of developments in dyeing and colouration.

7. Benjamin Franklin.

8. The finding and categorising and naming of (specifically) new species.

9. Snails and slugs.

10. Passeriformes or perching birds (songbirds is not strictly accurate, but give them a half).

QUIZ 124. THIS WAY AND THAT

All about travelling the globe in various directions, and how to get from A to B. The ability to see a map in your brain when asked geographical questions such as these would be a definite asset: they need some thinking about.

1. In 2008 a BBC programme followed Simon Reeve as he visited Namibia, Botswana, South Africa, Mozambique, Madagascar, Australia, Chile, Argentina, Paraguay and Brazil: what dictated his route?

2. Las Vegas, Nashville, Oklahoma City, San Francisco: which lies furthest north?

3. To travel overland from India to Turkey, what is the smallest number of other countries one would have to pass through?

4. To get from Serbia to Poland overland, one could go through Romania and the Ukraine. Which other two countries would also provide a more direct route?

5. Sail due west from Ireland and what is the first country one would encounter?

6. Sail east from Hawaii and what state or country's coastline will you hit?

7. Brussels, Frankfurt, Kiev, Prague: which is the furthest north?

8. Cape Town, SA; Santiago, Chile; Auckland, NZ; Hobart, Tasmania (Australia) – which lies furthest south?

9. The quickest route from California to Texas by land takes the traveller through which other two US states?

10. Panama, with its canal, links South America to Central and North America: which two countries lie to the north and south of Panama?

Answers to Quiz 123

1. Tom Watson. Watson won five Open Championships (he was a brilliant links player), and also won the Masters twice and the 1982 US Open. And he did it all with a smile and the utmost courtesy.

2. Thomas Cook. They don't make cabinets any more.

3. St Thomas Aquinas.

4. Hank Williams. Hiddleston sang the numbers himself, backed by the Saddle Spring Boys.

5. Tom Daley, Olympic medal-winning and World Champion diver.

6. Tom Lehrer, in 1959.

7. New England Patriots.

8. 'Green, Green Grass of Home' (1966).

9. Rage Against the Machine – their single, 'Killing in the Name', went to No. 1 on the back of an internet campaign to prevent the *X Factor* winner yet again having the Christmas No. 1.

10. Agatha Christie. Thomas and Tuppence Beresford appear in four novels (*The Secret Adversary*, *N or M?*, *By the Pricking of My Thumbs* and *Postern of Fate*) and a selection of short stories (*Partners in Crime*).

QUIZ 125. NEW YORK, NEW YORK

The Big Apple. (Why?) A set of questions on America's biggest and most glamorous city, and the world's biggest movie set.

1. What was New York's name when it was first colonised and developed by Dutch settlers in the early seventeenth century?

2. Which famous art museum opened in New York on 53rd Street in 1929?

3. Which New York landmark lies at the junction of Broadway and Seventh?

4. Which of the eight Ivy League colleges is based in New York City?

5. In which decade did the first part of the New York City Subway open?

6. Which of New York's boroughs covers the northernmost part of the city?

7. The New York Stock Exchange is the world's largest by market capitalisation: which exchange in the same city is the second largest?

8. What important New York transport link runs from Whitehall Terminal to St George Terminal?

9. Where in New York will you find the Swedish Cottage Marionette Theatre, the Angel of the Waters statue, the Diana Ross Playground and Belvedere Castle?

10. Which flagship department store stands on Herald Square in New York?

Answers to Quiz 124

1. They are the countries that lie on the Tropic of Capricorn, a set line of latitude to the south of the Equator.

2. San Francisco, comfortably – I was surprised how far north it is, only marginally south of Washington DC.

3. Two – Pakistan and Iran.

4. Hungary and Slovakia.

5. Canada.

6. Mexico.

7. Brussels is slightly further north than Kiev.

8. Hobart is comfortably further south than the other three.

9. Arizona and New Mexico.

10. Costa Rica and Colombia.

QUIZ 126. THEATRE

Another for the cultured types. A series of questions about drama and the theatre in general. Non-theatricals will score poorly on this, but some knowledge or interest should give a score of six or more.

1. Who is the daughter of Lady Bracknell in Oscar Wilde's *The Importance of Being Earnest*?

2. *The Room* (1957) was the first performed work by which major modern British playwright?

3. Which now discredited figure was the Artistic Director of the Old Vic theatre between 2003 and 2015?

4. Which play, with only two actors, opened in the West End in 1989 and is still running, making it the second-longest-running non-musical after *The Mousetrap*?

5. Who are Vladimir and Estragon?

6. Who wrote *Shopping and Fucking*, one of the more contentious plays of the 1990s, largely because of its attention-seeking title?

7. In what capacity did Cicely Berry earn plaudits galore for her work with the Royal Shakespeare Company?

8. *Look Back in Anger*, by John Osborne, gave rise to a spate of gritty, realist dramas that became collectively known by which term?

9. Who took the National Theatre to trial for obscenity in 1982 over their production of Howard Brenton's play, *Romans in Britain*?

10. Which major theatre can be found in Sloane Square, London?

Answers to Quiz 125

1. New Amsterdam; it was renamed when it came under English control after 1664. The land was gifted by the king to his brother James, Duke of York, hence New York.

2. Museum of Modern Art (MOMA).

3. Times Square.

4. Columbia (see below).

5. 1900s (1904).

6. The Bronx.

7. NASDAQ.

8. Staten Island Ferry.

9. They are all in Manhattan's Central Park.

10. Macy's, founded in 1858. By acquisition, it became affiliated to the Bloomingdale's chain, but it remains very much Macy's and the country's most prestigious department store. Macy's Thanksgiving Day Parade is one of the city's great events.

The Ivy League
The Ivy League began as an athletic league incorporating teams from eight privileged north-eastern universities, but the term is now used to refer to these universities in general.

The eight are:
Browns – Providence, Rhode Island.
Columbia – Upper Manhattan, New York City.
Cornell – Ithaca, New York State.
Dartmouth – Hanover, New Hampshire.
Harvard – Cambridge, Massachusetts.
University of Pennsylvania – Philadelphia, Pennsylvania.
Princeton – Princeton, New Jersey.
Yale – New Haven, Connecticut.

QUIZ 127. NICKS

We did this one for Nicole's birthday last year – a round on Nicks, Nicolases and Nicoles in a whole variety of roles.

1. Who hosted the Radio 1 Breakfast Show between 2012 and 2018?

2. Which Nick emulated his famous and more talented grandfather when he made his debut for the England Test Match cricket team in 2012?

3. Nicola Sturgeon is the leader of the SNP, but who leads the party in Westminster?

4. Nicky Wire is the bass player and lyricist with which Welsh rock band?

5. With Roy Keane and Paul Scholes both suspended, who played along-side David Beckham in central midfield in Manchester United's 1999 Champions League victory over Bayern Munich?

6. Who was the Artistic Director of the National Theatre from 2003 until 2015?

7. What is the 'secret' behind the best-selling author of psychological thrillers, Nicci French?

8. Nicola Roberts is a former member of which girl band?

9. Who played the villainous Millicent Clyde in the first *Paddington* movie?

10. Nicola Fairbrother won a silver medal at the 1992 Olympics in the lightweight judo division, where she was beaten by Spain's Miriam Blasco in the final. How did the story end: (a) she beat Blasco in the final in 1996; (b) she was later awarded a gold medal after Blasco tested positive for a banned substance; (c) they married each other; (d) Blasco was jailed for assaulting Fairbrother after a controversial defeat at the World Championships?

Answers to Quiz 126

1. Gwendolen Fairfax, who is the object of Jack/Ernest's affections, while Lady Bracknell's nephew, and Jack's friend, Algernon, is in love with Jack's ward, Cecily Cardew.

2. Harold Pinter; Pinter wrote twenty-nine published plays, including *The Caretaker*, *The Birthday Party*, *Betrayal* and *No Man's Land*, as well as numerous film screenplays, including those for *The Go-Between* and *The French Lieutenant's Woman*.

3. Kevin Spacey.

4. *The Woman in Black*, based on the Gothic mystery by Susan Hill.

5. The two tramps in Samuel Beckett's 1953 play, *Waiting for Godot*, one of the most influential works of the twentieth century.

6. Mark Ravenhill.

7. She was the company's voice coach from 1969 to 2014. She died in 2018, aged ninety-two.

8. Kitchen sink drama.

9. Mary Whitehouse; she lost.

10. Royal Court. It opened in 1870 and was purchased by the English Stage Company in 1956.

QUIZ 128. SPORT

All sorts of different sports, all sorts of different questions.

1. Running back LaDainian Tomlinson set a new National Football League record in 2006 with thirty-one of these. Thirty-one what?

2. Who are the three Brazilian drivers to have won the F1 World Driver's Championship?

3. Before the advent of the Super League, which club won seventeen Rugby League Championship titles, ten more than any other team, including every title from 1990 to 1996, the last before Super League.

4. Who is the only basketball player to have won the NBA's most valuable player six times?

5. US twins Mike and Bob Bryan have won sixteen important tournaments together doing what?

6. What name is given to the bowling style of a left-arm bowler who bowls with the same wrist action as a leg-break bowler?

7. Which team has played and lost in three Rugby Union World Cup Finals?

8. Why were the Russian ice hockey players who won the gold medal at the 2018 Winter Olympics designated 'Olympic Athletes from Russia'?

9. Whose six wickets won her the Player of the Match award as England defended an average total to beat India and win the 2017 Women's Cricket World Cup? Who captained the team?

10. What three surfaces are used for the four major tennis tournaments on the calendar?

Answers to Quiz 127

1. Nick Grimshaw.

2. Nick Compton. Comparisons with grandad aren't flattering. Denis Compton scored 5,807 Test runs at an average of 50.06, while Nick amassed only 775 at an average of 28.70.

3. Angus Robertson. The party holds thirty-five seats in the House of Commons, down from the 2015 peak of fifty-six. Scotland sends a total of fifty-nine MPs to the UK Parliament.

4. Manic Street Preachers. The band is a three-piece comprising Wire, James Dean Bradfield and drummer Sean Moore, Bradfield's cousin.

5. Nicky Butt. The full United team is printed below – have a stab at how many you can remember before you look at the list.

6. Nicholas Hytner, who has done great work in theatre, opera and film.

7. They are a husband-and-wife writing team.

8. Girls Aloud.

9. Nicole Kidman.

10. (c) they married each other.

This is the Manchester United team that won the Champions League in 1999. It wasn't their finest performance (that, arguably, came in the semi-final against Juventus), but they got the result.

Peter Schmeichel (captain)

Gary Neville   Jaap Stam   Ronny Johnsen   Denis Irwin

Ryan Giggs   David Beckham   Nicky Butt   Jesper Blomqvist

(sub: Teddy Sheringham)

Dwight Yorke   Andrew Cole (sub: Ole Gunnar Solskjær)

QUIZ 129. THIS OR THAT

These phrases are either the title of an Elmore Leonard novel, a best-selling Britpop album, or a film starring Steve McQueen.

1. *Get Shorty.*

2. *Dog Man Star.*

3. *Bullitt.*

4. *His 'n' Hers.*

5. *The Great Escape.*

6. *Tom Horn.*

7. *Cat Chaser.*

8. *Mother Nature Calls.*

9. *Rum Punch.*

10. *Hell is for Heroes.*

11. *A Storm in Heaven.*

12. *Out of Sight.*

Answers to Quiz 128

1. Touchdowns.

2. Emerson Fittipaldi (1972 and 1974); Nelson Piquet (1981, 1983 and 1987); Ayrton Senna (1988, 1990, 1991).

3. Wigan Warriors.

4. Kareem Abdul-Jabbar.

5. Playing tennis – they have won sixteen major titles as a pair; Mike has won a further two with Jack Sock (to 2018).

6. Chinaman.

7. France; they lost the inaugural final to New Zealand, to Australia in 1999 and to the All Blacks again in 2011.

8. Because Russia was still under an IOC ban – Russian entrants were allowed to compete under this designation in sports where they were deemed to be innocent of state-sponsored drug taking.

9. Anya Shrubsole; Heather Knight.

10. Grass (Wimbledon), clay (French) and hard courts (Australia and US Open).

QUIZ 130. HISTORY OF THE US

Some questions on the Founding Fathers and all that history stuff from across the pond. We get quite a few Americans bands and artists playing at the pub – they are all blown away by the fact that the pub is more than two hundred years older than the post-Native American version of their country.

1. What was the name given to the first ten amendments to the American Constitution signed by the legislature in 1791?

2. What was the name of the secret organisation within the thirteen colonies that aimed to resist unfair British taxation?

3. The Boston Tea Party was a 1773 incident in which opponents of the British colonial government destroyed a shipment of tea in Boston harbour: which colonial company owned the shipment?

4. Purchase of which tranche of land from France in 1803 doubled the size of the United States at one stroke?

5. The first armed conflict of the American Civil War was the bombard-ment of which stronghold near Charleston by Confederate Army forces?

6. What is the name given to the laws passed in the late nineteenth century that enforced segregation in the Confederate States?

7. American independence was declared in 1776, but in which year did George Washington take up office as the new nation's first president?

8. And who was Washington's vice-president and later his successor?

9. Which Democratic president preceded Abraham Lincoln, but was unable to find a compromise solution to the issue of slavery that dominated his time in office?

10. In the winter of 1777, British forces under Sir William Howe captured which crucial port city, a low point in the Revolutionary War for the American patriots?

Answers to Quiz 129

1. *Get Shorty* was an Elmore Leonard novel, made into a movie starring John Travolta in 1995, five years after the book.

2. *Dog Man Star* was the second album by British band Suede, released in 1994.

3. *Bullitt* was a 1968 Peter Yates film starring Steve McQueen.

4. *His 'n' Hers* was Pulp's fourth album and their most commercial to date – they benefited from the surge of Britpop even though they were around some time before most of the other bands in the movement.

5. *The Great Escape* was a 1963 all-star (including McQueen) film, but it was also the title of a 1995 album by Blur – give anyone who identified this TWO extra points.

6. *Tom Horn* was a 1980 Western starring Steve McQueen.

7. *Cat Chaser* was a 1982 book by Elmore Leonard. It was made into a film in 1989 starring Peter Weller and Kelly McGillis.

8. *Mother Nature Calls* was a Britpop album from the English band Cast.

9. *Rum Punch* was a 1992 Elmore Leonard novel filmed five years later by Quentin Tarantino as *Jackie Brown*.

10. *Hell is for Heroes* was a 1962 war movie with Steve McQueen.

11. *A Storm in Heaven* was the 1993 debut album by The Verve.

12. Elmore Leonard's *Out of Sight* (1996) was picked up immediately and came out as a movie directed by Steven Soderbergh in 1998, with George Clooney and Jennifer Lopez starring.

QUIZ 131. LAWMAKERS

Policemen, agents, sheriffs, spies – general knowledge questions about those who uphold the law and the safety of the nation.

1. Who was appointed head of the Metropolitan Police in April 2017?

2. Members of which private security firm formed in 1850 were used as Lincoln's personal guard during the US Civil War?

3. Who was the Tombstone Marshal who led the lawmakers at the legendary Gunfight at the O.K. Corral?

4. What initials are used to denote the intelligence unit that perpetrated the genocide known as 'the Great Purge' under Josef Stalin?

5. What was the name of the sheriff who hunted Billy the Kid?

6. How many deployable armed police officers are there in the UK? (stats as at March 2018). Are there 1,450; 4,100; 6,500; or 9,600?

7. With which movie franchise would one associate Sheriff J.W. Pepper, played by Clifton James?

8. In which US city and state can the headquarters of the CIA be found?

9. What is the name of the sheriff in the Bob Marley song, 'I Shot the Sheriff'?

10. What is the fourth arm of the Italian military (alongside the army, navy and air force), responsible for policing the military and some aspects of counter-terrorism and combat?

Answers to Quiz 130

1. Bill of Rights. These first ten amendments included the right to freedom of religion and speech (the first), the right to bear arms (second), the right to refuse to incriminate oneself (fifth), and the right to fair trial, by jury if appropriate (sixth and seventh).

2. Sons of Liberty.

3. British East India Company.

4. Louisiana Purchase – the land was enormous and included the entire states of Arkansas, Iowa, Kansas, Missouri, Nebraska and Oklahoma, as well as portions of nine others and a few bits of what is now Canada.

5. Fort Sumter.

6. Jim Crow laws.

7. 1789.

8. John Adams.

9. James Buchanan.

10. New York.

Here are the fifty states that make up the United States of America: Alabama; Alaska; Arizona; Arkansas; California; Carolina (North); Carolina (South); Colorado; Connecticut; Dakota (South); Dakota (North); Delaware; Florida; Georgia; Hawaii; Idaho; Illinois; Indiana; Iowa; Kansas; Kentucky; Louisiana; Maine; Maryland; Massachusetts; Michigan; Minnesota; Missouri; Mississippi; Montana; Nevada; Nebraska; New Hampshire; New Jersey; New Mexico; New York; Ohio; Oklahoma; Oregon; Pennsylvania; Rhode Island; Tennessee; Texas; Utah; Vermont; Virginia; Virginia (West); Washington; Wisconsin; Wyoming.

QUIZ 132. MOVIE MIX

Another cross-section of film questions.

1. In which 2007 film did Saoirse Ronan and Romola Garai play the same character aged thirteen and eighteen respectively?

2. *Live and Let Die* was the first Bond movie not to include which character, part of the MI6 head office set-up?

3. Who played Eminem's mum in the 2002 film *8 Mile*?

4. In which 1978 movie does Michael Myers go on a killing spree?

5. What was the title of the final Indiana Jones movie, released in 2008, nineteen years after the last of the original trilogy?

6. Emil Jannings plays a professor obsessed with a nightclub singer in *The Blue Angel* (1930): who plays the singer, Lola?

7. Robert De Niro and Leonardo DiCaprio have both enjoyed fruitful collaborative relationships with Martin Scorsese, but what was the only full-length feature film (up to January 2019) directed by Scorsese to feature both actors?

8. Who played Sheriff Will Kane's wife in the classic Western *High Noon*?

9. Who co-wrote and starred in *Bottle Rocket*, the directorial debut of Wes Anderson, and has worked on a number of further projects with the director?

10. If Tommy Lee Jones and Will Smith are Agents K and J, who is Agent L?

Answers to Quiz 131

1. Cressida Dick; she is the first female head of the Met.

2. The Pinkertons – the Pinkerton Detective agency was established by a Scot, Allan Pinkerton, in 1850.

3. Virgil Earp. The elder brother Virgil was the more experienced soldier and lawman, Wyatt was a conscripted Deputy, along with younger brother Morgan and their friend, Doc Holliday. Three of their opponents were killed while the rest fled the scene after a brief burst of gunfire that lasted no more than thirty seconds, according to eyewitness accounts.

4. NKVD – the unit was disbanded after the war and replaced by the Ministry of Internal Affairs.

5. Pat Garrett.

6. About 6,500.

7. James Bond. He first appeared as comic relief in *Live and Let Die* and reappeared in *The Man with the Golden Gun*. The character is as far removed from the tone and mood of Fleming's original concept as the film's ever got, and is about as funny as the bubonic plague.

8. Langley, Virginia.

9. John Brown: 'Sheriff John Brown always hated me – for what, I don't know.'

10. Carabinieri.

QUIZ 133. HARRY POTTER

Ten questions about the Harry Potter world. Some groan when we slip in a Potter question, but the books and films have pervaded every part of Western society, unlike any other series before or since.

1. What was the line-up for the Gryffindor Quidditch team in Harry Potter's first year at Hogwarts?

2. What is the name of Harry Potter's owl?

3. What is the name of the famous wandmaker with a shop in Diagon Alley in the Harry Potter books?

4. Which Mexican film director made the third film in the Harry Potter series, *Harry Potter and the Prisoner of Azkaban*?

5. What kind of creature is Firenze in the Harry Potter novels?

6. What is the name of the hero of the Fantastic Beasts stories, originally a 'non-fiction'-style guidebook to accompany the original novels, later films scripted by J.K. Rowling?

7. Which five wizards serve as Minister for Magic in the Harry Potter books?

8. What is the name of Rowling's play which opened in London's West End in summer 2016?

9. What are the names of Draco Malfoy's rather stupid companions in the Harry Potter books? (Bonus point for both first names!)

10. Who are the Hogwarts' Defence Against the Dark Arts teachers in the time period of the Harry Potter novels? (You should end up with eight names.)

Answers to Quiz 132

1. *Atonement* – both play Briony Tallis.

2. Q, the weapons and gadget expert. A character called the armourer appears in *Dr No*, then Desmond Llewelyn took over as Q until his death in 1999. John Cleese briefly took the role, then, in *Skyfall* (2012), a younger, tech-savvy Q appeared, played by Ben Whishaw.

3. Kim Basinger.

4. *Halloween*.

5. *Indiana Jones and the Kingdom of the Crystal Skull*.

6. Marlene Dietrich, in her most famous role and singing 'Falling in Love Again'.

7. *The Departed*.

8. Grace Kelly.

9. Owen Wilson.

10. Linda Fiorentino in *Men in Black*.

QUIZ 134. SCIENCE MIX

Another mixture of science questions. Just so we're clear – when we say science, we are including astronomy and natural history, so it's a broad interpretation.

1. Titan is a moon larger than the planet Mercury. Of which planet is it a satellite?

2. Is the diameter of Jupiter roughly eleven, eighteen or twenty-six times the size of that of earth?

3. What is the fourth fundamental state of matter, along with solid, liquid and gas?

4. Which controversial twentieth-century British scientist first coined the phrase Big Bang, but denied such an episode had ever taken place?

5. Which caring international body was founded by Henry Dunant? And to which British pioneer did he credit the inspiration for his work?

6. Which New Zealand-born scientist first differentiated between alpha and beta radiation while working in Canada, and later discovered and named the proton while at the University of Manchester?

7. What term is used to describe large-scale government-funded science projects, especially those from the Second World War era?

8. Species, _____, family, order, _____, phylum, kingdom. These are the first seven layers in the Linnaean taxonomic order. Which two are missing?

9. A mastodon is an extinct distant relative of which popular animal?

10. Which university, a specialist in the teaching of science, is third among British institutions behind Oxford and Cambridge in the QS world rankings?

Answers to Quiz 133

1. Oliver Wood (keeper). Angelina Johnson, Katie Bell and Alicia Spinnet (chasers). Fred and George Weasley (beaters) and Harry (seeker).

2. Hedwig.

3. Mr Olivander.

4. Alfonso Cuarón.

5. A centaur.

6. Newt Scamander.

7. Cornelius Fudge is the Minister for Magic in the early books, with Rufus Scrimgeour taking over when Fudge is discredited. After the Death Eaters torture and kill Scrimgeour, Pius Thicknesse becomes Voldemort's puppet. Kingsley Shacklebolt becomes Minister after the final battle, and in the epilogue, Hermione Granger is seen to have taken on the role.

8. Harry Potter and the Cursed Child.

9. Vincent Crabbe and Gregory Goyle.

10. Professors Quirrell, Lockhart, Lupin, Barty Crouch posing as Mad Eye Moody, Dolores Umbridge, Snape and Amycus Carrow.

QUIZ 135. GENERAL KNOWLEDGE

I wonder if a General Knowledge ever served in the military of some country? Unlikely; not a popular surname. Anyway, moving on, here's another mixed round.

1. The invention of the mini skirt and hot pants are both credited to which quintessentially English fashion designer?

2. Which internet entrepreneur bought the *Washington Post* newspaper for $250m cash in 2013?

3. Which famous nineteenth-century novel is subtitled *or The Modern Prometheus*?

4. The occult group, the Hermetic Order of the Golden Dawn, was formed by three members of which other organisation?

5. What word, from the Italian for a type of shell, was first used by Marco Polo to describe the delicate ceramics he saw in China?

6. Who was Becoming to the top of the book charts in 2018?

7. What would the now near-obsolete role of a stenographer be?

8. If N.W.A. were the most significant of the early L.A. hip-hop bands, who were the leaders of the parallel New York movement?

9. Which anti-crime scheme was adopted in the UK after British police officers visited Chicago in 1982?

10. Which element did Henry Cavendish describe as 'inflammable air'?

Answers to Quiz 134

1. Saturn. Saturn has over sixty moons, of which Titan is the largest, about five thousand kilometres across – only Ganymede, the largest moon of Jupiter, is larger.

2. About eleven times – Earth is 12,756 km, Jupiter 142,800 km.

3. Plasma.

4. Fred Hoyle.

5. The Red Cross. It was founded in 1863 and, like many international bodies, has its headquarters in neutral Switzerland, in Geneva. Dunant was inspired by the work of British nursing pioneer, Florence Nightingale.

6. Ernest Rutherford.

7. Big Science.

8. Genus and Class; for example, a leopard (*Panthera pardus*) is a species within the genus *Panthera*, which includes the extant big cats with the ability to roar. They belong to the family Felidae, which is all cats, within the order Carnivora (carnivorous mammals), within the class Mammalia (all mammals). The phylum (Chordata, in this case) is a more sophisticated biological distinction whereby a creature must possess five anatomical features, and the kingdom is Animalia, which is all animals.

9. Elephant.

10. Imperial College. The list, produced by a think-tank, includes five American universities, four British ones and a Swiss institute, so should be treated with suspicion.

QUIZ 136. WAR SONGS

We did a war-themed quiz for Armistice Day and the music round comprised questions on songs about war. This is it.

1. Who released a 1983 No. 1 album called *War*?

2. 'And I'll stand on your grave / 'Til I'm sure that you're dead.' Which anti-war song ends with this aggressive couplet?

3. What was John Lennon and Yoko Ono's 1971 Christmas hit? (be specific).

4. War Pigs was the opening track on which classic 1970 heavy metal album?

5. 'War Baby' (1986) was a solo No. 1 hit for which musician, now a BBC 6 music presenter? What was his earlier UK Top 10 hit with his band, riding the crest of the punk/pub rock wave.

6. 'War! Huh! What is it good for?'

7. Who took this song to No. 1 in the US and No. 3 in the UK in 1970?

8. On which label was it released?

9. For which band from the same label was the song originally written (and recorded, but not released as a single)?

10. Which singer-songwriter took the song back into the US Top 10 when he released it as a non-album single in 1986?

Answers to Quiz 135

1. Mary Quant; she came to prominence as an architect of the swinging sixties with her fresh look for women – Quant is still alive at the age of eighty-nine.

2. Jeff Bezos, the founder and CEO of Amazon.

3. Mary Shelley's *Frankenstein*; the book was published when Shelley was just twenty years old, but only carried her name from the second edition. It was Shelley's only major work, although she edited the works of her husband, the poet Percy Bysshe Shelley. She had great pedigree – her parents were the pioneering feminist writer Mary Wollstonecraft and the political thinker William Godwin.

4. Woodman, Westcott and Mathers were a splinter group formed from The Freemasons in 1887.

5. Porcelain.

6. Michelle Obama; it was the title of her autobiography.

7. A shorthand typist (accept typist).

8. Public Enemy. Their seminal second album, *It Takes a Nation of Millions to Hold Us Back*, was released in 1988, the same year as N.W.A. released *Straight Outta Compton*.

9. Neighbourhood watch.

10. Hydrogen.

QUIZ 137. LOAD OF BALLS

You may think that's the theme of the entire book, in which case I'm surprised you've got this far. In fact, this is a quiz about balls in general, whether its references in pop culture or people with entertaining surnames . . .

1. *Pelota* is the word for ball in which European language?

2. What is the name of the spin-off show from *Strictly Come Dancing*, presented on weekday nights by Zoë Ball?

3. What name is given to *France Football* magazine's prestigious annual award for the world's best player?

4. A 1987 starring role in which West End musical gave singer and actor Michael Ball his big break?

5. What political position did Ed Balls hold prior to losing his seat at the 2015 General Election?

6. Which singer, then with Big Brother and the Holding Company, performed a near-legendary rendition of the blues song 'Ball 'n' Chain' at the 1967 Monterey Pop Festival?

7. Who was actor Nicholas Ball's first wife: she is now married to a comedian and Knight of the Realm?

8. At twenty-one, Alan Ball was the youngest member of England's World Cup-winning team in 1966: for which club was he playing?

9. Which high-profile German midfield player moved from Bayern Munich to Chelsea on a free transfer in 2006?

10. Tommy Ball of Aston Villa, in the years after the First World War, is the only Football League player to date to (a) have been sent off in his only league appearance; (b) have played with a prosthetic leg; (c) have been murdered while still employed as a professional; or (d) have represented England, Scotland AND Wales?

Answers to Quiz 136

1. U2; it was the band's third album and included political anthems like 'New Year's Day' and 'Sunday Bloody Sunday'.

2. 'Masters of War' by Bob Dylan.

3. 'Happy Xmas (War is Over)' – extra point for the Xmas and the parentheses.

4. *Paranoid* by Black Sabbath.

5. Tom Robinson; he reached the Top 10 nine years earlier with the shouty anthem '2-4-6-8 Motorway'. Robinson was one of the first high-profile openly gay rock musicians – he even released a song called 'Glad to be Gay', a brave move in the 1970s.

6–10. Absolutely nothing; the song, 'War', was a hit for Edwin Starr on the Tamla Motown label, although it was original written for vocal group The Temptations. Bruce Springsteen released the 1986 version of the song, and includes it in many of his live shows. The song was written by Norman Whitfield and Barrett Strong, and a version by Frankie Goes to Hollywood was the B-side of their second single, 'Two Tribes'.

QUIZ 138. PEOPLE AND PLACES

A general round concerning places you may or may not have heard of. If you have, you'll do well, if not – good luck!

1. The Welsh call it Ynys Mon: what do the English call it?

2. The Messina Strait lies between mainland Italy and which of its sovereign islands?

3. Which large Middle Eastern country borders Armenia and Azerbaijan to the south?

4. The city state of Andorra lies near the border of which two European countries?

5. Which country would provide the quickest overland route from Greece to Romania?

6. Which country shares borders only with Montenegro, Kosovo, Macedonia and Greece?

7. A native Manx speaker would most likely be from where?

8. What is the collective name for the Sussex and Kent towns of Hastings, Rye, Hythe, Dover and Sandwich?

9. What is the name of the group of islands, jointly owned by Argentina and Chile, which lie off the southern tip of South America?

10. Tokyo is situated on which of the Japanese islands?

Answers to Quiz 137

1. Spanish.

2. *It Takes Two*: Strictly for addicts only.

3. Le Ballon d'Or.

4. *The Phantom of the Opera*.

5. Shadow Chancellor of the Exchequer.

6. Janis Joplin.

7. Pamela Stephenson, married to Billy Connolly.

8. Blackpool; he was sold soon afterwards to Everton and later played for Arsenal, Southampton (twice) and Blackpool again before taking up management. Ball became a legend for getting clubs relegated yet still being able to find another job. He died aged sixty-one, in 2007, the second member of the team to die after Bobby Moore.

9. Michael Ballack.

10. (c) He was shot in his garden after a dispute with his landlord, George Stagg.

Winners of *Strictly Come Dancing*
Natasha Kaplinsky, news presenter.
Jill Halfpenny, actress.
Darren Gough, former cricketer.
Mark Ramprakash, former cricketer.
Alesha Dixon, singer.
Tom Chambers, actor.
Chris Hollins, sports presenter.
Kara Tointon, actress.
Harry Judd, musician.
Louis Smith, former Olympic gymnast.
Abby Clancy, model.
Caroline Flack, TV presenter.
Jay McGuinness, singer.
Ore Oduba, sports presenter.

Joe McFadden, actor.

Stacey Dooley, TV presenter.

Only Aliona Vilani, of the celebrity dancers, has won the competition more than once (with Judd and McGuinness).

QUIZ 139. NUMBERS

Another of those incremental quizzes, starting with a one-point question and working up to the full ten-pointer.

1. What was David Bowie's first UK No. 1 album?

2. Who are the only two Rugby Union players to have scored more than five hundred points for England in full internationals?

3. What are the three novels that make up Philip Pullman's *His Dark Materials* trilogy?

4. Who were the four members of the classic 1960s/70s line-up of The Who?

5. Which other five US states share a land border with New York State?

6. What are the six noble gases?

7. According to 2016 statistics, what are the world's seven busiest airports?

8. What are the first eight books of the Old Testament?

9. Who are the nine British drivers to have won the Formula 1 World Driver's Championship?

10. Elvis has had the most UK No. 1 hit singles (twenty-one). Which ten artists are next in this list, with the last four having enjoyed nine No. 1s each?

Answers to Quiz 138

1. Anglesey, the island that stands as a county of Wales and is separated from the mainland by the Menai Strait.

2. Sicily, which appears on the map to be kicked by the boot of Italy; the town of Messina lies across the strait from the mainland.

3. Iran; it also borders Turkey to the north-west, and Iraq directly to the west, with Turkmenistan, Afghanistan and Pakistan sharing borders to the east.

4. Spain and France. Andorra is the largest (by area) of the six European microstates. The others are Liechtenstein, Malta, Monaco, San Marino and the Vatican City. The islands that make up Malta are by far the most populous of these, with 446,000 inhabitants.

5. Bulgaria.

6. Albania.

7. The Isle of Man, a UK territory in the Irish Sea.

8. The Cinque Ports, an old trade and military collaboration; New Romney was one of the original five but was replaced by Rye when it silted over.

9. Tierra del Fuego.

10. Honshu.

QUIZ 140. IDENTIFY THESE FICTIONAL CHARACTERS

1. Dr Robert Langdon.

2. Fanny Price.

3. Atticus Finch.

4. Bigwig, Hazel and Fiver.

5. Mr Micawber.

6. Count Alexei Kirillovich Vronsky.

7. Clarice Starling.

8. Iorek Byrnison.

9. Winston Smith.

10. Sherman McCoy, Larry Kramer and Peter Fallow.

Answers to Quiz 139

1. Aladdin Sane.

2. Jonny Wilkinson, Owen Farrell.

3. *Northern Lights*, *The Subtle Knife*, *The Amber Spyglass*.

4. Roger Daltrey, John Entwistle, Keith Moon, Pete Townshend.

5. Pennsylvania, New Jersey, Connecticut, Massachusetts, Vermont.

6. Helium, neon, argon, krypton, xenon, radon.

7. Hartsfield-Jackson, Atlanta; Beijing; Dubai; LA; Tokyo; O'Hare, Chicago; Heathrow, London.

8. Genesis, Exodus, Leviticus, Numbers, Deuteronomy, Joshua, Judges, Ruth.

9. Jim Clark, Graham Hill, John Surtees, Jackie Stewart, James Hunt, Nigel Mansell, Damon Hill, Lewis Hamilton, Jenson Button.

10. Second are The Beatles (seventeen); third equal are Cliff Richard and Westlife, whose first seven singles all topped the chart (fourteen); fifth is Madonna (thirteen); sixth are Take That (twelve); seventh is Scottish songwriter and producer Calvin Harris (ten); eighth equal are the four acts with nine, namely ABBA, the Spice Girls, Rihanna, Eminem. Stats are accurate to January 2019.

QUIZ 141. MORE GENERAL KNOWLEDGE

More bits and pieces of knowledge for you. You should aim for eight as a team; this isn't the hardest set of questions.

1. We heard much about President Trump's issues with CNN in the early days of his presidency: what does CNN stand for?

2. Bermuda, the Cayman Islands, St Lucia, Turks and Caicos: which of these is NOT a UK territory or dependency?

3. Nuclear-deterrent policies are based on the principle of fear of MAD: what is MAD?

4. Eugene Cernan was the most recent of only twelve men to do what?

5. *The Meltdown*, *Continental Drift* and *Collision Course* are all subtitles in which series of animated movies?

6. Who duetted on 'Up Where We Belong', a massive hit from the 1982 film *An Officer and a Gentleman*?

7. The French acronym FIDE is most commonly applied to the governing body of which sport or pastime?

8. Who played Dr Who in two films in the 1960s (*Dr Who and the Daleks* and *Daleks – Invasion Earth, 2150 A.D.*) that were made outside the official TV series?

9. How did American financier John Jacob Astor meet his death on 15 April 1912?

10. Which UK prime minister gave his name to a business bag that opens into two compartments?

Answers to Quiz 140

1. The main protagonist in Dan Brown's *The Da Vinci Code* and his other novels.

2. The heroine in Jane Austen's *Mansfield Park*.

3. A lawyer, the central character of Harper Lee's *To Kill a Mockingbird*.

4. Rabbits in *Watership Down*.

5. A clerk in Dickens' *David Copperfield* ('Something will come up' is his mantra).

6. A cavalry officer and the lover of Anna Karenina in Tolstoy's novel.

7. The FBI investigator in *The Silence of the Lambs*, played by Jodie Foster (and later by Julianne Moore in *Hannibal*).

8. The rightful King of the Panzerbjorn (armoured bears) in Philip Pullman's *His Dark Materials* trilogy.

9. The main protagonist in George Orwell's *Nineteen Eighty-four*.

10. The three principal characters in Tom Wolfe's *Bonfire of the Vanities*.

QUIZ 142. GERMANY

This counts as a sort of general knowledge round, except that all the questions are about Germany, so a mixture of history, geography and a couple of sport questions.

1. What is the large industrial area of Germany, which includes the cities of Dortmund and Essen?

2. What was the Austrian Royal House that controlled most of what is now Germany from 1438 to 1740?

3. Which of the German states was the dominant force in the new German Empire formed in 1871?

4. And who was the Chancellor who masterminded the formation of the Empire?

5. In which two sports have Germany won more Olympic gold medals than any other nation (general sport, not specific discipline; e.g. athletics, not the high jump)?

6. Who nailed his Protestant treatise, the Ninety-Five Theses, to the door of All Saints Church in Wittenberg?

7. Which city, the financial centre of Germany, has the country's busiest airport?

8. What name is given to the top division in German domestic football?

9. What new title did Adolf Hitler adopt after the death of President von Hindenburg in 1934?

10. What was the name of the East German secret service, effectively a parallel of the Soviet KGB?

Answers to Quiz 141

1. Cable News Network.

2. St Lucia is nothing to do with the UK; it is a sovereign island and one of the Lesser Antilles.

3. Mutually Assured Destruction.

4. Walk on the moon; Neil Armstrong and Buzz Aldrin were the first pair in 1969, Cernan and Harrison Schmitt the last in December, 1972.

5. *Ice Age*.

6. Joe Cocker and Jennifer Warnes.

7. Chess (it stands for Fédération International des Échecs).

8. Peter Cushing.

9. He went down with the *Titanic*.

10. (William) Gladstone.

Dr Who actors:
William Hartnell; Patrick Troughton; Jon Pertwee; Tom Baker; Peter Davison; Colin Baker; Sylvester McCoy; Paul McGann; Christopher Eccleston; David Tennant; Matt Smith; Peter Capaldi; Jodie Whittaker.

McGann appeared in just a single TV story, a 1996 one-off, but he has proved extremely popular as the Doctor in a number of audio adventures. In addition to the canon of twelve doctors is the War Doctor (John Hurt), who fits in between McGann and Eccleston and appeared in the fiftieth-anniversary storyline. Peter Cushing appeared in just the two movies and his timeline is not included in the official world of the show.

QUIZ 143. THIS OR THAT

The titles given in this selection of *bon mots* are either an album by Brazilian metal band Sepultura, a James Patterson novel in the Alex Cross series or a Hammer Horror film.

1. *Beneath the Remains.*

2. *Cat and Mouse.*

3. *Twins of Evil.*

4. *Along Came a Spider.*

5. *Demons of the Mind.*

6. *A-Lex.*

7. *The Big Bad Wolf.*

8. *Vampire Circus.*

9. *Hands of the Ripper.*

10. *Chaos A.D.*

11. *Mary Mary.*

12. *Machine Messiah.*

Answers to Quiz 142

1. The Ruhr.

2. House of Habsburg.

3. Prussia.

4. And it was Otto von Bismarck who was the prime mover in the unification of the German states, with Prussia at the head.

5. Canoeing and Equestrian.

6. Martin Luther. Protestantism ensued – cue very unhappy Catholic states; result: centuries of war and strife over some variations in liturgy . . . Okay, I'm oversimplifying.

7. Frankfurt.

8. The Bundesliga.

9. Führer (Supreme Leader).

10. Stasi.

The states of Germany (the country is the Federal Republic of Germany, and, like the US, is a federation of states that retain some authority to self-govern in certain areas of legislation) are: Baden Württemberg; Bavaria (Bayern in German, hence the name of the football team, Bavarian Munich); Berlin; Brandenburg; Bremen; Hamburg; Hesse; Lower Saxony; Mecklenburg; North Rhine-Westphalia; Rhineland Pfalz; Saarland; Saxony; Saxony-Anhalt; Schleswig-Holstein; Thuringia.

QUIZ 144. PEOPLE AND PLACES

A selection of geographical puzzlers. Nicole groans when the words 'geography' or 'map' are uttered, but I love a map. I can happily pore over an atlas for an hour or so, getting hopelessly distracted when I should be writing a quiz book.

1. Egypt, Kenya, Sudan, Tanzania: through which of these countries does the River Nile NOT flow?

2. Which five islands are the largest found in the Mediterranean Sea?

3. The state of Tamil Nadu reaches the southernmost tip of which large country?

4. Ibiza, Minorca and Majorca are the three main islands in which Mediterranean group?

5. Which city state lies within the borders of Italy to the south-west of the city of Rimini?

6. Prior to achieving independence in 1975, Angola was a colony of which European country?

7. Rhodes is the most significant of which Greek island group?

8. The power station on a promontory at Dungeness can be found in which English county?

9. Which strait at the tip of South America joins the Atlantic and Pacific Oceans?

10. What word for the vast plains of Central America comes from a Quechua word for 'flat place'?

Answers to Quiz 143

1. *Beneath the Remains* was the third album for Sepultura, and their first on the major metal label Roadrunner.

2. *Cat and Mouse* is the fourth novel in the Alex Cross series.

3. *Twins of Evil* was a 1971 Hammer film starring Peter Cushing as a vampire hunter dealing with two twins, one good, one evil, played by former models, Mary and Madeleine Collison.

4. *Along Came a Spider* (1993) was the first book about forensic psychologist Alex Cross, played in a 2001 film of the book by Morgan Freeman.

5. *Demons of the Mind* was a 1972 closed-house horror movie starring Robert Hardy and Michael Hordern.

6. You might think *A-Lex* would be an Alex Cross book, given the options here, but in fact it is the eleventh Sepultura album (2009) – a concept album based on Anthony Burgess's novel, *A Clockwork Orange*.

7. *The Big Bad Wolf* (2003) was Patterson's ninth Alex Cross novel.

8. *Vampire Circus* was a 1972 Hammer film about – you guessed it – a travelling circus full of vampires, come to wreak revenge on a village that killed the circus master's cousin. It's a pretty good effort, with a non-speaking appearance from Dave Prowse (Darth Vader) as a circus strongman.

9. *Hands of the Ripper* was a lame Hammer film from 1971.

10. Sepultura's fifth album, *Chaos A.D.*, saw the band shift away from the thrash metal of their earlier efforts.

11. *Mary Mary* is an Alex Cross novel – he is now working for the FBI.

12. Sepultura's most recent album, *Machine Messiah*, was released in 2017.

QUIZ 145. JACKS OF ALL TRADES

A selection of general questions on Jacks and Jackies. Inevitably, name-themed rounds are quite celebrity- and pop-culture driven, and this is no exception.

1. What is the name of actor/musician Jack Black's band?

2. Who is Jack Bauer?

3. Which footballer became the first £10,000 transfer when he moved from Bolton Wanderers to Arsenal in 1928?

4. Which rock star gave Johnny Depp inspiration for much of the look and mannerisms of his *Pirates of the Caribbean* character Jack Sparrow?

5. Which writer's most famous works are *Call of the Wild* and *White Fang*, tales of life in the Wild West during the Gold Rush?

6. Which England cricketer scored the most first-class centuries, a total of 199?

7. For which TV programme is the actor Jack Lord best remembered?

8. *One-Eyed Jacks*, a western, was the only film directed by which Academy Award-winning actor, who died in 2004, aged eighty?

9. Who was World Heavyweight Boxing Champion from 1919 to 1926?

10. Who made a pink Chanel suit and matching pillbox hat famous?

Answers to Quiz 144

1. Kenya.

2. Sicily is the largest, followed by the other major Italian island of Sardinia. Next is Cyprus (both parts included), and then Corsica, under French rule. The fifth is the largest of the Greek islands: Crete.

3. India; the Tamils are a native people who live manly in southern India and northern Sri Lanka, where they have been a militant majority, fighting a Civil War against the Sri Lankan government with acts of terror and atrocities on both sides.

4. The Balearic Islands.

5. San Marino.

6. Portugal; Angola, along with Mozambique, was Portugal's main foothold in Southern Africa.

7. The Dodecanese.

8. Kent: Dungeness is where the film-maker and garden designer Derek Jarman had his unique, windswept garden.

9. The Strait of Magellan, named after the explorer Ferdinand Magellan, who first made it around the tip of South America.

10. Pampas – the plains take in substantial parts of Argentina, all of Uruguay and a southern chunk of Brazil.

QUIZ 146. FA CUP

The FA Cup has lost its lustre in recent years, but I can remember it being the highlight of the football season, a big day out for two clubs after the league season finished, and an all-day TV extravaganza in a day when very little football was shown live.

1. In which year was the Cup Final first held at Wembley Stadium?

2. Which 'big club' won their last domestic trophy in 1955 when they lifted the FA Cup?

3. Barnsley, Birmingham City, Fulham, Middlesbrough: which is the only one of these clubs to have won the FA Cup?

4. Which two clubs played in the 'Stanley Matthews Final' of 1953, when that great player finally won a major medal, and played a significant part in his team's victory? Who might have felt slightly aggrieved at the attention lavished on Matthews, having scored a hat-trick in his side's 4–3 victory?

5. What do Kevin Moran, José Antonio Reyes, Pablo Zabaleta, Chris Smalling and Victor Moses have in common?

6. Where did the FA Cup Final take place between 2001 and 2006?

7. Which player holds the individual record for FA Cup winner's medals, with seven, earned with Arsenal and Chelsea?

8. Which club beat Manchester City in the 2013 FA Cup Final to become the first FA Cup winners to be relegated from the top flight in the same season?

9. Who scored in the FA Cup Final in 2007, 2009, 2010 and 2012?

10. To 2018, who were the last team from outside the top flight to contest an FA Cup Final (in 2008)? And who, in 1980, were the last second-tier side to win the competition?

Answers to Quiz 145

1. Tenacious D; the band is essentially Jack Black and Kyle Gass, with other musicians for touring purposes.

2. The lead character in 24, played by Kiefer Sutherland.

3. David Jack; Jack won three League titles and an FA Cup with Arsenal, to add to the two FA Cup wins he already had with Bolton.

4. Keith Richards, guitarist and songwriter with The Rolling Stones.

5. Jack London. *Call of the Wild* was written from the perspective of a sledge dog called Buck, who gradually goes feral in the harsh environment of the Yukon Gold Rush. It is still used as a set text.

6. Jack Hobbs; fifteen of those hundreds were in Test Matches, in which he scored 5,410 runs at an average of well over fifty.

7. Steve McGarrett in *Hawaii Five-0* (1968–90).

8. Marlon Brando.

9. Jack Dempsey.

10. Jackie Kennedy was dressed thus when her husband was assassinated.

QUIZ 147. MIDDLE NAMES

We have given you a set of middle names and a list of famous people. You have to match the middle name to its owner. Some of these people were always referred to inclusive of the middle name, others may be less familiar.

1. Albert.

2. Butler.

3. Byron.

4. Hubert.

5. Earl.

6. Winston.

7. Stanley.

8. Jackson.

9. Newbold.

10. Tiberius.

A. US president Carter.

B. Fictional prisoner Fletch, from TV sitcom *Porridge*.

C. Irish poet Yeats.

D. Olympic athlete and IOC bigwig Lord Coe.

E. John Lennon.

F. American icon James Dean.

G. Captain Kirk of the *Starship Enterprise*.

H. Ol' Blue Eyes Sinatra.

I. Action painter Pollock.

J. Former West Indian cricket captain Clive Lloyd.

Answers to Quiz 146

1. 1923.

2. Newcastle United.

3. Barnsley.

4. Blackpool (Matthews' team) beat Bolton Wanderers 4–3. Stan Mortensen scored three of Blackpool's goals. What is often forgotten (and yes, I am a Bolton supporter) is that the full back who Matthews tormented was a stand-in, as Tommy Banks was hampered by a serious injury and only carried on as a passenger up front because no substitutes were allowed in those days. For all that, Matthews was a wonderful player and deserved more reward for a fantastic and long career.

5. They were all sent off in an FA Cup Final. Moran was the first, playing for Manchester United against Everton (United still won); Reyes was sent off playing for Arsenal in 2005, Zabaleta for Manchester City in 2013, Chris Smalling for Manchester United in 2016 and Victor Moses for Chelsea in 2017.

6. The Millennium Stadium in Cardiff, during the refurbishment of Wembley Stadium.

7. Ashley Cole.

8. Wigan Athletic. Wigan had a relatively comfortable route to the final, but were expected to be pasted by a strong City side. Instead, they pulled off a remarkable win with Ben Watson's injury-time header.

9. Didier Drogba. His record in big matches is remarkable.

10. Cardiff City, who lost 1–0 to Portsmouth; West Ham United, who beat Arsenal 1–0 with a rare headed goal from Trevor Brooking.

QUIZ 148. MOVIE STUFF

We give you the casts of ten gangster films – all you have to do is identify the movie. This sounds as if it should be easy, but most people only remember the lead characters, so piecing together which Al Pacino film it is, for example, from the bit-part players can be quite tricky.

1. Robert De Niro; Ray Liotta; Joe Pesci; Lorraine Bracco, Paul Sorvino, Catherine Scorsese.

2. Paul Muni, Ann Dvorak, Osgood Perkins, Karen Morley, Boris Karloff.

3. Viggo Mortensen, Naomi Watts, Vincent Cassel, Armin Mueller-Stahl, Sinéad Cusack.

4. Tom Hanks, Tyler Hoechlin, Paul Newman, Jude Law, Daniel Craig, Stanley Tucci, Jennifer Jason Leigh.

5. Edward G. Robinson, Douglas Fairbanks Jr, Glenda Farrell.

6. Al Pacino, Steven Bauer, Michelle Pfeiffer, Mary Elizabeth Mastrantonio, Robert Loggia, F. Murray Abraham.

7. Robert De Niro, James Woods, Elizabeth McGovern, Treat Williams, Tuesday Weld, Joe Pesci.

8. Johnny Depp, Christian Bale, Marion Cotillard, Billy Crudup, Stephen Dorff, Channing Tatum.

9. Kevin Costner, Charles Martin Smith, Sean Connery, Robert De Niro, Andy Garcia, Patricia Clarkson.

10. Bob Hoskins, P.H. Moriarty, Helen Mirren, Bryan Marshall, Derek Thompson.

Answers to Quiz 147

1. H: Francis Albert Sinatra.

2. C: William Butler Yeats, by which full name he is often referred to, was a key Irish poet in the early twentieth century.

3. F: James Byron Dean, most famous for his role in *Rebel Without a Cause* (1955), released months before he died in a car crash, aged twenty-four.

4. J: Clive Hubert Lloyd was the captain of the all-conquering West Indies cricket team between 1974 and 1985. A left-handed batsman who hit the ball ferociously hard, he was a primary contributor to Lancashire's dominance of early domestic one-day cricket in the 1970s.

5. A: James Earl Carter.

6. E: John Winston Lennon – Lennon added Ono to his name to show his love for his wife, Yoko.

7. B: Norman Stanley Fletcher, as intoned by the sentencing judge at the start of every episode of the 1970s sitcom.

8. I: Paul Jackson Pollock – the artist was known by his middle name.

9. D: Sebastian Newbold Coe, former Olympic athlete and Conservative MP, and Chairman of the British Olympic Association etc. etc.

10. G: James Tiberius Kirk, as all good Trekkies would know.

QUIZ 149. ALL ABOUT ME

Match the individual to the title of his or her autobiography.

1. Roald Dahl.

2. David Niven.

3. Laurie Lee.

4. George Best.

5. Maya Angelou.

6. Anne Robinson.

7. Quentin Crisp.

8. Shirley MacLaine.

9. Dawn French.

10. Kate Adie.

A. *Memoirs of an Unfit Mother.*

B. *Out on a Limb.*

C. *Bring on the Empty Horses.*

D. *Dear Fatty.*

E. *The Naked Civil Servant.*

F. *Boy.*

G. *The Good, the Bad and the Bubbly.*

H. *I Know Why the Caged Birds Sing.*

I. *The Kindness of Strangers.*

J. *Cider with Rosie.*

Answers to Quiz 148

1. *Goodfellas* (1990, Martin Scorsese).

2. *Scarface* (1932, directed by the great Howard Hawks and with a screenplay by Ben Hecht).

3. *Eastern Promises* (2007, David Cronenberg).

4. *Road to Perdition* (2002, Sam Mendes).

5. *Little Caesar* (1931, Mervyn LeRoy).

6. *Scarface* (1983, Brian De Palma, script by Oliver Stone, a remake of the one in Question 2 and less satisfactory, despite Pacino's excellence).

7. *Once Upon a Time in America* (1984, directed by Sergio Leone, the spaghetti western director, and a gangster take on his earlier *Once Upon a Time in the West*).

8. *Public Enemies* (2009, Michael Mann's disappointing rendition of the John Dillinger story).

9. *The Untouchables* (1987, Brian De Palma again, a take on the Eliot Ness story drawn from Ness's own account, with Costner as the lawman).

10. *The Long Good Friday* (1979/80, John Mackenzie – it made Bob Hoskins into a star).

QUIZ 150. THE SECOND WORLD WAR

A history round entirely on the Second World War. We offered this one for VE Day. Scores ranged between one and ten, so who knows how it will pan out for you?

1. Where did the Allies' Operation Shingle land in Italy as the start of a push on Rome?

2. The Battle of Midway was a decisive turning point in the war, and was fought between the navies of which two countries?

3. Which crucial British outpost in the Pacific fell on Christmas Day 1941 after a seventeen-day attack?

4. After the resignation of Viscount Halifax as Foreign Secretary in December 1940, which future PM served in that role for the rest of the war?

5. Who was executed by his own countrymen on 28 April 1945?

6. In early 1941, which important port in modern Libya was taken from the Italian army by an Australian battalion with Allied air support?

7. Who was the Commander-in-Chief of the Allied forces in Europe during the latter part of the war?

8. The bombing of which German city in February 1945 has come to be regarded as one of the most morally debatable of the Allies' air raids in the latter part of the war?

9. Which two countries suffered the most casualties during the war, through a combination of military and civilian deaths, including famine and crimes against humanity?

10. What was the name of the August 1945 agreement between the Allied leaders concerning the post-war governance of Germany?

Answers to Quiz 149

1. F: Roald Dahl's account of his own childhood was published in 1984, six years before his death.

2. C: David Niven's anecdotal autobiography (1975) was a follow-up to the hugely successful *The Moon's a Balloon*.

3. J: Laurie Lee's *Cider with Rosie* (1959) is a twentieth-century classic – the book has sold over six million copies.

4. G: George Best's *The Good, the Bad and the Bubbly* was one of a number of accounts of his life.

5. H: Maya Angelou wrote *I Know Why the Caged Bird Sings*, her classic account of an African-American childhood in 1969, and a further five volumes followed.

6. A: Anne Robinson's self-deprecating *Memoirs of an Unfit Mother* recount her struggles with alcoholism.

7. E: Quentin Crisp's *The Naked Civil Servant* was a 1968 work made into a 1975 film with John Hurt as Crisp.

8. B: Shirley Maclaine has published a number of successful memoirs and self-help books: *Out on a Limb* was the fourth, published in 1983.

9. D: *Dear Fatty* was the 2008 memoir of comedian Dawn French, written as a series of letters.

10. I: Kate Adie's *The Kindness of Strangers* (2002) was her account of her time as a warzone reporter.

QUIZ 151. IDENTIFY

Here are ten names, some real, some fictional. We want to know who they were or what they did that made them famous or where they appear if they are fictional. I always allocate two points per question on these, and hand them out depending on the detail given. For example, if the name given were Grace Kelly and you just put 'actress', you would get a point. If you put 'Academy Award-winning actress who retired from the screen to marry Prince Rainier of Monaco', you would get both points. More is more, in this instance.

1. Catherine Middleton.

2. Clarice Cliff.

3. Macavity the Mystery Cat.

4. Rupert Giles.

5. Emily Davison.

6. Anthony Kiedis.

7. Billy Claiborne, Ike and Billy Clanton, Tom and Frank McLaury, Wes Fuller.

8. Derek and Clive.

9. Anne Hathaway.

10. Bob, Helen, Violet and Dash.

Answers to Quiz 150

1. Anzio beach head.

2. The US and Japan – the Japanese were attempting to wipe out American naval influence, but in the end the reverse came to pass.

3. Hong Kong.

4. Anthony Eden. He later became Prime Minister when Churchill retired, but became embroiled in the Suez Crisis and was forced to resign.

5. Benito Mussolini, the Italian fascist dictator.

6. Tobruk: the port eventually succumbed to Rommel's forces, but was recaptured later in 1942.

7. General Dwight D. Eisenhower, the future president.

8. Dresden.

9. Russia and China – the Chinese suffered massive losses to the Japanese.

10. The Potsdam Agreement.

QUIZ 152. MUSICAL NUMBERS

Another of those quizzes with one answer, then two, yada yada; you know the drill by now. Good luck – thirty out of fifty-five points is respectable here; there are lots of different genres and eras.

1. Dusty Springfield, however revered, had only one UK No. 1 single. What was it?

2. Amy Winehouse was only with us long enough to release two studio albums in her lifetime: what were they?

3. Only three artists have three entries in the Top 20 best-selling albums of the 2010s: who are they?

4. *Rolling Stone* magazine conducted a poll of the best live acts of all time. Take a stab at the top four.

5. Name the five members of The Jackson 5.

6. *Boy* was U2's debut album, released in 1980. What were the other five studio albums they released in the 1980s?

7. What are the seven albums released to date by Coldplay (to January 2019, last release 2015).

8. What were the eight singles that took Duran Duran into the top five of the UK charts? (For a bonus, name the two that reached No. 1).

9. What are Rihanna's nine UK No. 1 singles? (Includes three where she gets credit as a featured artist.)

10. Name the top ten best-selling albums in the UK in the 1970s (excluding Greatest Hits packages, but including Original Soundtracks, of which there are two in the list).

Answers to Quiz 151

1. Kate Middleton is Prince William's wife.

2. A 1920s Art Deco pottery designer.

3. A cat in T.S. Eliot's *Old Possum's Book of Practical Cats*.

4. Buffy's watcher (mentor and guardian) in *Buffy the Vampire Slayer*, played by Anthony Head.

5. Suffragette who was killed on the course at the Epsom Derby in 1913.

6. Lead singer in the Red Hot Chili Peppers.

7. The gang who duelled with the Earps and Doc Holiday in the Gunfight at the O.K. Corral.

8. Comic creation of Peter Cook and Dudley Moore.

9. American actress; also the name of Shakespeare's wife.

10. The Parr family, the Invincibles in the animated movies.

QUIZ 153. ELEMENTARY

A quiz on the world's greatest-ever detective. Shame he wasn't real. We are talking, of course, about Sherlock Holmes – a mixture here of straight questions about the books and ones on Holmes' various incarnations on TV and in film.

1. What was the occupation of Arthur Conan Doyle, creator of Sherlock Holmes?

2. *A Study in Scarlet* was the first of the four full-length Sherlock Holmes novels. In which decade was it published?

3. What is the name of the Scotland Yard detective who appears most frequently in the Sherlock Holmes stories?

4. *The House of Silk* (2011) was a new Sherlock Holmes story authorised by Conan Doyle's estate and written by which novelist and screenwriter?

5. Benedict Cumberbatch has made a modern Sherlock Holmes all his own, but who played the part in the 1980s for Granada TV, in a manner closer to the original stories?

6. Which two writers co-created the modern Sherlock?

7. The TV series *Arthur and George* starred Martin Clunes as Conan Doyle: on whose novel was it based?

8. Who played Holmes in a number of wartime dramas that paid little regard to Conan Doyle's work and were largely used as propaganda vehicles?

9. What name is given to the street urchins who help Holmes with his research and investigations?

10. What is the location in the Holmes story *The Final Problem*, where Holmes apparently falls to his death along with his nemesis, Professor Moriarty?

Answers to Quiz 152

1. 'You Don't Have to Say You Love Me'.

2. *Frank, Back in Black*.

3. Adele, Ed Sheeran, Michael Bublé.

4. Bruce Springsteen, The Rolling Stones, The Who, Pink Floyd.

5. Michael, Jermaine, Tito, Marlon, Jackie.

6. *October, War, The Unforgettable Fire, The Joshua Tree, Rattle and Hum*.

7. *Parachutes, A Rush of Blood to the Head, X&Y, Viva la Vida, Mylo Xyloto, Ghost Stories, A Head Full of Dreams*.

8. 'Girls on Film' (No. 5), 'Hungry Like a Wolf' (No. 5), 'Save a Prayer' (No. 2), 'Is There Something I Should Know?' (No. 1), 'Union of the Snake' (No. 3), 'The Reflex' (No. 1), 'Wild Boys' (No. 2), 'A View to a Kill' (No. 2).

9. 'Umbrella', 'Take a Bow', 'Only Girl (in the World)', 'What's My Name?', 'We Found Love' and 'Diamonds', plus 'Run this Town' (Jay-Z track), 'The Monster' (Eminem) and 'Wild Thoughts' (DJ Khaled).

10. *Bridge Over Troubled Water* (Simon & Garfunkel); *Tubular Bells* (Mike Oldfield); *Saturday Night Fever* (OST, Bee Gees and others); *Arrival* (ABBA); *Dark Side of the Moon* (Pink Floyd); *Grease* (OST); *Band on the Run* (Paul McCartney and Wings); *Rumours* (Fleetwood Mac); *Parallel Lines* (Blondie); *Atlantic Crossing* (Rod Stewart). The surprising omission here is *Bat Out of Hell* (Meatloaf) – it was a creeper seller and didn't really make the upper reaches of the charts for very long. As of 2019, however, nearly forty years on, only *Rumours* and *Dark Side of the Moon* have outsold Meatloaf's epic.

QUIZ 154. GAME OF THRONES

Moving swiftly on to a similar round, this time on TV's biggest *cause célèbre* of recent years, *Game of Thrones*. Like Harry Potter, this has been enough of a cultural phenomenon to justify its own section. Note, the quizzes were written before the last series aired, and I have tried to avoid too many spoilers.

1. The HBO series takes its name from the first novel in George R.R. Martin's series. What is the name given to the series as a whole? As of January 2019, when was the last novel in the series (the fifth of seven) released?

2. What is the name of the head of House Lannister at the beginning of *Game of Thrones* and what are his three children called?

3. Which of the major houses are based at Highgarden and Riverrun respectively?

4. Who is the leader of the Wildlings when Jon Snow first encounters them, and what is the name of the Wildling girl with whom Snow falls in love?

5. Which member of the *Game of Thrones* cast has won three Emmy Awards for Best Supporting Actor for his work in the show?

6. What is the name of the aggressive dragon ridden by Daenerys Targaryen?

7. Who is the head of House Bolton and what is the name of his psychotic son?

8. Which *Game of Thrones* character is known as Littlefinger?

9. Who are the six children, legitimate and otherwise, of Eddard Stark?

10. Who is the manipulative priest who arrives at King's Landing and insinuates himself into a position as head of the Faith Militant? Which British actor portrays this character?

Answers to Quiz 153

1. Doctor of Medicine.

2. It was published in 1887 (so 1880s); the other full-length novels were *The Sign of the Four* (1890), *The Hound of the Baskervilles* (1902) and *The Valley of Fear* (1915). The rest of the Sherlock Holmes canon were published as magazine stories in *The Strand* and later bound up into volumes of short stories.

3. Inspector Lestrade. There were a number of policemen who assisted Holmes in the books, but Lestrade was the most frequent and an object of Holmes' scorn more often than not.

4. Anthony Horowitz.

5. Jeremy Brett, with first David Burke and later Edward Hardwicke as Dr Watson.

6. Mark Gatiss and Steven Moffat.

7. Julian Barnes.

8. Basil Rathbone, with Nigel Bruce as a terribly British Dr Watson.

9. Baker Street Irregulars, led by urchin-in-chief Wiggins.

10. The Reichenbach Falls in Switzerland.

QUIZ 155. ONLY CONNECT . . .

Nine general knowledge questions that appear to have no connection. And yet they do. Only two out of twelve teams on the night we used the quiz got the connection. Which means it's a teensy bit tricky.

1. Who took over as editor of *Vogue* magazine in 1988 and still holds the post?

2. Which role in a Hitchcock film made a star of Anthony Perkins in 1960?

3. Whose goal-scoring record for Arsenal was broken by Thierry Henry in 2005?

4. What is the name of Albus Dumbledore's phoenix in the Harry Potter stories?

5. What was the name of the Biggest Dog in the World, in the 1973 family movie starring Jim Dale and featuring a cast of English eccentrics including Spike Milligan?

6. Who was appointed 1st Earl of Northumberland and Constable of England by King Henry IV, but was later killed in battle rebelling against the same king?

7. *Watermelon* and *Lucy Sullivan is Getting Married* were the first two novels by which successful Irish female novelist?

8. Which Bond movie features a muscled killer called Red Grant, played by Robert Shaw?

9. Which famous highwayman plays a key role in *Rookwood*, published in 1834, the first and best known of a series of Gothic novels by William Henry Ainsworth?

10. What's the connection?

Answers to Quiz 154

1. *A Song of Ice and Fire*. The books are *A Game of Thrones* (1996); *A Clash of Kings* (1999); *A Storm of Swords* (2000); *A Feast for Crows* (2005); *A Dance of Dragons* (2011). The sixth volume, *The Winds of Winter*, has long been anticipated, with a seventh, *A Dream of Spring*, some way off in the pipeline.

2. Tywin (Charles Dance in the TV show); Cersei (Lena Headey), Jaime (Nikolaj Coster-Walnau) and Tyrion (Peter Dinklage).

3. Tyrell and Tully.

4. Mance Rayder; Ygritte ('You know nothing, Jon Snow').

5. Peter Dinklage.

6. Drogon – Rhaegal and Viserion are the other two.

7. Roose, Ramsay.

8. Petyr Baelish.

9. Robb, Sansa, Arya, Brandon, Rickon and Jon Snow.

10. The High Sparrow; Jonathan Pryce.

QUIZ 156. WORDS, WORDS, WORDS

Words and their meanings, some technical, some just enhanced vocabulary. These rounds prove popular at the pub, even though the scoring is varied. I'm told you don't get wordy stuff in many pub quizzes, which is a shame, because words are terrific.

1. What does a paleontologist study?

2. If a dish contained eggplant and scallions on an Australian menu, what would it say on most English menus?

3. If the cervical vertebrae are in the neck and the lumbar are at the base of the spine, what sit in the middle of the back?

4. If you were asked to pay for something COD, what would that indicate?

5. A numismatist collects or studies what?

6. What is the German word used to describe a feeling of satisfaction at the misfortune of others?

7. Where are the intercostal muscles found?

8. Everyone loves a soufflé. What is the origin of the dish's name?

9. If a disease is widespread, it is an epidemic; if it is worldwide, it is a pandemic. What is it if it is specific to a certain area or people?

10. What are monotremes?

Answers to Quiz 155

1. Anna Wintour.

2. Norman Bates in *Psycho*; despite his best efforts to shake it, Perkins is remembered almost exclusively for this role.

3. Ian Wright, who in turn broke Cliff Bastin's near fifty-year-old record.

4. Fawkes.

5. Digby.

6. Henry Percy; his son, Henry Hotspur, also lost his life in the conflict.

7. Marian Keyes.

8. *From Russia with Love* (1963). It was the second Bond movie starring Sean Connery.

9. Dick Turpin.

10. All the questions or answers reference one of the co-conspirators in the Gunpowder Plot.

Here is a list of the official James Bond movies.

Sean Connery: *Dr No* (1962), *From Russia with Love* (1963), *Goldfinger* (1964), *Thunderball* (1965), *You Only Live Twice* (1967), *Diamonds are Forever* (1971).

George Lazenby: *On Her Majesty's Secret Service* (1969).

Roger Moore: *Live and Let Die* (1973), *The Man with the Golden Gun* (1974), *The Spy Who Loved Me* (1977), *Moonraker* (1979), *For Your Eyes Only* (1981), *Octopussy* (1983), *A View to a Kill* (1985).

Timothy Dalton: *The Living Daylights* (1987), *Licence to Kill* (1989).

Pierce Brosnan: *GoldenEye* (1995), *Tomorrow Never Dies* (1997), *The World is Not Enough* (1999), *Die Another Day* (2002).

Daniel Craig: *Casino Royale* (2006), *Quantum of Solace* (2008), *Skyfall* (2012), *Spectre* (2015), As yet unnamed (2020).

QUIZ 157. FOOD AND DRINK

Some questions for the epicurean types. These rounds are always popular – the subject eliminates book learning and is just pure general knowledge. You can be as thick as a whale omelette (*Blackadder*), but if you have worked in a kitchen at some point, you would still recognise it as an omelette.

1. If you ordered calamari in a restaurant, what would you be eating?

2. If you ordered Coquilles Saint Jacques in a restaurant, what would you get?

3. From what is the case to a haggis made? Is it (a) sheep's hide; (b) cow gut; (c) sheep's stomach; or (d) stretched pork skin?

4. Meringue is made from which two ingredients?

5. What is the Japanese name for a dish of specially prepared raw fish?

6. Gorgonzola and Roquefort cheese are both derived from which source?

7. Which Kent (Faversham)-based brewery lays claim to being Britain's oldest?

8. Bloody Mary, Harvey Wallbanger, Moscow Mule, Singapore Sling: which of these cocktails is not made with vodka as the base spirit?

9. If a Magnum is a double-sized bottle of Champagne, what is a bottle containing four standard bottles called?

10. Marsanne, Merlot, Sangiovese, Tempranillo: which of these is NOT a red wine grape?

Answers to Quiz 156

1. Fossils (technically, it is the study of pre-Holocene life, but fossils are the main source of study).

2. Aubergine and spring onion.

3. Thoracic vertebrae.

4. Cash on delivery.

5. Coins.

6. *Schadenfreude*.

7. Between the ribs.

8. From the French word for whisper, describing its lightness.

9. Endemic.

10. They are one of the three orders of mammals, the other two being placentals (which includes the majority of mammal species) and marsupials. Monotremes differ in that they lay eggs and hatch their young – they are made up of species of echidna and platypus.

QUIZ 158. THIS IS ENGLAND

The title here is not a nod to the racists, but a statement that this quiz is about the geography of England. We've set quite a few quizzes on world geography, so we thought it fair to concentrate on one closer to home.

1. Derby, Leicester, Lincoln, Nottingham: which of these lies furthest to the east?

2. What is the county town of Lancashire?

3. Which county lies between Hampshire and Devon on England's south coast?

4. Norwich is comfortably the biggest urban centre in the county of Norfolk: which other two Norfolk towns boast a population of over 30,000?

5. Which three National Parks in England and Wales cover an area of more than two thousand square kilometres?

6. What is the direct (as the crow flies) distance between Oxford and Cambridge? (Five miles either way, ten for a half-point.)

7. Apart from Lancashire, which county bears the red rose as its emblem?

8. In which UK city are the Co-op based?

9. The Georgian town of Darlington lies within the boundaries of which county?

10. Which two cathedral cities lie within the borders of the ceremonial county of Somerset?

Answers to Quiz 157

1. Squid.

2. Scallops (done the French way, with the scallop in a shell covered with creamy mushroom sauce and coated with crisped crumb).

3. It is traditionally a sheep's stomach.

4. Egg white and sugar (eggs is wrong, must be egg white).

5. Sashimi; sushi is wrong, that is the rice.

6. Ewe's milk; Gorgonzola is made near Milan, Italy, while Roquefort comes from the south of France.

7. Shepherd Neame.

8. Singapore Sling is a gin sling, made with gin, Cointreau, bitters, grenadine, pineapple juice and lime. The others are all vodka cocktails, with tomato juice (Bloody Mary), Galliano and orange juice (Harvey Wallbanger) or ginger beer/ale and lime (Moscow Mule).

9. Jeroboam.

10. Marsanne is a Northern Rhône grape used to make white wine, not red.

QUIZ 159. ALL SORTS

Another mish-mash of stuff.

1. Who made ready-to-wear haute couture fashionable in the 1960s with his Rive Gauche stores?

2. Launched in 2011 by Evan Spiegel, Bobby Murphy and Reggie Brown, which social media platform was the first to be targeted specifically at the mobile user?

3. What was Erica Jong's 1973 novel, celebrated for its honest and detailed portrayal of female sexuality?

4. In which part of the UK is the Green Man music festival held?

5. Both John F. Kennedy and his brother Edward represented which state in the US senate?

6. Which grime singer co-launched #Merky Books with publisher Penguin Random House in 2018?

7. What would a milliner make or sell?

8. Barack Obama was born nine days before me in Hawaii; but which state did he represent as a Senator from 2004 to 2008?

9. Pulteney Bridge, designed by Robert Adam, crosses the River Avon in which popular tourist city?

10. Where, near Bromley in Kent, is a major air show held annually?

Answers to Quiz 158

1. Lincoln.

2. Preston. Lancashire is a big county, and used to include both Manchester and Liverpool, but now they are separate Metropolitan areas (Greater Manchester and Merseyside).

3. Dorset; the coast runs, east to west, Kent, Sussex, Hampshire, Dorset, Devon, Cornwall.

4. Great Yarmouth and King's Lynn.

5. The Lake District, Yorkshire Dales and Snowdonia.

6. Sixty-seven miles.

7. Hampshire.

8. Manchester.

9. County Durham.

10. Bath and Wells.

There are thirteen National Parks in England and Wales (as opposed to Areas of Outstanding Natural Beauty): Lake District; Yorkshire Dales; Snowdonia; South Downs; Peak District; North York Moors; Brecon Beacons; Northumberland; Dartmoor; Exmoor; Pembrokeshire Coast; New Forest; Norfolk Broads.

QUIZ 160. MOVIE MIX

Another cross-section of movie questions, some old, some new(ish). You should aim for at least seven points here, they aren't all that tricky. Unless you never watch films or are twelve years old, in which case any film round would be tricky.

1. *Austin Powers: International Man of Mystery* was a surprise smash hit of 1997 – who played the title role?

2. Which film star played Charlie Chaplin in a 1992 biopic of the actor's life?

3. For which role in soft-core erotic films is Sylvia Kristel chiefly remembered?

4. Who played a former World Heavyweight Boxing Champion in the surprise 2009 hit *The Hangover*?

5. In which 1973 film did relative unknown Ted Neeley play Jesus Christ?

6. Who played 'Baby' in Howard Hawks' 1938 screwball comedy *Bringing Up Baby*?

7. In which Coen Brothers movie did Frances McDormand play a pregnant policewoman, being rewarded with an Academy Award for her work?

8. Who played a Spanish swordsman with a Scots accent in Russell Mulcahy's 1986 fantasy film *Highlander*?

9. Which cult eighties musical featured the voice of Levi Stubbs from the Four Tops as a murderous plant?

10. Grace Kelly played the lead female role in three Hitchcock films, opposite Ray Milland, James Stewart and Cary Grant respectively: what are the three films?

Answers to Quiz 159

1. Yves Saint-Laurent.

2. Snapchat.

3. *Fear of Flying*.

4. Brecon Beacons.

5. Massachusetts.

6. Stormzy.

7. Hats.

8. Illinois.

9. Bath.

10. Biggin Hill.

Here's an odd list.

In Britain there are eleven places with city status that do not have a cathedral: Bath (it has an abbey, not actually a cathedral, so technically is on this list), Cambridge, Hull, Lancaster, Newport, Nottingham, Plymouth, Salford, Southampton, Stoke-on-Trent and Wolverhampton.

Westminster Abbey would be precluded from a list of cathedrals for the same reason.

Conversely, to disprove the myth that a cathedral automatically makes a place a city, here are five towns that are home to a cathedral: Blackburn, Bury St Edmunds, Chelmsford, Guildford, and Southwell (in Nottinghamshire, with just over seven thousand inhabitants, but it does have Southwell Minster).

QUIZ 161. ODDS AND SODS

An odd-one-out round. Quite tough. Small pat on the back if you get more than six right.

1. Which of these counties does not boast a professional county cricket team: Gloucestershire; Oxfordshire; Sussex; Warwickshire?

2. Which of these is not a track on Meatloaf's original *Bat Out of Hell* album from 1977: 'Heaven Can Wait'; 'I'd Do Anything for Love'; 'Two Out of Three Ain't Bad'; 'You Took the Words Right Out of My Mouth'?

3. Which of these is not or was not a great classical pianist; Vladimir Ashkenazy; Daniel Barenboim; Lang Lang; Itzhak Perlman?

4. Which of these does not have a Red Sea coast: Eritrea; Egypt; Lebanon; Saudi Arabia?

5. Which of these is not a franchise in the National Football Conference, one of the two sections of the National Football League, the highest level of American Football: Atlanta Jackals; Philadelphia Eagles; Seattle Seahawks; Tampa Bay Buccaneers?

6. Which of these musicals does not have music written by Andrew Lloyd-Webber: *Cats*; *Evita*; *Les Misérables*; *Sunset Boulevard*?

7. Which of these is not one of Enid Blyton's Famous Five: Anne; Julian; Polly; Timmy?

8. Which of these does not touch the Equator: Brazil; Gabon; Indonesia; Nigeria?

9. Which of these players did not score a penalty in England's successful shoot-out against Colombia in the 2018 World Cup Finals: Harry Kane, Marcus Rashford, Jordan Henderson, Eric Dier?

10. Which of these artists is not a member of the '27 Club', the list of artists who died young at the age of twenty-seven: Kurt Cobain; Jim Morrison; Tupac Shakur; Amy Winehouse?

Answers to Quiz 160

1. Mike Myers; there were two sequels, *Austin Powers: The Spy Who Shagged Me*, and *Austin Powers in Goldmember*. Never got it, if I'm honest; much preferred Myers in *Wayne's World* and *So I Married an Axe Murderer*.

2. Robert Downey Jr. The film, directed by Richard Attenborough, also starred Chaplin's daughter, Geraldine, as her grandmother, Hannah.

3. Emmanuelle. Kristel appeared in the first four and the last of seven Emmanuelle films, as well as a version of *Lady Chatterley's Lover* and a soft-core take on the Mata Hari story.

4. Mike Tyson appeared as himself.

5. *Jesus Christ Superstar*, the film version of the Andrew Lloyd-Webber and Tim Rice musical. The musical was first released as a concept album before it was ever staged, with former Deep Purple frontman Ian Gillan as Jesus and Murray Head as Judas.

6. Baby was a leopard.

7. *Fargo*.

8. Sean Connery. Christoph Lambert played the main role. Despite hammy acting and a duff script, the film became a cult classic – largely because the Kurgan is a great bad guy.

9. *The Little Shop of Horrors*.

10. *Dial M for Murder*, *Rear Window* and *To Catch a Thief*.

QUIZ 162. LGBT

This was a round we included for the quiz immediately after Hastings Pride
– it was refreshingly well scored.

1. Where in 1969 did the Stonewall Riots take place after a police raid on
   a gay hang-out?

2. Who was prime minister when Section 28 was introduced, outlawing
   teachers from openly discussing gay issues in schools?

3. In which year was the first London Pride march, was it 1972, 1979, 1984
   or 1990?

4. Which gay symbol did Gilbert Baker design in San Francisco in 1978?

5. What occupation, previously closed to openly gay people, was made
   available in 2000?

6. What was the age of consent for a private homosexual relationship
   when it was first decriminalised in 1967?

7. According to Thomas Aquinas, what was the only sin of lust considered
   worse than sodomy?

8. In what year were same-sex relationships between women legalised in
   the UK?

9. Which world (G20) power was the first to formally legalise homosexu-
   ality (1880) and the first to make the age of consent equal?

10. Jóhanna Sigurðardóttir was the first openly gay head of government to
    be in power when she became prime minister of which country in
    2009?

Answers to quiz 161

1. Oxfordshire.

2. 'I'd Do Anything for Love' was on *Bat out of Hell II*; the seven tracks on the original were the title track, 'You Took the Words Right Out of My Mouth', 'Heaven Can Wait', 'All Revved Up with No Place to Go', 'Two Out of Three Ain't Bad', 'Paradise by the Dashboard Light' and 'For Crying Out Loud'.

3. Itzhak Perlman was a violinist.

4. Lebanon.

5. Atlanta Jackals; we made them up.

6. *Les Misérables* has music by Claude-Michel Schönberg.

7. Polly; the Famous Five are Julian, Anne, Dick, Georgina and Timmy the dog.

8. Nigeria.

9. Henderson missed his spot-kick, the other three and Kieran Trippier scored; fortunately for England, Uribe and Bacca also missed their kicks and England (deservedly) went through.

10. Tupac was twenty-five. Other members of the 27 Club include Brian Jones (Rolling Stones' guitarist), Janis Joplin, Pete Ham (of Badfinger), Jimi Hendrix and Richey Edwards (Manic Street Preachers).

QUIZ 163. ROBINS

Sounds like a neighbourhood playgroup. But it isn't. It's a quiz about people called Robin or Robbins.

1. Which TV presenter, best known for *Question Time*, also presented radio's *World at One* between 1979 and 1987?

2. Who was Robert, Earl of Huntingdon?

3. Robin Pecknold is the lead singer in which modern American folk band?

4. Who did the superhero Dick Grayson hang around with?

5. Who were Regal for a while and then had a Robin and a Kitten?

6. In which 1987 cult movie does Cary Elwes fall in love with Buttercup, played by Robin Wright?

7. *The Carpetbaggers*, *The Inheritors* and *The Betsy* were novels by which author, hugely popular in the 1960s and 70s but now largely unread?

8. Which of the Monty Python team played Sir Robin the Not-so-Brave in *Monty Python and the Holy Grail*?

9. What is the name of the character in *The Shawshank Redemption* played by Tim Robbins? Is it (a) Ellis 'Red' Redding; (b) Griffin Mill; (c) Andy Dufresne; or (d) Freddie Shaw?

10. Which South African-born cricketer made his Test Match debut against the then-mighty West Indies in 1988, five years after his elder brother Chris?

Answers to Quiz 162

1. San Francisco; liberal San Francisco was the trigger point for a number of gay rights protests – a few years after Stonewall, there were major disturbances when the murderer of Harvey Milk had his sentence reduced to manslaughter.

2. Margaret Thatcher.

3. 1972.

4. Rainbow banner.

5. Employment in the armed forces.

6. Twenty-one. It was lowered to eighteen in 1994, and to sixteen, the same as for heterosexual relationships, in 2000.

7. Incest. (I cannot print here some of the suggestions that were made at the quiz when I set this round.)

8. They were never illegal. One of our regulars, who is gay, was fuming when he was overruled on this by his (straight) teammates.

9. Japan.

10. Iceland.

QUIZ 164. WORLD CUP HEROES

Our second World Cup quiz is about record-breaking and brilliant individuals who have lit up the tournament over the years. Probably quite straightforward for a footie fan, less so if you do anything to avoid watching the TV once every four years.

1. Who became the top scorer at the World Cup Finals when he scored his sixteenth goal in 2016? And which Brazilian player's record did he beat?

2. Who (to 2018) is the only England player to score ten or more World Cup Finals' goals?

3. Which three players, all of whom played for Manchester United at some stage, have been sent off playing for England at the World Cup Finals?

4. Which German player has made the most World Cup Finals appearances (twenty-five)? And who heads the England list with seventeen (to 2018)?

5. Who came back from a ban for corruption in time to inspire his country to victory at the 1982 World Cup, when he scored a hat-trick against Brazil in a classic quarter-final match?

6. What was American midfielder Joe Gaetjens' claim to fame in the 1950 World Cup?

7. Which Brazilian prodigy was the youngest player to score in a World Cup Finals match when he scored, aged 17 and 239 days, against Wales in 1958?

8. Both Antonio Carbajal and Rafael Márquez have appeared in five World Cup Finals tournaments: for which country?

9. Of the players with ten or more World Cup Finals goals, Teófilo Cubillas is perhaps the one most people are least likely to remember. For which country did this brilliant player score ten goals in two finals tournaments?

10. At seventeen years and forty-one days, which Irishman remains the youngest player to appear in a Finals match?

Answers to Quiz 163

1. Sir Robin Day.

2. Robin Hood; he has various guises in the different versions of the stories, but most place him as a minor Saxon nobleman back from the Crusades.

3. Fleet Foxes.

4. Batman (Dick Grayson is Robin).

5. The Staffordshire car company, Reliant.

6. *The Princess Bride*. Written by William Goldman from his own novel and directed by Rob Reiner, the film plays fast and loose with classic adventure film tropes and is full of arch and quotable humour. A work of genius and a textbook on how to make a romantic comedy without any coarseness.

7. Harold Robbins.

8. Eric Idle.

9. Andy Dufresne.

10. Robin Smith. He played sixty-two Tests, scoring 4,236 runs at a time when England were a bit rubbish.

QUIZ 165. ROGERS

One of those names where there are as many people with the surname as with the first name, so there are questions here about both. A mix, some sport, some entertainment, some general.

1. Where did Roger Bannister memorably run the first sub-four-minute mile in 1954?

2. Who did everything Fred did, backwards and in heels, according to a famous quote?

3. With whom did the ventriloquist Roger de Courcy perform? Was it (a) Roland Rat; (b) Sid the Squirrel; (c) Nookie Bear; or (d) Bazooka Bear?

4. Don Rogers took Arsenal apart in the 1969 League Cup Final, enabling which then-Third Division club to win their only major trophy?

5. With which band has Roger Daltrey been the lead singer for over forty years?

6. In which year did Peter Mark Roget first publish his *Thesaurus*? Was it (a) 1852; (b) 1875; (c) 1922; or (d) 1946?

7. *South Pacific*, *The King and I*, *West Side Story*, *The Sound of Music*: which of these is not a Rodgers and Hammerstein musical?

8. Buster Crabbe played which hero in a 1939 Universal movie?

9. Who, in 1969, was insistent that he had to leave Durham Town?

10. Roger Waters became the de facto leader of Pink Floyd in 1968 after which troubled soul was excluded from the band?

Answers to Quiz 164

1. Miroslav Klose; Ronaldo.

2. Gary Lineker.

3. Ray Wilkins (1986), David Beckham (1998), Wayne Rooney (2006).

4. Lothar Matthäus; Peter Shilton.

5. Paolo Rossi.

6. Gaetjens scored the goal that saw the US to a massive shock – a 1–0 win over England. The English press were so incredulous they assumed the score was 10–1 to England!

7. Pelé; the best player to have ever played the game. Why so certain? He played in an era when he could be kicked with impunity and red cards were reserved for GBH; and he was instrumental in three World Cup wins. All the talk about the genius of the 1970 Brazilian side is over-stated; it comprised one genius and a handful of very good players who he took to a different level. He has conducted himself since retirement with consistent grace and dignity as an ambassador of the game. Forget the twentieth-century hype: Pelé was the best.

8. Mexico.

9. Peru – the attacking midfielder is their greatest player by some distance. Cubillas played in 1970 and again in 1978, when he orchestrated Peru's shock victory over a fancied Scotland team.

10. Norman Whiteside.

QUIZ 166. MUSIC MIX

A mixed music round. Two or three toughies in there – respect if you get both parts of No. 5.

1. If your album won a MOBO award, you would be recognised for what?

2. Who was Hardcore, Notorious, in the Bella Mafia and told the Naked Truth?

3. Who released two albums in 2005, the first, *Fijación Oral, Vol. 1* sung in Spanish, and the other, *Oral Fixation, Vol. 2*, sung in English? Where was this singer born?

4. Who took over Freddie Mercury's role in Queen from 2004 to 2009? With which two bands did this singer enjoy much commercial success in the 1970s?

5. What is the name of the Perth (Australia)-based prog-rock act that is primarily the work of Kevin Parker? Why might they be inclined to run away from Bradford Cox's experimental rock band from Atlanta, Georgia?

6. 'Eight Miles High', from the album *Fifth Dimension* (1966), was a song that influenced a plethora of psychedelic guitar bands. Which band released the song?

7. *Sgt Pepper's Lonely Hearts Club Band* (The Beatles), *Bridge Over Troubled Water* (Simon & Garfunkel), *Brothers in Arms* (Dire Straits), *(What's the Story) Morning Glory* (Oasis), *Back to Bedlam* (James Blunt): what's the connection, and which album will come next?

8. Who are the only two women to have scored more than twenty No. 1 singles on the US country chart?

9. Bob Dylan's 2015 album, *Shadows in the Night*, consists entirely of songs associated with which earlier popular artist?

10. Festival Republic, which runs Latitude and Reading/Leeds among others, was originally known by what name, taken from the famous north-west London music venue where the enterprise began?

Answers to Quiz 165

1. Oxford, at Iffley Road running track, with his friends Chris Brasher and Chris Chataway as pacemakers.

2. Ginger Rogers.

3. Nookie Bear.

4. Swindon Town; it was a fairy-tale season for the Wiltshire club, as they also won promotion from the third tier. They had to fight through a replay in four of their five ties en route to the final, beating Bradford City and Blackburn before knocking out top-flight Coventry City and then Derby County, who won the Second Division that season. In the semi-final they won away at top-tier Burnley, but lost the home leg by the same score, necessitating another replay. The final went to extra time after Arsenal scored a late equaliser, but Rogers ran a tiring defence ragged on a foul, muddy pitch to win Swindon their day of glory.

5. The Who.

6. 1852.

7. *West Side Story*. Arthur Laurents adapted the story from *Romeo and Juliet*, while Stephen Sondheim wrote the song lyrics and Leonard Bernstein the music.

8. Buck Rogers.

9. Roger Whittaker; Whittaker was a folk pop singer who was renowned for being an expert whistler.

10. Syd Barrett. Dave Gilmour came in on guitar and the band's most successful line-up was in place.

QUIZ 167. THIS OR THAT

India is the setting for the latest This or That. These words indicate either the surname of an Indian Test cricketer, one of the constituent states of India, or a Hindu sacred text (or major part thereof).

1. Viswanath.

2. Maharashtra.

3. Rig Veda.

4. Bihar.

5. Azharuddin.

6. Upanishads.

7. Uttarakhand.

8. Gujarat.

9. Pujara.

10. Aranyaka.

11. Purana.

12. Srikkanth.

Answers to Quiz 166

1. Music of Black Origin, established in 1996.

2. Lil' Kim; they are the titles of her four albums.

3. Shakira; Colombia.

4. Paul Rodgers. He'd been with Free and Bad Company previously, two bands which fused blues, Rodgers' primary love, and hard rock.

5. Tame Impala, and an impala would fear a Deerhunter, which is Cox's band. Sorry, I know, lame. Made me chuckle though.

6. The Byrds; it was written by Gene Clark, Roger McGuinn and David Crosby, and was influenced, like The Beatles' *Sgt Pepper's*, by the sitar playing of Ravi Shankar.

7. They are the best-selling albums of the 1960s, 70s, 80s, 90s and 2000s. Adele's 21 looks nailed on to be the best-seller of the 2010s.

8. Dolly Parton and Reba McEntire.

9. Frank Sinatra.

10. The Mean Fiddler Group.

QUIZ 168. EXPLAIN THESE NAMES OR TERMS

In other words, another 'Identify . . .' quiz, this time with a scientific leaning. Remember, more is more; don't short-change us on the detail.

1. Dmitri Mendeleev.

2. Lysozyme.

3. Pterodactylus.

4. Angiosperm.

5. Parthenogenesis.

6. Calvaria.

7. Oncology.

8. Krill.

9. Keck 1 and Keck 2.

10. Cetaceans.

Answers to Quiz 167

1. Gundappa Viswanath was a steady batsman in the Indian middle order in the 1970s; he scored over six thousand runs in ninety-one Tests.

2. Maharashtra is a large state in the west of India and the country's most heavily populated – partly because it includes the 18 million people who live in Mumbai.

3. The *Rig Veda* is one of the four canonical Hindu texts.

4. Bihar is a state in the north-east of India.

5. Mohammad Azharuddin scored over six thousand runs in ninety-nine Tests between 1984 and 2000.

6. The Upanishads are a series of philosophical Sanskrit writings.

7. Uttarakhand is a northern state in the Himalayas bordering Tibet.

8. Gujarat is the westernmost coastal state of India.

9. Cheteshwar Pujara is a current member of the Indian team: he has amassed over five thousand runs and, at thirty-one, has the power to add many more.

10. The Aranyakas explain the reasoning behind the belief in ritual sacrifice.

11. The Puranas contain much of the ancient lore and stories that form the basis of Hinduism.

12. Kris (Krishnamachari) Srikkanth was an attacking opening batsman in the 1980s, known mainly for his exploits in one-day cricket.

QUIZ 169. MOON

The moon is a ripe subject for a thematic quiz, as it has inspired artists of every form for an awfully long time, and plays an important part in mythologies of all kinds.

1. Which word indicating mental illness or, more commonly, abnormal behaviour derives from the notion of being touched by the moon?

2. Who played the character Alfie Moon in *EastEnders* from 2002 to 2005?

3. What name is given to the full moon closest to the autumnal equinox around the third week of September?

4. In Greek mythology, who is the goddess of the moon?

5. What name is given to the third part of Debussy's *Suite Bergamasque*, a piano composition interpreting a poem by Paul Verlaine?

6. *The Moon and Sixpence* was a 1919 novel by which English writer and one-time spy?

7. In which film was the song 'Moon River' first performed and by whom?

8. Which film won the 2016 Academy Award for Best Film?

9. Which Premier League club's fans sing the Rodgers and Hart classic 'Blue Moon' before each game.

10. How many moon landings were made by NASA between 1969 and 1972?

Answers to Quiz 168

1. Mendeleev developed the first draft of the Periodic Table.

2. This was the name given to the first natural antibiotic discovered by Alexander Fleming.

3. An extinct species of flying reptile.

4. Flowering, seed-producing plants – there are well over three hundred thousand known species.

5. Asexual reproduction without fertilisation.

6. Latin name for the skullcap in human anatomy.

7. Oncology is the medical discipline that covers the treatment and care of cancers.

8. Tiny crustaceans that form an important role at the bottom of the oceans' food chain; they have pharmaceutical uses as well as being used as bait and feed for aquarium fish.

9. Two enormous telescopes on Mauna Kea in Hawaii.

10. Aquatic mammals – dolphins, whales and porpoises.

QUIZ 170. CHARACTERFUL

A simple quiz. We give you three characters from a novel, and you just name the novel. Tricky, yes, because it relies on one of the team (a) having read the novel – they are all big sellers or classics – and (b) remembering the novel.

1. Marc-Ange Draco; Tracy di Vicenzo; Sir Hilary Bray (1963).

2. John Harmon; Lizzie Hexham; Bradley Headstone (1865).

3. Tom Joad; Jim Casy; Muley Graves (1939).

4. Dennis Simms; Miss Windsor; Darvesh Singh (2008).

5. Edmund Bertram; Mary Crawford; Mrs Norris (1814).

6. Rawdon Crawley; George Osborne; Becky Sharp (1847).

7. Jake Lovell; Billy Lloyd-Foxe; Tory Maxwell (1985).

8. Briony Tallis; Robbie Turner; Lola Quincey (2001).

9. Paul Atreides; Lady Margot Fenrig; Duncan Idaho (1965).

10. Charles Ryder; Julia Flyte; Rex Mottram (1945).

Answers to Quiz 169

1. Lunatic.

2. Shane Ritchie.

3. Harvest Moon.

4. Selene.

5. 'Clair de lune'.

6. W. Somerset Maugham.

7. *Breakfast at Tiffany's*; Audrey Hepburn.

8. *Moonlight*.

9. Manchester City.

10. Six.

'Moon River' was listed as the fourth most memorable movie song of the twentieth century in a list compiled by the AFI (American Film Institute). Here are the Top 10:

'Over the Rainbow' from *The Wizard of Oz* (1939) – Judy Garland (written by Arlen and Harberg).

'As Time Goes By' from *Casablanca* (1942) – Dooley Wilson (Herman Hupfeld).

'Singin' in the Rain' from the film of the same title (1952) – Gene Kelly (Nacio Herb Brown and Arthur Freed).

'Moon River' from *Breakfast at Tiffany's* (1959) – Audrey Hepburn (Henry Mancini and Johnny Mercer).

'White Christmas' from *Holiday Inn* (1942) – Bing Crosby (Irving Berlin).

'Mrs Robinson' from *The Graduate* (1969) – Simon & Garfunkel (Paul Simon).

'When You Wish Upon a Star' from *Pinocchio* (1940) – Ukulele Ike as Jiminy Cricket (Harline and Washington).

'The Way We Were' from film of the same title (1973) – Barbra Streisand (Marvin Hamlisch with the Bergmans).

'Stayin' Alive' from *Saturday Night Fever* (1977) – The Bee Gees (Gibb Brothers).

'The Sound of Music' from film of the same title (1965) – Julie Andrews (Rodgers and Hammerstein).

Personal faves would be 'I Could Write a Book' from *Pal Joey*; 'You're the One That I Want' from *Grease*; 'Cabaret' from *Cabaret*; 'Luck Be a Lady' from *Guys and Dolls*; 'Streets of Philadelphia' from *Philadelphia*; and, for a piece of pure movie cheese, 'Holding Out for a Hero' from *Footloose*.

QUIZ 171. NEW MOONS

Another moon quiz – I've used this theme twice over the last year or so, and it produced two good rounds with fairly even scoring.

1. Which TV series features a live-in housekeeper for the main character called Daphne Moon?

2. Which satellite of Jupiter is the largest moon in our solar system?

3. Who had a major hit, including a UK No. 1, with 'Can't Fight the Moonlight', the theme tune from the cult hit movie *Coyote Ugly*?

4. Australian Brendan Moon, at his peak in the 1980s, is regarded as a great in which sport?

5. Which ten-year-old won a Best Supporting Actress Academy Award for her role in the 1973 film *Paper Moon*?

6. The names of the moons of Uranus are drawn from Shakespeare plays and also the poem *The Rape of the Lock*, by which eighteenth-century satirical poet?

7. 'Giant steps are what you take, walking on the moon', sang Sting in the Police song. What's the next line?

8. Which crooner sang eight bars of 'Moon River' by Henry Mancini at the beginning of every episode of his nine-year TV show?

9. Charon is the largest moon of the dwarf planet, Pluto: what was Charon's role in Greek mythology?

10. What name is given to a waxing moon that is not yet full but larger than a semi-circle?

Answers to Quiz 170

1. They are all from *On Her Majesty's Secret Service* (Ian Fleming, 1963; the tenth James Bond novel and sixth film).

2. *Our Mutual Friend*, completed 1865, is Dickens' last finished novel and one of his finest.

3. *The Grapes of Wrath* (John Steinbeck's 1939 account of the struggles of ordinary people in the Great Depression).

4. *Boy in the Dress* (David Walliams, from 2008, one of a series of successful children's books by the comedian and actor).

5. *Mansfield Park* (1814; Jane Austen's third novel).

6. *Vanity Fair* (William Thackeray's coruscating 1848 novel of greed and ambition).

7. *Riders* (1985; the first of Jilly Cooper's Rutshire novels).

8. *Atonement* (Ian McEwan, 2001; a modern masterpiece, unlike the film).

9. *Dune* (Frank Herbert, 1965; ground-breaking sci-fi).

10. *Brideshead Revisited* (Evelyn Waugh's 1945 novel was turned into one of the UK's most memorable costume dramas, screened by Granada in 1981).

QUIZ 172. TV CRIME

There seems to be no end to the audience appetite for TV shows about crime, whether it be police procedurals, private-eye tales, gritty internal affairs and corruption dramas like *Line of Duty*, or gentle country murder mysteries. Here's another set of questions about a few of them.

1. What are the first names of the detectives Dalziel and Pascoe, played on TV by Warren Clarke and Colin Buchanan?

2. Which fictional seaside town was the setting for three drama series starring David Tennant and Olivia Colman as the lead police officers?

3. In the context of this round, who or what connects Shaun Evans and John Thaw?

4. What is the name of Helen Mirren's character in the various series of *Prime Suspect*?

5. What is the name by which we generally know DCI Stanhope of the Northumberland and City Police? Who plays Stanhope?

6. Joan Hickson, Geraldine McEwan and Julia McKenzie have all played which sleuth on TV?

7. The US TV series *Bones* is based on a series of books and characters created by which American crime writer?

8. Which three American cities have provided the setting for numerous series of *CSI: Crime Scene Investigation* (excluding the recent flop, *CSI: Cyber*)?

9. What was unusual about the early TV detective Ironside, played by Raymond Burr?

10. Which long-running crime series would end many of its episodes with the words, 'Book 'em, Danno!'?

Answers to Quiz 171

1. *Frasier*.

2. Ganymede.

3. LeAnn Rimes.

4. Rugby Union.

5. Tatum O'Neal.

6. Alexander Pope.

7. 'I hope my legs don't break, walking on the moon,'

8. Andy Williams.

9. He was the ferryman across the River Styx.

10. Gibbous.

Twelve deities

The twelve major deities on Mount Olympus in Greek mythology are these:

Zeus (Jupiter in Roman myths) – the head of the gods.
Hera (Juno) – Zeus's primary partner.
Poseidon (Neptune) – god of the seas and rivers.
Demeter (Ceres) – god of the earth and growing things.
Athena (Athena) – goddess of wisdom.
Apollo (Apollo) – god of light and the arts.
Artemis (Diana) – the huntress, goddess of virginity and purity.
Ares (Mars) – the god of war.
Aphrodite (Venus) – the goddess of love.
Hephaestus (Vulcan) – the Blacksmith, god of craftsmanship.
Hermes (Mercury) – the winged messenger and trickster.
Dionysus (Bacchus) – god of wine and revels.

In addition, there is Hades (Pluto), the god of the underworld and custodian of the dead, but he does not reside on Olympus. Charon (see Question 9 above) ferries the souls of the deceased to their new home, where unwanted visitors are kept at bay by Cerberus, Hades' three-headed dog.

QUIZ 173. NUMBERS

Another of those tricky blighters where you actually get fifty-five questions disguised as twelve. Now that's just mean, isn't it?

1. Apart from Cardiff and Swansea, which is the only town or city in Wales with a population of over a hundred thousand?

2. Which are the only two countries on the South American continent that do NOT share a border with Brazil?

3. Which are the three African countries with a four-letter name?

4. What are the four films starring both Humphrey Bogart and his second wife Lauren Bacall?

5. *Bleak Moments*; *High Hopes*; *Life is Sweet*; *Naked*; *Secrets and Lies*; *Career Girls*; *Topsy Turvy*; *All or Nothing*; *Vera Drake*; *Happy-Go-Lucky*; *Another Year*; *Mr Turner*. These are the twelve feature films made by Mike Leigh. In which five did Timothy Spall appear?

6. Which six clubs have contested every Premier League season since the competition began in 1993 until 2019?

7. Of the world's ten largest islands, three are sparsely populated Canadian territories (Baffin, Victoria and Ellesmere, at five, eight and ten). What are the other seven?

8. Which countries make up the G8 group of industrialised nations?

9. Name the nine footballers who have scored more than 150 Premier League goals. (Only one was still playing in 2018–19, although Harry Kane will doubtless join the list very soon.)

10. David Bowie was at his most prolific in the 1970s, releasing eleven albums. *The Man Who Sold the World* was the first in November 1970. What were the other ten?

Answers to Quiz 172

1. Andy Dalziel and Peter Pascoe.

2. *Broadchurch*, written by Chris Chibnall, who later became the *Dr Who* showrunner – hence the casting of Jodie Whittaker, who also had a major role in *Broadchurch*. The small world of TV.

3. They play the same character, Morse: John Thaw was the original grouchy Oxford cop, Evans plays his younger incarnation in the spin-off *Endeavour*.

4. Jane Tennison.

5. Vera, as played by Brenda Blethyn with fabulous world-weary candour in the series of that name.

6. Agatha Christie's Miss Marple.

7. Kathy Reichs. Reichs was herself a forensic pathologist, and the character of Temperance Brennan is based partly on her own experiences. As an in-show in-joke, Brennan writes a series of novels in the show about a forensic analyst called Kathy Reichs.

8. Las Vegas, Miami, New York.

9. He was in a wheelchair.

10. *Hawaii Five-O*.

QUIZ 174. MOVIES

This is a variant on the This or That-style quiz. Each of these twelve films starred Kevin Bacon, Mickey Rourke or Jeff Goldblum. Sort out who was in what – each star has four films on the list; there are no tricksy ones where two of them appeared.

1. *Mystic River* (2003).

2. *Independence Day* (1996).

3. *Rumble Fish* (1983).

4. *Animal House* (1978).

5. *The Fly* (1986).

6. *X-Men: First Class* (2011).

7. *Iron Man 2* (2010).

8. *Angel Heart* (1987).

9. *The Grand Budapest Hotel* (2014).

10. *The Rainmaker* (1997).

11. *Flatliners* (1990).

12. *The Big Chill* (1983).

Answers to Quiz 173

1. Newport.

2. Peru and Chile.

3. Chad, Mali, Togo.

4. *To Have and Have Not*; *The Big Sleep*; *The Dark Passage*; *Key Largo*.

5. *Life is Sweet*; *Secrets and Lies*; *Topsy Turvy*; *All or Nothing*; and *Mr Turner*.

6. Arsenal, Chelsea, Everton, Liverpool, Manchester United, Tottenham Hotspur. Of these, only Everton have flirted with relegation, and it is hard to see any of the other five disappearing from the top flight any time soon.

7. Greenland (1), New Guinea (2), Borneo (3), Madagascar (4), Sumatra (6), Honshu (7), Great Britain (9).

8. The US, Russia, Japan, UK, France, Germany, Italy, Canada.

9. Alan Shearer, Wayne Rooney, Andrew Cole, Frank Lampard, Thierry Henry, Robbie Fowler, Jermain Defoe, Sergio Aguero, Michael Owen.

10. *Hunky Dory*, *Ziggy Stardust*, *Aladdin Sane*, *Pin-Ups*, *Diamond Dogs*, *Young Americans*, *Station to Station*, *Low*, *Heroes*, *The Lodger*.

QUIZ 175. APPLES

We genuinely can't remember how we hit on apples as a theme, but we were pleased that we got a bit of variety out of it, rather than just questions about types of apple.

1. Which is the best-selling apple in the UK?

2. Which seven-minute song, the first released on the Beatles' Apple label, became the longest No. 1 single to that date when it hit the top of the charts in 1968?

3. Who co-founded Apple Inc. along with Steve Jobs and Ronald Wayne?

4. From where does the Braeburn apple originate?

5. Who is Apple Martin's mother?

6. Which family started brewing cider on their farm in Sandford, North Somerset, in 1904?

7. The apple is a deciduous tree belonging to which family of plants?

8. In which year was iTunes launched? Was it 1997, 2001, 2004 or 2009?

9. In which country did Kopparberg cider originate?

10. By what nickname is the pioneering nurseryman and early conservationist John Chapman known in popular culture?

Answers to Quiz 174

1. Kevin was in Clint Eastwood's thriller based on a novel by Denis Lehane.

2. Jeff was in Roland Emmerich's stinker of a blockbuster.

3. Mickey was in Coppola's coming-of-age drama based on S.E. Hinton's book.

4. Kevin was in John Landis's anarchic frat-house comedy.

5. Jeff was in the remake of a classic horror film.

6. Kevin was bad guy Sebastian Shaw in the fifth *X-Men* movie.

7. Mickey was the antagonist Vanko in the second *Iron Man* film.

8. Mickey was in Alan Parker's cult psycho drama with De Niro and Lisa Bonet.

9. Jeff was in Wes Anderson's quirky comedy drama.

10. Mickey was in another Coppola film, the John Grisham adaptation *The Rainmaker*.

11. Kevin was in Joel Schumacher's cult sci-fi film.

12. Jeff was part of the ensemble cast in Lawrence Kasdan's buddy drama.

QUIZ 176. CAMBRIDGE

The city of Cambridge, which is very beautiful, and its environs are the subject of this slightly random quiz. Expect a mixture of subjects, with a healthy smattering of geographical knowledge a useful asset.

1. A fast direct train from Cambridge to London would bring you into which London station?

2. The River Cam, which runs through Cambridge, joins the Great Ouse before it runs into which body of water at King's Lynn?

3. Which football club are known as The Posh?

4. What happens every year in the village of Cherry Hinton, a satellite of Cambridge?

5. In which Cambridgeshire village did Ian Huntley murder Holly Wells and Jessica Chapman?

6. Jeremy Paxman, a former student of St Catharine's College, is the host of TV quiz *University Challenge*. Who was his predecessor as the show's quizmaster?

7. Who led a rebellion against the Norman conquerors from his base on the Isle of Ely?

8. What happens at Fenner's in Cambridge?

9. In early 2013, Rowan Williams took up his new post as Master of Magdalene College, Cambridge. What was his previous job?

10. Who entered Parliament as the member for Cambridge in April 1640?

Answers to Quiz 175

1. Gala (including Royal Gala).

2. 'Hey Jude'; that record is now held by Oasis, with 'All Around the World'.

3. Steve Wozniak.

4. New Zealand; NZ produces splendid apples, if not that many of them – a bit like the UK. For sheer volume, China is way out ahead, producing ten times as many apples as the US, the second-biggest producer.

5. Gwyneth Paltrow; silly sausage.

6. Thatchers; the company is still owned by the descendants of William Thatcher.

7. Rosaceae.

8. The year was 2001; seems like a lifetime ago.

9. Sweden.

10. Johnny Appleseed – Disney made a short animated feature about him in 1948.

QUIZ 177. WTF?

Identify these apparently random words and make sense of the gibberish. This isn't so much vocabulary as knowledge of all things absurd and nonsensical.

1. Tinky Winky.

2. Oompa-loompa.

3. Ob-la-di, Ob-la-da.

4. Bada Bing.

5. Popocatépetl.

6. Bombalurina.

7. Jabberwocky.

8. Gabba Gabba Hey.

9. Yondu Udonta.

10. Pushmi-pullyu.

Answers to Quiz 176

1. London King's Cross, which serves most places north and east, as opposed to just east, which tend to be served by Liverpool Street.

2. The Wash, the large inlet at the northern end of East Anglia.

3. Peterborough United.

4. The Cambridge Folk Festival, first held in 1965.

5. Soham; the case dominated the news for a period in 2002 when the girls went missing before their bodies were found two weeks later. Huntley was found guilty in December 2003 and his girlfriend, Maxine Carr, was also jailed for giving him a false alibi.

6. Bamber Gascoigne, also a Cambridge graduate, from Magdalene College.

7. Hereward the Wake.

8. Cambridge University play cricket there; the ground has been in use since 1848.

9. Archbishop of Canterbury.

10. Oliver Cromwell.

QUIZ 178. MUSIC AND MOVIES

Pop stars and rock stars always fancy a bit of screen time, and a fair proportion of major artists have appeared in a movie at some stage in their career. For most of them, it was a terrible mistake; for others, it proved a mixed blessing, with some hits and some misses; and a rare one or two took to it rather well. All you have to do is match the rock or pop star to the film in which they appeared.

1. David Bowie.

2. Sting.

3. Madonna.

4. Ice Cube.

5. Joe Strummer.

6. Tina Turner.

7. Mariah Carey.

8. 50 Cent.

9. Ringo Starr.

10. Bjork.

A. *That'll Be the Day.*

B. *Mad Max Beyond Thunderdome.*

C. *Mystery Train.*

D. *Labyrinth.*

E. *Precious.*

F. *Spy.*

G. *Evita.*

H. *Dancer in the Dark.*

I. *Three Kings.*

J. *Lock, Stock and Two Smoking Barrels.*

Answers to Quiz 177

1. One of the four main characters in *Teletubbies*, alongside Dipsy, Laa-Laa and Po.

2. Willy Wonka's helpers in *Charlie and the Chocolate Factory*.

3. A song by the Beatles from the *White Album*, it was written by Paul McCartney and later became a hit for Marmalade.

4. Strip club in *The Sopranos*; the name comes from a catchphrase in *The Godfather*.

5. Popocatépetl is a volcano in Mexico – the volcano is active and is also the country's second-highest peak after Citlaltépetl.

6. A character in the musical *Cats*.

7. A poem by Lewis Carroll and film by Terry Gilliam; the poem was included in the 1871 work, *Through the Looking-Glass*, the follow-up to *Alice's Adventures in Wonderland*.

8. The slogan of the New York punk band The Ramones, chanted at the beginning of their shows.

9. A character in *Guardians of the Galaxy*.

10. A strange beast in the Dr Dolittle books by Hugh Lofting.

QUIZ 179. DRINK ADS

Booze companies have never been shy about throwing money at an advertising campaign, so the commodity has produced some of the more memorable TV ads over the years. How well do you remember them? (If you are over forty, this is an eight-or-nine-out-of-ten round.)

1. Which comedian appeared in a number of ads for John Smith's bitter?

2. I'll bet he drinks . . . what?

3. Which talking animal scored an advertising hit for Guinness?

4. Which beer boasted a bear?

5. Which German drink shares its emblem with our pub?

6. Whassup was a frequently heard refrain in the 1990s after it featured in an ad for which beer brand?

7. Which brewer couldn't give a XXXX?

8. What worked wonders?

9. Who claimed they stayed sharp to the bottom of the glass?

10. Britney, Beyoncé, P!nk, Taylor Swift: which hasn't featured in a Pepsi ad?

Answers to Quiz 178

1. D: Bowie appeared as the Goblin King in the 1986 Jim Henson fantasy.

2. J: Sting appears as JD, Eddie's father, whose bar is at risk after Eddie's foolhardy gambling, in Guy Ritchie's gangster movie.

3. G: Madonna was an obvious choice for Evita, and the film is serviceable. In her film roles, Madge has veered between deeply awful (*Shanghai Surprise*; *Body of Evidence*) and really very good (*Desperately Seeking Susan*; *A League of their Own*).

4. I: Ice Cube starred in *Three Kings* alongside George Clooney and Mark Wahlberg.

5. C: Joe Strummer sort of mumbled his way through his role in Jim Jarmusch's *Mystery Train* – he was no actor, but Jarmusch uses that quality cleverly in his films.

6. B: Tina Turner was fabulously over the top in the third *Mad Max* film – unfortunately, the rest of the film was a bit pants.

7. E: Mariah Carey was outstanding as a social worker in Lee Daniels' *Precious*.

8. F: 50 Cent is in *Spy*, the comedy vehicle for Melissa McCarthy and Miranda Hart, although whether he is acting is debatable, as he appears as himself.

9. A: Ringo is in *That'll be the Day* alongside David Essex and is really rather good, albeit a little older than the character he portrays.

10. H: Bjork starred in Von Trier's film, but did not enjoy the experience (which adds her to a list of actors who haven't enjoyed that particular experience). The film, and Bjork's own persona, are so quirky it is hard to assess whether she was a success or not.

QUIZ 180. ART PALETTE

Now we are going full-on with the culture. These will test your knowledge of fine art and history of art. Not your thing? Flip the page; this isn't the easiest round in the book.

1. Which of these four artists did NOT produce a work entitled *The Adoration of the Magi*: Bosch, Botticelli, Da Vinci, Delacroix?

2. The correct term for a horizontal projection from a building that is subtly braced as to appear self-supporting would be a baluster, a cantilever, a flying buttress or a purlin?

3. Jacopo and his sons Gentile and Giovanni were all members of which Italian Renaissance painting family?

4. American artist Winslow Homer produced most of his most famous works in his Prouts Neck studio, on the coast of (a) Maine; (b) West Virginia; (c) New Hampshire; or (d) Oregon?

5. John Piper is best known for designing what feature of Coventry Cathedral and Eton school?

6. Which US artist became known as a painter of London society in the late nineteenth century, as well as a chronicler of the First World War?

7. Which modern art movement was founded by Walter Gropius in Weimar just after the First World War?

8. Thomas Cole and others were affiliated to which nineteenth-century American landscape school?

9. *The Red Vineyard* was unique among Van Gogh's paintings in his lifetime. How?

10. What is the more popular name given to Whistler's 1871 painting *Arrangement in Grey and Black, No. 1*?

Answers to Quiz 179

1. Peter Kay – the ad in the swimming pool and the restaurant ones.

2. Carling Black Label – a whole series of ads depicting people doing extraordinary things were followed by that pay-off line.

3. A toucan – masterpieces of timing.

4. Hofmeister.

5. Jagermeister (but we don't stock it).

6. Budweiser; a series of laddish ads showing lazy people having larks.

7. Castlemaine; the Queensland brewer produced the second Aussie beer to make inroads into the UK, after Foster's.

8. Double Diamond; it didn't.

9. Harp lager; nice slogan, but actually the sharpness is dependent on how long you leave it, and the cleanliness of the glass as well as the product. I'm just saying!

10. Taylor Swift. Yet.

QUIZ 181. THREADS

This one needs a bit of explaining. The questions are deliberately sequenced so that the answers, or part of the question itself, reveal the solution to the conundrum posited by Question 12. If you can work out the thread, then it may make the solutions to some of the individual questions more accessible.

1. A one-off 1983 drama, *Woodentop*, was the start point for which police drama, which ran from 1984 to 2010?

2. Which classic 1967 film covers the coming-of-age of twenty-one-year-old Benjamin Braddock, played by Dustin Hoffman?

3. Who played the lead role in the eight series of the Showtime drama *Weeds*?

4. Which young actress, who made her name in *The Falling*, played the lead role in the critically acclaimed 2016 film, *Lady Macbeth*?

5. What kind of creature was Barney, the lead in *Barney and Friends*, a young children's programme that ran from 1992 to 2009?

6. Cuthbert was the first given name of which West Indian opening batsman, a member of Clive Lloyd's dominant team of the late 1970s and 80s?

7. Which children's TV series featured a policeman called Officer Dibble?

8. What was the name of the street close to Moorfields that became synonymous with hack writing and poor-quality publishing in the eighteenth century?

9. Which TV cook, who enjoyed a renaissance in recent years, published her first cookbook, the *Hamlyn All Colour Cookbook*, in 1970 when she was thirty-five years old?

10. Which charity, formed in 1969, is London's largest charity for the homeless?

11. Sand flies and black flies are varieties of biting insect coming under the umbrella of which common name?

12. Now deduce the three retro children's TV programmes referenced here.

Answers to Quiz 180

1. Delacroix is the odd painter out.

2. Cantilever.

3. Bellini; they were a key part of the Venetian school of Renaissance painting.

4. Maine. Homer trained in New York and worked in the north-east of England for a couple of years before moving back to the US. The studio is now owned by Portland Museum and is open to the public.

5. Stained glass; he was a notable landscape painter as well as a worker with glass.

6. John Singer Sargent; Sargent, American by nationality, was in style and influence a European painter, born in Florence and working most of his life across Europe.

7. Bauhaus.

8. The Hudson River School.

9. He sold it, the only painting he ever sold while he was still alive.

10. *Whistler's Mother*. Like Sargent, James McNeill Whistler was American-born, but chose to work in Europe, mainly in the UK.

QUIZ 182. MIXED SCIENCE

Another batch of science questions. We won't judge you whatever your score, as we reckon we would have got three, maybe four!

1. Which fêted microbiologist produced the first vaccine for rabies?

2. Who spent just over fifteen minutes in space on 5 May 1961? Was it Buzz Aldrin, Yuri Gagarin, John Glenn or Alan Shepard?

3. Bromine has a liquid form at standard temperature: which other metallic element shares this distinction?

4. In the cosmological equation about the expanding universe theory, $v = Hr$, what is H?

5. Which medical pioneer became the first female member of the Royal Statistical Society in 1859?

6. Which scientist (1745–1827) enabled the development of the internal combustion engine with his discovery of the combustibility of an air–methane mixture?

7. What was the principal invention of American scientist Charles Townes, now an integral part of much modern experimentation, including transmission of data via the internet?

8. Which word connects a small Eurasian wren with cave dwellers or hermits?

9. What part does the vas deferens play in the reproductive process of humans?

10. Which element, essential to healthy bones, is the most prevalent metal in the human body?

Answers to Quiz 181

1. *The BILL*; there were a staggering 2,425 episodes of *The Bill*.

2. *The Graduate*, wherein Anne Bancroft as the older woman, Mrs Robinson, helps BENjamin grow up.

3. Mary Louise Parker; WEEDs ran for 8 seasons and 102 episodes, and starred Parker as Nancy Botwin, a housewife turned drug-dealer to support her family – sound familiar? (It was before *Breaking Bad*.)

4. Florence PUGH.

5. BARNEY is a purple dinosaur.

6. CUTHBERT Gordon Greenidge; he scored 7,558 runs over a seventeen-year Test career and was one of the first destructive one-day-international opening batsmen.

7. Officer DIBBLE is in *Top Cat*.

8. GRUB Street.

9. MARY Berry, whose career resurgence with the *Great British Bake Off* must have surprised even her.

10. St MUNGO's.

11. MIDGEs.

12. The children's programmes are *BILL and BEN* (including Little WEED), *Trumpton*, with its fireman squad of PUGH (PUGH), BARNEY McGrew, CUTHBERT, DIBBLE, GRUB, and then *MARY, MUNGO and MIDGE*.

QUIZ 183. JULIE, JULIA, JOOLS . . .

Another name-themed round, this one based around Julies, Julias, Jools, and all derivatives thereof. We did this round in a café with no internet connection, so it's pretty straightforward; a team of four should get eight or nine of them correct.

1. 'I've been going out with a girl, her name is Julie . . .' Who sang this?

2. Which 1999 teen romance (based loosely on Shakespeare's *Taming of the Shrew*) saw Heath Ledger starring alongside Julia Stiles?

3. Julie Kavner is best known as the voice of which long-running cartoon character?

4. Julie Christie won an Academy Award for which of the following films: *Darling*; *Doctor Zhivago*; *Far from the Madding Crowd*; *The Go-Between*?

5. Who starred as Julia Child, the American cordon bleu chef, in the 2009 film, *Julie and Julia*?

6. Julia Gillard was the twenty-seventh prime minister of which country from 2010 to 2013?

7. Which rhyming picture book by Julia Donaldson (and illustrated by Axel Scheffler) has racked up sales of over 13 million copies worldwide since its first publication in 1999?

8. Juli Inkster has won seven important titles and a further twenty-six others in which sport?

9. Who was the keyboard player in indie band Squeeze from their formation in 1974 until 1981?

10. Poppy Honey; Daisy Boo; Clarrie Teardrop; River Rocket: which of these is not the name of one of the children of Jamie Oliver and his wife Jules?

Answers to Quiz 182

1. Louis Pasteur.

2. It was Alan Shepard and the trip made him the first American in space.

3. Mercury, as used in thermometers.

4. Hubble's constant, named after Edward Hubble, the astronomer, who devised the equation.

5. Florence Nightingale.

6. Alessandro Volta; he is also credited with inventing the battery and was admired and patronised by Napoleon Bonaparte.

7. Laser.

8. Troglodytes – it is an old name for a hermit and *Troglodytes troglodytes* is the Latin name for a wren.

9. It carries sperm from the epididymis ready for ejaculation.

10. Calcium.

QUIZ 184. NOVEMBER 5

It was Bonfire Night, and we had run out of bonfire questions because Hastings has its own Bonfire Night (Sussex bonfires, they are a big local thing) a few weeks prior to this. So we put a general quiz together on things that happened on 5 November.

1. Who fell off his boat in 1991, never to be seen again?

2. Which new mobile operating system was unveiled by Google in 2007?

3. In which Russian city did the October Revolution of 1917 begin, instigated by Lenin on 5 November?

4. Who was formally elected to an unprecedented third term in office as US President in 1940?

5. Which Danish international goalkeeper begat another one in 1986?

6. René Goscinny, who died in 1977, was half of the famous writer/illustrator team behind which series of comic books?

7. Susan Anthony became the first woman to do what in the United States in 1872, a 'crime' for which she was fined $100?

8. Which American songwriter, producer, guitarist and wife beater was born in 1931?

9. Nat Turner was sentenced to death in Virginia in 1831 for what crime?

10. Which jockey, born in 1935, rode nine Epsom Derby winners, including Sir Ivor and the legendary Nijinsky?

Answers to Quiz 183

1. Jilted John, a recording name for comedian and writer Graham Fellows, aka John Shuttleworth.

2. *10 Things I Hate About You*.

3. Kavner is the voice of Marge Simpson, as well as her sisters, Patty and Selma Bouvier.

4. *Darling*, opposite Dirk Bogarde; Christie also earned nominations for *McCabe & Mrs Miller*, *Afterglow* and *Away from Her*.

5. Meryl Streep in one of her many Oscar-nominated roles; Amy Adams played Julie, the modern-day cookery writer who undertakes a project to cook all of Julia's recipes.

6. Australia.

7. *The Gruffalo*; the pair have collaborated on a number of successful projects, including *Room on the Broom* and *The Gruffalo's Child*, a follow-up to the original book.

8. Golf.

9. Jools Holland, now a music TV presenter (*The Tube* and *Later with Jools Holland*).

10. Clarrie Teardrop (we made that one up).

QUIZ 185. ARTS AND LITERATURE

Here's a funny round. Oh no, hang on, it's just a quiz about funny. You need to match the author to the comic work of their creation. One clever-clogs team got the lot.

1. Beryl Bainbridge.
2. Jonathan Coe.
3. Helen DeWitt.
4. Roddy Doyle.
5. Stella Gibbons.
6. Jerome K. Jerome.
7. David Lodge.
8. Spike Milligan.
9. John Kennedy Toole.
10. Geoffrey Willans.

A. *Three Men in a Boat.*

B. *Cold Comfort Farm.*

C. *Down with Skool!*

D. *Puckoon.*

E. *The Van.*

F. *A Confederacy of Dunces.*

G. *Nice Work.*

H. *The Rotters' Club.*

I. *The Bottle Factory Outing.*

J. *Lightning Rods.*

Answers to Quiz 184

1. Robert Maxwell; did he fall? Really?

2. Android, the non-geeks' alternative to Apple.

3. St Petersburg (Petrograd).

4. Franklin D. Roosevelt; Roosevelt's grip on the presidency led to the enactment of the 22nd Amendment in 1947, limiting candidates to two terms of office.

5. Peter Schmeichel and his wife Bente produced Kasper Schmeichel, currently of Leicester City – Schmeichel elder has since remarried.

6. *Asterix the Gaul*. There are now thirty-seven volumes in the series; the first twenty-four were written by Goscinny in his lifetime and all twenty-four were illustrated by Albert Uderzo.

7. Vote, in Rochester, New York.

8. Ike Turner.

9. Provoking a slave rebellion.

10. Lester Piggott. Piggott also won the 1,000 Guineas twice, the 2,000 Guineas five times, the Oaks six times, and was eight times a winner of the St Leger, for a total of thirty Classic wins.

QUIZ 186. SPORT MIX

Another sporting miscellany, nothing too tricky. Aim high – seven is okay, eight or nine is better. Obvs.

1. Of the seventy-six women's tennis major tournaments since 2000, what percentage have been won by the Williams sisters? Is it 22 per cent, 39 per cent, 48 per cent or 61 per cent?

2. Alpine skiing is made up of which two disciplines?

3. England's Georgia Hall was a popular home winner of which competition in 2018?

4. In which sport and with whom do England contest the annual sports fixture called the Calcutta Cup?

5. What was Gary Anderson accused of doing to upset his opponent, Wesley Harms, during their encounter at the 2018 Grand Slam of Darts?

6. What term is used in baseball when a batter hits a home run with all three bases occupied, thereby scoring four points for the team?

7. In which sport might the Magic come up against the Wizards and the Timberwolves take on the Grizzlies?

8. Which top-flight English Rugby League club play on the same site as a Test Match cricket ground?

9. The 2013 film *Rush* documented the rivalry between which two Formula 1 drivers?

10. What connects the National Hockey League franchises the Senators, the Jets, the Oilers and the Flames?

Answers to Quiz 185

1. I: Bainbridge's *The Bottle Factory Outing* is a hilarious but ultimately tragic view of the lives of two working-class girls.

2. H: *The Rotters' Club* was a 2001 nostalgic work by Jonathan Coe, who wrote a 2004 sequel, *The Closed Circle*.

3. J: Helen DeWitt's *Lightning Rods* is a unique view on sexual division in the workplace.

4. E: *The Van* is Roddy Doyle's follow-up to *The Commitments*.

5. B: *Cold Comfort Farm* is a comedy classic written in 1932 by Stella Gibbons.

6. A: *Three Men in a Boat* is Jerome K. Jerome's 1889 account of a boating holiday.

7. G: *Nice Work* was the final part of Lodge's campus trilogy, after *Changing Places* and *Small World*.

8. D: *Puckoon* is a comic work by Spike Milligan.

9. F: Toole's *A Confederacy of Dunces* was published and won a Pulitzer Prize eleven years after he took his own life.

10. C: Geoffrey Willans created the character of Molesworth in the book *Down with Skool!* – the book was illustrated by Ronald Searle.

QUIZ 187. FRANCE

Vive la France. Here is a Francophile mix of sports and current affairs and geography questions on our sometime rival and erstwhile allies across the Channel.

1. Which French king earned the name the Sun King after he ruled his country from 1643 to 1715?

2. Who was the first Frenchman to become top scorer for a season in the English Premier League?

3. Who was crowned King of Italy in May 1805 and remained king until being deposed in 1814?

4. On which date does the French Republic celebrate the storming of the Bastille prison?

5. Which French Rugby Union club won the first of a hat-trick of European Champions trophies in 2013?

6. Which town in south-central France became the centre of government of the country between 1940 and 1944 during the German occupation?

7. Who did Emmanuel Macron defeat in the final run-off for the French presidency in 2017?

8. Which coastal city boasts France's third busiest airport, after Charles de Gaulle and Orly in the Paris region?

9. Which is the only one of the thirteen administrative regions of France not on the European mainland?

10. Who was elected President of the Paris Commune, the most powerful body in post-revolutionary France, in August 1792, from which time he presided over the Reign of Terror until his own arrest and death in July 1794?

Answers to Quiz 186

1. Thirty-eight per cent – they have won thirty out of seventy-six, with Serena accounting for a remarkable twenty-two of those. She has won twenty-three in all, but the first was the US Open of 1999.

2. Downhill and slalom.

3. Golf's Women's British Open Championship.

4. Rugby Union; Scotland.

5. Farting!

6. It's a familiar sporting term: a Grand Slam.

7. Basketball. Those two fixtures would see an Orlando team play one from Washington DC, and the Minneapolis-based Minnesota Timberwolves clash with the team from Memphis, Tennessee.

8. Leeds Rhinos play at Headingley.

9. James Hunt (Chris Hemsworth) and Niki Lauda (Daniel Bruhl) – the film was directed by Ron Howard and written by Peter Morgan (*The Queen*, *Frost/Nixon* and TV's *The Crown*).

10. They all play in Canada; in Ottawa, Winnipeg, Edmonton and Calgary respectively. There are seven Canadian teams in all, but we thought the Toronto Maple Leafs, Montreal Canadiens and Vancouver Canucks would give too much of a clue.

QUIZ 188. MOVIE MIX

A veritable mix of movie memories, mostly from a little further back, when movies were made using cameras, not computers.

1. *Arthur* was a hit 1981 comedy, with comedian/actor Dudley Moore as a drunken playboy finding his feet with the aid of his butler, Hobson. Which archetypally English old stager played the butler?

2. What part was played by Omar Sharif in a 1969 biopic and by Benicio del Toro in a Steven Soderbergh film about the same character in 2008?

3. Who played Elizabeth I's spymaster Francis Walsingham in *Elizabeth* (1998) and *Elizabeth: The Golden Age* (2007)?

4. The odd 1968 film *Head*, written by director Bob Rafelson and Jack Nicholson, was a vehicle for which Anglo-American pop group?

5. *Jewel of the Nile* (1985) was a sequel to which adventure movie starring the same lead couple (Michael Douglas and Kathleen Turner) from the previous year?

6. British character actor Ralph Brown played which part in the 1988 film *Buster*, starring Phil Collins?

7. *Father of the Bride* (1991) saw actor/comedian Steve Martin stepping into whose shoes from the 1950 original?

8. Which actress hit the high spot of her career in three Mel Brooks' comedies (*Blazing Saddles*, *Young Frankenstein* and *High Anxiety*) in the mid-1970s?

9. *Gregory's Girl* (1981) and *Local Hero* (1983) were low-key triumphs for which Scottish writer-director?

10. In Kenneth Branagh's 1993 version of Shakespeare's *Much Ado About Nothing*, Branagh plays Benedick himself. Who stars opposite him as Beatrice?

Answers to Quiz 187

1. Louis XIV; seventy-two years is the longest reign of any European monarch – not that Louis knew much about the first few years: he was only four when he ascended to the throne and his mother, Anne, acted as Regent until he came of age.

2. Thierry Henry; influential as he was, Eric Cantona was never top scorer.

3. Napoleon Bonaparte.

4. The fourteenth of July – as you would know if you'd been paying attention to the earlier rounds.

5. Toulon, who had famously signed England's influential outside half Jonny Wilkinson. A mark of the man's influence is that fans of two French rugby clubs sang 'God Save the Queen' after his final match.

6. Vichy.

7. Marie Le Pen.

8. Nice.

9. Corsica.

10. Robespierre.

QUIZ 189. MIXED BAG

Another general knowledge round, with a mix of categories and a mix of difficulties.

1. A traditional pirate hat would be an example of a bromby, a deerstalker, a fedora or a tricorn?

2. Who was the running mate and vice-president of President George H.W. Bush who acquired a reputation for not being the brightest page in the book?

3. For what did Andy Coulson serve five months of an eighteen-month prison sentence in 2014?

4. Who is the Greek god of wine and revelry?

5. What is the significance of the following numbers: 13, 21, 34, 55, 89, 144?

6. David Polonsky added the artwork to turn which famous war diary into a graphic novel published in 2018?

7. Someone with a knack for prestidigitation would be very good at what?

8. *The Fall of the House of Usher*, *The Masque of Red Death* and *The Pit and the Pendulum* are among the better-known works of which American writer?

9. Conservative Party leadership elections are overseen by the Chair of which influential committee?

10. Who wrote the novel on which the famous Hitchcock film *The 39 Steps* was based?

Answers to Quiz 188

1. Sir John Gielgud; he stole every scene he was in of Steve Gordon's film.

2. Che Guevara; technically Soderbergh's version of events was two films, as it was released in two parts.

3. Geoffrey Rush; the first of Shekhar Kapur's duology was terrific, the second less so.

4. The Monkees; a very strange experience.

5. *Romancing the Stone*.

6. Brown played Ronnie Biggs.

7. Spencer Tracy; the remake was a surprisingly good stab at recreating the original in a modern context. Shame about *Father of the Bride 2*.

8. Madeline Kahn.

9. Bill Forsyth; the films were a highlight of British indie film making in the 1980s.

10. Emma Thompson.

QUIZ 190. MUSIC BOOKS

Ten musical big hitters; ten life stories. Simply match the star to the book. This proved tricky for our regulars – so maybe six is a respectable score.

1. Patti Smith.

2. Bruce Springsteen.

3. Keith Richards.

4. Sting.

5. Anthony Kiedis.

6. Nikki Sixx.

7. Jay-Z.

8. Woody Guthrie.

9. Kristin Hersh.

10. Johnny Marr.

A. *Scar Tissue.*

B. *Decoded.*

C. *Rat Girl.*

D. *Life.*

E. *Set the Boy Free.*

F. *Bound for Glory.*

G. *Born to Run.*

H. *The Heroin Diaries.*

I. *Broken Music.*

J. *Just Kids.*

Answers to Quiz 189

1. A tricorn – any hat with the brim turned up on three sides making a triangular shape.

2. Dan Quayle; other aspects of his life suggest he wasn't as stupid as the media made him out to be, but it did appear that every time he opened his mouth there was comedy gold waiting to come out.

3. His part in the phone-hacking scandal that brought about the closure of the *News of the World*.

4. Dionysus, known as Bacchus in the Roman stories. His role seems to have been mainly getting pissed with his hangers-on, the Satyrs.

5. They are a Fibonacci sequence, where each number from the third onwards is a sum of the previous two.

6. *The Diary of Ann Frank*.

7. Magic tricks – it is a formal word for a sleight of hand.

8. Edgar Allan Poe.

9. The 1922 Committee, currently chaired by Sir Graham Brady (at March 2019).

10. John Buchan. Robert Donat played the central character Richard Hannay in Hitchcock's 1935 film, and Kenneth More (1959) and Robert Powell (1978) played the part in later versions. Rupert Penry-Jones played Hannay in a 2008 TV movie.

QUIZ 191. MIXED BAG

Once more unto the breach, dear friends – here's yet another mixed bag of a round to test your general knowledge. If you've been found wanting, you've probably thrown the book away, so, for you die-hards, gird your loins and get stuck in.

1. What was traditionally used to bind legal documents?

2. Lisa Gherardini is a familiar, even iconic face: explain.

3. The vizsla, similar to a pointer, is a dog breed of which EU nation?

4. Which Marvel character was introduced into the Marvel Universe in 2019, played by Brie Larson? In which 2018 film does another character send her a message?

5. Which European political leader faced trial for sex with an under-age Moroccan belly dancer in 2011?

6. Who was the face of *The Apprentice* when it launched in the US in 2004?

7. Which commuter was first used in court in 1903 to illustrate the ordinary person going about their everyday business?

8. Before calculators were deemed acceptable to use in GCSEs and other exams, what was the only tool available for solving calculus equations?

9. Which radio series is based in the fictional county of Borsetshire?

10. What term was given to the police method of confining demonstrators in a restricted space or a long time, as used in the 2010 Tuition Fees protests?

Answers to Quiz 190

1. J: Patti Smith's award-winning *Just Kids* was published in 2010.

2. G: Bruce Springsteen's autobiography was *Born to Run* – not the hardest one to guess.

3. D: *Life* was the prosaic title of Keith Richards' 2009 book.

4. I: Sting wrote *Broken Music* (2004) – it was a bit dull.

5. A: Anthony Kiedis of Red Hot Chili Peppers wrote *Scar Tissue* (2005).

6. H: Nikki Sixx's time in Motley Crue is documented in *The Heroin Diaries* (co-written with Ian Gittins, the Sparkle Fairy).

7. B: Jay-Z was *Decoded* in 2011.

8. F: *Bound for Glory* was a song and a book by American folk legend Woody Guthrie.

9. C: *Rat Girl* was the memoir (and a good one) of Kristin Hersh of Throwing Muses.

10. E: Former Smiths' guitarist and songwriter Johnny Marr put pen to paper (or, more likely, fingers to keyboard), for *Set the Boy Free* (2016).

QUIZ 192. SCIENCE

There are many complex aspects to the world of science and neither of us understand any of them. So we just set the questions, hope we haven't got it wrong, and let you all make fools of yourselves while pretending we knew the answers all along.

1. The taxonomic order Chiroptera is essentially comprised of which mammals?

2. If the perigee is the closest point of the moon to the earth during its orbit, what is the name given to the furthest point?

3. What SI unit is used to measure frequency?

4. Which German scientist devised the laws of planetary motion and linked the movement of tides to phases of the moon?

5. Which nineteenth-century scientist gave his name to a form of food preservation still effective today?

6. The work of Georges Cuvier on extinction made him one of the founders of which modern science?

7. What product made from natural fibres, now an integral part of daily life, was developed by Cai Lun in China around the end of the first century?

8. Which species of bird has the longest wingspan, touching twelve feet on rare occasions?

9. Marie Stopes (1880–1958) was a controversial figure whose main work was in fighting for better understanding of what topic?

10. Rust, in almost all its forms, is a hydrated form of which compound?

Answers to Quiz 191

1. Red tape, hence the modern phrase for overweening bureaucracy.

2. She was the model for Leonardo da Vinci's *Mona Lisa*.

3. Hungary.

4. Captain Marvel, and Nick Fury messages her at the end of *The Avengers: Infinity War*.

5. Silvio Berlusconi (of course it was).

6. Donald Trump; imagine voting in Alan Sugar as prime minister. Actually, don't, it's too disturbing.

7. The man on the Clapham omnibus.

8. Logarithm (log) tables.

9. *The Archers* was launched in 1951 and has run for nearly nineteen thousand episodes.

10. Kettling.

QUIZ 193. MIXED BAG

Don't read this drivel, just do the quiz . . .

1. Dolores Haze is the twelve-year-old lead female character in which controversial 1955 novel?

2. What did the Australian MP Larissa Waters become the first woman to do in Parliament in May 2017?

3. Most modern cars are fitted with ABS. For what does ABS stand?

4. Indiana-born Bruce Nauman is famous for (a) campaigning for LGBT rights; (b) playing basketball; (c) installation art; or (d) the longest ever speech in the House of Representatives.

5. Which former UK prime minister gave his name to a type of tea?

6. The 2005 Ridley Scott film *Kingdom of Heaven* concerns which military conflict?

7. Whose song, 'We Belong Together', from *Toy Story 3*, won an Academy Award for Best Original Song?

8. Norwegian Trygve Lie was the first person to hold which office: (a) President of the European Council; (b) Secretary-General of the United Nations; (c) President of UEFA; (d) President of the Nordic Council?

9. Which popular culinary flavouring is derived from the fruits of an orchid?

10. Whose shoes carry a distinctive red sole? Is it Christian Louboutin, Jimmy Choo, Christian Dior or Patrick Cox?

Answers to Quiz 192

1. Bats.

2. The apogee.

3. Hertz.

4. Johannes Keppler.

5. Louis Pasteur, as in pasteurisation.

6. Paleontology.

7. Paper.

8. (Wandering) albatross.

9. Birth control.

10. Iron oxide.

Planets of the solar system

Earth – the 'third rock from the sun'. The simplest calculation of distance from the sun is to judge everything by how far away the earth is, so earth is 1AU. The earth has only one satellite, the moon.

Mercury is closest to the Sun at 0.4AU, relatively small, and has no satellites.

Venus is roughly equidistant between Mercury and Earth at 0.7AU; it is extremely hot and has no moons.

Mars has two small satellites, is the most similar to Earth in its composition, and is 1.5AU from the sun.

Jupiter is the first of the outer planets, sitting much further away from the sun (5.2AU). It is vast; its mass is believed to be more than double that of the other planets combined. Jupiter has seventy-nine known satellites, some almost planet size.

Saturn is 9.5 AU away from the sun, has sixty-two satellites of varying size, and also has its distinctive rings, composed mainly of ice.

Uranus has twenty-seven satellites that have been recorded, and is much colder than the other planets, showing little sign of geological activity. It is 19.2AU away from the sun.

Neptune is the furthest planet, a massive 30.1AU from the sun, and has fourteen satellites that we know about.

There was once believed to be a ninth planet, Pluto, but with new classifications introduced earlier this century (2006), it was downgraded to a dwarf planet (essentially a giant asteroid).

QUIZ 194. GEOGRAPHY

Most cities were built near a water source or on a water source. Match the city to the river that runs through it. This should be one of the easier quizzes in the book.

1. Budapest, Hungary.
2. Glasgow, Scotland.
3. Florence, Italy.
4. Basel, Switzerland.
5. Liverpool, England.
6. Melbourne, Australia.
7. Nashville, US.
8. St Louis, US.
9. Quebec, Canada.
10. Paris, France.

A. Cumberland.
B. Seine.
C. Yarra.
D. Clyde.
E. St Lawrence.
F. Danube.
G. Rhine.
H. Mississippi.
J. Arno.
K. Mersey.

Answers to Quiz 193

1. *Lolita* (by Vladimir Nabokov), the object of Humbert Humbert's obsession.

2. Breastfeed.

3. Anti-lock Braking System – this was first toyed with as far back as the 1920s but became commercially available on a large scale in the 1970s.

4. Nauman is an installation artist.

5. Charles Grey, the 2nd Earl Grey; Grey was prime minister from 1830 to 1834, and his Premiership encompassed the Abolition of Slavery Act of 1833.

6. The Crusades, with Orlando Bloom as Balian of Ibelin. If you watch it, give it the whole evening and watch the epic Director's Cut.

7. Randy Newman; it was his second win, after he won the same award for 'If I Didn't have You', from *Monsters Inc.* in 2002.

8. Lie was the first Secretary-General of the United Nations.

9. Vanilla pods.

10. Louboutin has that distinctive signature.

QUIZ 195. MIXED BAG

Another mixed round, and you should be able to get around eight out of ten on this one; it's not too tricky.

1. How many courses of action are open to someone faced with a Hobson's choice?

2. Who was the first Director of the FBI after helping form it in 1935?

3. Which warm, dry wind of the Rocky Mountains shares its name with a helicopter?

4. In which French region is Chablis made?

5. To whom was Brad Pitt married when he started his affair with Angelina Jolie?

6. Which character is shot in the opening half of the British crime drama *The Blue Lamp* (1949), only to be resurrected for his own series on TV?

7. Rambutan: is it (a) an Islamic Holy Day; (b) a fruit similar to a lychee; (c) a Malaysian stringed instrument; or (d) the oldest (field) hockey club in the world?

8. Which country has won the most gold medals in the Olympic Field Hockey tournament?

9. The name of which Norwegian army officer, executed for collaboration with the Nazis, is synonymous with being a traitor?

10. What term, used to describe the virtual reality created by computers, was coined by science-fiction writer William Gibson in his 1984 novel *Neuromancer*?

Answers to Quiz 194

1. F: Budapest is one of four capital cities served by the River Danube (the others are Vienna, Bratislava and Belgrade).

2. D: The Clyde and its famous dockyards are a crucial part of Glasgow's history.

3. J: The River Arno adds to the beauty of medieval Florence.

4. G: The Rhine empties into the North Sea near Rotterdam in the Netherlands; it also flows through a number of major German cities, including Cologne, and the Swiss city of Basel.

5. K: Liverpool is on the Mersey – you knew this, right?

6. C: The river that flows through Melbourne is the Yarra, formerly known as the Yarra Yarra.

7. A: The River Cumberland serves the city of Nashville, Tennessee.

8. H: The Mississippi includes St Louis along its seemingly endless journey across the US.

9. E: The St Lawrence River flows through Quebec, as well as forming part of the border between Canada and the US.

10. B: Paris is on the Seine – we knew this one as well, yes?

QUIZ 196. ARTS AND LITERATURE

A cheeky round on the more erotic aspects of literature and books. Oh, go on, don't be shy; we'll bet most of you have read at least one of them . . .

1. What is the name of the main female protagonist of *Fifty Shades of Grey*?

2. In which 1973 Martin Amis novel does Charles Highway become sexually obsessed with a young woman?

3. The name of the band Steely Dan comes from (a) a translation of a short story by the Marquis de Sade; (b) a predatory cruiser in the film *Midnight Cowboy*; (c) a metal vibrator in *The Naked Lunch* by William Burroughs; or (d) a freight train on the Pennsylvania to New York railway line?

4. How many strokes of the brush did Melissa P. need, and when did she need them?

5. *Written on the Body* was an explicit 1992 novel by which mainstream female award-winning author?

6. What was Daniel Defoe's 1722 novel about the life of an initially innocent young woman who falls into prostitution and disrepute?

7. Which award, given by the *Literary Review*, has been won by Sebastian Faulks, A.A. Gill, Melvyn Bragg, Iain Hollingshead and Ben Okri, among others?

8. What connects the writings of Henry Miller with a map of the earth?

9. What was the 1748 erotic novel by John Cleland about a young woman who becomes the object of lust for a variety of society types?

10. *Dead Until Dark* (2001) is the first in a successful series of vampire erotica featuring Sookie Stackhouse. They are the source for which successful TV series?

Answers to Quiz 195

1. One. Hobson was a coachman who would tell customers they could hire any horse as long as it was the one near the door.

2. J. Edgar Hoover.

3. Chinook.

4. Burgundy (Bourgogne France-Comté).

5. Jennifer Aniston.

6. PC George Dixon (played by Jack Warner), who became the central character in *Dixon of Dock Green*.

7. Rambutan is a fruit.

8. India; they won seven out of eight between 1928 and 1964, being beaten only by arch-rivals Pakistan in 1960, and they won again in 1980.

9. Vidkun Quisling.

10. Cyberspace.

Directors of the FBI

Hoover held the post from 1935 until 1972, and the seven subsequent Directors, not including stand-ins, have been:

Clarence Kelly (retired).

William Webster (he left to run the CIA; the only man to hold both jobs).

William Sessions (fired by Bill Clinton).

Louis Freeh (resigned).

Robert Mueller (who investigated Russian interference in the 2016 presidential election).

James Comey (sacked by Trump).

Christopher Wray.

QUIZ 197. CATCHPHRASES

TV shows are littered with quotable catchphrases, aped by children in school, colleagues at work, and mates in the pub. An entire generation of 'plonkers' owe that epithet to *Only Fools and Horses*, and 'Doh!' became the self-admonishment of choice for hundreds of thousands of *Simpsons* viewers. See if you can sort these out (expect to score high; it's not that difficult).

1. In which TV comedy show was Arabella Weir obsessively asking 'Does my Bum Look Big in This?'

2. 'Ooh, you are awful . . . but I like you.' Which dragged-up comedian used this catchphrase?

3. Who was the only Gay in the village, and who played him?

4. Who ended his TV comedy show with the phrase 'May your God go with you'?

5. Who would frequently call who a 'stupid boy' in *Dad's Army*?

6. 'Nice to see you, to see you . . . nice.' Whose line in which TV show?

7. 'I don't believe it.' Who uttered this incredulous statement in which comedy series and who played him?

8. Who frequently asked us whether we thought she was bovvered and expressed dismay that we were taking liberties?

9. Who frequently declared that he had a cunning plan, but invariably didn't?

10. Who would often ask that his shorts be eaten?

Answers to Quiz 196

1. Anastasia Steele.

2. *The Rachel Papers*.

3. The name Steely Dan comes from a vibrator in the *Naked Lunch*, Burroughs' 1959 hallucinogenic masterpiece.

4. One hundred, before bedtime.

5. Jeanette Winterson; her narrator is neither named nor identified by gender, and the book chronicles the affair between this character and a married woman.

6. *(The Life and Times of) Moll Flanders*.

7. *Literary Review*'s Bad Sex in Fiction Award (Bad Sex Award is enough); the 2015 winner was Morrissey for a scene in his debut novel – he was VERY CROSS.

8. His main works were called *Tropic of Cancer* and *Tropic of Capricorn*, two of the defining lines of latitude on maps of the earth.

9. *Fanny Hill*; one of the most banned books in literary history.

10. *True Blood*.

QUIZ 198. PREMIER LEAGUE

I'm torn on this subject. It is probably the highest-quality sporting entertainment this country has known, but it is also a venal, self-serving, nauseous homage to the power of money, with enough media backing to distort all it touches.

1. Who were the first winners of the Premier League and in which season did it start as a competition?

2. Which two sides have won the competition on one solitary occasion (to 2017–18, so Liverpool will make it three if they win in 2019)?

3. Who is the only player to captain a Premier League-winning club but never win a full international cap?

4. Which four Italian managers have won the Premier League title?

5. Who was the club's top scorer when Arsenal won their first Premier League title in 1998?

6. Who is the only player from outside the UK to feature in 500 Premier League matches?

7. Which Dutchman was the first non-English top scorer in the Premier League? And who was the first non-European to head the list?

8. Alex Ferguson won thirteen Premier League titles. Which other two managers have three each (to 2018)?

9. In 1999–2000 the Premier League's top scorer came from the club that finished seventh, Sunderland. Who was he?

10. Surprisingly, only one Italian player has won a Premier League winner's medal, in 2012. Who was it? And which two players from Iceland and Uruguay are their country's only representatives on the list?

Answers to Quiz 197

1. *The Fast Show*. Weir and Caroline Aherne were the main female presence in a sketch-show line-up that included Paul Whitehouse, John Thomson, Charlie Higson, Simon Day and Mark Williams.

2. Dick Emery – his show ran from 1963 to 1981. Much of it would be unacceptable now, but it was hugely influential.

3. Daffyd Thomas, played in *Little Britain* by Matt Lucas.

4. Dave Allen, the Irish comedian. His show consisted of a few sketches linked by Allen telling funny stories in a raconteur style while sitting in an armchair drinking. It was hilarious.

5. Captain Mainwaring (Arthur Lowe) would say this to Private Pike (Ian Lavender).

6. Bruce Forsyth in *The Generation Game*.

7. Victor Meldrew in *One Foot in the Grave*; Richard Wilson.

8. Catherine Tate in the guise of lazy teen Lauren Cooper.

9. Baldrick in *Blackadder*.

10. Bart Simpson.

QUIZ 199. FOOD AND DRINK

Another mixed section on things to eat and drink. It's making us hungry going through this. Time for breakfast . . .

1. What name would be given to a creamy soup made from seafood, more usually lobster or crab?

2. What is the term for the preferred Italian method of serving pasta slightly firm to the bite?

3. What is the principal ingredient of the Mexican dip, guacamole?

4. If you order polpette in an Italian restaurant, what will you be served?

5. What name is given to a Russian buckwheat pancake, often served topped with caviar?

6. Anise, cardamom, cinnamon, fennel: which of these is NOT an ingredient in Chinese Five Spice powder?

7. The cocktail Black Russian comprises vodka, cola and which liqueur?

8. What is the base flavour of Chartreuse, Cointreau and Grand Marnier?

9. What is the signature red wine grape of France's Burgundy region?

10. What was invented/discovered by a Benedictine monk called Dom Perignon in the late seventeenth century?

Answers to Quiz 198

1. Manchester United, 1992–3.

2. Blackburn Rovers and Leicester City.

3. Steve Bruce.

4. Carlo Ancelotti (Chelsea 2010); Roberto Mancini (Man City, 2012); Claudio Ranieri (Leicester, 2016); Antonio Conte (Chelsea, 2017).

5. Dennis Bergkamp.

6. Mark Schwarzer, the Australian goalkeeper, who made most of those appearances with Middlesbrough and Fulham.

7. Jimmy Floyd Hasselbaink (with Leeds United, 1998–9, and again with Chelsea in 2000–1); Didier Drogba (Chelsea, 2006–7 and 2009–10).

8. Arsène Wenger and José Mourinho.

9. Kevin Phillips.

10. Mario Balotelli; Eiður Guðjohnsen and Diego Forlán.

Top 10 Premier League appearances (as of 22 March 2019)

Gareth Barry 653 (Aston Villa; Manchester City; Everton; West Bromwich Albion).

Ryan Giggs 632 (Manchester United).

Frank Lampard 609 (West Ham United, Chelsea, Man City).

David James 572 (Liverpool, Aston Villa, West Ham, Manchester City, Portsmouth).

Gary Speed 535 (Leeds United, Everton, Newcastle United, Bolton Wanderers).

Emile Heskey 516 (Leicester City, Liverpool, Birmingham City, Wigan Athletic, Aston Villa).

Mark Schwarzer 514 (Middlesbrough, Fulham, Chelsea, Leicester City).

James Milner* 510 (Leeds, Newcastle United, Aston Villa, Manchester City, Liverpool).

Jamie Carragher 508 (Liverpool).

Phil Neville 505 (Manchester United, Everton).

Top 10 Premier League scorers

Alan Shearer 260 (Blackburn Rovers, Newcastle United).

Wayne Rooney 208 (Everton, Manchester United).

Andrew Cole 187 (Blackburn, Fulham, Manchester City, Portsmouth).

Frank Lampard 177 (the only player on both lists).

Thierry Henry 175 (Arsenal).

Robbie Fowler 163 (Liverpool, Leeds, Manchester City, Blackburn).

Jermaine Defoe 162 (West Ham, Portsmouth, Tottenham Hotspur, Sunderland, Bournemouth).

Sergio Aguero* 161 (Manchester City).

Michael Owen 150 (Liverpool, Newcastle United, Manchester United, Stoke City).

Les Ferdinand 149 (QPR, Newcastle United, Spurs, West Ham, Leicester City, Bolton Wanderers).

*Still playing. My guess would be that Milner will reach fifth place behind James, and Aguero will overtake everyone except Shearer and maybe Rooney. Harry Kane is currently on 125, and could possibly catch Shearer, unless he goes abroad.

QUIZ 200. HISTORY

War, specifically battles. It's a depressing truth that we study the history of our species by reviewing and analysing conflict, war, conquest and enslavement, rather than focusing on peace and harmony.

1. In which country is the site of the Battle of Waterloo?

2. Pearl Harbor is in which US state?

3. Napoleon's greatest victory was in defeating a combined Russian and Austrian army at Austerlitz, then part of the Holy Roman Empire but now lying in which EU member state?

4. The disastrous Gallipoli campaign of the First World War took place in which modern country?

5. General Hannibal of Carthage gave the Romans a runaround before he was defeated by Scipio at the Battle of Zama. Both Zama and Carthage are in which modern African country?

6. The Confederates finally packed in the American Civil War at the Battle of Appomattox Court House. In which state is this?

7. Marston Moor, a decisive battle of the English Civil War, is in which county?

8. The Battle of Balaclava, famous for the Charge of the Light Brigade, was part of a struggle for which port city during the Crimean War?

9. Who was the losing US general at the Battle of Little Bighorn in 1876?

10. The Battle of Lepanto of 1571 was the last major naval engagement fought mainly by rowing vessels as opposed to sailing vessels, and resulted in a victory for the Venetian alliance against which opposition?

Answers to Quiz 199

1. Bisque.

2. *Al dente*.

3. Avocado.

4. Meatballs. We do them with pork and beef, and occasionally lamb with pistachio.

5. Blini – they are also delicious with smoked salmon.

6. Cardamom (mainly Indian) – the other two are pepper and cloves.

7. Kahlua – most self-respecting Russians would pass on the cola and just have the vodka and kahlua.

8. Orange.

9. Pinot noir.

10. Champagne.

Top guacamole recipe

Finely chop (or blitz in a food processor, but not a blender) one large red chilli, two shallots, a clove or two of garlic, salt, pepper and a pinch of paprika.

Take two avocados, ripe but not mushy, and mash them with a fork, not in a processor or a blender. Mix in the other ingredients without pulping the avocado, add the juice of half a lemon – if you are not serving immediately leave the avocado stones in; it helps keep the mix fresh.

Serve with crudités or tortilla chips, or on toasted bruschetta.

QUIZ 201. MIXED BAG

Another melange of non-related trivia. Be ready for anything, and be happy with a score of eight out of ten.

1. Sarah-Jane Hutt was the most recent (1983) of four British winners of which title?

2. What term is used for an attempt to freeze out a vote by using delaying tactics during a Senate debate?

3. In 2011, Colombian singer Shakira married which Barcelona and Spain footballer, ten years her junior?

4. Which German/Frankish saint is celebrated on the night of 30 April and the daytime of 1 May?

5. Which Dublin-born poet and playwright, also an MP for Stafford for a number of years, wrote the satirical plays *The Rivals* and *A School for Scandal*?

6. What was unique about the nomination of Nick Drnaso's *Sabrina* for the Man Booker Prize longlist?

7. In what commodity would a sommelier possess expertise?

8. Which business, now the second largest of its kind in the world and owned by Whitbread, was founded by brothers Bruno and Sergio in Lambeth in 1971?

9. In which Shakespeare play are Benedick and Beatrice tricked into admitting they love one another, in spite of their constant bickering?

10. The Battle of Bosworth field was a decisive battle in the War of the Roses. In which modern English county did it take place?

Answers to Quiz 200

1. Waterloo is smack bang in the centre of Belgium.

2. Hawaii; Pearl Harbor was the US Pacific naval base, and was the easiest and most vulnerable target when the Japanese decided to attack the Americans. The attack led to the immediate entry of the US into the war and was therefore a key turning point in the conflict.

3. Czech Republic.

4. Turkey. The Ottoman forces successfully beat off a huge allied army, consisting mainly of Australian and New Zealand troops.

5. Tunisia. Carthage was one of the few city states to successfully challenge and resist the Roman Empire for a while – the city was initially part of the widespread Phoenician Empire.

6. Virginia. The court house where General Lee surrendered to Ulysses S. Grant is now at the centre of a small national park.

7. North Yorkshire. Marston Moor saw a major turnaround in the war when the newly revamped Parliamentarian army under Sir Thomas Fairfax routed the king's army.

8. Sebastopol, the major Black Sea port.

9. General Custer, who was a bit of a wally, not an Errol Flynn-style dashing hero.

10. The Ottoman Empire. Sailing ships were already replacing galleys in most navies.

QUIZ 202. WHO?

Another identification round; this time, all the characters are from the movies. Please identify the movie in which the character appears and who plays or voices the character.

1. Marty McFly.

2. Durand Durand.

3. Axel Foley.

4. Roy Batty.

5. Audrey II.

6. Roxie Hart.

7. Snake Plissken.

8. Fanny Brice.

9. Bill the Butcher.

10. Adrian Cronauer.

Answers to Quiz 201

1. Miss World. Eric Morley launched the annual beauty pageant in 1951 and it still takes place, albeit with attempts to make it less leery.

2. A filibuster.

3. Gerard Piqué.

4. Saint Walpurga.

5. Richard Brinsley Sheridan (1751–1816).

6. It was the first graphic novel to be so nominated.

7. Wine – the sommelier is the wine waiter in a posh restaurant.

8. Costa Coffee.

9. *Much Ado about Nothing*.

10. Leicestershire.

Booker Prize (later Man Booker Prize) winners

In 2014, the entry qualification changed to any novel in the English language, whereas previously only Commonwealth authors were eligible. The years 2016 and 2017 saw American authors scoop the prize.

2018 *Milkman* by Anna Burns.
2017 *Lincoln in the Bardo* by George Saunders.
2016 *The Sellout* by Paul Beatty.
2015 *A Brief History of Seven Killings* by Marlon James.
2014 *The Narrow Road to the Deep North* by Richard Flanagan.
2013 *The Luminaries* by Eleanor Catton.
2012 *Bring Up the Bodies* by Hilary Mantel (2).
2011 *The Sense of an Ending* by Julian Barnes.
2010 *The Finkler Question* by Howard Jacobson.
2009 *Wolf Hall* by Hilary Mantel.
2008 *The White Tiger* by Aravind Adiga.
2007 *The Gathering* by Anne Enright.
2006 *The Inheritance of Loss* by Kiran Desai.
2005 *The Sea* by John Banville.
2004 *The Line of Beauty* by Alan Hollinghurst.
2003 *Vernon God Little* by DBC Pierre.

2002 *Life of Pi* by Yann Martel.

2001 *True History of the Kelly Gang* by Peter Carey (2).

2000 *The Blind Assassin* by Margaret Atwood.

1999 *Disgrace* by J. M. Coetzee (2).

1998 *Amsterdam* by Ian McEwan.

1997 *The God of Small Things* by Arundhati Roy.

1996 *Last Orders* by Graham Swift.

1995 *The Ghost Road* by Pat Barker.

1994 *How Late It Was, How Late* by James Kelman.

1993 *Paddy Clarke Ha Ha Ha* by Roddy Doyle.

1992 *Sacred Hunger* by Barry Unsworth; and *The English Patient* by Michael Ondaatje.

1991 *The Famished Road* by Ben Okri.

1990 *Possession* by A. S. Byatt.

1989 *The Remains of the Day* by Kazuo Ishiguro.

1988 *Oscar and Lucinda* by Peter Carey.

1987 *Moon Tiger* by Penelope Lively.

1986 *The Old Devils* by Kingsley Amis.

1985 *The Bone People* by Keri Hulme.

1984 *Hotel du Lac* by Anita Brookner.

1983 *Life and Times of Michael K* by J.M. Coetzee.

1982 *Schindler's Ark* by Thomas Keneally.

1981 *Midnight's Children* by Salman Rushdie.

1980 *Rites of Passage* by William Golding.

1979 *Offshore* by Penelope Fitzgerald.

1978 *The Sea, The Sea* by Iris Murdoch.

1977 *Staying On* by Paul Scott.

1976 *Saville* by David Storey.

1975 *Heat and Dust* by Ruth Prawer Jhabvala.

1974 *The Conservationist* by Nadine Gordimer; and *Holiday* by Stanley Middleton.

1973 *The Siege of Krishnapur* by J.G. Farrell.

1972 *G.* by John Berger.

1971 *In a Free State* by V.S. Naipaul.

1970 *Troubles* by J.G. Farrell.

1970 *The Elected Member* by Bernice Rubens.

1969 *Something to Answer For* by P.H. Newby

QUIZ 203. THIS OR THAT

Another round of choices, choices, choices. On this occasion, you have to decide whether these good folks are country singers, members of the US Senate (past or present) or porn stars.

1. Traci Lords.
2. Rose Long.
3. Loretta Lynn.
4. Brandi Carlile.
5. Brandi Love.
6. Olympia Snowe.
7. Rocco Siffredi.
8. Orrin Hatch.
9. Heidi Heitkamp.
10. Shooter Jennings.
11. Marilyn Chambers.
12. Jewel.

Answers to Quiz 202

1. Michael J. Fox's character in the *Back to the Future* films.

2. A character in Roger Vadim's *Barbarella* (1969), played by Milo O'Shea – the character gave his name to the 1980s pop group, with the end 'd' dropped.

3. Eddie Murphy's character in the *Beverly Hills Cop* series.

4. Rutger Hauer's character in *Blade Runner* (Ridley Scott, 1982).

5. The killer plant in the 1986 musical comedy *Little Shop of Horrors*, voiced by Levi Stubbs.

6. Renée Zellweger's part in *Chicago* (Rob Marshall, 2002).

7. Kurt Russell's character in *Escape from New York* (1981) and *Escape from L.A.* (1986), both directed by John Carpenter.

8. Barbra Streisand's character in *Funny Girl* (1968).

9. Daniel Day-Lewis's character in Scorsese's *Gangs of New York* (2002).

10. Robin Williams' DJ character in *Good Morning, Vietnam* (1987).

QUIZ 204. SCIENCE

The appliance of. Natural history, bit of physics, some astronomy – it's all Greek to me. Actually, scratch that, I'd be much better off with Greek . . . We would have scored five on this round. Miserable.

1. What is the brightest star seen by the naked eye from earth, found in the constellation Canis Major?

2. What comes between Family and Species in the taxonomical categories?

3. What is measured in becquerels?

4. Why did G.W. Carver promote the growing of peanuts and sweet potatoes as well as cotton at the turn of the last century?

5. Whose work included the concept of electronegativity, the alpha-helix structure of proteins, and progress in the battle against sickle-cell anaemia?

6. What common mathematical constant is often referred to as Archimedes' Constant, after its Greek originator?

7. What was the main purpose of Thomas Savery and Thomas Newcomen's early steam engines?

8. Kestrels belong to which genus of birds of prey?

9. What is the famous observatory in Cheshire, now administered by the University of Manchester?

10. What is the largest species of extant penguin? And what is unique to the group about the Galapagos penguin?

Answers to Quiz 203

1. Traci Lords was a famous porn star turned mainstream actress who took her name from Jack Lord, the policeman in *Hawaii 5-O*.

2. Rose Long succeeded her husband Huey as the Senator for Louisiana in 1836 – she was the third woman to sit in the Senate.

3. Loretta Lynn is a country legend, still performing at eighty-six.

4. Brandi Carlile is a pop/country crossover singer – her 2007 album *The Story* is a classic of modern Americana.

5. Brandi Love is a porn star, a latecomer to the industry; she made her name as a 'Cougar'.

6. Olympia Snowe was the Republican Senator for Maine from 1995 to 2013.

7. Rocco Siffredi took his name from an Alain Delon character in a gangster film. He is an Italian porn actor and director.

8. Orrin Hatch was elected as a Republican Senator for Utah in 1977 and retained that position until his retirement in 2019, making him the longest-serving Senator in history.

9. Heidi Heitkamp was a Democratic Senator from 2013 to 2019 in the state of North Dakota.

10. Shooter Jennings is a country singer and producer, and the son of superstar Waylon Jennings and singer Jessi Colter.

11. Marilyn Chambers was the star of the 1972 film, *Behind the Green Door*, one of the porn industry's best-known early films. She died in 2009, aged fifty-six.

12. Jewel is a country singer who has also acted – she made her debut in *Ride with the Devil*, a 1999 American Civil War film with Tobey Maguire.

QUIZ 205. GENERAL KNOWLEDGE

A collection of assorted questions on assorted topics.

1. By what name is the International Criminal Police Organisation better known?

2. Chipping Campden and Chipping Norton are beautiful Cotswold towns: what is the meaning of the term 'Chipping' in this context?

3. Apart from a cheesy song by The Village People, what is the YMCA?

4. What was Michael Moore's 2002 documentary about guns in the United States, motivated by and beginning with an infamous school shooting?

5. Joey Bishop, Bing Crosby, Dean Martin, Frank Sinatra: which of these entertainers was NOT a member of the Rat Pack?

6. *The Thin Man* (1934) was the first in a series of six films based on the private detective created by which American crime author?

7. Why is the notion of Alfred Nobel giving his name to a peace prize somewhat ironic?

8. To which piece of music did Torvill and Dean skate when they won their Olympic gold medal?

9. Who was the manager of The Beatles who died of a drug overdose in 1967?

10. Which British fashion designer committed suicide in 2010, the day before his mother's funeral?

Answers to Quiz 204

1. Sirius A, the Dog Star.

2. Genus.

3. Radioactivity.

4. Carver worked out that soil deteriorated with annual usage, and that rotating cotton with nitrogen-yielding crops was a huge benefit. This principle is still applied in agriculture today.

5. Linus Pauling.

6. Pi – as a general rule, if you can only think of one possible answer to a question, there's a good chance it's the correct one.

7. Pumping water from mines.

8. Falcons; kestrels are the smallest falcons, a genus that also includes hobbies and peregrine falcons – peregrines are the fastest creatures on earth when they dive, regularly reaching speeds of 200 mph.

9. Jodrell Bank.

10. The Emperor Penguin is the largest, while the Galapagos is the only one living in the northern hemisphere.

QUIZ 206. MUSIC MIX

An assortment of music questions across all genres.

1. Hank Williams was a pioneer of what style of music? Who played Williams in *I Saw the Light*, a 2016 film about his life?

2. What is the name of the biggest music festival in the US, held every year in Milwaukee, Wisconsin?

3. *(But Tuesday is Just as Bad)* is the subtitle of which famous and much covered T-Bone Walker song?

4. Sam Phillips was the first man to record Carl Perkins, Elvis Presley, Roy Orbison and Johnny Cash, among others. What was the name of his independent record label based in Memphis, Tennessee?

5. Which songwriter gave up a modest recording career and has enjoyed eight No. 1 singles and five Ivor Novello awards, penning singles like 'Can't Get You Out of My Head', 'I Kissed a Girl', 'About You Now' and 'Toxic'? Which female pop artists reached No. 1 in the UK with the songs listed?

6. Glam rocker Alice Cooper; singer and producer Peter Gabriel; soul singer Lionel Richie; keyboard player and songwriter Stevie Wonder: who is the senior high and who is the office junior?

7. If 'Innuendo' was one of the band's two non-collaborative UK No. 1 singles, what was the other?

8. Which acronym took Usher to the top of the US and UK charts in 2010? And which Black Eyed Pea gave him a helping hand?

9. Which innovative musician and producer's credits include *Fear of Music* (Talking Heads), *The Unforgettable Fire* (U2) and *Laid* (James)? With which band did he come to prominence as a synthesiser wizard?

10. When Steve Marriott left the Small Faces, the band recruited a new guitarist and new singer. Who were they? Who was the band's drummer, who would later replace Keith Moon in The Who?

Answers to Quiz 205

1. Interpol.

2. Marketplace (market is fine).

3. The Young Men's Christian Association; the song was a huge hit, reaching No. 2 in the US and topping the charts in the UK in early 1979. The six characters in this American band, aimed at the gay disco market, were a motorcycle cop, a Native American, a GI, a construction worker, a cowboy and a leather-clad rocker. 'YMCA' and the follow-up, 'In the Navy', are still played at parties and sung at sporting events.

4. *Bowling for Columbine*.

5. Crosby was a contemporary, but not one of the Rat Pack.

6. Dashiell Hammett.

7. Nobel invented dynamite – he later came to regret his innovation when he saw the nefarious uses to which humanity put his science.

8. Ravel's *Bolero*.

9. Brian Epstein.

10. Alexander McQueen.

QUIZ 207. IN WHICH YEAR . . .

This is tricky. You have to name the exact year in which these events took place. The figure in parentheses is the leeway you are given to get half a point.

1. The first CD released (one year).

2. Instagram launched (one year).

3. Princess Diana born (one year).

4. Paula Yates died from a heroin overdose (two years).

5. *Dr Who* relaunched on the BBC, with Christopher Eccleston in the role (one year).

6. Prince William married Catherine Middleton (one year).

7. James Dyson established his company (two years).

8. Amazon sold its first book online (two years).

9. Netflix commenced streaming entertainment (one year).

10. Kanye West married Kim Kardashian (one year).

Answers to Quiz 206

1. He was a massively influential country singer, and he was played by Tom Hiddleston in the film.

2. Summerfest.

3. 'Call It Stormy Monday' (accept 'Stormy Monday').

4. Sun Records.

5. Cathy Dennis; Kylie Minogue, Katy Perry, Sugababes and Britney Spears.

6. Cooper is the eldest, born in 1948. Richie was born in 1949, while the other two were born in 1950, Gabriel a few months prior to the youngest of the four, Stevie Wonder. Stevie seems to have been around longer than the others because he started as a harmonica-playing child prodigy.

7. 'Bohemian Rhapsody'; the band is Queen – they also reached No. 1 with David Bowie, singing 'Under Pressure'.

8. OMG; will.i.am.

9. Brian Eno, Roxy Music.

10. Ronnie Wood and Rod Stewart – neither was especially small, so the band changed their name to simply The Faces. Kenney Jones.

QUIZ 208. NEW ZEALAND

Accusing a New Zealander of being an Aussie is like calling a Canadian American. The only thing the Kiwis enjoy more than putting one over on the old country is putting one over on their larger, noisier neighbour. Here's a series of questions on this beautiful country.

1. Auckland is by far New Zealand's most populous city, but what is the official capital?

2. Name the two official spoken languages of New Zealand?

3. The New Zealand men's Rugby Union team are known as the All Blacks. What name is given to the women's team?

4. Wairau River, Maipo Valley, Martinborough, Hawke's Bay: which of these is NOT a highly rated New Zealand wine region?

5. Like the UK, New Zealand has a centre-left Labour Party. What is the name of the main party to the right of centre?

6. Which New Zealand soprano sang Handel's 'Let the Bright Seraphim' at the wedding of Prince Charles and Lady Diana Spencer?

7. How many times have the New Zealand football team qualified for the World Cup Finals?

8. Valerie Vili won a gold medal at the Beijing Olympics and successfully defended her title in London under her married name of Valerie Adams. In which athletic discipline?

9. Who is the most-capped New Zealand Rugby Union player, who also holds the world record for the number of Tests played as captain of his team?

10. Who gives his name to the narrow strait between New Zealand's North and South Island?

Answers to Quiz 207

1. 1982; it was developed jointly by Philips and Sony, while Denon developed the CD-ROM in the same year.

2. 2010. It was originally an app for Macintosh users, with an android version coming eighteen months later. Facebook purchased the interface for about one million dollars in 2012.

3. 1961, about six weeks before Nick.

4. 2000 – the coroner ruled the death not to have been suicide. Paula used to have a house in Hastings round the back of our pub.

5. 2005; Eccleston thereby became the Ninth Doctor – no one anticipated the scale of the show's revival.

6. 2011.

7. 1987.

8. 1994. Jeff Bezos's company is now the biggest online retailer in the world. We just wish they would share a bit of that wealth with the tax collectors.

9. Reed Hastings and Marc Randolph started the company in 1997, but they commenced streaming services in 2007.

10. 2014. They now have children: Nori, Chicago and Saint.

QUIZ 209. MIXED BAG

A completely random selection of bits and pieces. You should be able to manage seven or eight out of ten on this one.

1. What was the name of the ship on which William Bradford and his followers set sail to form the first American colony in 1620?

2. What do John McCain and Mitt Romney have in common?

3. Which Bond film was named after Ian Fleming's Caribbean home?

4. Which Gaelic word has transferred into English as one of many names for the May Day festival?

5. Which novel concerns the relationship between a deformed former conjuror called Erik and a young opera singer called Christine?

6. Which song did Donald Trump allegedly eulogise when he called the President of Egypt after his election victory?

7. If you were in a position of authority and displaying nepotism, what would you be doing?

8. Which city boasted a football team called the Chargers and a baseball team named the Padres from 1969 until 2017, when the Chargers relocated to LA?

9. Teams compete for the annual race, run since 1715, named Doggett's Coat and Badge. In which sport?

10. Where did the Parsees mainly resettle when they were forced out of Persia in the eighth century?

Answers to Quiz 208

1. Wellington. Auckland is the only New Zealand city with over a million inhabitants – there are just seven with over a hundred thousand. Wellington and Christchurch have around four hundred thousand each. Both Wellington and Auckland are on the more populous North Island, Auckland to the north-west and Wellington on the south-east tip.

2. English and Maori.

3. Black Ferns.

4. Maipo Valley is in Chile. The Wairau River runs through the South Island, creating the fertile Marlborough region; Martinborough is a wine area near Wellington, and Hawke's Bay is a large wine-growing region up the east coast of the North Island.

5. The National Party; the current prime minister, Jacinda Ardern, represents the Labour Party – she won the 2017 election after nine years of National Party governance.

6. Kiri Te Kanawa.

7. Twice. In 1974 they suffered heavy defeats to Scotland, the Soviet Union and Brazil (tough group!), but in 2010 they did much better, drawing all three games with Slovakia, Italy and Paraguay. It wasn't quite enough for them to make the knockout rounds, which would have been a major achievement – maybe a little more ambition against a poor Paraguay team would have served them better.

8. Shot putt; Adams came back to the Olympics in Rio in 2016 and won a silver medal – she is also a four-time World Champion.

9. Richie McCaw; 148 caps, 110 of them as captain, and two World Cup victories.

10. The explorer James Cook.

QUIZ 210. ARTISTS

Another set of artists to match to one of their works – this lot are trickier.

1. Hans Holbein the Younger.

2. Henri de Toulouse-Lautrec.

3. Rembrandt van Rijn.

4. Marcel Duchamp.

5. Wassily Kandinsky.

6. J.M.W. Turner.

7. Gustav Klimt.

8. John Everett Millais.

9. Paul Cézanne.

10. Edvard Munch.

A. *At the Moulin Rouge.*

B. *The Kiss.*

C. *The Blue Rider.*

D. *The Order of Release.*

E. *The Fighting Temeraire.*

F. *The Ambassadors.*

G. *Vampire.*

H. *Belshazzar's Feast.*

I. *The Bathers.*

J. *Bicycle Wheel.*

Answers to Quiz 209

1. The *Mayflower*.

2. They were the two Republican candidates defeated by Barack Obama, McCain in 2008, Romney in 2012.

3. *Goldeneye*; Fleming was in Naval Intelligence during the war and Operation Goldeneye was a plan to scupper Spanish support for Germany in the event of Franco abandoning Spain's charade of neutrality (they gave covert support to Germany but never formed an actual alliance). Fleming later used the name for his Jamaican home, and it was adopted for the 1995 film starring Pierce Brosnan as James Bond.

4. Beltane.

5. *The Phantom of the Opera*.

6. 'Walk like an Egyptian' by The Bangles. (Not sure I believe that particular bit of Trump-bashing, but the man himself never lets the truth get in the way of a good story, so why should I?)

7. Favouring family and friends.

8. San Diego.

9. Rowing.

10. India.

QUIZ 211. NUMBERS

You love these, right? How could you not love the chance to pick up fifty-five points in one round? Except you probably won't. Thirty-five to forty is a good score.

1. What was the only novel written by poet and playwright Oscar Wilde?

2. Which two films won Jack Nicholson a Best Actor Academy Award?

3. What were the first three albums released by indie rock band The xx?

4. Which four English counties share a land border with Wales?

5. Name the five US states with a seaboard on the Gulf of Mexico.

6. Which six songs took Blondie to the top of the UK singles chart?

7. Which seven countries have lost more than one World Cup Final?

8. Name the 'A8' countries that joined the European Union in 2004 along with Cyprus and Malta.

9. Name Abba's nine No. 1 UK singles.

10. Jan Kodeš (Czechoslovakia, 1973) was the first European player to win the Wimbledon Men's Singles title in the post-1968 Open era. Who are the other ten Europeans to have followed suit?

Answers to Quiz 210

1. F: Holbein was a major portrait painter of the early sixteenth century – he worked extensively in England under the patronage of, first, Thomas More and, later, Thomas Cromwell.

2. A: Toulouse-Lautrec painted numerous depictions of Parisian nightlife in the late nineteenth century – he died in 1901, aged only thirty-six.

3. H: Rembrandt painted *Belshazzar's Feast* in the 1630s and it was acquired by the National Gallery in London in 1964.

4. J: Duchamp was an influential twentieth-century painter and sculptor, a prime mover in the notion of conceptual art.

5. C: *Der Blaue Reiter* was a 1903 work by Wassily Kandinsky that gave its name to a German art movement in the early twentieth century.

6. E: Turner's painting (full title, *The Fighting Temeraire, Tugged to Her Last Berth to be Broken Up*), was voted the nation's favourite in a 2005 poll.

7. F: Klimt's *The Kiss* is his most enduring work.

8. D: Millais was a major member of the Pre-Raphaelite movement, although this particular painting represented a shift away from the conventional subject matter of the movement.

9. I: *The Bathers* is one of Cézanne's best-known works – it is the biggest of a series of paintings depicting bathers, and it hangs in Philadelphia.

10. G: Norwegian Edvard Munch is better known for his disturbing portrait *The Scream*. *Vampire* (also known as *Love and Pain*) was painted two years later, in 1895.

QUIZ 212. THE UNITED STATES

Ten questions on the history of the good old US of A. If you're not American, I would expect you to get five or six; if you are American, probably three or four. Only kidding – students of American history should get all of these.

1. What act by the United States sparked the war with Mexico from 1846 to 1848?

2. What post did Jefferson Davis hold from 1861 to 1865?

3. How many amendments to the US constitution have been accepted by both Houses?

4. What began on Thursday, 24 October 1929?

5. Prohibition in the US was introduced in 1920. What was the name of the legislation that backed up the initial constitutional amendment and in which year was it repealed?

6. Where did Rosa Parks refuse to give up her seat to a white person on 1 December 1955?

7. What was James Earl Ray's contribution to American history on 4 April 1968?

8. What was the name given to the major civic proposal, incorporating a number of social and economic reforms, put forward by Roosevelt's government in 1933?

9. A new internal security organisation, the FBI, was launched in 1935. Who was the first head of the organisation?

10. How did the 22nd Amendment of 1951 directly affect the presidency?

Answers to Quiz 211

1. *The Picture of Dorian Gray.*

2. *One Flew Over the Cuckoo's Nest* and *As Good As It Gets*.

3. *xx*; *Coexist*; *I See You*.

4. Herefordshire; Shropshire; Gloucestershire; Cheshire.

5. Texas, Louisiana, Mississippi, Alabama, Florida.

6. 'Heart of Glass'; 'Sunday Girl'; 'Call Me'; 'Atomic'; 'The Tide is High'; 'Maria'.

7. Argentina; Brazil; Czechoslovakia; Germany (including West Germany); Hungary; Italy; the Netherlands.

8. Czech Republic; Hungary; Estonia; Latvia; Lithuania; Poland; Slovakia; Slovenia.

9. 'Waterloo'; 'Mamma Mia'; 'Fernando'; 'Dancing Queen'; 'Knowing Me, Knowing You'; 'The Name of the Game'; 'Take a Chance On Me'; 'The Winner Takes It All'; 'Super Trouper'.

10. Björn Borg; Boris Becker; Stefan Edberg; Michael Stich; Richard Krajicek; Goran Ivanišević; Roger Federer; Rafael Nadal; Novak Djokovic; Andy Murray.

QUIZ 213. GENERAL KNOWLEDGE

We've run out of intros for the general rounds, so you may as well just crack on . . .

1. If spumante is fully sparkling Italian wine, what term is given to semi-sparkling wine, where the bubbles cease soon after pouring?

2. In the US Constitution, who presides over the Senate and has a nominal casting vote?

3. By what name is widowed, Somali-born fashion model and philanthropist Zara Mohamed Abdulmajid better known?

4. Which philosopher and occultist served as an adviser to Queen Elizabeth I and was also the subject of an opera project by Damon Albarn?

5. Who was the first woman to win an Academy Award for Best Director and for which film?

6. How did the BBC respond when Director of School Broadcasting, Mary Somerville, became pregnant in 1928?

7. Which word, often used in a socio-political context, means fear of strangers?

8. Which publication, founded in 1821, dropped Manchester from its name in 1959?

9. Which City of London institution is based at 10 Paternoster Square?

10. What aspect of the weather is measured with an anemometer?

Answers to Quiz 212

1. Annexation of the Republic of Texas; President James K. Polk sent troops to support the annexation, and the impoverished Mexicans were quickly defeated, ceding a large chunk of what is now southern California and most of New Mexico, as well as accepting the loss of Texas.

2. President of the Confederate States.

3. Twenty-seven; the most recent 27th Amendment was ratified in 2002 and means that any salary changes for elected members of the Federal government do not come into place until their next term, meaning they need to get re-elected to get the money they voted themselves – clever.

4. The Wall Street Crash; this came five days before Black Tuesday, when the biggest hit rocked the stock market.

5. The Volstead Act: Prohibition was repealed in 1933.

6. Montgomery, Alabama.

7. He assassinated Martin Luther King Jr, massively increasing the likelihood of everything he feared coming to pass.

8. The New Deal.

9. The FBI was a revamp of the Bureau of Investigation, launched in 1908. The inaugural head of the FBI, J. Edgar Hoover, ensured the new body had far greater powers than its predecessor.

10. It limited the period of office to two full terms of four years.

QUIZ 214. PEOPLE AND PLACES

Sort of a general knowledge round, except that all the questions are about geography. So, a geography round. But about places, not rocks, fossils, topography and all that stuff. We got there eventually.

1. Which lake in Russia lays claim to being the world's deepest?

2. The western portion of Malaysia, containing the capital city, Kuala Lumpur, lies south of Thailand on the Malay Peninsula. Which other major city lies on the southern tip of this peninsula?

3. If Kyushu and Shikoku are to the south, and Hokkaido to the north, what is in the middle?

4. The Aegean Sea is a part of the Mediterranean lying between Greece and which other country?

5. Guernsey, Jersey, Lundy, Sark: which of these is NOT part of the Channel Islands group?

6. According to the most recent statistics, which are the six most populous African countries?

7. Sardinia is an Italian island in the Mediterranean: what is the French-controlled island immediately to the north?

8. Which river, the world's longest tributary, joins the Mississippi just north of St Louis?

9. What is the world's biggest land-locked country (by area)?

10. In which country is Lake Disappointment?

Answers to Quiz 213

1. Frizzante.

2. The vice-president.

3. Iman; she married David Bowie in 1992.

4. John Dee; Albarn's opera was written for the Manchester International Festival in 2012, and later performed at the London Coliseum, home of the English National Opera.

5. Kathryn Bigelow for *The Hurt Locker* in 2009; she remains the only female winner of the Best Director award. There have been only four other female nominees: Lina Wertmüller (*Seven Beauties*, 1976); Jane Campion (*The Piano*, 1993); Sofia Coppola (*Lost in Translation*, 2003); Greta Gerwig (*Lady Bird*, 2017).

6. They introduced maternity leave.

7. Xenophobia.

8. The *Guardian*.

9. London Stock Exchange.

10. Wind speed.

QUIZ 215. STEVE! STEVE!

Sorry to reference the annoying adverts. This is, of course, a quiz about Steves, Stevies, Stevens, Stephens and all things Steve-related.

1. 'Not Waving, But Drowning' is a famous 1957 piece by which poet?

2. American Steve Cauthen won which major British sporting event in 1985 and 1987?

3. Which boy-band icon died of a heart attack in 2009, aged just thirty-three?

4. Which unseeded American player won the 2017 US Open Ladies' Singles title?

5. Steve Tyler, still going at sixty-nine, is the lead singer in which American rock band?

6. What is the more common British name for St Stephen's Day?

7. Who played Mr Pink?

8. In their World Cup squad of 1986, England had two players with the same first name and surname. Which name?

9. Which classical actress made her breakthrough and earned a BAFTA nomination opposite Alan Rickman in *Truly, Madly, Deeply*?

10. What is the rock-and-roll alter-ego of Michael Barratt, who had four UK No. 1 hits in the early 1980s?

Answers to Quiz 214

1. Lake Baikal.

2. Singapore.

3. Honshu; these are the largest of the Japanese islands.

4. Turkey.

5. Lundy; the two main bailiwicks of the Channel Islands are Jersey and Guernsey, with Alderney and Sark being counted as part of Guernsey. Lundy is a separate island in the Bristol Channel off the North Devon coast, and is essentially a nature reserve.

6. Nigeria, Ethiopia, Egypt, Democratic Republic of Congo, South Africa, Tanzania; if you got more than three of these, well done!

7. Corsica.

8. Missouri; it rises in the Rockies and flows through Montana, North and South Dakota, Nebraska, Iowa and Kansas, before entering the state of Missouri and joining the Mississippi.

9. Kazakhstan; it is over a million square miles, much of it desert and mountain.

10. Australia. Of course it is.

QUIZ 216. SPORT

A mixture of sport questions, across a broad spectrum of different sports. It's a fact that few people are genuine sports enthusiasts rather than just devotees of one particular game. I consider myself a sports fan, but come the Olympics you would have to pay me to watch Weightlifting or Equestrian sports (even though I love horse racing). I love basketball and baseball but not American Football, and I struggle with both codes of Rugby. Each to their own, I s'pose.

1. Which Australian tennis player won the first Open Era Wimbledon Men's Singles title in 1968?

2. Who was the manager of Ipswich Town when they won their only Football League title in 1962?

3. What is the equivalent of the Ryder Cup in professional Ladies' Golf?

4. Which country provided a historic warm-up for the 2019 Ashes series when they played their first ever Test match against England?

5. In which year were NBA professionals first allowed to compete at the Olympics, with a Dream Team led by Michael Jordan carrying all before them? And who beat the US in the 2004 semi-finals before beating Italy in the Final, the only year the US haven't won the competition in the pro era? Was it Argentina, Lithuania, Russia or Serbia?

6. Wycombe Wanderers; Norwich City; Leicester City; _____; Aston Villa; Sunderland; Ireland; Nottingham Forest. Whose League and international management career does this list cover, and which is the missing club?

7. In 2018, the Capitals beat the Golden Knights to win their sport's premier trophy, taking the title that the Penguins had held for the last two years. What's the sport?

8. The Aviva Stadium in Dublin is home to both the Ireland Rugby Union and the Ireland football team. By what name was it formerly known (and still is, colloquially)?

9. In their 2020 European Championships qualifier against the Czech Republic, England had two eighteen-year-olds on the pitch for the first time. Who were they?

10. Following in the footsteps of Martina Navratilova, which Czech tennis player won four major titles between 1981 and 1987, missing out only on the Wimbledon title? Who was her protégée, who made up for that by winning her only major title on the grass at Wimbledon?

Answers to Quiz 215

1. Stevie Smith.

2. The Epsom Derby, aboard Slip Anchor and Reference Point, both trained by Henry Cecil. Reference Point was the last horse to win both the Derby and the St Leger, which is two furlongs more and a bigger test of stamina.

3. Stephen Gately.

4. Sloane Stephens; she proved it was a genuine improvement by reaching the final of the French Open the following year, but lost to Simona Halep.

5. Aerosmith.

6. Boxing Day.

7. Steve Buscemi, in Tarantino's *Reservoir Dogs*; the other colours were White (Harvey Keitel), Orange (Tim Roth), Blonde (Michael Madsen, scary), Blue (Edward Bunker) and Brown (Tarantino himself).

8. Gary Stevens (one of them threw in an initial and became known as Gary A. Stevens).

9. Juliet Stevenson.

10. Shakin' Stevens: 'This Ole House', 'Green Door', 'Oh Julie' and 'Merry Christmas Everyone'. Truly, there is no accounting for the taste of the record-buying public.

QUIZ 217. HALLOWE'EN

Hallowe'en quizzes are usually about horror movies and things that go bump. This one was just a general knowledge round (sort of), with a bonus-point task. What is the three-word phrase prompted by the clues and answers.

1. *Frozen in Time*, *Above the Below* and *Vertigo* were all performance feats by which magician and illusionist?

2. What is Clint Eastwood's profession in the classic Western, *The Good, the Bad and the Ugly*?

3. What is the prestigious professional body for magicians in Britain?

4. Which 490 BCE battle ended with a soldier called Pheidippides running to Athens to inform the government of their army's victory?

5. Which French word is used in English to define manual dexterity or slickness in performing sleight-of-hand tricks?

6. What was the 1955 Academy Award-nominated film starring William Holden, Kim Novak and Rosalind Russell?

7. Which German physician and astronomer gave his name to a form of animal magnetism nowadays associated with hypnosis?

8. Gertrude Jekyll, Queen of Sweden and Munstead Wood are all examples of what?

9. Which magician shares his name with a famous literary character?

10. What is the name of the butler in *Cinderella*, often played by a woman?

11. Bonus question: what is the theme of this round – only a specific three-word phrase will do?

Answers to Quiz 216

1. Rod Laver.

2. Alf Ramsey; it got him the England job, and it remains the only League title for the Suffolk club, although they finished second in consecutive seasons (1980–1 and 1981–2) under another future England manager, Bobby Robson.

3. The Solheim Cup.

4. Ireland.

5. 1992 in Barcelona; Argentina.

6. Martin O'Neill; Celtic.

7. Ice hockey; the Washington Capitals beat the Vegas Golden Knights, preventing a hat-trick for the Pittsburgh Penguins.

8. Lansdowne Road.

9. Jadon Sancho started and Callum Hudson-Odoi came on as a second-half substitute.

10. Hana Mandlíková; Jana Novotna. Novotna lost two tight finals, to Steffi Graf in 1993 and Martina Hingis in 1997, and it looked like her chance had gone at nearly thirty years old in an era where young players were the dominant force. In 1998 she beat a teenage Venus Williams and took revenge on Hingis to earn a place in the final against sixteenth seed, Nathalie Tauziat, a final she won in straight sets before soaking the Wimbledon grass with tears. Bless.

Olympic host cities

1896	Athens.
1900	Paris.
1904	St Louis.
1908	London.
1912	Stockholm.
1920	Antwerp.
1924	Paris.
1928	Amsterdam.

1932	Los Angeles.
1936	Berlin.
1948	London.
1952	Helsinki.
1956	Melbourne.
1960	Rome.
1964	Tokyo.
1968	Mexico City.
1972	Munich.
1976	Montreal.
1980	Moscow.
1984	Los Angeles.
1988	Seoul.
1992	Barcelona.
1996	Atlanta.
2000	Sydney.
2004	Athens.
2008	Beijing.
2012	London.
2016	Rio de Janeiro.
2020	Tokyo.
2024	Paris.
2028	Los Angeles.

QUIZ 218. MOVIES

Film stuff – a mixture of questions about films, more old than new.

1. Which American writer connects *Barefoot in the Park* (1967), *The Odd Couple* (1968) and *California Suite* (1978)?

2. Ian Fleming, creator of James Bond, was also the unlikely author of the source book for *Chitty Chitty Bang Bang*. Which other children's writer adapted the book for the 1968 film version with Dick Van Dyke?

3. *Enemy at the Gates*, a 2001 film starring Joseph Fiennes and Jude Law, is an account of which action during the Second World War?

4. Which rock star appeared as the lead singer in the band playing at the students' ball in the film version of *Harry Potter and the Goblet of Fire*?

5. Alan Alda, Jeff Goldblum, Samuel L. Jackson, Sam Neill: which of these actors was NOT in the first *Jurassic Park* film (1993)?

6. *Silkwood* was a 1983 nuclear drama starring Meryl Streep and Kurt Russell. Who directed the film and who co-starred as Streep's gay flatmate?

7. *First Blood* (1982) was the first film featuring which action character, played by Sylvester Stallone?

8. Macaulay Culkin came to prominence as a child star in which 1990 family entertainment?

9. Who played Jimmy Porter in the 1959 film version of John Osborne's kitchen sink drama *Look Back in Anger*?

10. Which part was played by Albert Finney in *Murder on the Orient Express* (Sidney Lumet, 1974)?

Answers to Quiz 217

1. David Blaine.

2. BOUNTY Hunter.

3. The Magic Circle.

4. MARATHON.

5. Legerdemain.

6. PICNIC.

7. Franz Mesmer.

8. ROSES, specifically David Austin roses.

9. David Copperfield.

10. BUTTONS.

11. Trick or Treat – alternate questions are about tricks or chocolate bars. (See above – Bounty, Marathon, Picnic, Roses and Buttons. Yummy.)

QUIZ 219. MIXED BAG

Encore une fois, mes amis. You should manage seven out of eight on this one.

1. What is the main ingredient of the Italian drink, a Bellini, popularised by Harry's Bar in Venice?

2. Which future US president was vice-president to Dwight D. Eisenhower between 1952 and 1960?

3. Which American design company produced the first denim jeans?

4. The manuscript seller Nicolas Flamel later acquired a reputation as a practitioner of which medieval skill. Was it (a) lute playing; (b) espionage; (c) alchemy; or (d) necromancy?

5. Who is the only actor to win three or more Academy Awards for Best Actor (up to and including 2018)?

6. Which two actors won an Academy Award for their screenplay to *Good Will Hunting*, the 1997 film in which both appeared alongside Robin Williams?

7. Why would someone suffering from ablutophobia not be too pleasant to have around?

8. Charles Baudelaire was best known for what in the nineteenth century?

9. New York State lies on one side of Niagara Falls: which Canadian province lies on the other?

10. Spider, squirrel, proboscis and rhesus are species of which animal?

Answers to Quiz 218

1. Neil Simon, the playwright and scriptwriter; he won Academy Award nominations for his screenplays to *The Odd Couple* and *California Suite*, and the same recognition for *The Sunshine Boys* (1975) and *The Goodbye Girl* (1977).

2. Roald Dahl.

3. The siege of Stalingrad.

4. Jarvis Cocker, the former singer with Pulp, later solo artist and radio presenter.

5. Alan Alda.

6. Mike Nichols and Cher.

7. John Rambo.

8. *Home Alone.*

9. Richard Burton; *Look Back in Anger* was premiered at the Royal Court in 1956. The critical description of Osborne as an 'angry young man' gave rise to the use of that expression for a wave of 1950s realist drama.

10. Hercule Poirot.

QUIZ 220. WOMEN'S MOVEMENT

This one we did for International Women's Day (the Monday after) – a quizzical tribute to brave and influential women. Most teams scored five to seven points.

1. What limit was put on women who were given the vote in Britain in 1918?

2. Which country, in 1893, became the first to give women the vote in a national election?

3. The first example of what medical facility was opened by Margaret Sanger in Brooklyn in 1916?

4. Which amendment to the American constitution allows the right to vote regardless of gender?

5. In 1888, Annie Besant encouraged which group of labourers to strike for better pay and conditions?

6. What was Eve Ensler's controversial off-Broadway play of 1996, which has since become an oft-performed feminist classic?

7. Who wrote the early feminist work *The Vindication of the Rights of Woman*?

8. Who was the first female professor at the University of Paris, the Sorbonne, when she replaced her own husband in 1906?

9. What did Jeanette Rankin of Montana achieve in November 1916?

10. What was Theodore Melfi's 2016 film about the forgotten work of pioneering female mathematicians at NASA in the early 1960s?

Answers to Quiz 219

1. Prosecco (usually with peach juice or liqueur).

2. Richard Nixon; even during this early part of his career, Nixon earned a reputation for mendaciousness and the nickname Tricky Dicky.

3. Levi Strauss; Strauss and his partner, Jacob W. Davis, began manufacturing denim work trousers in 1873.

4. Alchemy.

5. Daniel Day-Lewis. He won for *My Left Foot* (1989), *There Will be Blood* (2007) and *Lincoln* (2012). He won a BAFTA for the same three roles and also for *Gangs of New York* (2002).

6. Matt Damon and Ben Affleck.

7. They would be averse to bathing.

8. Poetry: Baudelaire's 1857 work, *Les Fleurs du mal* (Flowers of Evil), was one of the most influential works of French literature in the nineteenth century.

9. Ontario. Niagara Falls is actually comprised of three falls: Horseshoe, American and Bridal Veils.

10. Monkey.

QUIZ 221. TV CHEFS

It used to be just cookery demonstration programmes, then they became high-budget cookery-cum-travel programmes, then – with the advent of reality TV – they became cookery-skills elimination contests.

1. Which TV show was developed by Franc Roddam and first aired in the UK in July 1990?

2. There are five UK restaurants with three Michelin stars: three are in London, the other two are in which Berkshire village?

3. What song did Keith Floyd insist was used as his signature tune on his cookery programmes?

4. Who's *Invitation to Indian Cooking* (1973) changed the American perception of what was authentic Indian cuisine, and whose 1982 BBC TV show made Britain realise there was more to it than Saturday night at the local Curry Cabin?

5. What was the title of Jamie Oliver's first book and TV show?

6. Hugh Fearnley-Whittingstall is behind which cookbook and restaurant brand and template for self-sufficiency, originally based in Netherbury in Dorset?

7. What do comedian and singer Ade Edmondson, Emma Thompson's sister, Sophie, and rugby player Phil Vickery have in common?

8. In 2012 the Hand and Flowers in Marlow, on the River Thames in Buckinghamshire, became the first pub to gain two Michelin stars. Which chef earned this accolade for his food?

9. What was Nigella Lawson's first cookbook, published by Chatto & Windus in 1998?

10. Which South African-born food entrepreneur replaced Mary Berry as a judge on *The Great British Bake Off*?

Answers to Quiz 220

1. They were required to be over thirty and with self-supporting means.

2. New Zealand.

3. Birth control clinic.

4. The 19th Amendment, ratified in 1920.

5. Match workers. The strike brought the Bryant and May factory to a close until they agreed concessions for the workers.

6. *The Vagina Monologues*.

7. Mary Wollstonecraft.

8. Marie Curie.

9. She became the first woman elected to Congress; in 1922 Rebecca Felton became the first female Senator, representing Georgia. There are currently twenty-five female Senators out of a hundred incumbents – seventeen of the twenty-five are Democratic Senators.

10. *Hidden Figures*, starring Taraji P. Henson, Octavia Spencer and Janelle Monáe as the three scientists.

QUIZ 222. MUSIC MIX-TAPE

You get knocked down, but you get up again. And you face the next musical challenge. You hate us because last time you only got five when we said you should get seven, so you're thinking, 'I'll show those smug bastards; next time I'll get nine, and they won't think they're so clever . . .' Shhh. There's no need to be angry; we do this for you: we want you to enjoy yourselves.

1. Who styled himself Slim Shady on an early album, and what is his real name?

2. Under what name did Tina Weymouth and her husband Chris Frantz record as their main side-project from Talking Heads?

3. André 3000 and Big Boi have both enjoyed solo success in the hip-hop arena. By what name were they known when they operated as a duo?

4. What was David Bowie's final album, released two days before his death in January 2016?

5. Who were the only one of the British electronic bands from the 1980s to properly break the US market, reaching No. 1 on both sides of the Atlantic with their 1993 album *Songs of Faith and Devotion*?

6. What was Bob Dylan's first soundtrack album from 1973, who directed the film, and what was the name of the character Dylan played in the film?

7. A number of major rock figures have died aged twenty-seven. Which of these singers never reached that age: Kurt Cobain, Jimi Hendrix, Buddy Holly, Amy Winehouse?

8. Imagine, if you will, a rap supergroup featuring Shawn Carter, William Drayton Jr, Aubrey Graham, Curtis Jackson III and O'Shea Jackson Snr. Who are we watching?

9. Who assembled a host of stars for a one-off televised concert at Old Trafford Cricket Ground to raise money to help victims of the suicide bomb attack at the Manchester Arena in May 2017?

10. Which boy band, fostered by Simon Cowell, were the first to have their first four albums debut at No. 1 on the US album chart?

11. Bonus: what song did we reference in the intro to this round?

Answers to Quiz 221

1. *Masterchef*; the brand went international with the launch of *Masterchef: Australia* in 2009, and is now seen in every major country.

2. Bray, where you can choose to eat at either Heston Blumenthal's Fat Duck, or at The Waterside Inn, opened by Michel and Albert Roux in 1972, and now run by Alain Roux.

3. 'Peaches' by The Stranglers.

4. Madhur Jaffrey.

5. *The Naked Chef*.

6. *River Cottage*.

7. They all won *Celebrity Masterchef*.

8. Tom Kerridge.

9. *How to Eat*; a former journalist, Nigella published her first cookbook at the age of thirty-eight. Like Jamie Oliver, she is not a highly trained, technically accomplished chef, but a good writer and charismatic presenter with a proper feel for the food ordinary people who can't afford £300 dinners want to eat.

10. Prue Leith.

QUIZ 223. THIS OR THAT

These twelve thingummyjigs are either a South American football team, a terrorist organisation or a Nobel Laureate.

1. Colo Colo.

2. Shining Path.

3. Grazia Deledda.

4. Kawabata.

5. Penarol.

6. Independiente.

7. Boko Haram.

8. Odysseas.

9. Hezbollah.

10. Botafogo.

11. Lashkar.

12. Shmuel Agnon.

Answers to Quiz 222

1. Eminem; Marshall Mathers.

2. Tom Tom Club – they wanted an outlet to explore their own ideas without David Byrne's overwhelming presence.

3. Outkast.

4. *Blackstar* – it shot straight to No. 1 in pretty much every territory.

5. Depeche Mode – the Human League hit the US Top 10 with 'Dare', but never really followed up on that success.

6. *Pat Garrett and Billy the Kid*, directed by Sam Peckinpah. Dylan played an odd character called Alias (James Coburn played Garrett and country singer Kris Kristofferson had his first major non-musical film role as Billy).

7. Holly was still only twenty-two when he died in a plane crash in 1959.

8. Jay-Z, Flavor Flav, Drake, 50 Cent and Ice Cube.

9. Ariana Grande, whose show at the Arena had just finished when the bomb went off.

10. One Direction.

11. 'Tubthumping' by Chumbawamba contains that opening sentence in the first person.

QUIZ 224. TV DRAMAS

Simple concept, this one. We give you four members of the cast of a major modern TV drama and all you need to do is name the drama. Easy peasy lemon squeezy. But not all of them are that easy. Aim for eight points.

1. Peggy Olson, Joan Harris, Sally Draper, Lane Pryce.

2. Ellie Miller, Beth Latimer, Rev Paul Coates, Susan Wright.

3. Elizabeth Urquhart, Corder, Mattie Storrin, Sir Bruce Bullerby.

4. Leo McGarry, Josh Lyman, Donna Moss, Will Bailey.

5. Seth Bullock, Alma Garret, Doc Cochran, Joanie Stubbs.

6. Ash Morgan, Stacie Monroe, Albert Stroller, Danny Blue.

7. Louis Litt, Donna Paulsen, Rachel Zane, Mike Ross.

8. Dale Cooper, Shelly Johnson, Audrey Horne, Norma Jennings.

9. Claire Underwood, Zoe Barnes, Doug Stamper, Remy Danton.

10. Miles Stewart, Anna Forbes, Milly Nassim, Edgar Cooke.

Answers to Quiz 223

1. Colo Colo is a Santiago-based Chilean football team.

2. Shining Light are a pseudo-Communist Peruvian terrorist militia.

3. Italian Grazia Deledda won the Nobel Prize in 1926.

4. Japanese novelist Yasunari Kawabata won the Nobel Prize in 1968.

5. Penarol are a Uruguayan football team based in the capital city, Montevideo.

6. Independiente are a football team based in the Avellaneda district of Buenos Aires.

7. Boko Haram are an extreme Islamic group operating in northern Nigeria, and spreading into Chad, Niger and Cameroon.

8. Odysseas Elytis (1979) is one of only two Greek winners of the Nobel Prize for Literature.

9. Hezbollah are a Lebanese resistance movement whose military wing is regarded as a terrorist organisation by most Western governments.

10. Botafogo are one of Brazil's premier football clubs, based in a beach area of Rio de Janeiro.

11. Lashkar are a Pakistan-based terrorist group – a branch of this organisation carried out the 2006 Mumbai train bombings.

12. Austrian-born Shmuel Agnon, winner of the 1966 Nobel Prize for Literature, remains the only Israeli citizen to receive the prize.

QUIZ 225. MORE ALLSORTS

Another mix of questions for you to puzzle over. It's not the trickiest – a team of four should aim for eight of ten.

1. Which term derives from the affliction that overtook a man who stole a glance at the naked Lady Godiva as she rode through Coventry to absolve her husband's tenants of their debts.

2. The actress Lynne Frederick was married briefly to David Frost after being left a widow by her first husband. Who was the first husband, who died of a heart attack aged fifty-four in 1980?

3. What kind of dog is called a levrette in France?

4. What did the Titan Prometheus steal from the gods to give to mankind, incurring Zeus's wrath and a terrible punishment?

5. Which 1920s comic actor was accused and tried of the rape and subsequent death from a ruptured bladder of actress and society girl Virginia Rappe?

6. Who drove the Compact Pussycat in the *Wacky Races*?

7. If you saw *Cave Canem* written on a gate, what would you be worried about?

8. Who played Princess Amidala in the middle trilogy of *Star Wars* films?

9. Who was the Communications Officer aboard the *Starship Enterprise* in the original *Star Trek*?

10. Which spice consists of the unopened dried flower buds of a tropical evergreen tree of the myrtle family?

Answers to Quiz 224

1. *Mad Men*: played by Elisabeth Moss, Christina Hendricks, Kiernan Shipka and Jared Harris respectively.

2. *Broadchurch*: Olivia Colman, Jodie Whittaker, Arthur Darvill, Pauline Quirke.

3. *House of Cards* (UK): Diane Fletcher, Nick Brimble, Susannah Harker, David Ryall.

4. *The West Wing*: John Spencer, Bradley Whitford, Janel Moloney, Joshua Malina.

5. *Deadwood*: Timothy Olyphant, Molly Parker, Brad Dourif, Kim Dickens.

6. *Hustle*: Robert Glenister, Jaime Murray, Robert Vaughn, Marc Warren.

7. *Suits*: Rick Hoffman, Sarah Rafferty, Meghan Markle, Patrick J. Adams.

8. *Twin Peaks*: Kyle MacLachlan, Madchen Amick, Sherilyn Fenn, Peggy Lipton.

9. *House of Cards* (US): Robin Wright, Kate Mara, Michael Kelly, Mahershala Ali.

10. *This Life*: Jack Davenport, Daniela Nardini, Amita Dhiri, Andrew Lincoln.

QUIZ 226. WORDS – LANGUAGES

The word quizzes are always popular, and usually quite well scored. Some of the questions are greeted with groans, but then, when the team stop and talk about it, they work out the answer even if it's something they think they don't know.

1. What is the national language of Pakistan?

2. What is the first language, other than English, spoken by Harry Potter in J.K. Rowling's books?

3. Gary Lineker, the *Match of the Day* presenter, is fluent in which second language?

4. The *Bhagavad Gita* is a 700-verse sacred Hindu text: in which language was it written?

5. In 1649, Alexander Ross produced the first English translation, via a French edition, in itself a translation, of which major religious work?

6. What is the main language of the Republic of Moldova?

7. What writing system is used in Russia, large parts of Eastern Europe, Central Asia and Northern Asia?

8. Most South American countries use a form of Spanish. Guyana has ties with Britain and uses English, while Surinam and Brazil use, respectively, which other two European languages?

9. English is the most common language in the US, with Spanish a comfortable second. What is third, with an estimated 3.4 million speakers in 2016?

10. Which European language would be of most use on a holiday to Laos and Cambodia?

Answers to Quiz 225

1. Peeping Tom – the man, Tom the Tailor, is said to have been struck blind for his impropriety.

2. Peter Sellers.

3. A greyhound.

4. Fire.

5. Fatty Arbuckle.

6. Penelope Pitstop.

7. A dog – it means 'beware the dog'.

8. Natalie Portman.

9. Lt Uhuru.

10. Clove.

The cars and drivers in the Wacky Races

Car 00   Dick Dastardly and Muttley in The Mean Machine.

Car 1   The Slag Brothers in The Boulder Mobile.

Car 2   The Gruesome Twosome in The Creepy Coupe.

Car 3   Professor Pat Pending in The Convert-a-Car.

Car 4   The Red Max in The Crimson Haybaler.

Car 5   Penelope Pitstop in The Compact Pussycat.

Car 6   Sergeant Blast and Private Meekly in The Army Surplus Special.

Car 7   The Ant Hill Mob in The Bulletproof Bomb.

Car 8   Luke and Blubber Bear in The Arkansas Chuggabug.

Car 9   Peter Perfect in The Turbo Terrific.

Car 10   Rufus Ruffcut and Sawtooth in The Buzzwagon.

QUIZ 227. MIXED BAG

A trickier set. Anything more than six out of ten is good going.

1. Which clouds are most likely to be accompanied by thunder? Is it alto-stratus, nimbostratus or cumulonimbus?

2. Which country supplies over 90 per cent of the world's opium?

3. What is the name of the dog who featured on the classic HMV logo?

4. Along with chlorine, which element is the other main constituent of table salt?

5. What connects Tom Hardy and Spandau Ballet?

6. Which is London's oldest restaurant, open since 1798? Is it The Ivy, Rules, The Savoy or L'Escargot?

7. What is the field of expertise of a hippologist?

8. Which TV programme is set in Wisteria Lane in the fictional town of Fairview, Eagle State?

9. 'I have climbed to the top of the greasy pole.' So said which British Prime Minister on taking office in 1868?

10. Which film did the Coen Brothers remake in 2010 with Jeff Bridges in the lead role of Sheriff Rooster Cogburn?

Answers to Quiz 226

1. Urdu.

2. Parsil tongue – he speaks to the snake that he releases at the zoo.

3. Spanish, from his time playing for Barcelona between 1986 and 1989.

4. Sanskrit.

5. The *Koran*, or *Qur'an*.

6. Romanian. Moldova is the only other country where Romanian is a principal language.

7. Cyrillic.

8. Dutch and Portuguese.

9. Mandarin. Pretty much every US city has a decent-sized Chinese quarter.

10. French. Both countries were part of the extensive French territories (Indochine) in Southeast Asia. The post-war conflict in neighbouring Vietnam was initially between the French and the Vietnamese fighters under Ho Chi Minh, who eventually won their independence and formed the communist northern part of the country in 1954, some time before US intervention.

QUIZ 228. NEW ENGLAND

A quiz on the north-eastern states of the US, the area where the pilgrims first landed and that retains that slightly anglophile feel and atmosphere today. They are among the most affluent and comfortable of US states, as well as the most liberal. As the quiz was set around Thanksgiving, we've thrown in a couple of questions about the holiday at the end.

1. Connecticut: New Jersey; Plymouth; Rhode Island. Which of these was not an early Puritan colony?

2. What is the state capital of New Hampshire, sharing its name with a large English city?

3. Which New England state was the first to join the Union after the original thirteen states: it is the second-least populous state of the US after Wyoming?

4. Which state lies furthest to the north on the East Coast of the United States?

5. What is the biggest city in the six states of New England?

6. Which New England state is the smallest in the US?

7. 'Yankee Doodle' is the anthem of which New England state?

8. When does Thanksgiving fall in the United States?

9. Thanksgiving was originally (a) a celebration of American Independence; (b) a celebration of the landing of *The Mayflower* in America; (c) a harvest festival; or (d) a celebration of the abolition of slavery?

10. Which US president made Thanksgiving a federal holiday in 1863?

Answers to Quiz 227

1. Cumulonimbus.

2. Afghanistan.

3. Nipper.

4. Sodium; NaCl is the formula for common salt – sea salt has a slightly different composition.

5. Both Hardy and the Kemp brothers (who were in Spandau Ballet) have played the Kray twins. The Kemps played the two brothers (Gary was Ronnie, Martin was Reggie) in Peter Medak's 1990 biopic, while Hardy played both parts in *Legend*, Brian Helgeland's 2015 version of the story based on John Pearson's biography, *The Profession of Violence*.

6. Rules, opened by Thomas Rule on Maiden Lane in Covent Garden.

7. Horses.

8. *Desperate Housewives*.

9. Benjamin Disraeli.

10. *True Grit*. John Wayne played the part, arguably his most memorable, in Henry Hathaway's 1969 original, with Kim Darby as Mattie Ross and country singer Glen Campbell as Texas Ranger La Boeuf. The 2010 version had Hailee Stanfield and Matt Damon in those roles.

QUIZ 229. *ENCORE DU STUFF*

Over to you.

1. Jilly Cooper's longer novels are often grouped together as the Rutshire Chronicles. Which was the first of this sequence, in 1985?

2. Which of these four gents was never married to Elizabeth Taylor: Richard Burton, Eddie Fisher, Mike Todd or Ted Turner?

3. If you attended the ENT department in a hospital, what part of your body would be afflicted?

4. The crow, the dove, the hawk, the peacock: which of these is not a constellation in the night sky of either hemisphere?

5. Hammer Horror stars Peter Cushing and Christopher Lee both appeared in which award-winning 1948 film as Osric (a courtier) and a spear carrier (no spoken words) respectively?

6. If he was played by Alan Alda in the long-running TV series, who played him in the 1970 film directed by Robert Altman?

7. Which literary character was portrayed by Nicole Kidman in Stephen Daldry's *The Hours* (2002)?

8. What is the only poker hand that beats four of a kind?

9. Grey, John Snow, St Chad's and Ushaw are a few of the individual colleges that make up which British university.

10. In fashion terms, what is an 'lbd'?

Answers to Quiz 228

1. New Jersey.

2. Manchester.

3. Vermont.

4. Maine.

5. Boston.

6. Rhode Island.

7. Connecticut.

8. The fourth Thursday in November.

9. It was originally a harvest festival.

10. Abraham Lincoln.

States that comprise New England

Maine (capital Augusta, largest city Portland, one Republican senator, one
  Democrat-leaning Independent).

Vermont (capital Montpelier, largest city Burlington, one Democrat senator and one Democrat-leaning Independent).

New Hampshire (capital Concord, largest city Manchester, two female
  Democrat senators).

Massachusetts (capital and largest city Boston, two Democrat senators).

Rhode Island (capital and largest city, two Democrat senators).

Connecticut (capital Hartford, largest city Bridgeport, two Democrat
  senators).

QUIZ 230. SCI-FI MOVIES

A bit of a personal specialist subject for the setters, but we've tried to ensure it isn't too much of a demonic selection. We've stuck to the major franchises in the main.

1. *The Wrath of Khan* was the second (and many believe the best) in which sequence of sci-fi movies?

2. Which author connects the films *Blade Runner* and *Total Recall*?

3. Who was The Omega Man in the 1971 post-apocalyptic sci-fi film of that name?

4. Who starred as the unnamed Mariner in the 1995 post-apocalyptic adventure *Waterworld*?

5. Originally a radio play that caused alarm in some who heard it, which story was filmed by Byron Haskin in 1953 and Steven Spielberg in 2005?

6. The TV series *Westworld* was developed from the 1973 film version of a Michael Crichton novel. Who starred in the film as a killer android gunslinger?

7. By what name is the character Erik Lehnsherr better known in the movies in which he has appeared?

8. Alec Guinness played Obi-Wan Kenobi in the original *Star Wars* trilogy. Who took the role of the younger Obi-Wan in the later prequel trilogy?

9. Which American actress had an early starring role as Gertie, a five-year-old, in *E.T. the Extra-Terrestrial*?

10. Zhang Yimou's martial arts epics were the Chinese Academy Award nominations for 2002, 2004, 2006. *Hero* and *Curse of the Golden Flower* were the first and last; what was the middle film, from 2004?

Answers to Quiz 229

1. *Riders*; the others are *Rivals* (1988), *Polo* (1991), *The Man Who Made Husbands Jealous* (1993), *Appassionata* (1996), *Score!* (1999), *Jump!* (2010) and *Mount!* (2016). *Pandora* (2002) and *Wicked!* (2006) feature many of the same characters, but are not technically part of the same series.

2. Ted Turner.

3. ENT is ear, nose and throat (sinuses is fine, it covers all those areas).

4. The hawk. Corvus (the crow), Pavo (the peacock) and Columba (the dove) are all constellations in the Southern sky.

5. *Hamlet*, directed by and starring Laurence Olivier.

6. Donald Sutherland (the character is Hawkeye Pierce in *M*A*S*H*).

7. Virginia Woolf.

8. A straight flush – five consecutive cards in the same suit.

9. Durham.

10. A little black dress.

Poker hands in descending order

Five of a kind (only relevant if wild cards are played; unlikely in professional or casino poker).

Straight flush (same suit, sequential).

Four of a kind.

Full house (two of one card and three of another, e.g. two fours and three jacks).

Flush (same suit, non-sequential).

Three of a kind.

Two pairs.

One pair.

High card.

QUIZ 231. MODERN AMERICA

A section on more recent American history, mainly from the 1950s and 60s. Sort of stuff your mum and dad might remember.

1. Which US astronaut orbited the earth in *Friendship 7* in 1962?

2. Where, in November 1978, did 909 Americans, members of Jim Jones's religious cult, The People's Temple, apparently commit suicide?

3. Which US president's 'big idea' was the Great Society, a set of reforms to eliminate poverty and discrimination?

4. In which theatre of war did the US intervene in June 1950?

5. Who was shot by Palestinian activist Sirhan Sirhan in Los Angeles in 1968?

6. For what were Julius and Ethel Rosenberg executed in the US in 1953?

7. What took place in White Lake, New York State, between 15 and 19 August 1969?

8. What did Ray Kroc open in Des Plaines, Illinois, in April 1955?

9. The Vietnam War officially ended with the fall of Saigon to the People's Army and the Viet Cong: in which year?

10. Hawaii was the last and fiftieth US state to be admitted to the Union: what was the forty-ninth?

Answers to Quiz 230

1. The original *Star Trek* movies. The six movies in the original run of films were *Star Trek: The Motion Picture*, *The Wrath of Khan*, *The Search for Spock*, *The Voyage Home*, *The Final Frontier* and *The Undiscovered Country*.

2. Both are based on stories by Philip K. Dick. *Blade Runner* was an adaptation of *Do Androids Dream of Electric Sheep?* while *Total Recall* was based on *We Can Remember it for You Wholesale*.

3. Charlton Heston.

4. Kevin Costner.

5. *War of the Worlds*. The radio broadcast was directed by Orson Welles, and the end of the first half with a radio voice announcing a Martian landing sent a few of the more gullible listeners into a panic.

6. Yul Brynner.

7. Magneto in the *X-Men* films, played by Ian McKellen.

8. Ewan McGregor.

9. Drew Barrymore.

10. *House of Flying Daggers*.

QUIZ 232. BUNGS AND BRIBES

We promised the good folks a brown-envelope quiz – not sure they were expecting a round on stationery and another on bungs and illegal payments.

1. Which naval administrator admitted in his diary for 1663 to taking sweeteners to ease the tax burden on importers?

2. In 1973, US vice-president Spiro Agnew resigned from office after a federal corruption investigation, including the receipt of over a hundred thousand dollars in bribes. Who replaced him?

3. During the legal battle between Alan Sugar and Terry Venables when both were involved with Tottenham Hotspur, which manager was alleged to 'like a bung' as part of transfer negotiations, including the purchase of England striker Teddy Sheringham?

4. In 1919, the Eight Men Out scandal rocked the world of baseball. Which team saw eight of its players banned for life for throwing a game against the Cincinnati Reds?

5. In the wake of the cash-for-questions affair during John Major's time as prime minister, who defeated the incumbent Tory MP for Tatton, Neil Hamilton, standing on an anti-corruption platform, with the Labour and Lib Dem candidates standing down?

6. The payments, allegedly made by a lobbyist, Ian Greer, were made on behalf of which overseas businessman?

7. For which football manager's demise was Norwegian agent Rune Hauge responsible?

8. Peter Swan, an England international who may well have made England's 1966 World Cup squad, was one of three players banned from football for eight years after betting against their own team before a game against Ipswich. What was the club?

9. Which British pharma giant was fined nearly half a million dollars by the Chinese Government in 2014 for bribing medical staff and institutions?

10. Which South African cricket captain was given a life ban for match-fixing in 2001?

Answers to Quiz 231

1. John Glenn.

2. Guyana. Jones' activities were investigated by US representative Leo Ryan, who was then murdered as he tried to leave Jones' compound, before the entire cult consumed poisoned drinks.

3. Lyndon B. Johnson.

4. Korea.

5. Robert F. (Bobby) Kennedy.

6. Passing atomic secrets to the Soviet Union.

7. Woodstock Festival; the festival was commemorated in a 1970 documentary and the famous song by Joni Mitchell. Ang Lee made a 2009 film (*Taking Woodstock*) about the idea for and development of the festival.

8. The first McDonald's.

9. 1975.

10. Alaska.

QUIZ 233. DOUBLE DAVE

There were so many good Dave questions when we did this section, we had enough for two rounds. So here's the second.

1. Which two Davids have sat as Prime Minister of the United Kingdom?

2. Who is the only person to have won a BAFTA for a programme made in black and white, colour, HD and 3D? What birthday did he celebrate in May 2016?

3. *Eraserhead* was the debut feature film by which maverick director? Which 1980 film (with almost exclusively British actors) gave him his commercial breakthrough and an Academy Award nomination?

4. Which 1970s sitcom was adapted by David Nobbs from his own novels? Who was the star of his 1989 series about social climbers in Yorkshire, *A Bit of a Do*?

5. Michael Scott is the US equivalent of which UK TV comedy character? Who played Michael for seven seasons of the US show?

6. Who climbed a White Ladder to the top of the UK albums in 1999–2000? What was the only UK Top 10 single from the album?

7. Who is the only manager called Dave or David to win the FA Cup? With which club did he win the trophy?

8. Betsey Trotwood is the aunt and Agnes Wickfield the second wife of which titular literary character? Who is the book's chief villain, who lent his name to a 1970s prog-rock band?

9. Who is the MP for Haltemprice and Howden in Yorkshire, and from what ministerial post did he resign in 2018?

10. Who beat Nikolai Valuev to win the WBA Heavyweight title in 2009, and who in turn beat this boxer to unify four world title belts?

Answers to Quiz 232

1. Samuel Pepys.

2. Gerald Ford. He subsequently followed Nixon into office after the president also fell into disgrace, thereby serving in both roles, vice-president and president, without ever fighting an election.

3. Brian Clough.

4. Chicago White Sox.

5. Martin Bell. The former BBC journalist won handsomely, with the help of Alastair Campbell, who persuaded Labour and the Lib Dems to withdraw their candidates. Bell kept his pledge to relinquish the seat in 2001, instead standing against Eric Pickles in Essex. Tatton, a safe Tory seat, was won back for the Conservatives by George Osborne.

6. Mohamed Al-Fayed.

7. George Graham. Hauge was the rogue agent who arranged the bung that caught Graham out.

8. Sheffield Wednesday. Had he not been banned, Swan might well have partnered Bobby Moore in England's defence at the 1966 World Cup.

9. GlaxoSmithKline.

10. Hansie Cronje. He died in a plane crash the following year.

QUIZ 234. MIXED SPORTS

Sixteen answers here, with the first question demanding five names. Ten is a decent score. A broad knowledge of all sports, not just the most popular ones, is an asset.

1. Who are the five drivers with four or more Formula 1 World Championship titles?

2. If your captain is handed the Webb Ellis Trophy, what have you won?

3. Which coach/quarterback combination has seen the New England Patriots become the major team of twenty-first-century American Football, with nine Superbowl appearances in that timespan (to 2018)?

4. Which two teams beat Germany in the 2018 World Cup as the holders made their earliest exit from a Finals tournament since 1938?

5. Kasey Keller, Brad Friedel and Tim Howard were the three dominant US goalkeepers of the 1990s and 2000s. Which of the three won the most caps?

6. Allianz Arena, Flushing Meadow, Roland Garros, Wimbledon. Which of these has never been a venue for one of the four major tennis tournaments?

7. Which French tennis player won two major tournaments in 2006 and later became coach to Andy Murray?

8. Where were the 1964 Olympic Games held, the first time they had been held on this particular continent?

9. Who won Team GB's only gold medal at the 2018 Winter Olympics, and in which event?

10. Why was no Stanley Cup awarded to the winners of America's premier ice hockey competition, the National Hockey League, in 2004–5?

Answers to Quiz 233

1. David Lloyd George (1916–22) and Cameron (2010–16).

2. David Attenborough; his ninetieth.

3. David Lynch; *The Elephant Man*.

4. *The Fall and Rise of Reginald Perrin*, starring Leonard Rossiter; David Jason.

5. David Brent (in *The Office*); Steve Carell.

6. David Gray, 'Babylon': Gray's album was a word-of-mouth creeper; it had been out for a year before it hit the charts.

7. Dave Sexton; Chelsea in 1970 when they beat Leeds United 2–1 in a replay after a 2–2 draw. It was one of the most famous finals, remembered for some good football and also as one of the dirtiest games of the televised era – in 2019 it would have ended eight a side.

8. Charles Dickens' David Copperfield; Uriah Heep.

9. David Davies; Brexit Minister.

10. David Haye; Wladimir Klitschko.

QUIZ 235. JESUS

This isn't a religious round, although there are references. Think of it more like the name rounds; it just so happens the name in this instance is Jesus.

1. Which is the only Gospel to mention the three wise men who came to the infant Jesus bearing gifts? Who was the third of them, along with Caspar and Balthazar?

2. The authors of the *Book of Common Prayer* and the *Rime of the Ancient Mariner* are both alumni of Jesus College, Cambridge. Who are they?

3. Which TV show features a show-within-the-show called *Jesus and Pals*? In the episode 'Red Sleigh Down', Jesus is killed in a raid to rescue which character?

4. Who paid Palmeiras thirty-two million euros for Gabriel Jesus in 2017? What shirt number does he like to wear in honour of his namesake?

5. Whose painting from 1475, *The Adoration of the Magi*, has a prominent place in the Uffizi Gallery in Florence? Members of which Italian family, patrons of the artist, are featured prominently in the painting?

6. According to the Sermon on the Mount, what reward awaits the meek and the peacemakers?

7. If you have five unleavened loaves, each weighing 1.8 kilograms, two tuna of 4 kilograms each, and three large bream totalling 7.6 kilograms, how much food, in weight, does everyone get?

8. Which great Italian director made the 1977 mini-series, *Jesus of Nazareth*, starring Robert Powell as Jesus? Which portly English character actor, winner of two Best Supporting Actor awards, played Herod?

9. Who released the album *Yeezus*, in 2013, to widespread acclaim? The album was co-produced by Rick Rubin and released on which label, founded by Rubin in the early 1980s?

10. What word is given to a piece of art depicting the Virgin Mary cradling the dead body of Jesus? Who sculpted one of the most famous ones in 1498–9; it now sits in St Peter's Basilica in the Vatican?

Answers to Quiz 234

1. Michael Schumacher, Juan Manuel Fangio, Lewis Hamilton, Alain Prost, Sebastian Vettel.

2. The Rugby Union World Cup.

3. Bill Belichick and Tom Brady.

4. Mexico and South Korea; a sharp fall from grace for the side that won so gloriously in 2014.

5. Howard, with 121, Keller won 102, while Friedel, probably the best keeper of the three, won 80.

6. The Allianz Arena is a German football ground, home to Bayern Munich.

7. Amélie Mauresmo. She beat Justine Henin in the final of both the Australian Open and Wimbledon, the latter after going a set down.

8. Tokyo.

9. Lizzy Yarnold, skeleton; she retained the gold medal she won in Sochi in 2014.

10. There was no competition that year; it was the year of the NHL Lockout, when the players went on strike for over three months.

QUIZ 236. NAME THE BAND

We give you the members of the band, you just give us the name of that band. This one is for the younger elements. Do not attempt this section if you stopped buying music around 1990.

1. Damon Albarn, Graham Coxon, Alex James, Dave Rowntree.

2. George Daniel, Adam Hann, Matty Healy, Ross MacDonald.

3. Tom Fleming, Ben Little, Chris Talbot, Hayden Thorpe.

4. Dr Dre, Easy-E, Ice Cube, DJ Yella, MC Ren.

5. Robbie Bennett, Adam Granduciel, Charlie Hall, Dave Hartley, Anthony LaMarca.

6. Matt Berninger, Aaron and Bryce Dessner, Bryan and Scott Devendorf.

7. Ana Matronic, Babydaddy, Paddy Boom, Del Marquis, Jake Shears.

8. Greg Churchouse, Pete Ellard, Roy Stride.

9. Chester Bennington, Rob Bourdon, Brad Delson, Joe Hahn, Mike Shinoda.

10. Kevin Baird, Sam Halliday, Alex Trimble.

Answers to Quiz 235

1. Matthew; Melchior.

2. Thomas Cranmer, the Archbishop of Canterbury in the latter years of Henry VIII's reign, and Samuel Taylor Coleridge, the romantic poet.

3. *South Park*; Santa Claus.

4. Manchester City; thirty-three. Jesus has thirteen international goals already (January 2019) – he is only twenty-one. Even at that money, City may have a bargain.

5. Botticelli; the Medici family.

6. They shall inherit the earth and be called children of God respectively.

7. This is a reference to the feeding of the 5,000. We got that, right? Five loaves at 1.8 kilograms is 9 kilograms; two tuna at 4 kilograms is 8 kilograms; add 7.6 kilograms of bream, which makes a total of 24.6 kilograms of food, or 24,600 grams. That makes 4.92 grams each for 5,000 people.

8. Franco Zeffirelli; Peter Ustinov.

9. Kanye West; Def Jam.

10. *Pietà*; Michelangelo.

QUIZ 237. THIS OR THAT

This one is a quiz salad, with potatoes, tomatoes and apples in equal measure. It's up to you to pick out each ingredient.

1. Merlin.

2. Baldwin.

3. San Marzano.

4. Sungold.

5. Anya.

6. Jonagold.

7. Jersey Royal.

8. Early Girl.

9. McIntosh.

10. Black Oxford.

11. Purple Majesty.

12. Black Krim.

Answers to Quiz 236

1. Blur: one of the prime movers of Britpop, they count as Grand Old Men now.

2. Manchester band, The 1975. Three albums so far, all immediately No. 1.

3. Wild Beasts; five albums, bit of a cult band.

4. N.W.A. – the big hitters of the 1990s L.A. rap scene.

5. War on Drugs – their 2014 album, *Lost in the Dream*, was voted album of the year in a number of publications.

6. The National, gloomy New York art rockers.

7. Scissor Sisters: early 2000s doyens of the disco scene.

8. Scouting for Girls: cheeky London popsters.

9. Linkin Park – Bennington hanged himself in 2017.

10. Two Door Cinema Club – Northern Ireland indie band.

QUIZ 238. DO THE MATHS

This isn't science general knowledge; there's actually a bit of working out involved in one or two of the questions, so pencils and paper at the ready. Try and go old school – no calculators or other mathematical aids.

1. The sum of the squares of the two shorter sides of a right-angle triangle is equal to the square of the hypotenuse, or longer side. Whose work?

2. What is the square root of 225?

3. What device did William Oughtred invent in 1622 that significantly increased mathematical calculation speeds?

4. And whose work on developing logarithm tables prompted Oughtred's work?

5. Add the horsemen of the apocalypse to Tarantino's hateful party and multiply by French hens. What have you got?

6. $V = ®r2h$. What is this formula?

7. What name is given to a parallelogram with unequal adjacent sides and no right angles?

8. What is the tenth prime number?

9. Add the Fellowship of the Ring to a Rugby League team and divide by a Field Hockey team – what's the result?

10. What is the mean, median, mode and range of the following set of numbers: 11, 16, 14, 24, 11, 11, 18.

Answers to Quiz 237

1. Merlin is a potato variety, a yellow-skinned, red-spotted all-rounder.

2. Baldwin is a bright-red New England winter apple.

3. San Marzano is a variety of Italian plum tomato from a small town near Naples.

4. Sungold is a sweet, orange-tinged tomato.

5. Anya is a knobbly, tasty salad potato grown for Sainsbury's and named after the Chairman's wife, Lady Anya.

6. Jonagold is a sweet American hybrid apple developed from Golden Delicious.

7. Jersey Royal is a new potato with a Protected Designation of Origin, which means that any attempt to replicate the potato cannot use the name.

8. Early Girl is a medium to large hybrid tomato.

9. McIntosh is a tart apple grown widely in Canada.

10. Black Oxford is a New England apple with a dark-purple, black-tinged skin.

11. Purple Majesty is a standard potato with naturally occurring purple skin and flesh.

12. Black Krim is a Russian tomato with deep-purple flesh and a black tinge to the outer.

QUIZ 239. MIXED BAG

Let's go round again. Bit of sport, bit of pop culture, bit of general – the whole world is here. Aim for seven out of ten.

1. The Spanish natural phenomenon known as the solano is (a) a hot spring; (b) a freak coastal storm; (c) a hot dusty wind; (d) a perfect rainbow following a period of drought?

2. What is the name of Batman's butler?

3. United in . . . what, according to the motto of the European Union?

4. What substance, found in the fourth stomach of a young calf, has milk-curdling properties and is also used in the production of cheese?

5. What was the tallest building in the European Union, pre-Brexit?

6. Which UK city provided the backdrop for Jodie Whittaker's historic first appearance as a female Dr Who?

7. Astrakhan is a kind of (a) goat's cheese; (b) tea; (c) vodka; or (d) wool?

8. The Courtauld Gallery forms part of which neo-classical building on the Strand, formerly the home of the Inland Revenue and the Registry of Births, Marriages and Deaths?

9. In 1941, David Stirling of the Scots guards formed which elite military unit?

10. In horse racing, what is the name of the sharp left-hand final bend on the Derby course at Epsom?

Answers to Quiz 238

1. This is Pythagoras' theorem.

2. Fifteen.

3. The slide rule.

4. John Napier; logarithm tables were actually first compiled by Henry Briggs in 1617, but Napier's work was the basis of the charts.

5. Four horsemen + Hateful Eight = 12 × Three French hens = 36.

6. The volume of a cylinder.

7. Rhomboid (rhombus is wrong).

8. Prime numbers are numbers not divisible by any two others, so we go 1, 2, 3, 5, 7, 11, 13, 17, 23, and then 29, which is the tenth. After 2, all primes are odd numbers.

9. There are nine travellers in *The Fellowship of the Ring* and thirteen in a Rugby League team = 22. Divide by eleven in a hockey team = 2.

10. The numbers total 105 and there are seven of them, so the mean (average) is 15. The median is the middle number if the seven are ranged lowest to highest – so 14 is the median. The mode is the most commonly occurring number, so that would be 11. The range is the difference between the lowest and highest, so it is 13 (24 – 11).

QUIZ 240. BOOKS DO FURNISH A ROOM

Books Do Furnish a Room is a novel by post-war English novelist Anthony Powell, part of a twelve-book sequence called *A Dance to the Music of Time*. The statement is true – ask any editor or photographer of a lifestyle magazine; they commonly use strategically placed books in the eyeline to enhance a visual. Anyway, moving on, here are ten questions on books, some classic, some modern.

1. *Farmer Giles of Ham* is a story in medieval style written in 1937 by which well-known fantasy author?

2. Which Roman Catholic novelist wrote the screenplay for the classic spy noir film *The Third Man*.

3. *Jumping the Queue* (1983) was the first published adult novel by Mary Wesley, at the age of seventy-one. What was the 1984 follow-up, the most successful of her ten novels?

4. Which Victorian novel concerns the life and career of Michael Henchard?

5. The famous stage direction, 'Exit, pursued by a bear' comes from which Shakespeare play?

6. *At Risk* was the debut 2004 novel of successful thriller writer Stella Rimington. What was her previous job?

7. Which huge and influential French novel was published in seven parts between 1913 and 1927?

8. Multiply the Gentlemen of Verona by Chekhov's sisters and add the number of *Narnia* books: what have you got?

9. *Leaves of Grass* is a well-known volume of poetry, much revised and rewritten after its initial 1855 publication by which American writer?

10. Who wrote the novel on which the massively successful musical *Les Misérables* is based?

Answers to Quiz 239

1. Solano is a hot dusty mainland wind.

2. Alfred Pennyworth; he was played by Alan Napier in the 1960s *Batman* series and film with Adam West, by Michael Gough in the Tim Burton *Batman* films and by Michael Caine in the *Dark Knight* trilogy. Jeremy Irons plays the part in the recent DC movies.

3. United in diversity.

4. Rennet.

5. The Shard, near London Bridge in south-east London.

6. Sheffield; it explains how the Doctor picks up Whittaker's own accent and her new companions are partially defined by their connection to the city.

7. It is wool from karakul sheep.

8. Somerset House; the main courtyard is traditionally converted into an ice rink for the Christmas season.

9. The SAS; it was formed during the Second World War, then made part of the Territorial Army in 1947, before becoming the 22nd Special Air Services corps, part of the army proper in 1950, from when it was developed into the covert unit it remains today.

10. Tattenham Corner. Just as with human runners, the way a bend is run can define the outcome of a close race.

QUIZ 241. ODDS BODKINS

An odd-one-out round. Again, be careful, there are a couple of sneaky ones in here.

1. Charing Cross, Fenchurch Street, Kings Cross, Marylebone: which of these London stations is NOT one of the four featured on a standard Monopoly board?

2. Chemistry, Economics, Peace, Poetry: for which of these is a Nobel Prize NOT awarded?

3. Charles Bronson, James Garner, Steve McQueen, Robert Vaughn: which one of these actors was NOT one of the original *Magnificent Seven*?

4. Denmark, Lithuania, Malta, Netherlands: which of these countries does NOT use the euro as its currency?

5. Instagram; Messenger; Spotify; WhatsApp: which of these is NOT a subsidiary of Facebook?

6. Winston Churchill, Margaret Thatcher, Franklin D. Roosevelt, John F. Kennedy, Nelson Mandela: which of these was NOT one of the four people chosen by a computer algorithm for the BBC's twentieth-century-icon poll in 2019?

7. Teams in the MLS in North America mainly take American-style team names, but a few borrow historic European names. Which of these is NOT an MLS team: DC United, Real Salt Lake, Sporting Kansas City, Seattle Wanderers?

8. Brian Jones, Jimmy Page, Mick Taylor, Ron Wood: which of these never played guitar for The Rolling Stones?

9. Austria, Croatia, Slovenia, Switzerland: which of these countries does NOT share a border with Italy?

10. Gauteng, KwaZulu-Natal, Limpopo, Transvaal: which of these is not a province of South Africa?

Answers to Quiz 240

1. J.R.R. Tolkien; Tolkien was a significant Anglo-Saxon and medieval scholar who taught at Pembroke College, Oxford, where he began writing his great works.

2. Graham Greene; most of Greene's screenplays were adapted from his own novels. As a novelist, he put down the story of *The Third Man* in prose form before developing it into a screenplay. The novella was later published, but only after the film came out. Directed by Carol Reed, the latter is a masterpiece of suspense and one of the defining works of the film noir heyday.

3. *The Camomile Lawn*.

4. Thomas Hardy's *The Mayor of Casterbridge*, about a man who sells his wife and spends the rest of his life hating himself for it. It was a characteristically bleak view of humankind from Hardy.

5. *A Winter's Tale*; Antigonus, a courtier, is instructed to abandon a baby to die, but protects the girl until he is chased (and presumably killed) by a bear.

6. Head of MI6.

7. *A la récherche du temps perdu* (Remembrance of Things Past) by Marcel Proust.

8. Two Gentlemen of Verona × three Sisters = 6 + seven *Narnia* books = 13.

9. Walt Whitman.

10. Victor Hugo.

QUIZ 242. LIGHT ENTERTAINMENT

'Light Entertainment' is a vague term to describe anything that doesn't obviously come under another TV category. It includes game shows, magazine programmes that aren't specifically news driven, music shows, chat shows, comedy shows that don't use a dramatic format so aren't sitcoms, and reality TV, although that has become such a large part of TV it probably needs its own category.

1. Who presented the BBC's principal film magazine show from 1972 to 1998?

2. Alistair Leslie Graham first appeared on Channel 4's magazine comedy show *The 11 O'Clock Show*. By what name do we know this individual?

3. *The Tube* was launched by Tyne Tees Television in November 1982. Who were the programme's two principal hosts?

4. Whose *Big Show* has topped the TV light entertainment rankings for the last three years?

5. Whose chat show preceded Graham Norton's in the prestigious BBC late-night Friday slot?

6. Which TV presenter once opened the batting for Barnsley Cricket Club alongside future Test Match umpire and fellow resident of Cudworth, Dickie Bird?

7. Which comedy duo's purple patch started in 1968 when they were given a regular slot on the BBC working with writer Eddie Braben?

8. What was Simon Fuller's UK talent contest from 2001 to 2003, which paved the way for the *X Factor* and a host of other derivative shows?

9. *Comic Relief*, launched in 1985 as part of the push for funds to help with famine in Ethiopia, was the brainchild of writer Richard Curtis and which comedian?

10. Which TV entertainment concept was devised by John de Mol Jr in the Netherlands and launched there in 1999?

Answers to Quiz 241

1. Charing Cross – the fourth station on the board is Liverpool Street.

2. Poetry – there is a Literature prize, which can go to a poet, but not a prize specifically for poetry.

3. James Garner; the other four were Yul Brynner, James Coburn, Horst Buchholz and Brad Dexter.

4. Denmark still use krone.

5. Spotify; as we know, most of the Western world is owned by Google or Facebook.

6. Kennedy. Apparently, Margaret Thatcher made a greater contribution to the twentieth century than Kennedy.

7. Seattle Wanderers; the Seattle team are called the Sounders.

8. Jimmy Page; he was the guitarist first with the Yardbirds and later with Led Zeppelin.

9. Croatia – Slovenia is in the way.

10. Transvaal was dissolved as an administrative division post-apartheid. Limpopo and Gauteng are both within the territory that was Transvaal.

QUIZ 243. DOGS

We do a charity quiz every year, which is 'presented' by our lovely Romanian rescue dog, Martha, and the proceeds go to the charity that rescued Martha and a host of other dogs from kill shelters in Eastern Europe.

1. Which comic-book character owns a dog called Snowy?

2. What is the name of the three-headed canine guardian of the under-world in Greek mythology?

3. And what is the name of a similar guardian in the Harry Potter books?

4. Which author wrote about Know-Nothing Bozo, the Non-Wonder Dog?

5. Who wrote about a rabid St Bernard called Cujo?

6. Argos was a faithful hound in Greek mythology who waited an awful long time for his dad to come home. Who was his dad?

7. Which family own a Newfoundland called Nana?

8. In which classic novel of 1889 by Jerome K. Jerome does a dog called Montmorency go on a journey down the Thames?

9. Bulls-Eye was a dog belonging to Bill Sikes in which Charles Dickens' novel?

10. Who wrote the novel, later turned into a successful stage play, *The Curious Incident of the Dog in the Night-Time*?

Answers to Quiz 242

1. Barry Norman; he was replaced by Jonathan Ross, who presented the show until 2010, when Claudia Winkleman took over. From 2016 to 2018 the show used a variety of non-permanent presenters, and in December 2018 the show was cancelled after forty-six years.

2. This is the full name of Sacha Baron Cohen's character, Ali G.

3. Jools Holland and Paula Yates.

4. Michael McIntyre's.

5. Jonathan Ross'.

6. Michael Parkinson; Parky was often wheeled out as a celebrity cricket enthusiast and proved himself extremely knowledgeable, although he does suffer from 'Trueman's disease', whereby no current player could ever match up to those of the past, i.e. his own heyday.

7. Morecambe and Wise; their glory days were the BBC years from 1968 to 1977 – they never seemed such a natural fit with ITV when they moved across from 1978 until 1983.

8. *Pop Idol*; the first ground-breaking series launched the careers of both Will Young and Gareth Gates, who finished first and second respectively.

9. Lenny Henry.

10. *Big Brother*.

QUIZ 244. MOVIE MIX

Another movie round – once again, this is more for the avid movie watcher than the two-cinema-trips-a-year crowd. If you are a movie buff, go for eight out of ten; otherwise five out of ten is perfectly acceptable.

1. Roger Vadim's *Barbarella* (1967) was an erotic sci-fi romp which served as a vehicle for which American actress, Vadim's wife at the time?

2. What part was played by Rex Harrison in the 1963 epic *Cleopatra*, with Elizabeth Taylor as the eponymous Egyptian ruler?

3. *The Enforcer* (1976) and *Dead Pool* (1988) are both films starring which on-screen detective?

4. In *Harvey* (1950), a social comedy with James Stewart in the lead role, who or what was Harvey?

5. The 1953 film *Kiss Me Kate* is based on a musical which, in turn, is based on which play by William Shakespeare?

6. *The Color of Money* (Martin Scorsese, 1986), starring Paul Newman, was a sequel to which earlier Newman film, directed by Robert Rossen and released in 1961?

7. *Fletch* (1985) and *Fletch Lives* (1989) were essentially vehicles for which comic actor?

8. Who, as Wayne Szalinski, first shrunk his kids, then blew one up?

9. Who or what is Mikey (Bruce Willis) in the 1989 comedy *Look Who's Talking*?

10. If it was played by Charles Laughton in 1935, and Trevor Howard in 1962, who played the part in 1984?

Answers to Quiz 243

1. Tintin; there are twenty-three comic albums in the series, with another unfinished work that was completed and published after the death in 1983 of the character's creator, Hergé.

2. Cerberus.

3. Fluffy; he appears in *Harry Potter and the Philosopher's Stone*, guarding the trapdoor to the underground chamber.

4. Douglas Adams; he appears in the fourth volume of the *Hitchhikers' Guide to the Galaxy* series, *So Long, and Thanks for all the Fish*.

5. Stephen King.

6. Odysseus; the hound recognises the returning wanderer when even his wife has her suspicions.

7. The Darling family in *Peter Pan*.

8. *Three Men and a Dog*.

9. *Oliver Twist*.

10. Mark Haddon. The theatrical version was written by Simon Stephens and won numerous awards to go with the Whitbread Award for novel of the year that Haddon's book picked up in 2003. The title comes from a comment by Sherlock Holmes in the story, 'The Adventure of Silver Blaze'.

QUIZ 245. NAME THE YEAR

Another round of guessing the year. We are often surprised how far out some teams get with these questions. Generally, the scores are decent – averaging six or seven out of ten on a round – but occasionally there is a collective memory dysfunction. Once again, the figure in parentheses is the leeway you are given to get half a point.

1. Sir Stanley Matthews plays his last League game; Joan Rivers makes her TV debut; the first US ground troops land in Vietnam; *Highway 61 Revisited* is released; cigarette advertising is banned on British TV (two years).

2. Israel invades Lebanon after Hezbollah capture two soldiers; the Winter Olympics are held in Turin; Saddam Hussein is sentenced to death; Arsenal lose to Barcelona in the Champions League final (one year).

3. The Macintosh personal computer is launched by Apple; Tommy Cooper suffers a fatal heart attack live on TV; *Ghostbusters* and *Gremlins* are released on the same day in June; the original Band Aid Christmas single is released to overwhelming sales (one year).

4. The controversial Section 28 law is passed by the UK government; the Soviet Union begins withdrawal from Afghanistan; Ayrton Senna wins his first F1 Drivers' World Championship; Roy Orbison dies of a heart attack (one year).

5. Benedict XVI becomes the first Pope to resign since 1415; the Syrian government murders nearly 1,500 people with banned chemical weapons in a suburb of Damascus; Justin Rose becomes the first winner of the US Open since 1970; Daft Punk release their defining album *Random Access Memories* (one year).

6. Disney's *101 Dalmatians* is released; the US launches the ill-fated Bay of Pigs operation against Cuba; the UK makes its first application for membership of the EEC; Tottenham Hotspur win the Double of League Title and FA Cup (one year).

7. *Family Guy* debuts on Fox TV; *Shakespeare in Love* wins Best Film at the Academy Awards; Jill Dando is shot dead on her front doorstep; Napster launches; Vladimir Putin becomes acting President of Russia on New Year's Eve (one year).

8. Poland and nine other states join the EU; Chechen rebels take over a thousand people hostage in a school; deaths of Ronald Reagan, Marlon Brando and Brian Clough; seventeen-year-old Maria Sharapova shocks Serena Williams to win the Wimbledon Ladies Singles Final (one year).

9. Fourteen unarmed marchers killed in Ireland in the Bloody Sunday massacre; Uganda begins expelling 50,000 British Asians; Gene Cernan becomes the last man (thus far) to walk on the moon; the year begins with T. Rex's *Electric Warrior* atop the album charts and ends with Jimmy Osmond at No. 1 in the singles chart with 'Long Haired Lover from Liverpool' (two years).

10. Trygve Lie becomes the first Secretary-General of the UN; Italy votes to become a republic, not a monarchy; *It's A Wonderful Life* premieres in New York; Airborne is the last grey to win the Derby and goes on to complete a rare double by winning the St Leger (two years).

Answers to Quiz 244

1. Jane Fonda.

2. *Julius Caesar* (Richard Burton was Mark Antony).

3. Harry Callahan, or Dirty Harry, played in five films by Clint Eastwood. First came *Dirty Harry* (1971), then *Magnum Force* (1973). The fourth film in the series was *Sudden Impact* (1983), which Eastwood directed himself.

4. An invisible rabbit.

5. *The Taming of the Shrew*.

6. *The Hustler*. In the earlier film, Newman is Fast Eddie Felson, an up-and-comer on the pool scene; in *The Color of Money* he is the old lag, with Tom Cruise as the new kid on the block.

7. Chevy Chase.

8. Rick Moranis (in *Honey, I Shrunk the Kids* and *Honey, I Blew Up the Kid*).

9. A young baby whose voice is heard only by his babysitter James (John Travolta).

10. Anthony Hopkins – the part is Captain Bligh in various versions of *Mutiny on the Bounty* (the Hopkins film was entitled simply *The Bounty*).

QUIZ 246. PEOPLE AND PLACES

More geographical gems from the vaults. What vaults? Must stop writing such nonsense.

1. Which of the Great Lakes in North America claims the greatest surface area?

2. The tiny kingdom of Brunei lies within one of the land masses that make up which Asian country?

3. Aalborg, Bergen, Esbjerg, Odense: which of these is NOT in Denmark?

4. Syracuse and Palermo are cities found on which Mediterranean island?

5. Barcelona is the centre of which semi-autonomous region of eastern Spain?

6. The Galapagos Islands, famous as a location of Darwinian research, are currently administered by which South American country?

7. Ljubljana and Skopje are the capital cities of which two European countries, both formerly part of Yugoslavia?

8. The Ebro is the longest river in which European country?

9. Which Caribbean capital lies closest to the city of Miami at the southern tip of Florida?

10. Which archipelago lies between Orkney and the Faroe Islands?

Answers to Quiz 245

1. 1965.

2. 2006.

3. 1984.

4. 1985.

5. 2013.

6. 1961.

7. 1999.

8. 2004.

9. 1972.

10. 1946.

Instances of clubs winning the Double of League title and FA Cup in England

1888–9 Preston North End.

1896–7 Aston Villa.

1960–1 Tottenham Hotspur.

1970–1 Arsenal (and again in 1997–8 and 2001–2).

1985–6 Liverpool.

1993–4 Manchester United (and again in 1995–6 and their treble-winning year of 1998–9).

2009–10 Chelsea.

At the time of writing, Manchester City have won the League Cup for 2018–19 and are still in the FA Cup, the Champions League and the Premier League title race.

The feat of winning the Double is quite rare in most major European leagues, although Juventus have dominated a weak Italian domestic scene to the extent that they have won the Double in 2015, 2016, 2017 and 2018. Bayern Munich have won the Double eleven times, out of the fourteen times the feat has been accomplished in the Bundesliga era.

In Scotland, Rangers head Celtic 18–17 on Double-winning seasons, but Celtic are strong favourites to win the title in 2019 and are in the Scottish Cup semi-final, whereas Rangers are eliminated. The only other team to win the Double in Scotland was Aberdeen in 1983–4 when Alex Ferguson was their manager.

QUIZ 247. FOOD AND DRINK

1. Where the French would enjoy their hors-d'oeuvres, what would the Italians eat?

2. In Eastern Mediterranean cookery, dolmades are pockets of rice mixed with meat and/or vegetables and wrapped in what?

3. Hoisin sauce, a common ingredient in Asian cuisine, is made from (a) dried fish; (b) macadamia nuts; (c) soya bean; or (d) gingko bark?

4. A side dish of cucumber and yoghurt in Greek cuisine is known as tzatziki. By what name is a very similar dish often served as an accompaniment to curry known?

5. Shea butter, often used in cosmetics, is (a) a synthesised goat curd; (b) a tree sap; (c) emulsified corn oil; or (d) a nut fat from an African tree?

6. Cross a raspberry bush with a blackberry bush and what do you get?

7. Which spirit is the principal ingredient of a margarita cocktail?

8. Pernod (French) and Ouzo (Greek) share which principal flavouring?

9. White wines made in the Chablis region to the north of Burgundy are made from which white grape?

10. In 2015 it was announced that The Glenlivet had overtaken which other famous brand as the world's biggest-selling single malt whisky?

Answers to Quiz 246

1. Lake Superior.

2. Malaysia; it is on the island of Borneo, surrounded by the Malaysian portion of that island; the rest of the island is part of Indonesia.

3. Bergen is in Norway.

4. Sicily; Palermo, the capital, is on the north coast, while Syracuse is to the south-east of the island.

5. Catalunya (or Catalonia).

6. Ecuador – they are off the Ecuadorian coast in the Pacific, sitting almost on the Equator, whence Ecuador gets its name.

7. Ljubljana is the capital of Slovenia, and Skopje of the Socialist Republic of Macedonia.

8. Spain.

9. Nassau in the Bahamas.

10. Shetland or the Shetland Islands, comprising a large mainland and some fourteen other inhabited islands.

QUIZ 248. LYRICS

I'm terrible at these rounds; I just leave them to the other team members. You can ask me obscure stuff about band members and names, and which track was on what album, but I just cannot connect lyrics unless I hear the tune. These are all first lines of really well-known tunes, but very few teams will get ten out of ten.

1. 'There's a lady who's sure, all that glitters is gold.'

2. 'There's a fire starting in my heart.'

3. 'When the night has come and the land is dark, and the moon is the only light we'll see.'

4. 'I don't like your little games, don't like your tilted stage.'

5. 'It doesn't hurt me. Do you wanna feel how it feels?'

6. 'Feel it comin' in the air, and the screams from everywhere.'

7. 'When we first came here, we were cold and we were clear.'

8. 'Confidence is a preference for the habitual voyeur.'

9. 'She was more like a beauty queen from a movie scene.'

10. 'I'll sing it one more time for you, then we really have to go.'

Answers to Quiz 247

1. Antipasti.

2. Vine leaves.

3. (c) It is a soya bean derivative, with chilli, vinegar, garlic and often sugar added.

4. Raita.

5. (d) It is the oil from the nuts of the African Shea tree.

6. Loganberries.

7. Tequila.

8. Aniseed; absinthe and sambuca, and the French spirit pastis, all have anise as the predominant flavour.

9. Chardonnay. Most fine Chablis wines are not as heavily oaked as most white Burgundies, often not at all.

10. Glenfiddich. By 2018, Glenfiddich had resumed its place at the top of the list.

Classic margarita

Chill the glass in the fridge, then run a lime wedge around the edge before dipping the rim in salt.

Mix one part of Tequila with half a part of Cointreau and half a part of lime juice in a shaker with lots of ice.

Strain into a glass and garnish with a wedge of lime on the rim of the glass.

(If you are using cheap Tequila, maybe add half a part of sugar syrup.)

QUIZ 249. STUFF

All sorts of stuff, about different things, in no particular order.

1. What does one traditionally receive for finishing last in a tournament or competition, or, indeed, a quiz?

2. Which small marine creatures make up the genus hippocampus?

3. Which long-haired small dog was bred as a sentinel or alarm dog in the monasteries of Tibet?

4. Which position is currently held by Mark Carney?

5. Who was the enlightened chief mistress to French King Louis XV from 1745, who also served as a trusted adviser and a valued lady of the court?

6. What is Article 50?

7. Which common phrase is derived from the turning area of a Navy punishment whip?

8. What was Arlene Foster's political role in the UK Parliament during all the Brexit votes and negotiations?

9. In 1987, which American singer became the first female artist to be inducted into the Rock and Roll Hall of Fame?

10. The okapi, discovered by Europeans for the first time around 1900 in Africa, is a relative of which more familiar animal?

Answers to Quiz 248

1. 'Stairway to Heaven' (Led Zeppelin, from *Led Zeppelin IV*, 1971).

2. 'Rolling in the Deep' (Adele, 2010, from *21*).

3. 'Stand By Me' (Ben E. King, 1961, written with Leiber and Stoller).

4. 'Look What You Made Me Do' (Taylor Swift); it was the lead single from her 2017 album, *Reputation*.

5. 'Running Up That Hill' (Kate Bush) was from her 1985 masterpiece *Hounds of Love*.

6. 'Run This Town' (Jay-Z with Rihanna and Kanye West, 2009, from *Blueprint 3*).

7. 'Spectrum' was a single from Florence + the Machine's second album, *Ceremonials*, released in 2011.

8. 'Parklife' is the title track from Blur's 1994 album.

9. 'Billie Jean' (Michael Jackson), was a single from his mega seller, *Thriller* (1982).

10. 'Run' is from Snow Patrol's 2003 album, *The Last Straw*, and was also a hit for Leona Lewis, the 2006 *X Factor* winner.

QUIZ 250. SHAKESPEARE QUOTES

No apologies for another round on Shakespeare; he's the best. This quiz is all about quotes from Shakespeare's plays, and words and expressions that have entered the language via his work.

1. 'Devil incarnate'; 'Wild goose chase'; 'When hell freezes over'; 'Foregone conclusion'. Which of these phrases did not enter the language via Shakespeare's work?

2. What, according to Iago in *Othello*, is 'the green-eyed monster'?

3. In which Shakespeare play does the word flibbertigibbet first appear?

4. 'Knock knock, who's there . . .?' We all know the old kids' jokes, but in which Shakespeare tragedy does this line appear in a rare comic moment?

5. The phrase 'the game is afoot' was first used in *Henry IV Part 1*. Which other famous literary character is known for using this phrase?

6. Who took the phrase 'brave new world' from Shakespeare's *The Tempest* and used it as the title of a 1932 novel?

7. In which of Shakespeare's Roman plays does a major character say; 'Cry havoc! And let slip the dogs of war'?

8. 'Neither a borrower nor a lender be.' In which Shakespeare play does an old bore called Polonius give this advice to his son?

9. 'But soft, what light through yonder window breaks? It is the east, and . . . is the sun'? Who is getting all lyrical about whom?

10. 'Break the ice', 'kill with kindness' and 'cold comfort' are all phrases that first appeared in which Shakespeare play, unpopular now for its blatant misogyny?

Answers to Quiz 249

1. A wooden spoon; or at The Stag, a mug to remind you how dismal was your failure. I believe they can be found on eBay for 40p.

2. Sea horses.

3. Lhasa Apso.

4. Governor of the Bank of England; Carney, a Canadian with British and Irish citizenship, was appointed in 2013 in succession to Mervyn King.

5. Madame de Pompadour.

6. The clause in the EU constitution that allows any member state to leave.

7. 'No room to swing a cat', the cat not being a cat but a cat o' nine tails, or flail.

8. Foster is the leader of the DUP, whose support for the Conservative government gave them a working majority in Parliament, but not for most of the votes on Theresa May's Brexit deal.

9. Aretha Franklin.

10. The giraffe.

QUIZ 251. DAN

Another name round. Dan, Danny, Daniel and all things Danworthy. This wasn't a name we had any personal acquaintance with until we met the chap who runs the café opposite our house – a splendid fellow in every way. We dedicate this round to 'Uncle Black Pudding', as he is known to Martha, and to the lovely Lisa.

1. Journalist, radio-show host, comedian and football pundit Danny Baker is an avid supporter of which football team?

2. Barry George was tried and convicted of whose murder in 2001, prior to being acquitted in 2008?

3. What is the name of Kylie Minogue's sister? (Must be spelt correctly to get full point.)

4. Which Liberal Democrat MP was Chief Secretary to the Treasury in David Cameron's coalition government between 2010 and 2015?

5. What is Desperate Dan's favourite food?

6. In Dante's *Divina Comedia*, how many circles of the Inferno, or hell, are depicted?

7. 'Daniel is leaving tonight on a plane . . .': who wrote these words?

8. Scottish sailor Alexander Selkirk is believed to have been the main inspiration for which literary character, created by Daniel Defoe in 1719?

9. Which seventy-year-old American romantic novelist is the biggest-selling author in history to still be living (as of 1 January 2019)?

10. Who made his name as the Cat in the sci-fi sitcom *Red Dwarf*?

Answers to Quiz 250

1. 'When hell freezes over' is not from Shakespeare; the phrase has no certain origin but dates from the early twentieth century, and was also the name of an Eagles tour and live album.

2. Jealousy; Iago plays on Othello's jealousy until he strangles his own wife, believing false reports of her infidelity.

3. *King Lear*; Edgar, masquerading as Mad Tom, refers to the 'foul fiend, Flibbertigibbet'.

4. *Macbeth*.

5. Sherlock Holmes.

6. Aldous Huxley.

7. *Julius Caesar*; the lines are spoken over Caesar's body by Mark Antony, announcing his intention to incite the mob to take revenge on Caesar's killers.

8. *Hamlet*; Polonius advises Laertes thus in a scene intended to illustrate what an interfering bore he is.

9. Romeo about Juliet, when he sees her on her balcony.

10. *The Taming of the Shrew*. Attempts have been made to stage the play in a better light, but there is no escaping the misogyny. Other representations of women by Shakespeare gainsay this view, so maybe it was a temporary disillusionment with women on the playwright's part.

QUIZ 252. THE APPLIANCE OF SCIENCE

Here we are again, in over our heads. You?

1. Geodesy is the science of measuring what?

2. Christiaan Barnard was the first man to perform what in 1967?

3. What would you measure in kilograms per cubic metre?

4. What did Wilhelm Roentgen discover in 1895?

5. Wilder Penfield's contribution to medicine was as (a) a gynaecologist; (b) an anaesthetist; (c) a patron of hospital building; or (d) a brain surgeon?

6. Who is credited with solving quadratic equations for the first time? Was it (a) the Greek scholar Euclid; (b) the Alexandrine Diophantus; (c) the Indian Brahmagupta; or (d) the Frenchman Pierre de Fermat?

7. John Harrison made the first device for measuring longitude at sea. What was Harrison's profession?

8. Condors are classified among which genus of bird?

9. What is the name of the University of California's famous observatory situated on Mount Hamilton to the east of San Jose?

10. What feature is unique to four species of echidna (spiny anteater) and the platypus?

Answers to Quiz 251

1. Millwall.

2. Jill Dando; the media frenzy around this case made impartiality difficult.

3. Dannii Minogue.

4. Danny Alexander.

5. Cow pie; Desperate Dan appeared in the first edition of the *Dandy* comic in 1937 – he was their showpiece character until the comic stopped publication in 2012.

6. Nine.

7. Bernie Taupin, Elton John's lyricist, in the 1973 song, 'Daniel', from *Don't Shoot Me, I'm Only the Piano Player*.

8. Robinson Crusoe.

9. Danielle Steel.

10. Danny John-Jules.

QUIZ 253. ACRONYMS

This quiz is about abbreviations, so should suit those who enjoy the modern vogue for writing nothing out in full. CGAF? Then move swiftly on . . .

1. The CBI is an industrial think-tank – for what does it stand?

2. If you are in correspondence with UCAS, what are you probably trying to do?

3. Most people are familiar with the tech company IBM, but for what does IBM stand?

4. In the world of transport, what is the LNER?

5. What abbreviation would traditionally be used to indicate that a reader of a manuscript should continue reading rather than stop at the end of a page?

6. If you are a member of RIBA, what is your profession?

7. TSB, now part of Lloyds TSB, is short for what?

8. If an IT lady offers to sort out your SEO's, what does she mean?

9. For what does BDE stand, a twitter meme coined by Tyrell Grant?

10. If you get a text or see a tweet with IMHO on it, what is the person at the other end letting you know?

Answers to Quiz 252

1. The shape and gravity of the earth.

2. A heart transplant.

3. Density.

4. X-rays; Roentgen was a German engineer and scientist who stumbled upon the discovery that electromagnetic waves leave an imprint when passed through a vacuum. His work earned him the first Nobel Prize in Physics.

5. (d) A brain surgeon – he devised much more accurate maps of the brain in the 1930s and 40s.

6. Brahmagupta.

7. A clockmaker.

8. Vultures.

9. The Lick Observatory, home of the Shane telescope.

10. They are the only mammals that lay eggs.

QUIZ 254. NOVEMBER 23

Well, what else do you use for a theme on a quiet Monday in November? This is all about stuff that happened on 23 November, or about people who were born or died on that day.

1. Where did a famous trial commence on this day in 1945?

2. Which piece of ground-breaking software was launched on this day in 1985?

3. Who did Lieutenant Philip Mountbatten marry on this day in 1947?

4. Protests in which city on this day, in 1989, led to a peaceful transition away from communism that came to be known as the Velvet Revolution?

5. The opera *Fidelio* was performed for the first time on this day in 1805. Who was the composer of this, his only foray into opera?

6. Native American protesters occupied the site of which high-profile American prison on this day in 1969?

7. Which historic English building suffered 50 million pounds' worth of damage on this day in 1992?

8. Which Egyptian became the first Arab leader to meet with the Israelis when he met prime minister Menachem Begin on this day in 1977?

9. Which great Russian novelist died in 1910, aged eighty-two?

10. Which perfect 10 was born on this day in 1956?

Answers to Quiz 253

1. Confederation of British Industry.

2. Get into university – UCAS is the Universities and Colleges Admissions Service.

3. International Business Machines; the corporation was founded in New York in 1911 and adopted its current name in 1924.

4. London North Eastern Railway.

5. PTO – please turn over.

6. Architect.

7. Trustee Savings Bank; a trustee bank traditionally wasn't run by a commercial board and quoted on the Stock Exchange, nor was it run as a mutual, like most of the old building societies. Instead, a group of trustees would oversee the customers' investments and act as guarantors.

8. Search Engine Optimisation.

9. Big Dick Energy – a modern equivalent of chutzpah.

10. That the content is In My Humble Opinion.

QUIZ 255. ONLY CONNECT

Answer the first nine questions and see if you can spot the connection between them. If you get the connection early and know the subject, it may help you with one or two of the trickier questions.

1. Which mythological creature has the upper body of a human and the lower body and legs of a horse?

2. Who rescued the chained Andromeda from Poseidon's sea serpent?

3. Which navigational instrument was alluded to by Isaac Newton and developed in the 1730s by John Hadley and Thomas Godfrey?

4. Which creature's unique characteristic is assisted by a lattice of guanine nanocrystals forming a layer over their skin?

5. Whose fifth album, *The Raven*, was released in 1979, featuring the singles 'Nuclear Device' and 'Duchess'?

6. Who, according to mythology, killed the Lernaean Hydra?

7. 'Aquarius' is a song from which hippie musical, launched off Broadway in 1967?

8. Which modern English word derives from *fornax*, the Latin for oven?

9. *Mons Mensae*, to give it a Latin name, overlooks which coastal city?

10. What's the connection?

Answers to Quiz 254

1. Nuremberg; the main Nuremberg Trial of the twenty-four most prominent surviving Nazi leaders started in 1945 and ended on 1 October 1946 (see below).

2. Microsoft Windows.

3. Princess Elizabeth (later Queen Elizabeth II).

4. Prague, in Czechoslovakia.

5. Beethoven. He wrote the opera in 1805, roughly the middle of his prolific career.

6. Alcatraz.

7. Windsor Castle.

8. Anwar Sadat.

9. Leo Tolstoy.

10. Bo Derek, star of the film 10, co-starring Dudley Moore and Julie Andrews and directed by Andrews' husband, Blake Edwards.

Nuremberg trials

Of the twenty-four tried, twelve were sentenced to death: Martin Bormann was missing, and was later discovered to have been already deceased, while Hermann Göring managed to commit suicide on the eve of his execution. On 16 October 1946, the following ten were hanged for war crimes and crimes against humanity:

Hans Frank (politician), Wilhelm Frick (politician), Alfred Jodl (military), Ernst Kaltenbrunner (military, SS), Wilhelm Keitel (military), Joachim von Ribbentrop (politician), Alfred Rosenberg (ideologist and politician), Fritz Sauchel (politician), Arthur Seyss-Inquart (politician), Julius Streicher (politician).

Robert Ley was already dead; he committed suicide a few days into the trial, so it could not proceed. One other defendant, Gustav Krupp, was arraigned in error, as he was paralysed and had relinquished control of his munitions factory to his son, Alfried.

Ten others were indicted and tried. Three were acquitted: Hans Fritzsche (propagandist); Franz von Papen, he was later retried and sentenced to hard labour, then re-acquitted; Hjalmar Schacht (financier) – Schacht was a controversial choice for the twenty-four, given that he finished the war in a concentration camp himself.

The other seven were given prison sentences of varying length: Karl Donitz (military), Walther Funk (politician), Rudolf Hess (politician), Baron von Neurath (politician), Erich Raecher (military), Baldur von Schirach (propagandist), Albert Speer (financier).

QUIZ 256. SPORT MIX

On sport. Mixed. One or two are quite tricksy. Aim for six or seven out of ten.

1. What role in tennis history did Carlos Ramos play in 2018?

2. The Epsom Derby, the Cheltenham Gold Cup, the St Leger, the 2,000 Guineas: which of these is NOT one of the five horse-racing classics?

3. Who was the only Liverpool player in England's 1966 World Cup-winning team?

4. After a fight against depression, Tyson Fury made his heavyweight comeback in December 2018. Who did he fight, failing to regain the title after a contentious split decision made the fight a draw?

5. Which team have won the Major League Soccer Cup (confusingly for English football fans, it isn't a Cup, it's a league with a post-season play-off) most times (five) since the competition's inception in 1993 (up to 2018)?

6. What did Robert Parish do 1,611 times, a lot more than anyone else?

7. Who captained the winning South African team at the 1995 Rugby Union World Cup, and who presented him with the trophy?

8. In Test Cricket, who is the only batsman with over ten thousand runs to have also taken over two hundred and fifty wickets?

9. Conversely, who is the only bowler with over four hundred wickets to have also scored over five thousand runs? (Ian Botham didn't quite make it to four hundred wickets . . .).

10. Which Swedish golfer recorded the best-ever return against par (-20) in a major tournament when he won the 2016 Open Championship?

Answers to Quiz 255

1. CENTAUR.

2. Perseus; CASSIOPEIA, wife of King Cepheus of Ethiope, boasts that her daughter Andromeda is more beautiful than the Nereids, the servants of the sea god, Poseidon; the god sends a monster to claim penance and Andromeda is chained to a rock as a sacrifice. Perseus flies in on the winged horse, Pegasus, and rescues the maiden. A famous painting by Lord Leighton depicts this – the Ethiopian Princess is a naked white woman. See if you can spot the flaw!!

3. SEXTANT; the instrument was used to calculate the angle between the horizon and a celestial object, thus allowing the user to determine distances at sea.

4. CHAMELEON.

5. The Stranglers; (RAVEN).

6. Herakles; it was the second of his Labours for the cowardly King Eurystheus (HYDRA/SERPENT).

7. *Hair*; (AQUARIUS).

8. FURNACE.

9. Cape Town; Mons MENSAE is Table Mountain.

10. All the questions or answers reference a constellation.

QUIZ 257. ZODIAC

If you keep the Chinese Zodiac in mind, that may give you a head start here. All the questions or answers reference one of the twelve signs.

1. The theft of which animal is at the centre of the 1984 comedy film, *A Private Function*, starring Michael Palin and Maggie Smith?

2. Who had a UK No. 1 single in 1979 with a song about a school shooting in San Diego?

3. In which mythology does the Midgard Serpent surround the earth and lie with its own tail in its mouth?

4. What did Tiger Roll win in April 2018?

5. Which of the Weasley children went to work as a Dragon Keeper in Romania after leaving Hogwarts?

6. 'Little Red Rooster' (1964) was the second UK No. 1 single for which durable band?

7. Which Greek god has the horns and lower body of a goat?

8. The mustang, an iconic breed of horse found mainly in the American West, was first brought to North America by which settlers?

9. Her performance in *Atonement* earned Saoirse Ronan an Academy Award nomination as a teenager. Which two later films earned her Best Actress nominations in 2016 and 2018?

10. Who mounted a challenge to Jeremy Corbyn's leadership of the Labour Party in 2016, but lost heavily in the subsequent vote?

Answers to Quiz 256

1. He was the umpire with whom Serena Williams had a heated row during the US Open Final, when she was beaten by Naomi Osaka. Neither the umpire nor Serena came out of the contretemps well.

2. The Gold Cup at Cheltenham is a jumping event under National Hunt rules – the classics are all flat races. The 1,000 and 2,000 Guineas are run over two days in May at Newmarket; the Oaks and the Derby are run at Epsom in June, and the St Leger takes place in September at Doncaster. The 1,000 Guineas and the Oaks are for three-year-old fillies only, the 2,000 Guineas and Derby are for colts of the same age, while any three-year-old thoroughbred can run in the St Leger.

3. Roger Hunt.

4. Deontay Wilder.

5. LA Galaxy.

6. Play basketball in an NBA match.

7. Francois Pienaar; Nelson Mandela.

8. Jacques Kallis.

9. Kapil Dev.

10. Henrik Stenson.

QUIZ 258. FILM SHOW

Another selection of film questions, with a few more up-to-date ones. There is more than a nod to the Academy Awards in this round; it was part of our Oscar's Night quiz.

1. Alastair Sim memorably dragged up to play the headmistress of St Trinian's School in the series of films about that peculiar establishment. Who did the same in the 2007 reboot?

2. When *Chicago* won the 2003 Academy Award for Best Film, it was the first musical to win the award for thirty-five years. What was the 1968 winner?

3. Adaptations of which Thomas Hardy novel were made with Julie Christie in 1967 and Carey Mulligan in 2015?

4. Who played the psychotic JD in the blacker-than-black 1989 comedy *Heathers*? Was it Matthew Broderick, Jeff Goldblum, Mickey Rourke or Christian Slater?

5. Who played the poet Geoffrey Chaucer in the entertaining medieval fantasy *A Knight's Tale* (2001)?

6. Who was nominated for an Academy Award as Best Supporting Actress in 1986 for her debut film role in Spielberg's *The Color Purple*?

7. Who is the only actor to win the Academy Award for Best Actor two years running?

8. What was Kathryn Bigelow's award-winning 2008 drama about a team of bomb disposal experts working in Iraq?

9. Who has a cameo role in *Mamma Mia!* (2008) as a piano player in the 'Dancing Queen' sequence? Is it Benny Andersson, Jamie Cullum, Jools Holland or Elton John?

10. Which rock star played Australian bushwhacker Ned Kelly in a 1970 film directed by Tony Richardson?

Answers to Quiz 257

1. A pig.

2. The Boomtown Rats ('I Don't Like Mondays'); it was the band's second UK No. 1, after 'Rat Trap' the previous year. The Boomtown Rats were fronted by Bob Geldof, who would later be instrumental in Live Aid.

3. Norse.

4. The Grand National.

5. Charlie.

6. The Rolling Stones; The Stones had eight No. 1s, all in the 1960s: 'It's All Over Now', 'Little Red Rooster' (1964); 'The Last Time', '(I Can't Get No) Satisfaction', 'Get Off of My Cloud' (1965); 'Paint It Black' (1966); 'Jumpin' Jack Flash' (1968); 'Honky Tonk Women' (1969).

7. Pan.

8. Spanish.

9. *Brooklyn*, in which she played a young Irish girl moving to New York to find work and happiness, and *Lady Bird*, Greta Gerwig's film about a young woman reaching adulthood and trying to resolve a troubled relationship with her mother.

10. Owen Smith.

QUIZ 259. PAIRS

There are ten questions here. Each of questions 1 to 5 is linked to one of questions 6 to 10, either through the clue or through the answer. It might help . . . Otherwise, just treat this as general knowledge and see how you get on.

1. Who was Thelma to Susan Sarandon's Louise?

2. Which Italian club wore black armbands in memory of Ray Wilkins, the England footballer who died in 2018?

3. Orville Burrell, trade name Shaggy, had four UK No. 1 hits. What was the first: a cover of a Folkes Brothers' song that topped the chart in 1993?

4. Who starred as a Fire Chief in *Roxanne*, a 1987 modern remake of Edmond de Rostand's play *Cyrano de Bergerac*?

5. Who won a gold medal in the Heptathlon at the 2000 Sydney Olympics?

6. Which third love won the 1997 PGA Championship and captained the US Ryder Cup teams of 2012 and 2016?

7. Who is Norville Rogers?

8.9. Bodie and Doyle.

10. What is the first name of Mr Micawber in Dickens' *Old Curiosity Shop*?

Answers to Quiz 258

1. Rupert Everett.

2. *Oliver!*, directed by Carol Reed. Only a handful of musicals were even nominated in the intervening years: *Hello Dolly, Fiddler on the Roof, Cabaret* (unlucky enough to be released in the same year as *The Godfather*) and *All That Jazz*. The musical all but disappeared as a milieu for serious film-makers in the 1980s and 1990s, with Disney's *Beauty and the Beast* (1991) the closest thing nominated. The comeback began in 2002 with Baz Luhrmann's *Moulin Rouge!* before Rob Marshall's *Chicago* picked up the big one the following year.

3. *Far from the Madding Crowd* – both played Bathsheba Everdene, the central character.

4. Christian Slater. Haven't seen it? Missed a treat.

5. Paul Bethany, who meets the hero, played by Heath Ledger, on his journey to a tournament and joins his small band of followers.

6. Oprah Winfrey.

7. Tom Hanks for *Philadelphia* and *Forrest Gump* in 1993 and 1994.

8. *The Hurt Locker*.

9. Benny Andersson; it wasn't a trick question – he also wrote additional music for the film to supplement the Abba songs.

10. Mick Jagger.

QUIZ 260. MUSIC MIX

Another mixed round, this time all music questions.

1. Which UK band released their seventh album, *In Rainbows*, in 2007 as a download that allowed consumers to pay the price they thought appropriate?

2. Which DJ's voice was the first to be heard on Radio 1?

3. James Blunt; Chris Martin; Shakira; Kanye West. Who is the elder statesperson?

4. Who was country music's Man in Black? What was the 2005 film about his life?

5. Who formed Foo Fighters in 1994? With which band was he previously the drummer?

6. Which five great artists formed the supergroup The Travelling Wilburys in 1988?

7. If Roger Taylor and John Deacon are the rhythm section, who were the other two members of the original band?

8. How did Lady Gaga and Bradley Cooper hit the top of the UK singles chart in 2018?

9. Nick Cave and the Bad Seeds released their first album in 1984. What was Cave's band prior to forming the Bad Seeds?

10. Which two female artists have won two Grammy Awards since 2000 for their own albums (as performing artists, not as producers or song-writers); the only two women to do so since the awards began?

Answers to Quiz 259

1. Geena Davis.

2. AC Milan – Wilkins had three seasons in Milan after five at Manchester United. Many (including me) would argue he played his best football as a youngster at Chelsea.

3. 'Oh Carolina'. 'Boombastic', 'It Wasn't Me' and 'Angel' were the other three chart-toppers.

4. Steve Martin, opposite Darryl Hannah – it was a good film, but, better still, check out Gerard Depardieu in a straight version of De Rostand's work.

5. Denise Lewis. Team GB won eleven gold medals in Sydney and twenty-eight overall – it may not seem a lot by recent heady standards, but after a miserable showing at Atlanta in 1996 (one gold, fifteen medals) it was comforting for British sports fans.

6. Davis Love III.

7. Shaggy from *Scooby-Doo*.

8. Lewis Collins and 9. Martin Shaw – they were the actors who played Bodie and Doyle in *The Professionals*, with Gordon Jackson as their handler.

10. Wilkins Micawber.

Question 1 pairs with 6 (Davis); 2 with 10 (Wilkins); 3 with 7 (Shaggy); 4 with 9 (Martin) and 5 with 8 (Lewis).

QUIZ 261. THE SEA, THE SEA

All things seaside. It seemed an appropriate round to include during the week we had a Hastings quiz, it being a seaside town 'n' all.

1. The title of this round was also the title of a 1978 Booker Prize-winning novel by which author, one of the leading twentieth-century British writers?

2. Portland Bill and its famous lighthouse lie on a promontory to the south of which Dorset coastal town?

3. What is the name of the nearby beach that lent its name to a 2007 novella by Ian McEwan?

4. Used as the Blackpool Tower theme by the resident organist for four decades, which song was written in 1907 by John Glover-Kind and recorded two years later by Mark Sheridan?

5. Seaweed is a multicellular form of what kind of botanical life?

6. Which culinary marine creatures with collectable shells form the taxonomic family Pectinidae?

7. Which 2000 film by Danny Boyle starring Leonardo DiCaprio was based on a novel by Alex Garland?

8. If Torquay lies at the north end of Tor Bay, and Paignton sits in the centre, which small harbour town lies at the southern end?

9. Cromer, Sheringham and Blakeney are small towns on the north coast of which county?

10. Vodka with cranberry juice and grapefruit juice is a cocktail known by which name?

Answers to Quiz 260

1. Radiohead.

2. Tony Blackburn.

3. James Blunt was born in 1974 – the others were all born in 1977.

4. Johnny Cash; *I Walk the Line*.

5. Dave Grohl, Nirvana.

6. Bob Dylan, George Harrison, Jeff Lynne, Roy Orbison, Tom Petty. They posed as a band of Wilbury Brothers and adopted the names Lucky, Nelson, Otis, Lefty and Charlie T. respectively on their debut album *Travelling Wilburys Vol. 1*. After Orbison's death the following year, they released another album, perversely entitled *Vol. 3*, using the names Clayton (Lynne), Spike (Harrison), Boo (Dylan) and Muddy (Petty).

7. Brian May and Freddie Mercury – the band is Queen.

8. They starred together in *A Star is Born* and the single from the soundtrack, 'Shallow', topped the charts, as did the soundtrack album.

9. The Birthday Party.

10. Taylor Swift and Adele.

QUIZ 262. SCIENCE

Another mix of science, some physics and chemistry, some medicine and natural history.

1. In Greek medicine, black bile, yellow bile, phlegm and blood were collectively known as what?

2. Tungsten, hydrogen and astatine: what?

3. Henry, hour, kelvin, litre, lux, mole, newton, pascal, tesla, volt. Eight of these are official SI scientific units – which two are not?

4. In the early 1940s, the American scientists Florey and Chain synthesised what medical product, researched previously by Alexander Fleming?

5. Chinese scientist Tu Youyou synthesised artemisinin from sweet wormwood, thereby achieving a major breakthrough in the treatment of which global disease?

6. Which Greek scholar wrote the definitive early mathematical work, *Elements*?

7. The electric lightbulb and the phonograph were both patented inventions by which American innovator?

8. Kiwis, emus and rheas make up part of the group of ratite birds, all flightless, along with which other family, comprising two species, common or Somali?

9. Roughly how many species of spider are native to the UK? Is it 140, 340, 650 or 1,650?

10. Beavers, guinea pigs, hedgehogs, squirrels: which of these mammals is NOT a rodent?

Answers to Quiz 261

1. Iris Murdoch.
2. Weymouth.
3. Chesil beach.
4. 'I Do Like to Be Beside the Seaside'.
5. Algae.
6. Scallops.
7. *The Beach*.
8. Brixham.
9. Norfolk.
10. Sea Breeze.

The *Rough Guide* website lists the top seaside resorts in the UK, and the friendly shabby-chic of Hastings earned the town seventh place. Here are the Top 20:

Tynemouth, Tyne and Wear.
Southwold, Suffolk.
Porthmadog, Snowdonia.
Whitstable, Kent.
Aberystwyth, mid-Wales.
Shanklin, Isle of Wight.
Hastings, East Sussex.
Pittenweem, Fife.
Crosby, Merseyside.
Gardenstown, Aberdeenshire.
Tenby, South Wales.
Lochiver, West Highlands.
Folkestone, Kent.
New Brighton, Merseyside.
Bournemouth, Dorset.
Margate, Kent.
Portmeirion, Snowdonia.
Filey, North Yorkshire.
St. Ives, Cornwall.

QUIZ 263. NUMBERS

Here we go on a trek through the numbers to get to the magic fifty-five points. You probably won't reach that, but forty is still a really good effort on these rounds.

1. Which country produces the most bananas?

2. Which two Southern states border the most other states in the US, eight apiece, including each other, Kentucky and Arkansas?

3. If H denotes Huron in the mnemonic HOMES, and S stands for Superior, what are O, M and E?

4. Which four US presidents have been assassinated while in office?

5. Which five African countries have a Mediterranean coastline?

6. According to 2018 stats, what are the world's six biggest car manufacturers?

7. What are the seven deadly sins?

8. New York and Los Angeles are comfortably the two most populous cities in the US. What are the next eight on the list, which includes three Texan cities?

9. What are the nine albums released by Radiohead, either in hard format or digital download, up to 2016?

10. Name the ten clubs to have won the top flight of English football on four or more occasions.

Answers to Quiz 262

1. Humours; they were the core of human activity, according to early Greek medicine. The blood, produced by the liver, was the source of energy and social behaviour. Yellow bile was the source of aggression and anger, black bile of melancholy and depression, and phlegm of weakness and apathy.

2. 'What' is both a clue and the answer; the chemical symbols for these three elements (Tungsten = W, Hydrogen = H, Astatine = At) spell WHAT.

3. Hour and litre.

4. Penicillin.

5. Malaria; the discovery led to the use of artemisinin to treat malaria sufferers in developing countries, saving untold numbers of lives. Tu Youyou was awarded the Nobel Prize for Medicine in 2015.

6. Euclid.

7. Thomas Edison.

8. Ostriches.

9. There are 650. And Nicole is scared of all of them.

10. Hedgehogs are not rodents (although porcupines are).

QUIZ 264. AUSTRALIA

Many of us have relatives who live or have lived in Australia, and our two countries retain strong cultural and familial ties. But how much do we know about Australia?

1. Who is the current Head of State of Australia?

2. Who was the poster girl for Australian athletics who won the 400 metres at the Sydney Olympics in 2000?

3. What percentage of the population of Australia live in Sydney and its surrounds? Is it 8 per cent, 12 per cent, 20 per cent or 32 per cent ?

4. Brisbane is the principal city and capital of which Australian state?

5. What is the flight time between Sydney on the east coast of Australia and Perth on the West coast?

6. Geelong, Toowoomba, Larimba, Wollongong: which of these is not a town or suburb in Australia?

7. Which major piece of architecture was designed by Danish architect Jørn Utzon and officially opened in 1973?

8. Terence Stamp walking down the main street of a rough Australian mining town in full drag: what's the movie?

9. In which year did the six separate colonies in Australia join together to form the Commonwealth of Australia? Was it 1847, 1886, 1901 or 1920?

10. Who did Australia beat in the final of the 2015 Cricket World Cup?

Answers to Quiz 263

1. India.

2. Tennessee and Missouri.

3. Ontario, Michigan and Erie – they are the Great Lakes.

4. Abraham Lincoln, William McKinley, James Garfield, John F. Kennedy.

5. Morocco, Algeria, Tunisia, Libya, Egypt.

6. Toyota, Volkswagen, AG-Daimler (accept Mercedes), General Motors, Ford, Honda.

7. Lust, gluttony, greed, sloth, wrath, envy, pride.

8. Chicago, Houston, Philadelphia, Phoenix, San Antonio, San Diego, Dallas, San Jose.

9. *Pablo Honey, The Bends, OK Computer, Kid A, Amnesiac, Hail to the Thief, In Rainbows, The King of Limbs, A Moon Shaped Pool.*

10. Manchester United, Liverpool, Arsenal, Everton, Aston Villa, Sunderland, Chelsea, Manchester City, Newcastle United, Sheffield Wednesday.

QUIZ 265. THIS OR THAT

Here we go again. This time you have to choose whether the word given is an Italian wine grape, a type of pasta or a character from Mozart's *The Magic Flute*.

1. Barbera.

2. Farfalle.

3. Sarastro.

4. Grillo.

5. Nebbiolo.

6. Papageno.

7. Tamino.

8. Capellini.

9. Orecchiette.

10. Sangiovese.

11. Monostasos.

12. Pappardelle.

Answers to Quiz 264

1. Her Majesty, the Queen; the last public vote on the Australian constitution was in 1999, when 55 per cent voted in favour of retaining the current system rather than Australia becoming a full republic. It's largely a titular concern, as Australia has full and total control over its own affairs.

2. Kathy Freeman.

3. Twenty per cent – Sydney accounts for just over 5 million of Australia's 25-plus million inhabitants.

4. Queensland.

5. Five hours.

6. Geelong is in Victoria, fifty miles south of Melbourne; Wollongong is fifty miles down the coast from Sydney in New South Wales; Toowoomba is in Queensland, eighty miles west of Brisbane. We made Larimba up.

7. Sydney Harbour Bridge.

8. *Priscilla, Queen of the Desert*.

9. 1901.

10. New Zealand.

QUIZ 266. THE HORROR!

This was a Hallowe'en quiz, surprise, surprise. It is actually a books round, being about literary horror and best-sellers.

1. In which year was Bram Stoker's *Dracula* first published? Was it 1846, 1875, 1897 or 1910?

2. 'The horror! The horror!' is a famous line towards the end of which book by Joseph Conrad?

3. *Interview with the Vampire* (1976) is the first of a series of erotic vampire novels by which author?

4. *The Vampire Lovers* (1970) was the first in Hammer Horror's Karnstein trilogy and is loosely based on the novel by which Victorian master of gothic suspense fiction? Was it (a) J. Sheridan Le Fanu; (b) M.R. James; (c) Wilkie Collins; or (d) Anne Radcliffe?

5. What was Stephen King's first published novel in 1974, when he was aged twenty-six? It was turned into a celebrated movie two years later, which cemented his reputation.

6. Which series of scary stories by R.L. Stine sold over 350 million copies when they were published between 1992 and 1997?

7. Richard Bachman is a pen name used for seven novels by which high-profile horror writer?

8. In the 2011 National Theatre adaptation of *Frankenstein* by Nick Dear, which two actors interchanged the roles of Dr Frankenstein and the monster?

9. Who directed the 1987 film *Hellraiser*, as well as writing the screenplay from his own short novel *The Hellbound Heart*?

10. Which iconic horror movie was based on a 1971 novel by William Peter Blatty?

Answers to Quiz 265

1. Barbera is a red wine grape from Piedmont in northern Italy.

2. Farfalle is butterfly-shaped pasta.

3. Sarastro is the bad guy in *The Magic Flute* – it is a bass part; the bad guys are often bass parts.

4. Grillo is a Sicilian white wine grape, used on its own or in blends – it is the principal grape in Marsala wine.

5. Nebbiolo is another Piedmont red grape, making fuller wines than Barbera.

6. Papageno is the central comic character in *The Magic Flute*; he is also sung by a bass.

7. Prince Tamino, a tenor part, is the hero of *The Magic Flute*.

8. Capellini is a pasta that comes in long, thin strands.

9. Orecchiette means 'little ears' and this pasta bears that shape.

10. Sangiovese is a common Italian red wine grape, used notably in making Brunello di Montalcino.

11. Monostasos, a tenor, is the Chief of the Slaves in service to Sarastro in *The Magic Flute*.

12. Pappardelle is a ribbon pasta, similar to tagliatelle but wider strands.

QUIZ 267. JOBS

What we do for a living. We are publicans – how about you?

1. What was Jimmy Carter's famous mode of employment prior to becoming a politician and president of the United States?

2. Who is Joe Wurzelbacher?

3. Who would you get to shoe your horses?

4. If the NFFO are looking after your interests, what is most likely to be your profession?

5. If you carry the letter FRCVS after your name, what is most likely your profession?

6. Cordwainers and curriers both work with which material?

7. Which football team are known as the Blades and why?

8. If you train at LAMDA, what do you aspire to be?

9. Which are the only branch of the military to have won the FA Cup?

10. 'The first thing we do, let's kill all . . .', says Dick the Butcher in *Henry VI, Part 2*. Kill all what?

Answers to Quiz 266

1. 1897.

2. *Heart of Darkness*.

3. Anne Rice; it was made into a 1994 film by Neil Jordan, with Tom Cruise and Brad Pitt.

4. J. Sheridan Le Fanu; the other two were *Lust for a Vampire* and *Twins of Evil*, both 1971.

5. *Carrie*.

6. *Goosebumps*.

7. Stephen King. The best known of the Bachman books is *The Running Man*, the sci-fi tale that was the basis for the film starring Arnold Schwarzenegger.

8. Benedict Cumberbatch and Jonny Lee Miller.

9. Clive Barker. Barker successfully combined writing horror and fantasy fiction with writing and producing low-budget horror movies.

10. *The Exorcist*, William Friedkin's 1973 masterpiece, with Linda Blair as the teenager possessed by a demon.

QUIZ 268. CHAMPIONS LEAGUE

A quick round on the Champions League and its predecessor, the European Cup – for purposes of simplicity, we have just referred to the competition as the Champions League.

1. Real Madrid have won the Champions League a record thirteen times: who come second on the list with seven wins?

2. How many times have English clubs won the Champions League, and which club accounts for two of those victories?

3. Who did Celtic beat in the final when they became the first British club to win the trophy in 1967? And who beat them when they made their second final appearance in 1970?

4. In 2005, when Liverpool came back from 3–0 down to win their fifth Champions trophy, which much-maligned goalkeeper saved a penalty during the game and two more in the shoot-out? And which prolific striker missed the one in the game and the crucial one in the shoot-out?

5. Which manager and captain combined to lead Real Madrid to three consecutive Champions League trophies between 2016 and 2018? And who came off the bench to score twice and seal the hat-trick in the 3–1 win over Liverpool in 2018?

6. Which three clubs have won the Champions League on one occasion, and also remain the only team from their country to win the competition?

7. Who scored a late goal and then put away the winning penalty when Chelsea won the Champions League in a shoot-out over Bayern Munich in 2012? Who masterminded Chelsea's victories despite only being a caretaker manager?

8. From 2006 to 2009, Arsenal, Liverpool, Chelsea and Manchester United lost four successive Champions League finals. Which were the four victorious teams?

9. A handful of players played in all five of Real Madrid's consecutive European Cup wins from 1956 to 1960. Who was also still around for their 1966 victory? And which two Milan players sit just behind him, alongside Cristiano Ronaldo, with five winners' medals?

10. Who was the first manager to win the Champions League three times?

Answers to Quiz 267

1. A peanut farmer.

2. Joe the Plumber: in the 2008 American presidential election he was involved in an exchange with Barack Obama that was seized upon by the conservative media as an indication that Obama was a socialist.

3. A farrier.

4. The NFFO is the National Federation of Fishermen's Organisations.

5. You would be a vet, FRCVS means a Fellow of the Royal College of Veterinary Surgeons.

6. A cordwainer is a shoemaker, while a currier treats tanned leather to make it workable, so the answer is leather.

7. Sheffield United; the name stems from Sheffield's associations with the steel industry, including cutlery and knife making.

8. An actor (LAMDA is the London Academy of Music and Dramatic Arts); alumni include Jim Broadbent, Brian Cox, Diana Dors, Chiwetel Ejiofor, Rory Kinnear, David Suchet, Donald Sutherland, Harriet Walter, Ruth Wilson and current president, Benedict Cumberbatch.

9. Royal Engineers; they lost to The Wanderers in the very first Final in 1872, and to Oxford University in 1874, before defeating Old Etonians after a replay in 1875.

10. The lawyers.

QUIZ 269. NOT SO CHRISTMAS CAROLS

Carols of all sizes and sorts, but not the Christmassy kind. We threw this one in as a cheeky round in the Christmas quiz last year.

1. Who is Charles Lutwidge Dodgson?

2. Who was appointed poet laureate in 2009?

3. Which Bond movie with Roger Moore in the title role co-starred Carole Bouquet as feisty Melina Havelock?

4. Andy Carroll moved to Liverpool for £35 million in January 2011: two years later he made a permanent move to which club for less than half that amount?

5. Who played the title character in Todd Haynes' 2015 social drama, *Carol*?

6. Singer-songwriter Carole King began her career as part of a songwriting duo writing hits for other people with her then-husband. Who was the husband?

7. Carole Lombard was a great comic actress and wit who died aged thirty-three in a plane crash in 1942. Who was her husband, who was reputedly never the same after he lost her?

8. Who was Karol Wojtyla, 1920–2005?

9. Which Carol did the maths on *Countdown*?

10. Bob Carolgees was a contributor to Chris Tarrant and Lenny Henry's cult children's show *Tiswas*. What was the name of the puppet that comprised the main part of his act?

Answers to Quiz 268

1. AC Milan.

2. Twelve – Liverpool have won five, Manchester United three, Nottingham Forest two (so they are the correct answer), Aston Villa one, Chelsea one.

3. Celtic beat Internazionale 2–1 in 1967, with goals from Tommy Gemmell and Stevie Chalmers. In 1970, Gemmell scored again, but this time it was the opposition, Feyenoord, who came back from a goal down to win 2–1.

4. Jerzy Dudek; Andriy Shevchenko.

5. Zinedine Zidane and Sergio Ramos; Gareth Bale.

6. Steaua Bucarest (Romania), Red Star Belgrade (Yugoslavia/Serbia), Celtic (Scotland).

7. Didier Drogba; Roberto Di Matteo.

8. Barcelona beat Arsenal 2–1, AC Milan gained their revenge on Liverpool, winning 2–1, Manchester United beat Chelsea on penalties, and then Barcelona also beat Manchester United.

9. Francisco Gento; Alessandro Costacurta and Paolo Maldini.

10. Bob Paisley with Liverpool.

QUIZ 270. HISTORY

A general round, but about history. No specialist knowledge required, but please bring a sharp pencil, together with your brain and memory.

1. What title did Oliver Cromwell take as de facto ruler of England from 1653?

2. Who was appointed by Congress to command the Continental Army at the start of the American Revolutionary War?

3. What name was given to the main crossing point between East and West Berlin on Friedrichstrasse?

4. Which iconic American motor vehicle first reached the market in October 1908?

5. Which US city was plagued by gang wars between the Irish North Siders and the Italian South Siders during the 1920s and 1930s? Who was the best known of the heads of the Italian faction?

6. In which city did a fire in the Cocoanut Grove nightclub kill 492 people in November, 1942?

7. What was the last Chinese Imperial dynasty, lasting from the mid-seventeenth century until the formation of the Republic in 1912? Was it the Hang, Tan, Yuan or Qing?

8. In which era on earth did humans first appear? Was it the Jurassic, Paleozoic, Pleistocene or Silurian?

9. Which African country became the first African Republic to proclaim independence in 1847 after it was colonised by freed slaves and Afro-Caribbean refugees fleeing from the United States?

10. Which English poet died of septicaemia from an infected mosquito bite while serving in the Royal Navy in 1915?

Answers to Quiz 269

1. Dodgson is the real name of Lewis Carroll.

2. Carol Anne Duffy – the first woman to hold the post.

3. *For Your Eyes Only*, the twelfth Bond movie.

4. West Ham United.

5. Cate Blanchett plays the older woman going through a divorce, engaged in an affair with a younger woman, played by Mara Rooney.

6. Gerry Goffin. King had 188 US chart hits and 61 UK chart hits – this made her the most successful female songwriter of the latter half of the twentieth century. Their hits together include 'Will You Still Love Me Tomorrow' (banned for its assumption of casual sex), 'The Loco-Motion', 'Chains', 'Some Kind of Wonderful', 'Up on the Roof', 'One Fine Day', 'Oh No, Not My Baby', '(You Make Me Feel Like a) Natural Woman' and 'Pleasant Valley Sunday'.

7. Clark Gable.

8. Pope John Paul II.

9. Carol Vorderman.

10. Spit the Dog.

QUIZ 271. STUFF ABOUT ALIENS

That's a fib. This was an opening round of an April Fool's Day Quiz, with a deliberately misleading header. We are so naughty.

1. If an era is a vast measurement of time on earth and a period is a slightly less vast one, what is the next largest measure?

2. What took David Weir thirty-eight minutes less than Stephen Kiprotich in London in 2012?

3. Who was shot by Jack Ruby?

4. The Indian city of Chennai in the state of Tamil Nadu in the south was formerly known in English by which name?

5. Which sports star spent six years in prison for raping a Miss Black America contestant in 1991?

6. 'It's doubtful that anyone with an internet connection at his workplace is writing really good fiction.' Whose acerbic take on modern mores was this in *Ten Rules for Writers*? Was it (a) Martin Amis; (b) Philip Pullman; (c) Jonathan Franzen; or (d) Margaret Atwood?

7. Bijouterie is (a) the practice of studding the navel; (b) costume jewellery; (c) an accessories store; or (d) smoked pork?

8. Who is Jane Porter, later Jane Clayton?

9. '*Sangre azul*' is the original Spanish for which phrase used to describe those of aristocratic appearance, supposedly reflecting the way veins show under pale skin?

10. Which religious movement grew out of a Bible study group founded by Charles Taze Russell in Pittsburgh in the 1870s, and took its current name in 1931?

Answers to Quiz 270

1. Lord Protector. Cromwell was one of the Parliamentarians who signed Charles II's death warrant in 1649. For four years, the country was ruled by a Parliament known as the Rump Parliament (many former members were dead or excluded). In 1653, Cromwell, the dominant voice in the Rump, became Lord Protector and de facto ruler. On his death, his son, Richard, became a reluctant successor, pending the Restoration of the monarchy in 1660.

2. George Washington.

3. Checkpoint Charlie.

4. Ford Model T.

5. Chicago; Al Capone.

6. Boston; following on from a fire in Mississippi that killed 209 people in 1940, the Cocoanut Grove incident led to major reforms of safety regulations.

7. It was the Qing dynasty.

8. Pleistocene; it lasted from about two and a half million years ago until around 11,700 years ago.

9. As the name suggests, it is Liberia.

10. Rupert Brooke. Edward Thomas and Wilfred Owen were also killed in the First World War, in more direct military circumstances, while Siegfried Sassoon and Robert Graves were among the survivors who wrote of the scarring experience of the trenches and warfare.

QUIZ 272. MOVIES – OH DANNY BOY

This wasn't one from the pub. It was written for a special 2012 Olympic Quiz that a PTA asked Nick to do, and was relevant at the time, as Boyle directed the opening ceremony at the London Olympic Stadium. We've simply updated the CV.

Danny Boyle has made twelve full-length feature films between 1994 and 2017. Can you fill in the gaps from this list of Boyle's films and their stars?

1994 *Shallow Grave* (Christopher Eccleston, Ewan McGregor and Kerry Fox).

1996 _____ (Ewan McGregor, Robert Carlyle, Jonny Lee Miller, Kelly MacDonald).

1997 *A Life Less Ordinary* (Ewan McGregor and _____).

2000 _____ (Leonardo DiCaprio and Virginie Ledoyen).

2002 *28 Days Later* (_____).

2004 *Millions* (Alex Etel).

2007 *Sunshine* (_____).

2008 _____ (Dev Patel).

2010 *127 Hours* (_____).

2013 _____ (James McAvoy, Vincent Cassel, Rosario Dawson).

2015 *Steve Jobs* (_____ and Kate Winslet, written by _____).

2017 *T2* (Ewan McGregor, Robert Carlyle, Jonny Lee Miller, Kelly MacDonald).

Answers to Quiz 271

1. Epoch.

2. The London Marathon – Weir won the wheelchair race, which finishes some time before the foot race.

3. Lee Harvey Oswald, the shooter of JFK. Conspiracy theories abound . . .

4. Madras; most of the name changes were less drastic – Calcutta to Kolkota, for example, although Bombay to Mumbai threw a few folk.

5. Mike Tyson. Tyson was convicted in 1992 and served just under three years of a six-year sentence before resuming his career. He converted to Islam in prison, but it didn't improve his behaviour – he was later disqualified from a title fight for biting off part of Evander Holyfield's ear, and threatened to eat Lennox Lewis' children.

6. Jonathan Franzen. He has a point – it can be a distraction – but cutting yourself off from the internet wouldn't help much in writing a quiz book.

7. It is costume jewellery.

8. Tarzan's Jane; Tarzan's real name is John Clayton II, Viscount Greystoke.

9. Blue bloods.

10. Jehovah's Witnesses.

QUIZ 273. BARN DANCE

Not a quiz about line dancing or banjo strumming or anything even remotely similar. Nope, it's another name quiz, with 'Barn' as the key four letters.

1. Where was former England footballer John Barnes born?

2. Who devised the bouncing bomb used in the famous Dambusters raid?

3. Name all Barney McGrew's colleagues.

4. What is the name of Barney Rubble's adoptive son?

5. Who played J.R. Ewing's rival Cliff Barnes in *Dallas*?

6. *A Tale of the Riots of Eighty* is the subtitle of which Charles Dickens novel featuring the Willets, the Vardens and the Chesters as well as the titular family?

7. Which football team first gained entry to the League under colourful manager Barry Fry in 1990–1?

8. Barnes, in south-west London, is a district within which London Borough?

9. Which is the largest bookselling chain in the Western economy?

10. Which North Devon town on the River Taw lays claim to being the oldest borough in the UK?

Answers to Quiz 272

1. The 1996 film was *TRAINSPOTTING*.

2. CAMERON DIAZ was in *A Life Less Ordinary*.

3. The 2000 DiCaprio movie was *THE BEACH*, based on Alex Garland's novel.

4. CILLIAN MURPHY was in the chilling dystopian horror, *28 Days Later*.

5. CILLIAN MURPHY was also in *Sunshine*.

6. Dev Patel was in the Academy Award-winning *SLUMDOG MILLIONAIRE*.

7. JAMES FRANCO was in *127 Hours*.

8. The 2013 film was *TRANCE* (don't be embarrassed at not remembering this; it was Boyle's worst film by a distance).

9. and10. MICHAEL FASSBENDER played Steve Jobs and the script was by legendary American screenwriter AARON SORKIN. Since compiling the quiz, the release date has been set (May 2019) for Boyle's next project, a Richard Curtis-scripted comedy, *Yesterday*.

QUIZ 274. SCIENCE AND NATURE

This is the last science round in the book. I know, I know, I'm fighting back the tears myself . . .

1. CV is a recommended form of exercise for the heart and lungs. For what is CV actually short?

2. What can a dendrochronologist tell you and how?

3. What non-SI unit is used to express the weight equal to 1,000 kg?

4. Galen, an influential Roman physician who was among the first to link diet and health, began his research while working with which subject group? Was it (a) pregnant mothers; (b) legionnaires; (c) galley slaves; or (d) gladiators?

5. Who proposed and published the first law governing the behaviour of gases in 1662?

6. Whose work, *Book of Calculation*, introduced Indian systems and revitalised European mathematics? He gave his name to a famous mathematical progression.

7. What was Noyce and Kilby's massive contribution to twentieth-century progress?

8. Koalas, possums, wombats and Tasmanian devils are all part of which class of mammals?

9. Fructose or fruit sugar, bonded to glucose, produces what?

10. Equidae, the horse family, includes which other two types of animal alongside the various species of horse?

Answers to Quiz 273

1. Jamaica.

2. Barnes Wallis.

3. Pugh, Pugh, Cuthbert, Dibble, Grubb.

4. Bamm-Bamm. Fred and Wilma Flintstone have a daughter, Pebbles, and two pets, Dino (a dinosaur that behaves like a dog) and Baby Puss (a rarely seen sabre-toothed tiger). Barney and Betty Rubble adopt the unnaturally strong Bamm-Bamm, and have a pet kangaroo hybrid called Hopparoo.

5. Ken Kercheval.

6. *Barnaby Rudge*; the story is set during the Gordon Riots of 1780 when, under the pretence of supporting Lord George Gordon's anti-Catholic campaign, mobs looted and rioted in London while the government dithered.

7. Barnet. Fry managed Barnet in two spells (with an odd year at Maidstone in between), then later managed Southend United, Birmingham City and Peterborough United, where he remains Director of Football.

8. Richmond.

9. Barnes and Noble.

10. Barnstaple.

QUIZ 275. DECEMBER 25

Not exactly a Christmas round, but one about people who were born or died on Christmas Day.

1. Who was the Naked Civil Servant, born 1908?

2. The Godfather of Soul, died 2006?

3. Which East European leader was tried and summarily executed, along with his wife, in 1989? What change in the law was made as a result?

4. Which cricketer, born in 1984, one of his country's greatest exponents of the sport, retired from the international scene in 2018?

5. Born in 1899, who hit the big screen big time with his performances in *High Sierra* and *The Maltese Falcon* in 1941?

6. Who was crowned Holy Roman Emperor in 800 CE?

7. Bass guitar player Noel Redding, born 1945, is best remembered for his work with which rock icon?

8. What was stolen (or reclaimed, depending on your perspective) from Westminster Abbey by Scottish nationalists in 1950?

9. Carrie, born 1949?

10. Which actor and comedian, who died in 1946, had a problem with working with dogs and children, and refused to drink water 'because fish **** in it'?

Answers to Quiz 274

1. Cardio-vascular.

2. The age of a tree by examining the rings in the trunk.

3. Tonne; as opposed to the old ton, which was equal to 2,240 pounds. The use of the ton as a commercial weight was barred by the 1985 Weights and Measures Act.

4. (d) Gladiators.

5. (Robert) Boyle, he of Boyle's Law: The absolute pressure exerted by a given mass of an ideal gas is inversely proportional to the volume it occupies if the temperature and amount of gas remain unchanged within a closed system.

6. Fibonacci.

7. The microchip.

8. Marsupials; the word comes from the name for the pouch in which most carry their young.

9. Sucrose.

10. Donkeys (including asses) and zebras.

QUIZ 276. MUSIC

Another round on the wild world of pop and rock. We have had some fantastic bands play at the pub in our first two years – none of them are mentioned here.

1. Who was the first female DJ to host the *Radio 1 Breakfast Show*?

2. Madonna had seven UK No. 1 singles between 1985 and 1990, but then waited until 1998 for her next, from the *Ray of Light* album. What was it, and what was her last UK No. 1 single, in 2005, from the album *Hard Candy*?

3. What did 'Dancing Queen' achieve that Abba's seven other UK No. 1 singles failed to do?

4. Whose 2009 debut album, *Sigh No More*, peaked at No. 2 in the chart in both the UK and the US, and what was the 2012 follow-up, which went one better and topped both charts?

5. Of the ten artists with the most No. 1 singles on the Billboard Hot 100 to January 2019, six were female artists. Who are the six?

6. Under what name does Annie Clark record and with whom did she release a 2012 collaboration called 'Love This Giant'?

7. What colour brought Coldplay into the mainstream? What was the title of their 2000 debut album from which this song was taken?

8. In the 1990s and 2000s, Rick Rubin produced six albums on the American label with which recording legend?

9. Which hard-rock band's classic line-up included Scott Gorham, Brian Robertson on twin lead guitar and Brian Downey on drums? Who was the charismatic bass player and singer and main songwriter?

10. Whose *Miseducation* from 1998 remains her only completed solo album? With which band did she first come to public attention?

Answers to Quiz 275

1. Quentin Crisp. *The Naked Civil Servant* was his 1968 autobiography, made into a 1975 film starring John Hurt.

2. James Brown. With his band, The Famous Flames, Brown was a pioneer of funk and gospel-influenced soul music.

3. Nicolae Ceaușescu, the former head of communist Romania, virtually a dictator to his people; the abolition of capital punishment.

4. Alastair Cook – Cook scored 12,472 Test Match runs, the most by any Englishman, with thirty-three hundreds. He wasn't even a part-time bowler, but brought himself on for a giggle as a 2014 Test against India was heading for an inevitable draw. Cue great hilarity as Cook took his only Test wicket.

5. Humphrey Bogart.

6. Charlemagne; a classic example of 'if you can only think of one answer, it's probably that one'. We wouldn't ask a question about a Holy Roman Emperor unless it were Charlemagne.

7. Redding made up the Jimi Hendrix Experience along with drummer Mitch Mitchell and – obviously – Jimi Hendrix.

8. The Stone of Scone.

9. Sissy Spacek, who played the title role in the 1976 film of that name.

10. W.C. Fields.

QUIZ 277. CHRISTMAS FOOD (SORT OF)

This constitutes selling a round under pretences. Some of the questions are nothing to do with food, even though that is the theme. All will become clear . . . and think of the theme before you answer the questions.

1. Anatolia is the ancient name for the Asian part of which modern country?

2. Which two brands enjoy over 40 per cent of the UK sales of port wine?

3. Nougat and which two other ingredients are mixed with chocolate to make a Toblerone bar?

4. A really bad film, or turkey, can win which award, presented annually the day before the Academy Awards? Who won the Best Actress Award at both ceremonies in 2010 for *Blind Side* and *All About Steve*?

5. What is the rich fruit cake dusted with icing sugar eaten as a Christmas treat in Germany? Which city has a festival celebrating the cake as part of its annual Striezelmarkt?

6. What seasonal treat is taken from the *Castanea sativa* tree? What part of the tree do we actually eat?

7. Who plays Professor Sprout in the Harry Potter films, and what is her teaching discipline?

8. Terry's Chocolate Orange was first produced in which decade and in which English city?

9. Edgar Froese, who died in 2015, was the main man in which pioneering electronic band formed in the 1970s? Being invited to write the score to the fifth game in which popular game franchise gave them a late career pay-day in 2013?

10. What are the two ingredients of the cocktail, popular at Christmas, called a snowball? (Correct spelling for full marks.)

Answers to Quiz 276

1. Zoë Ball (co-host in 1997 and on her own from 1998 to 2000).

2. 'Frozen'; '4 Minutes'.

3. 'Dancing Queen' was the only Abba single to top the Billboard Hot 100.

4. Mumford & Sons; 'Babel'.

5. Mariah Carey (eighteen); Rihanna (thirteen); The Supremes, Madonna (twelve); Whitney Houston (eleven); Janet Jackson (ten). The Beatles head the list with twenty, Elvis has eighteen, Michael Jackson thirteen and Stevie Wonder ten.

6. St. Vincent; David Byrne.

7. Yellow; *Parachutes*.

8. Johnny Cash.

9. Thin Lizzy; Phil Lynott. The band's heyday saw the 1976–7 albums *Jailbreak*, *Johnny the Fox* and *Bad Reputation*, while the 1978 live album, *Live and Dangerous*, confirmed their reputation as a top live act.

10. Lauryn Hill; the Fugees.

QUIZ 278. PEOPLE AND PLACES

Geography stuff. It's okay, you can relax soon; only two more quizzes to go.

1. Which is the largest area of inland water in mainland Britain?

2. What are the only two land-locked countries on the continent of South America?

3. Svalbard, an archipelago roughly halfway between the northernmost point of Europe and the North Pole, belongs to which European country?

4. The lagoon surrounding Venice is part of which body of water, in turn part of the Mediterranean Sea?

5. What is the principal city in the Basque region of northern Spain?

6. Which South American country is bordered by Colombia to the west, Brazil to the south and Guyana to the east?

7. Lake Balaton is the largest lake in central or western Europe. In which country does it lie?

8. Which river empties into the Atlantic in New York Bay?

9. The Three Gorges Dam in China is the world's largest. What river does it span?

10. Which land-locked lake lies over 1,300 feet below sea level and is the lowest body of water on the earth?

Answers to Quiz 277

1. Turkey.

2. Taylor's and Cockburn's. Port is a Protected Designation of Origin product, which means that only a product made in the specific region where it originated is allowed to use the name. Champagne, Stilton cheese and Prosciutto are all examples of PDO products.

3. Almond and honey.

4. The Golden Raspberry; Sandra Bullock.

5. Stollen; Dresden.

6. Chestnut; the seed.

7. Miriam Margolyes; herbology.

8. The 1930s (1932); York. Terry's other best-known product, All Gold, also came out in the 1930s. The firm has been sold a number of times since, and the York factory was closed down by Kraft in 2005.

9. Tangerine Dream; *Grand Theft Auto V*. The group were at their height in the 1970s, with Froese, Peter Baumann and Christopher Franke as a trio.

10. Advocaat and lemonade.

QUIZ 279. CRYPTIC CAROLS

Here are the names of twelve Christmas Carols laid out in cryptic form. All you need to do is deduce which carol is hidden in the clue. Some are less obvious than others.

1. Willoughby out for a posh dinner.

2. Clarion call for the loyalists.

3. Cheering for Adebayor and Petit.

4. No one talks to this one.

5. Ben, BB and Albert?

6. Well it wasn't Liam's brother, I know that much.

7. Cloudless nocturnal surprise.

8. Quiet in the dark.

9. One day in Jerusalem.

10. Stable break.

Answers to Quiz 278

1. Loch Lomond, to the north-west of Glasgow in Scotland.

2. Bolivia and Paraguay.

3. Norway – it was once a Dutch territory known as Spitzbergen. We were quite surprised when we read this – weren't aware Spitzbergen wasn't a 'thing' any more.

4. The Adriatic Sea; it is the portion of the Mediterranean that lies between Italy and Croatia.

5. Bilbao; the Basque region extends into southern France, around the coastal towns of Biarritz and Bayonne.

6. Venezuela.

7. Hungary.

8. The Hudson; it flows down from the upstate Adirondack Hills.

9. The Yangtze. The Yangtze River basin is home to a third of the population of China, which means about half a billion people.

10. The Dead Sea.

QUIZ 280. LAST WORDS

I shall leave the final words to the various people whose last words are laid out below. For my part, as Question 10 attests, the rest is silence.

1. 'After all, tomorrow is another day.' These are the closing lines to which book and even more famous film?

2. 'The creatures outside looked from pig to man, and from man to pig, and from pig to man again; but already it was impossible to say which was which.' The doom-laden ending to which dystopian novel?

3. 'May only goodness and kindness pursue me all the days of my life, and I will dwell in the house of the Lord for the length of days.' To what are these the closing words?

4. 'I have offended God and mankind because my work did not reach the quality it should have.' Who is being unnecessarily modest in his last words?

5. 'When you ain't got nothing, you got nothing to lose / You're invisible now, you got no secrets to conceal.' These are the last words, chorus excepted, of which Bob Dylan song?

6. 'Money can't buy life.' Which iconic singer, who died in 1981?

7. 'Last words are for fools who haven't said enough.' Which nineteenth-century political thinker, who changed the world with his writing?

8. 'I should never have switched from Scotch to Martinis.' Which actor from Hollywood's golden age and professional boozer?

9. Which sports star died allegedly uttering the words 'at least I get to see Marilyn'?

10. Whose last words are 'The rest is silence'?

Answers to Quiz 279

1. Holly (Willoughby) and the Ivy (posh London restaurant).

2. O Come, All ye Faithful.

3. O Come, O Come Emmanuel (Petit and Adebayor are both former Arsenal players).

4. Coventry Carol (as in sent to Coventry).

5. We Three Kings (Ben E. King, soul singer; B.B. and Albert King, both blues guitarists).

6. The First Noel.

7. It Came Upon a Midnight Clear.

8. Silent Night.

9. Once in Royal David's City.

10. Away in a Manger.

Answers to Quiz 280

1. *Gone with the Wind* (Margaret Mitchell). The words are uttered by Scarlett O'Hara, consoling herself that she still has Tara and she may yet win back her beau, Rhett Butler.

2. *Animal Farm* (George Orwell). I remember reading the book as a teenager and being distraught at the bleakness of the ending.

3. Psalm 23; the one that begins 'The Lord is my Shepherd, I shall not want.'

4. Leonardo da Vinci.

5. 'Like a Rolling Stone'. Arguably Dylan's most famous song – the renowned music journalist Greil Marcus deemed it worthy of an entire book.

6. Bob Marley. Lots of people answered John Lennon, but he died in 1980, and, given the circumstances, probably didn't have time for famous last words.

7. Karl Marx.

8. Humphrey Bogart. This is probably apocryphal – I am always a bit suspicious when people are credited with deathbed witticisms.

9. Joe DiMaggio, Monroe's ex-husband. DiMaggio was Monroe's second husband and their liaison was short-lived. He was replaced by another celebrity, the playwright Arthur Miller. It is often mistakenly written that the marriage between the two was an "older man" scenario, but Miller was only eleven years older than Marilyn – the differential was actually less than that between Marilyn and Di Maggio, the retired baseball player, who was twelve years older than his wife.

10. Hamlet's. 'O, I die, Horatio. / The potent poison quite o'ercrows my spirit. / I cannot live to hear the news from England. / But I do prophesy the election lights / On Fortinbras. He has my dying voice. / So tell him, with th' occurrents, more and less, / Which have solicited. The rest is silence.'